Praise for Cristina Rathbone's *On The Outside Looking In*:

"Cristina Rathbone's *On the Outside Looking In* is a moving and often lyrical story about some of the most admirable and tragic characters I can imagine, and a brilliant expression of empathy. I can't imagine anybody reading this book without being moved, not only to tears, but to action. This is one of the most powerful works of protest literature since Richard Wright's *Native Son.*"—David H. Bradley, author of *The Chaneysville Incident: A Novel* (Winner of the Pen/Faulkner Award)

"I read this book ravenously and it affected me on every single page. In a hard-hearted era, when we hear about inner-city children mostly as a force of 'super-predators,' *On the Outside Looking In* reminds us just how much more complex and wrenching life really is among this caste of untouchables."—Samuel G. Freedman, author of *Small Victories*

"A heartbreaking yet uplifting story about the children and staff of West Side High School."—Sol Stern, *The Wall Street Journal*

"The kids open their chaotic inner lives to Cristina Rathbone in ways that are extraordinarily intimate and deeply poignant. Rathbone understands the power of narrative. She uses the stories of students' lives outside the classroom to fuel the book, but it is by contrasting her more ordinary, middle class rebellion with theirs that she unearths the unsettling truth that these kids aren't so different from the rest of us. Or they wouldn't be, given half a chance. What makes the book heartbreaking is the realization of how much normalcy it takes to sustain the most ordinary ambitions: love, family, work."—Rebecca Johnson, *Vogue*

"*On the Outside Looking In* will raise the consciousness and the conscience of Americans. Cristina Rathbone eloquently reveals how the subtle and complex forces of poverty and social disadvantage impact the lives of teenagers, including their performance in school. This book ought to reach the widest possible audience—its real human stories will surely help to galvanize efforts to improve the chances in life for young people who struggle to survive against discouraging odds."—William Julius Wilson, author of *The Declining Significance of Race*

"Cristina Rathbone's sympathy for students does not prevent her from showing some of them at their very worst: going into crack houses, dealing heroin, beating up their classmates. But she never lets these students become the one-dimensional addicts, pushers and thugs of so many political speeches. Always they have their full human complexity, always they are individuals who might have had very different fates had they not been born into such grim circumstances."—Stephen O'Conner, *The New York Times Book Review*

"Cristina Rathbone has guts, analytical deftness and a superbly loving imagination. She sets a whole new standard for poverty journalism." —Benjamin DeMott, author of *The Imperial Middle*

"*On the Outside Looking In* gets past the stereotypes and makes these kids lives real, makes it obvious their lives are in flux. As sad as some of their tragedies are, there is a sense of possibility and change. This book is both heartbreaking and revelatory, and it deserves to be read."—Jessica Seigel, *Newsday*

"This is one brave book. It is peopled by kids most of us are afraid of—gang girls, drug dealers, thugs-in-the-making. They are, however, still kids, and they go to a school which believes that they are not irredeemable, and Cristina Rathbone has had the courage and the patience to take the full measure of their humanity. She furnishes us with an eccentric hero—Ed Reynolds, the principal of West Side High School, in Manhattan—and shows us the daily tug-of-war between the secure environment of the school and the ruinous one of the streets. There are moments of real exhilaration, when a child discovers the possibility of another kind of life. The kids are sustained by an antic gallows humor; but what's most terrible is how they have come to accept the inevitability of catastrophe. Their sense of doom turns out to be accurate, and perhaps self-fulfilling. 'The pull of their chaotic pasts was just to strong,' Rathbone writes.

"This is not a book that secretly glories in the failures of the poor. Rathbone has no ideological brief, and no blueprint for reform. It is, if anything, a parable about the weakness of the most powerful institution we have to shape the lives of children, in the face of the pathologies that now grip our inner cities."—James Traub, author of *City On a Hill*

"Superb."—James North, *The Philadelphia Inquirer*

"What emerges most powerfully is the grace and resiliency of the young people she befriended and the generosity of spirit possessed by truly heroic teachers and the school's tireless principal, Ed Reynolds."—*Booklist*

"This is a story that reaches out, grabs the reader by both lapels, and never lets go. Cristina Rathbone is a writer of exceptional talent. *On the Outside Looking In* is a book that I would be proud to have written myself."—Leon Bing, author of *Do or Die*

"It's the level of honesty and admittedly imperfect objectivity that make Rathbone's experiment a success. She contrives no happy endings for students who cannot find them. Neither does she paint a hopeless picture to assail or depress us. Her version of the facts is refreshing."—*Kirkus Reviews*

"While Ms. Rathbone writes about the rare opportunity of being let into the hearts and minds of a group of alternative school students in New York City, the truth is that the youth she writes about are typical of so many inner-city students who are trying to make it under extraordinary conditions. Ms. Rathbone captures the subtleties that make these youth complex, dangerous, beautiful and real. I highly recommend *On the Outside Looking In* to educators of teachers, parents and human-service providers. The book's insights can only but sensitize the adult who genuinely wants to reach today's youth."—Michael Borrero, Ph.D., Director, Institute for Violence Reduction

"Cristina Rathbone's book is a window onto a world of trouble and courage, where the twin struggles to teach and learn are won only against overwhelming odds. Here is a cogent argument for the small, active, involved alternative school, often a teenager's last hope, the only defense we currently offer against the apathy and ignorance always ready to lay claim. You'll find yourself rooting for these kids to get their diplomas, to climb one more rung on the ladder, to achieve the stability so many of us take for granted. Rathbone shows us human needs we dare not deny."—Hettie Jones, author of *How I Became Hettie Jones*

"*On the Outside Looking In: A Year in an Inner-City High School,* is a gritty and unsentimental book that sadly is as accurate a summary of the school system today as *Up the Down Staircase* was in more hopeful times."—Neal Travis, *New York Post*

"Cristina Rathbone's journey into a tough American high school transcends the cliché of the touring journalist reporting back to a voyeuristic public. Her passion to see these kids from the inside and her commitment to understand the social contexts in which they enact their lives creates complex, humanizing confrontations on every page.

"Rathbone documents the lives of young people negotiating the difficult passage toward identity, purpose, and integrity. For many of them the choice to be nobody or somebody bad, rather than not quite anybody at all, becomes an alluring option. For others the sustained struggle to construct a self in a society eager to throw them away is absolutely dazzling.

"Rathbone illuminates the modern predicament for our young people—valorized as consumers, demonized as criminals, they look uneasily toward a future which they fear has no room for them at all. Acutely aware that they are throw-away children—immigrant, African-American, from disorganized or deteriorating families, too poor to matter much—many give up. In the most insistent and dogmatic 'edspeak,' these youngsters are 'at-risk.' Rathbone shows us how, in spite of the wholesale abandonment by a self-indulgent adult society, they might also become valuable people and people 'of promise.' It is the tension between the stereotyped dead-end vision of these kids and their daily efforts to imagine a life of hope, dignity, and respect that animates this breath-taking book.

"Like Dickens and de Tocqueville, whose American journeys in the last century challenged us to look at ourselves in new and surprising ways, Rathbone's outsider perspective—she is a young, self-described brown-skinned woman raised in London and living in New York—provides more than a thick description of some distant and abstract subculture. *On the Outside Looking In* is finally a mirror held up to our American dream—what we behold is a frighteningly fragile future and a world in desperate need of repair."—William Ayers, author of *A Kind and Just Parent: The Children of Juvenile Court*

On the Outside Looking In

On the Outside Looking In

A YEAR IN AN INNER-CITY HIGH SCHOOL

Cristina Rathbone

Atlantic Monthly Press
New York

Published simultaneously in Canada
Printed in the United States of America

FIRST PAPERBACK EDITION

Library of Congress Cataloging-in-Publication Data
Rathbone, Cristina.
On the outside looking in : a year in an inner-city high school / Cristina Rathbone
p. cm.
ISBN 0-87113-736-4 (pbk.)
1. Education, Urban—United States—Case studies. 2. Socially handicapped youth—Education (Secondary)—United States—Case studies. 3. West Side High School (New York, N.Y.) I. Title.
LC5131.R38 1998
373.747'1—dc21 97-33528
CIP

DESIGN BY LAURA HAMMOND HOUGH

The Atlantic Monthly Press
841 Broadway
New York, NY 10003

99 00 01 02 10 9 8 7 6 5 4 3 2 1

For my mother, Margarita, my father, Tim,

and my editor, husband, and best friend, Anton

What do I want

Out of life?

To finish high school

Learn to drive

And to marry Jasmine

And there you have it

Almost everything you wanted

To know about me

But were afraid to ask.

—West Side Student

To the Reader

The names of the students and of certain other people in this book have been changed and certain information that might identify them is disguised.

Prologue

AFTER TEN YEARS in New York I had lived in four different corners of Brooklyn, in Hell's Kitchen, on the Lower East Side, the Upper West Side, and in a tall apartment building in midtown Manhattan. As freely as anyone, I had traveled from the city's wealthiest enclaves to some of its poorest neighborhoods, and had rubbed shoulders with just about every kind of New Yorker. Professionally, too, my job as a reporter had allowed me to approach a broad section of humanity. But despite the fact that I had friends and acquaintances from all walks of life, and that I had written about helicopter pilots, perfume creators, and tugboat men, I had never so much as spoken to an inner-city teenager. Friends advised caution, and the cumulative representations in the media, of politicians, and of sociologists encouraged me to keep my distance. Like so many middle-class New Yorkers, I began to feel entirely reasonable in stepping aside, crossing the street, or leaving the train to avoid groups of kids.

In time, this response became second nature to me. Not because I didn't like teenagers. Fundamentally, anyway, I have always loved their vertiginous swings between blustery arrogance and crippling lack of identity. It was just that the distance between my life and theirs was such that I slipped into the prevalent and only semiconsciously held belief that avoiding them was the only smart thing to do.

Of course, I had the statistics to excuse this behavior: if I shied away, it was because people were quick to remind me that while violent crime was on the decline overall, crime among teenagers was skyrocketing, and that one out of four young African American men was in prison, on probation, or on parole. Almost every day there was a story in the papers to remind me: GANG DUO NABBED IN TORTURE!, TEEN SLAIN OVER GAME!, KILLERS! and MONSTER! were just a few of the headlines from one month's youth-related stories. Editorials, frequently, were worse. I read the following in the *New York Post*:

> The courts can't handle them. The cop's hands are tied. Yet they rob, rape even kill—only to be tossed back on the street unpunished. They are teenage felons. Boys as young as 13.
>
> Now word is coming down from Albany that New Yorkers have even more reason to be afraid: A dramatic surge in crime committed by youth 13 to 19 is on the way.
>
> Hold on. It gets worse.
>
> Criminal justice experts have put a date on the expected arrival of this youthful terror spree: 1995.
>
> Yup, next year . . .

That such graphic demonization should exist in the tabloids was to be expected, but the same attitude was prevalent elsewhere as well. Even the most mainstream of rap lyrics boasted of the danger of life on the streets. And, as if inner-city youth were a health hazard that had to be buried somewhere far away to make the world safe again, our political leaders leapt over one another to be the first on the bandwagon promoting adult trials and sentences for juvenile offenders. The problem was as insoluble as it was rampant, it seemed. Kids were self-destructing; we would all do best to wash our hands of them as soon as possible.

It wasn't until one afternoon when I found myself crossing the street to avoid a boisterous group of teenage girls that I shocked myself out of the knotted assumptions I had unwittingly twisted myself into. The girls were angry, that much was clear. Teasing and cursing at passersby, they seemed living proof that teenagers had become more antisocial than ever. But the question of whether this was an insane response to a sane world, or a sane response to an insane one, had yet to be answered. It never even seemed to have been asked. By the time I got back to my apartment I had made up my mind to address the issue by spending the upcoming year in a New York City high school.

As a journalist more interested in the lives of students than in the methods used to educate those lives, I'd had difficulty finding a school I could comfortably spend a year in. There was no shortage of options. The New York City school system is the largest in the nation. The high school sector alone was responsible for 280,000 students that year, and its 180 facilities include almost every kind of institution. At the top of the pile are the four specialized high schools, the city's pride and joy: Fiorello H. LaGuardia High School of Music and Art and Performing Arts, Bronx High School of Science, Brooklyn Technical, and Stuyvesant, all of which are among the most successful schools in the country. But students are admitted to these schools only on the basis of a competitive exam, and kids brilliant or studious or disciplined enough to get in weren't the ones skating on the thin ice of possible trouble that I was interested in. Besides, in an increasingly minority-based school system, these schools had the reverse problem. Stuyvesant's enrollment was a scant 4.5 percent black and 3.9 percent Hispanic, and only Brooklyn Technical approached a true reflection of the city's population with 37 percent of its students being African American and 14 percent Hispanic.

At the lower end of the pyramid were the basic neighborhood comprehensive, or zoned, high schools. Created at the optimistic turn of the century, these facilities were initially seen as a way to expose large numbers of students to society's most advanced technologies. At the time they had been filled with state-of-the-art laboratories and trade and sports facilities. Once heralded as the cornerstone of American democracy, however, these schools are now attended predominantly by kids whose parents aren't energetic or savvy enough to manipulate the system. The scale of these schools—some have more than 4,000 students enrolled—had increasingly led to the kind of dismal and institutionalized anonymity that necessitates metal detectors at their front doors. Many were overcrowded, underfunded, and notoriously dangerous; in a recent study by the U.S. Centers for Disease Control and Prevention, more than one-third of students said they were physically threatened during the school year, and one in five admitted to carrying weapons to school. Considering the continuously negative press these schools received, it seemed unlikely that a journalist would be welcomed inside for a year.

In fact, I never even got in the door. Instead, the Board of Education steered me to the middle ground, to the schools called "option high schools." Using citywide, standardized reading test scores, these schools maintained an academic balance by admitting 16 percent of their students at an above-average level, 68 percent within the average range, and 16 percent at below average. My contact at the board was pleased to provide me with a list of five or six that might be amenable to my project. I visited them all. And though the buildings were large, well equipped, and clean on the whole, and the students polite and well behaved, each one left me feeling smothered, suffocated, and downright hostile by the end of the day.

Not that they were bad places to go to school. For the most part, in fact, they were far more successful than average. Once I was even taken to a large, bright, well-furnished auditorium to watch an impressively vibrant multicultural show. The school was proud of having children who spoke a total of fifty-five languages, and many of them were on display that day, as traditional dances from Spain, Africa, and northern Europe blended with neo-Aztec rituals from Mexico and sequences of traditional Japanese and Korean singing. It was just that from the minute I arrived to the minute I left, the crisp discipline and anxious hand-wringing that had accompanied my request to spend a year there, as well as the strict outlines of what I would and would not be able to do, left me deflated and depressed: I would not be able to interview any of the school's difficult pupils; could not write anything that might be construed as being detrimental to the school; could not speak, unaccompanied, to any student either on or off the school grounds; and could not, ever, use the school's name.

Then an acquaintance who had covered education in the press for years suggested I visit Ed Reynolds, the principal of an alternative school in midtown Manhattan. At first I thought he was sending me to one of the new minischools that had adopted alternative educational methods. Largely funded by a grant from the Annenberg Foundation, these schools epitomized the latest trend in educational reform, where staff members, parents, and students worked together to build a more creative learning environment. They were exciting new places with sharp new ideas and sturdy financial backing, but they were increasingly falling into the "option school" section, creaming at least "average" students from a below-average pool. It didn't take me long to realize that Ed's school was something different. Largely composed of students that even the worst zoned schools rejected, West Side was far closer to the bottom of the heap and seemed almost as marginalized and neglected as the kids it served.

Still, as soon as the elevator doors opened onto the sky-blue corridors I knew I had found my school. The receptionist's desk was decorated with a vase full of tissue-paper daisies, and when I asked her to please tell Ed Reynolds I was there, she called me *Corazón* and *Dear* and *Honey* all in one breath. In contrast to the other schools I'd seen, there was a constant, roiling ebullience in the hallways too, a boisterous intimacy which seemed to prohibit the kinds of tensions that smoldered in the semidarkness of the option schools' old, well-polished corridors.

Ed was as welcoming as he was wry. An Irish American who loved to talk, he spoke with passion about what had come to be the crux of my own motivation for the project: how, far from reaching out to its marginal teenagers, society was starting to hold them responsible for the drug abuse and violence and appalling deprivation that created so many of their problems in the first place. And though he seemed receptive to my still vaguely conceived plan that I spend a year at his school trying to bride the gap that had led to such demonization, he wanted me to know what I was getting myself into as well. He spoke of the problems that beset so many of his kids, of the poverty and instability, and how so many felt they had no control over their lives. One afternoon he told me, hands clasped on his lap, that he had lost ten students during the previous year to violence in their neighborhoods: that six had been shot, one had died of AIDS, and one had had his legs amputated by a subway car while running from the cops after a bungled robbery attempt. I nodded, trying to look sad and wise, as though I'd heard it all before and I understood, when actually I wanted to flee. But these were the kids I had been wondering about, I told myself—kids who had already bumped against the limits society placed on them, who had in some cases run afoul of the law, and yet who were still struggling to keep one foot in the mainstream. West Side was not a typical, troubled New York City high school. It could in no way claim to be representative. But it was one of the few places that welcomed kids who were cut off from the rest of society. Kids on the outside who still wanted to get in.

1

ED REYNOLDS, THE principal of West Side High School, was in no position to start registering kids for classes on the first day of school. A mad flurry of royal-blue SWA graffiti tags had appeared mysteriously the night before, scrawled across the walls of the seventh floor. So instead of preparing for the onrush of students in the stately way befitting a principal, he had spent most of the last hour on his knees, scrubbing. He was using a can of soap named Staci. The label read: "Vandal mark remover. A required product for hotels, restaurants, institutions, schools and motels." Ed had bought a whole crate of it on special offer. But despite its robust claim, the Staci didn't seem to be working. After nearly fifty minutes of scrubbing, the blue ink still hovered there, translucent now, as though painted on with watercolor: SWA—Spicks With Attitude.

Ed was proud of his school, even if their last building had been condemned two years before. They were currently housed in a temporarily leased space in midtown Manhattan, a kind of homeless shelter for a school with no place else to go. Right in the heart of the fashion district, and with the Mary McFadden showroom across the street and Macy's and Madison Square Garden just a few blocks away, it was an odd location, not typical Board of Education real estate. But then West Side was not a typical public high school. Long used as a place for dumping troubled kids, it was a school for those the Board of Education wanted to forget. And if that was why Ed's students had to commute a hundred or so blocks from Washington Heights and Harlem, while their old school building sat empty, then Ed was determined that at least the walls would be clean.

Given the current situation, there was little else to make his students feel wanted. It would be one thing if they had the whole building. As it was, they were huddled into three floors of an otherwise perfectly normal, twelve-story office building. The rest of the floors housed a variety of businesses—each good object lessons for the students, it was true—but it wasn't as if they could provide what the school really needed, like a lunchroom, cooking facilities, an auditorium, science labs, music rooms, or even a gym. The school was so stripped of perks, in fact, that unless you knew it was there you would walk right past the tiny blue metal sign that hung from the top of a gray side door next to a coffee shop and a subway entrance to the uptown A train. "West Side High School," the sign read in murky letters, "500 8th Avenue."

On the first day of school in the fall of 1994, however, you couldn't miss the place. By 8:00 the school's elevator operator still hadn't arrived, and though security had taken over, the new walkie-talkies they were using didn't work and they were forced to communicate through the open shaft of the unused freight elevator instead: "We need you down here in the lobby!" "I'm on seven now—coming right down!" The process was excruciatingly slow, and with nowhere else to go a sizable crowd of frustrated students had ballooned out of the too small lobby and onto the sidewalk. By the time I walked out of the Thirty-fourth Street subway station they were mingling as best they could with truckers eating their breakfasts out on the street and with the photographers, stylists, models, and well-dressed salesgirls clicking by on their way to Macy's just two blocks away.

Behind on their high school credits at nineteen, twenty, or twenty-one, West Side students were older than most high schoolers in the city. Most had once been dropouts, chronic absentees, or hyperactive loudmouths—the kind of brashly egotistical kids who can disrupt an entire class, or an entire year of school if left unchecked. So it wasn't that surprising to see that even after two years they were not a particularly welcome addition to the heart of the prosperous, crowded, grimly busy world of New York's garment district. Their numbers alone intimidated the elderly seamstresses who hobbled past on their way to open-plan sweatshops, and their hooded stares and languid postures, postures that somehow seemed insolent if you happened to be hurrying past on your way to work, drove many commuters to cast their eyes to the ground and scurry across the street.

Dragging at coffee through a hole in the lid, I glanced apprehensively from one huddle of students to another. Across the street a boy in a yellow baseball hat and matching yellow shorts gave a handful of cigarettes to another boy whose jeans hung low enough to reveal the ZIMM lettering across his shimmering red boxer shorts. Over by the pay phones another cluster of boys in oversized black canvas jackets and heavy black jeans were engaged in a surly dance with their beepers, looking down at them before turning to the phone, punching a series of numbers in, and then hanging up, immediately, long before there was time for words to be spoken. Nearby, the girls were dressed in the same oversized jeans and stuffed nylon jackets as the boys. Topped with hollow, hooped gold earrings and brightly painted lips, they surveyed the street with an almost macho, proprietorial ease, until one of them saw me staring and pursed her lips, cocked her knee, placed a hand on her hip, and said, "Yeah?" I turned away as though our meeting of eyes had been a mistake. I was so relieved when I recognized a boy standing in front of a corrugated iron garage door that I raised my arm to wave at him. When he didn't respond, I pretended I was fixing my hair instead.

Ed had told me to meet him up on the seventh floor of the school at 8:00. It was nearly 8:30 now, and the elevator was still horrendously backed up. I went to the coffee shop on the corner, bought another cup of coffee for myself and one for Ed, lingered a little while longer, and finally decided to take the stairs. Seven stories up the hallways were as packed as the sidewalk had been, and I was surprised to see so many little children among the crowds. Some were tiny, just a few weeks old in body holders. Others were older, three or four perhaps, and they wandered around among the students' legs at about calf height, expectant at first, probably thinking they were at a party, but then becoming frustrated when they realized there would be no balloons or cake.

"Momma momma I'm bored I wanna go," one pudgy three-year-old with bows in her hair told her mother, tugging at her elbow.

"So do I, girl. Believe me, so do I," the not quite fifteen-year-old mother said without even looking up from the pile of school papers in her hand. Another little girl still wobbly on her feet had decided to sit down on the floor. With little else to distract her she had started to play with the Velcro on her Reebok sneakers, pulling the flaplike tongue up and then sticking it back down, until her mother, standing in line for a train pass at the other side of the room, shouted at her, "Come over here, now-now-now—*now!*" Five minutes later, when Ed asked the young mother how her summer had been she looked away and said, simply: "Bad."

"Bad?" Ed asked softly.

"You don't know how bad, Ed. It was hard."

Ed was still down on the floor scrubbing away at the SWA tags when I spotted him. He seemed glad, if a bit surprised, to see me, though the coffee I offered him was clearly something he didn't have time for right then. Sitting behind a desk a few yards away, the receptionist kept answering the phone, then cupping the receiver and shouting across the hall to ask Ed whatever the person on the other end wanted to know. Teachers approached with requests for chalk or student lists. Some handed him papers to sign, others needed keys to the book room, the weight room, or one of the storage cupboards in Ed's office. Every seven or eight minutes a new load of incoming students poured out of the tightly packed elevator in a sea of freshly ironed Guess jeans and Nike sneakers and bright red and yellow T-shirts. As they unfolded themselves from the overfull elevator amid clouds of "Shit!" and "Damn, man!" Ed would lumber to his feet and greet them with the casually welcoming markers of a favorite uncle.

"Maria, your hair looks nice," he said to a passing girl, whose scowl eased into a smile. "Thanks, Ed," she said, swinging her hips.

"Enrique! Has Angelique been looking after you this summer?" he asked a tall boy with a ribbon mustache whose heavily tattooed arm was draped clumsily on his tiny girlfriend's shoulder. "How's your mother, Dayna?" "Halloo, Tamiqua!" "Baldwin, welcome." "Keeping out of trouble, Rahim—What? No? Rahim—Rahim—Rahim!" he said, clasping his cheeks with the flats of his palms in mock horror.

Down a few feet from him a girl with white acrylic nail extensions an inch and a half long was trying to press the bell for the elevator. "Could you press the elevator for me?" she asked a woman who had been storming up and down the corridor ever since I had arrived. But the woman ignored her. She was chasing after her son's records for the third day in a row, she told anyone who looked like they might be able to help her. Where could she find a copy of her son's transcript?

Ed stayed where he was, down on the ground with a rag in his hand. Pools of sweat had formed under his arms, dyeing his mauve shirt purple. He rolled his eyes. "Know who she is?" he asked me when she was well out of earshot. "She's the mother of a student who killed another student uptown last semester. Can you believe that? Killed him—and now she's mad that we can't complete his paperwork in five minutes."

It was nine-thirty by then, and Ed had given me the bucket and cloth and two cans of Staci to carry, trailing behind him as he made his way, late, to his classroom. He wasn't all that surprised to find that it was filled with sixty or seventy chairs. The room was painted mauve, nearly the same color as his shirt, and was wider than it was long, with three windows looking out onto the sweatshops of West Thirty-fifth Street. It would have been a nice room if it weren't so cluttered, and I spent the next few minutes arranging the chairs into a rough kind of circle while Ed dumped the orange milk crate he had been hefting around all morning onto a desk at the front and started in on some paperwork.

The building was beginning to fill up. I couldn't see what caused it from where I had taken a seat in the back of Ed's classroom, but the level of noise in the corridor had exploded. The flat sound of palmed high fives snapped into the room, coupled with laughter and sometimes a screech from a girl welcomed just a little too enthusiastically. Groups of students ran laughingly by in a blur, their sneakers squeaking against the linoleum floor, and every now and then one of Ed's advisees swaggered or shimmied into the room, each with their assumed persona etched as clearly on their face as if they were carrying a sign around their neck.

Cristy Rivera was the first of his kids to appear in his classroom that day. A big girl with a pale face and traces of a downy black mustache highlighted by two shades of deep-purple lipstick, she rolled into the room like a star onto a sit-com set, her book bag in one hand, a yellow Styrofoam plate with three wedges of carrot cake in the other.

"Hi Ed!" she announced, walking over to a seat in the the center of the room, and throwing her bag onto the empty chair beside her. "Hey Ed, it's me, Cristy," she said again, when he didn't answer right away. "I told you I'd be back."

Ed cupped his face in his hands. "Oh no," he groaned. "I dreamt your mother took you back to Salvador."

"Nope. Guess you weren't so lucky," Cristy laughed. But she quickly grew serious when a skinny young man in a yellow sweatshirt and a fancy, fitted blue baseball cap came in. When he started to sit down in the chair next to her she flared her nostrils and pursed her lips and then said: "Yo! Yo! That chair's for Mama—out!" It spoke wonders for her size that the boy stood, unquestioningly, and moved to another seat.

Next in was a six-foot-tall, broad-shouldered young man and a skinny boy in an orange jacket and orange jeans and a snappy pair of rectangular wire-rimmed orange shades. They had been complaining loudly about how long it had taken them to make their way through the confusion downstairs, so by the time they made their entrance Ed had known they were coming for some time and was prepared. "Maurice and Rasheem," he told me, arching his eyebrows in expectation.

"Damn man, I seen a kid pull a snake out of his pocket down there, Ed. An actual live snake," the tall one, Maurice, said by way of a hello. "A python."

His friend Rasheem laughed in agreement. He adjusted his hat and then glanced around the room. "Uh," he said as he caught my eye. "Uh."

Ed was soon surrounded by a shifting group of seven or eight students vying for his attention. Unlike regular schools, every student at West Side had individually scheduled class programs. In an environment where a twenty-year-old may have two high school credits and a sixteen-year-old thirty, a generalized grade system couldn't work. And though it led to increased paperwork, the personalized system was essential for making sure each student received the classes they needed. But paperwork was clearly not something Ed enjoyed or was particularly good at. I could tell by the way he hunched over his orange milk crate, tense and worried, and by the alarmingly casual way he rectified mistakes: drawing a hasty line through an erroneous figure, scrawling a signature or a note on a scrap of discarded paper taped over the top with an explanation, as if to say, "I am the principal. This will pass."

Ed didn't notice when Lucille Andrews came in five minutes later with her puffy blond caretaker from the residential home for disturbed teenagers where she lived. I had met them both the week before at an orientation for new students, and Lucille had been scared then. Clinging to the same man's arm, almost in tears, she had explained to

Ed that she didn't want to go to West Side, that she just wanted to go back to her center, because she just knew by looking around that she would be the youngest one in the school.

"What are you, fifteen?" Ed had asked. Lucille looked nineteen or twenty. "Fourteen?"

"Thirteen," Lucille had said very quietly, her eyes fixed on the floor. Ed couldn't believe it. He glanced up at her guardian, who nodded. "We'll keep that secret then," he said, clearly dismayed. "OK? No one will have to know."

But today she was all dressed up in a pink felt beret studded with sparkling, multicolored gems, a pink sweatshirt, and baggy white jeans, and from the moment she sat down she flashed lusty glances and provocative smiles in Maurice's direction. Her guardian had to wait for her paperwork to be completed before he could leave. But he was so involved in the sports section of his paper that he didn't notice when Lucille slid out of her seat a few minutes later. Strolling to the open door she turned around for all the world like a model on the runway and, curling her finger, beckoned Maurice outside. When he got back five minutes later he was smiling bashfully, shaking his head, and adjusting the bandanna that was wrapped around the hundreds of multicolored elastic bands in his hair.

"You dis me and I'm gonna pull a Lorena Bobbit on joo," Lucille said to him, wagging her finger from the doorway.

"Damn, she shady," he said to Rasheem once she was out of sight. "She half-and-half—one day cool, the next all lovey-dovey. I tell you something, nigger: that relationship ain't going to last long."

Then he tugged at the front right pocket of his jeans and twisted his beeper so he could see the digital screen on top. I had begun to recognize the quick grasping motion kids made toward their hip, and then the flick of the wrist and the glance to the top edge of the matchbox-sized transmitter. Beepers weren't allowed at West Side, but all the kids seem to have them: there were neon green, pink, and blue ones, and white ones, and clear ones that showed the inner wiring like a miniature Pompidou Center. Some carried the digital message on the top, others on the side, and still others were covered in homemade designs painted on with Liquid Paper. One was even painted like the American flag, and its owner somehow managed to persuade Ed to let him use the classroom phone to respond to a beep that he swore was from his mother. But Sandra Quintana, the girl for whom Cristy had been saving a chair for close to an hour, was the only one who brazenly wore her beeper on the outside of her pocket and left the setting on "beep." Hers was plain black, but it was a Motorola, the Rolls-Royce of beepers, which said all it needed, and it went off as she strolled in, about half an hour later, in a succession of high-pitched, second-long squeals.

"Hi Ed!" she said exactly the same way Cristy had, and then casually stopped the tiny alarm and looked down to her hip, shrugging as if the number she read there wasn't important.

"Ms. Quintana!" Ed replied, putting on a French accent as he looked up from the crowd around his desk. "Oooh la la."

"—I ain't taking no first period, Ed, come on, B! I gotta pick up my girl in the mornings," a young man said when he finally saw the schedule Ed had outlined for him.

"Tell me, James. How do you spell success?" Ed asked him.

"S-u-c-c-e-s-s," Sandra sang out as though she were in kindergarten. "Don't dis us, Ed."

But he had leapt out of his chair by then, no small feat as he hardly fit into it in the first place, and he'd had to do a slippery little side shimmy to squeeze out of the gap between chair and table and then thrust his weight forward before he toppled over. At the board he erased the graffiti written on it with the edge of his hand without paying it the slightest bit of attention, and with the tiny fragment of chalk, which was all he could find, he started to write.

"This is how you spell success," he said. "D-I-P-L-O-M-A. Remember that when you get up in the mornings and you'll be out of here by June."

"Tha's whack, Ed," Sandra said.

"He a corny nigger," someone else agreed.

"Nah, nah, he cool. Ed, you cool," Maurice announced. "Seriously he is," he said to Lucille, who had sunk her face down into her crossed arms on the desk by then. "He joke around and stuff. He ah-ight."

No one seemed to notice me sitting pertly there, in my own little chair at the back of the room. Or if they did they simply assumed I was meant to be there and ignored me, and perhaps because I was feeling shy and wary I was content to sit back and watch a lanky boy in a red satin ice hockey shirt give up the battle for Ed's attention and focus on a girl across the other side of table instead.

"You wearing enough rings?" he asked. The girl extended her fingers, looked down at her hand, and smiled at the clumps of silver rings she had bunched there.

"Yeah," she said.

"What's with the silver thing? That a new trend? Yo Ed, you heard about that? A new trend in silver?" Ed didn't hear him. "I don't know, man," the boy said pensively then, stroking the inch of thick gold rope that stuck out from under the neckline of his hockey shirt. "Silver's attractive but . . . problem is . . . no value."

A few of Ed's advisees had managed to register for a full complement of classes by then and had already left, their schedules tucked carefully into their wallets or their back pockets along with their free student travel passes, but most hadn't even begun. And apart from an occasional and random attempt at progress—a "Yo Ed, you finished with me yet?" shouted in no particular direction—most kids seemed pretty happy just to let time slide by as they waited, not very hopefully, for whatever was supposed to happen. One rolled small bits of paper into pellets, another chewed his way down to the end of a brown plastic coffee stirrer, but most just stared at the wall or watched a clump of skinny black girls in tight jeans and high heels catch up on neighborhood gossip as they picked at their McDonald's sausage-and-egg biscuits, conscientiously raising their little fingers like dainty old women at a tea party.

Then a security guard in a too tight uniform burst into the room. I had seen him earlier in the day, leaning against the open doorway downstairs, hitching his pants over his rock-hard belly as he eyed the girls. But he ignored them now as he dodged through the desks and then peered out of first one, then another, then the third window to the street below. A carload of nonmatriculating kids from "uptown" had pulled up outside, he said under his breath. Those that heard him shut up. Alarmed, Ed stepped out of his chair, more quickly than he had before, and joined the guard at the window. The kids in the car could be here to cause trouble. It had happened before. When the school still had the run of a grand old building on 102nd Street and Amsterdam

Avenue two boys had driven to West Side looking to avenge a shooting from the night before. They waited all day, until they saw the boys they were looking for. Then they jumped out of their car and started shooting. "Nobody was hurt, thank God." Ed had told me. "But the point is that as friendly as we are, we are always on the alert for that kind of danger."

I didn't know how many people in the room had heard that story, but most were sitting silently now, somber and edgy. Boys slid low into their seats as if stretching, girls made as if they were doing their nails, and every now and then they shot glances at one another as though asking, "You know anything about this?" For a full minute and a half there was no sound in the room except the frantic crackle and burst from the old radios that the security team had finally pulled out, in desperation of ever getting the new sets to work. This time it turned out to be nothing. Perhaps thirty seconds later the car drove away. The security guard, who I would find out later was named Louis, left, and Ed went back to his desk and tried to complete the registration process for at least a few more of his kids.

But any cohesion the class had managed to maintain until then had evaporated. In relief or frustration or fear or celebration kids leapt out of their seats and jabbered. Jokes were made, stories told about high drama out on the streets over the summer—daring trips to the all-white Brighton Beach, cars being stolen, cops evaded. And an hour later Maurice and Rasheem and Sandra and Cristy and Lucille were still sitting there, ostensibly struggling to fill out their for the most part incomprehensible registration forms. By then Maurice was musing about setting fire to the school. Sandra sympathized but asked him to wait until she had graduated. Cristy said that he better make sure she wasn't in the building before he struck the match, and Lucille just smiled softly. Rasheem raised a long thin finger in the air like a comic-book professor and inquired politely of Ed how many credits he might need to complete his education. And even the boy who until then had been keeping himself happy by chewing his coffee stirrer removed it now to ask, over and over, and never with any change of inflection: "Yo Ed! Where's my papers at, Ed? Yo Ed! Where's my papers at, Ed? Yo Ed! Where's my papers at, Ed?" until Ed—almost drowning in the chaos of reverberating *Yo Ed!*s—put an end to it all by stretching his great belly to an almost flat line, raising his hands up palm outward, and admitting defeat. He was up to his elbows in his students' original transcripts, the closely guarded notches on their ladders to graduation, and the files inside his orange milk crate were in total disarray. Loose pages were everywhere, and many of them were covered with yellow Post-it notes scrawled across with phrases like "Credits missing from American history," "Transfer sheet not found," "RCT English passed?" or, in big letters and underlined, "RCTs?"

"OK OK OK, I'm going to tell you what," he said. "In one month's time I'm going to turn fifty. October ninth. Fifty years old. And if by then, by the time I turn fifty, all your records aren't in total order, then—I'm really going to go out on a limb here—I'll buy you all tickets to the Broadway show *Les Misérables.*"

The class groaned. "Shit sounds whack to me," someone said.

2

IN THE COBBLE Hill neighborhood of Brooklyn, where I lived, my alarm went off at 6:30 every morning those first few weeks. Wide-eyed and anxious, I struggled into one of my four appropriately bland "school outfits" and then rushed to the station, where I boarded an overcrowded, overheated train to Manhattan. I was so tense I often had stomach cramps by the time I climbed out of the subway at 8:00. Ed had invited me into the school without consulting anyone on his staff, and I was unsure about how I would be greeted. Unlike the Annenberg schools, which receive a major concession from the teacher's union, allowing them to bypass seniority rules and choose instructors committed to new teaching methods, West Side's staff was made up more or less equally of teachers who had requested the school, teachers who had happened upon it and grown to love it, and teachers placed there by the central bureaucracy who would clearly have preferred to be someplace else. They were of every kind: from a retired nun and a fresh-faced college grad to an older man who looked like he would be both happier and better off at home in bed. Some of them, I knew, were uncomfortable with my presence at the school and would not appreciate my attending their classes, but most seemed more or less accustomed to Ed's whims, of which, apparently, I was the latest, and welcomed me to their own patch of the school in the early-morning staff meetings.

Esther was usually the first to arrive. A perpetually surprised looking, heavily mascaraed, Puerto Rican art teacher, she had greeted me with a huge smile almost from the first day. She sat up at the front of the room with Ed most of the time, and because I preferred the anonymity of the back I tended to sit next to Linda, one of the school's social workers, or with the two math teachers named David and their friend Albert, who had been the lead guitarist in a very famous rock band before coming to West Side.

In a school as unregimented as West Side, these meetings provided the only structured forum for teachers and administrators to exchange information, test new ideas, and work out problems. These ranged from the relatively minor—whether a group of students should attend a new documentary on Malcolm X during class time—to more serious disagreements over disciplinary issues, administrative deadlines, and elections for the school-based management team. In the course of the year, issues would arise that would resonate well beyond the confines of the large corner room in which they were held. But for the most part the meetings focused on the more mundane process of going through daily "notices"—long lists of administrative requests and scheduled events mimeographed in slightly blurred purple print—and generally ended with a quiet, if vaguely sardonic, synchronization of watches. West Side had no school bells, so it was important that everyone was running on a more-or-less similar schedule. Like patrolmen in old-fashioned TV cop shows, teachers shook out their wrists from their shirt sleeves when Ed announced the time and adjusted their watches before dispersing through the school's three floors to their Family Group rooms, where the real day would begin.

Every day, Family Group—a forty-minute stretch from 8:52 to 9:32—was spent talking. Discussions developed according to the students' impulses, and no subject was out of bounds unless an individual student made it so. Sports, fashion, sex, politics, history, race, and class blended together under the guidance of the group leader. Each ran their group differently, and though initial matches between student and teacher were random, the system was fluid enough to give students the opportunity to shift to the instructor who most suited them.

Rochelle, an old-fashioned English teacher, attracted the type of kid who needed crisply delineated structure. Janina, a Polish-born special-education teacher with a pale moon face and a huge bright smile, liked the unsynchronized girls, those who flew from one mood to another in the blink of an eye. The young mothers tended to spend most of their time with Marie, the health teacher. The quiet ones, those at West Side because they had been bullied and harassed in larger schools, took to the more extravagant teachers, like either of the Davids. And most of the kids who actually did the bullying or the disrupting sought refuge with Ed. In a last-chance high school, his was the last-chance Family Group.

Unmanageable by anyone but him, some of his advisees were sent straight from the criminal-justice system; others arrived as a result of a superintendent's suspense meaning that Ed got a call one day from his boss, the superintendent of alternative schools, saying James Maloy, for example, had just been thrown out of his zoned school for assaulting his teacher with a chair, can you fit him in? The rest were simply kids that no one else could handle in the school. Banished from other teachers' Family Groups, they hid out there like fugitives until whatever storm they had created blew over. Ed was loath to give up on any student, and it was perhaps because of this that his Family Group had become so unwieldy. In the fall of '94 it was close to five times the size most people thought it should be. On paper at least, he had seventy-four advisees. Nineteen, he said, were not around; but that still left fifty or so: thirty-three who would turn up regularly and another eleven who would be in and out. Far too many no matter how you looked at it. But even though Ed often compared himself to the Old Woman who lived in a shoe, a feeling of unity prevailed that generally prevented serious conflicts from erupting. Kids were sometimes angry, frequently sullen, and almost always unreliable, and it was rare to engage the whole class at once; but more often than not issues would arise that would surprise everyone, and sometimes great whirling debates would engulf the whole class.

At first I found the dynamics of this group as difficult to master as I had when I had been the students' age myself. The boys were pleased enough to spend a few minutes flirting with me in the morning, but they always dropped me when their friends arrived, and then disappeared after Family Group to who knew where. Sandra and Cristy, the two beefy girls who had sat in the middle of the classroom on that first day, were so clearly in charge of the girls that it seemed pointless to approach anyone else without at least their tacit consent. They were brutally self-sufficient, though, and because they didn't invite me to do otherwise, I kept my distance.

Sensing the difficulties I was having, Ed tried to help by handing the group over to me one morning, suggesting I use the time to discuss my plans for this book. For close to twenty minutes I chattered on as best I could, trying hard not to sound foolish. But when I finished and Ed asked, no one expressed the slightest bit of curiosity.

"You wouldn't be interested in reading it at all—even if it were about yourselves?" Ed asked again. After a long pause, a girl so large that the class had nicknamed her Moby let out a sigh, shrugged, and removing a saliva-coated pencil from her mouth said: "As long as it weren't no great, fat, Bible type of book I might," which was about as enthusiastic a response as I got all month.

As a result I spent most of my time those first few weeks shadowing Ed on his journeys through the school day. He was hardly ever in his office. He spent a fair deal of time in meetings with teachers or individual students, quietly discussing a problem so troubling that no one else would be allowed to hear. But mainly he roamed the corridors, jubilantly shouting out students' names as he shooed them into their rooms. Geographically, anyway, the school was not hard to figure out. West Side occupied the seventh, tenth, and eleventh floors, and each of the three was arranged identically: a central square corridor, off of which lay three or four classrooms to a side. Because there was only one elevator, the place got congested between classes, and though Ed had two deans and four security guards to clear the halls, it seemed as if he got his energy jostling for position with the kids. Round and round he would go, a giant, floating bubble weighed down only by a pocketful of subway tokens, which he handed out to anyone who needed them. Usually he stopped moving only when someone from the Board of Education called to complain that one of their thousands and thousands of standard operating procedures had been broken or bent or just totally ignored. This happened every other week, at least, and Ed never paid them much attention. He was always very polite and responsive when they called. He would apologize and slap his head in grief at everything he had forgotten to do, or would sigh as if in sudden understanding of what it was exactly that they had wanted him to do. Then, after apologizing some more, he would hang up the phone, perform a mincing little ballet step to parody his own simpering manner (surreal to see such tiny, trippingly dainty leaps on such a large man), and with a laugh forget the whole thing, turning his attention again to his frantic chase around the tenth floor.

At that point I would usually retire to the staff cafeteria: two regular-sized classrooms on the eleventh floor that had paintings instead of maps or charts on the walls and a fully equipped but nonfunctioning kitchen in the back. After two years the Board of Education had yet to hook the stoves up to gas lines, but the room provided a good getaway from the kids, who were still keeping their distance. Finally, though, after two or three weeks of numbing indifference punctuated only by the occasional question as to where I was from ("London—that London, France?") and who I was ("I don't mean no disrespect, Tina, but are you white or what?") familiarity began to work its magic.

It started with little things. In Ed's Family Group Enrique confided that he smoked weed every morning before coming into school; James that he had been a basketball star; and an impossibly charming con artist, named Nino, confessed he had lost his job the previous summer as a result of falling in love and forging business checks in order to buy his girlfriend presents worthy of her. Rasheem, I discovered, was the resident artist; Maurice, the womanizer; and Nicole, the wildcat whose recent escape from a foster home upstate she was never too shy to discuss. She brought in sliced pickles for breakfast every morning, extra sour, and ate them one by one from a Styrofoam cup with a plastic lid. Cristy preferred plate-sized cinnamon rolls, while a boy named Julio liked fried egg sandwiches with melted American cheese. He thought himself the smartest kid in New York because he had stopped selling heroin in favor of a mixture of legal substances disguised by a local Dominican crew to look just like the real thing. In this way he was able to earn a minimum of three hundred dollars a day without ever risking incarceration, he said.

Soon I began to feel completely at home in Ed's Family Group. Partly this was because my mother is Cuban. Growing up in London I had almost always been the only brown-skinned person in the room. Now, however, I was surrounded by people whose skin tones echoed my own, and was almost invisible at school where, apart from one Caucasian and a pair of Philippine twins, the student population was more or less evenly divided between Latino and African-American. I could speak Spanish, too, passingly well, and it was thrilling to be able to understand the fluent waves of Spanglish the kids whispered in defiance of their teachers' for the most part English-only ears.

It was the kids' edgy and off-balanced energy though that most resonated with my own memories of adolescence. I had been what might now be called an at-risk child myself, though the numbers of safety nets strung beneath me would have prevented even a bruising if I had ever fallen. Bright but undisciplined, and brash and loud, I created rebellions and student strikes and general disorder in high schools all over England for the five years it took me to graduate. I jumped out of windows to escape dreary classes, locked teachers in closets, hid cheap, strong liquor under my bed in boarding school, and smoked anything I could get my hands on that stood even the slightest chance of getting me high. By the time I was fifteen I was hitchhiking to distant towns, sneaking out to local pubs, and having sex—to ward off boredom mostly, I think, but also because, for some reason or other, and despite all my parents' love and affection, I simply didn't care.

I was finally thrown out of the third school after a four-hour-long interrogation with two members of the local drug squad revealed that I had been smoking marijuana in the woods nearby with a friend. Shortly after that I found myself in my fourth and final establishment—one for "difficult students" in London. There, the classes were small, the rules few, and almost all of the students rejects from someplace else. And though that school was private—I still don't dare ask my father what my almost entirely wasted education ended up costing him—it was similar in many ways to West Side, where 85.5 percent of the students had dropped out or been kicked out of two or more high schools before arriving.

But there the similarities ended. Unlike my schoolmates, West Side's student body was overwhelmingly poor. Poor enough for access to a phone to be a luxury. Every day after Family Group Ed made phone call after phone call for a never-ending stream of his students: to their parents, their children, their foster-care agencies, welfare offices, parole officers, judges, or sometimes even just to their friends who hadn't shown up at school that day. Because almost all lived in single-parent families in public housing, or in group or foster homes funded by the state, I wasn't surprised to learn that most also qualified for both a free breakfast and lunch; only 11.6 percent of West Side students received them, but over 80 percent would have if everyone eligible had claimed them. The forms they had to fill out asked tricky personal questions in big bold letters. Questions like whether a student lived in foster care or at home, and whether they lived with one parent or two, and if those parents were receiving public assistance, how much they received, and whether or not it was supplemented with food stamps. Because many kids lived lives of such desperation that they lied even to each other about where they lived and with whom, most of them sneered when Ed handed the forms out one morning before surreptitiously shoving them deep into the bottom of their bags. "I ain't going to fill out that shit for no free prison food," one young man said, throwing his crumpled application into the garbage can. "Rather go hungry, Ed. Damn!"

I had been just as invested in the power of my own indomitability when I was a teenager, and had spent an equal amount of time exploding in similar spurts of frustrated energy and pride. But, from the moment they'd been born, the circumstances surrounding these students' lives could not have been more different from my own. And to begin with, anyway, the resulting sense of unfamiliar familiarity often led to confusion. I passed kids in the corridors who carried suits carefully folded in their book bags for job interviews later in the day but who looked and dressed and talked and carried themselves in just the same way as a boy who had just been transferred in from another school for attacking a teacher with an ice pick. And I met girls like Lucille, whose enormous intelligence had long ago been sharpened to inflict the most possible pain. Once, during my second week there, she persuaded me to borrow a pair of scissors for her, which she then pocketed and denied ever seeing. That was one of the worst episodes of my time at West Side. I knew that at least once in her life she had become violent enough to attempt murder. I never discovered the details, though later she would hint that her intended victim had been her mother. Whatever the case, she now had a huge, rusty pair of scissors tucked away. For days I fretted, begging for them back, smiling ingratiatingly all the while, not wanting to offend so close to the beginning of the year. When I finally gave up and told Ed all about it he got them back as casually and gracefully as I had been awkward. I was so embarrassed that I didn't turn up at school for three days.

But things like that happened all the time at first. They were bound to, given the fact that, aside from my instincts, I had no idea what I was doing or even what to expect. I had lived in the Crown Heights section of Brooklyn for nearly three years. In a neighborhood where windows were burst out by gunfire, and crack vials piled up in the corner of the hallway outside my apartment, I had had plenty of time to see the results of danger and violence and deprivation. I had had a knife stuck to my throat one evening as I walked into my apartment building, and like anyone else living in a less than desirable location I had spent a great deal of time, in between looking for work and going to movies and falling in love, planning ways of moving to some place in the city were I'd be able to go buy a pack of cigarettes after dark without worrying about it for an hour beforehand.

At a low point I had even witnessed what I now refer to as "the children's riot," during which the local half-wit—a young man kept happy and financially afloat by merchants on the local shopping strip of Washington Avenue—was attacked by a group of eleven-year-old kids. Their voices hadn't broken yet, and I remember thinking how strange and pathetic it sounded when they sat on the corner and dissed passersby with their little-girl voices. There were no guns or knives involved in the incident. Instead, the elementary school children threw plastic milk crates at the fully grown but hopelessly retarded young man until his head split open. Arms flailing, mouth agape, he rushed into the liquor store for protection. When they realized that the door had been locked behind him the boys started to throw bricks and bottles and a couple of twisted hubcaps at the store window until the glass broke against the thick steel mesh that stood behind it. I was inside the store at the time, trying to keep both the man-boy's head still and the elderly store owner calm. And the strangest thing of all, even through the fear and the panic inside that always dusty, overpriced, understocked liquor store, the thing that scared me most was that I had known one of the children still heaving and wrenching at the metal grid outside. Just six months before he had been a friend of mine. He and his best friend, Leston, had used my video camera to record rap songs they made up during the day at school, and to tell stories that they'd act out, using my boyfriend's clothes and my hats to dress up in. Now, just half a year later, here he was, smashing glass. I had no idea what had happened to him in that time. I knew only that at some point during the summer his grandmother had given up on him and had stopped calling him in for dinner every evening out of their third-story window.

But now, at West Side, I was beginning to fill in the previously invisible narratives that transformed a kid like Eric from a bright and imaginative boy to a bully. And as I started, piece by piece, to fit together the jigsaw puzzle that made up the contours of some students' lives—lives that ran parallel to but separately from my own—all I really learned was to grow ever more respectful of the complexity of things. A student's not turning up for school was irresponsible behavior, which, if frequent enough, would be sufficient for their removal from a neighborhood school. But it was not unusual for a kid to miss school at West Side because his best friend had been shot, or because he was arrested, or his mother had nearly died the night before from an asthma attack, a disease that strikes disproportionately among the poor in New York City, most particularly in Washington Heights, where the majority of the kids were from. And because for the most part these lives remained hidden, or at least only partially exposed, what you were left with, if you were Ed or a teacher at West Side, were the symptoms: erratic behavior, bloody-minded wrongheadedness, self-destruction, and a long string of problems so numerous and weighty that a friendly place to go to school and a good ear often didn't seem like enough help.

I will never forget one morning when a seventeen-year-old girl I had never seen before turned up at Ed's Family Group drunk. Still carrying a bottle wrapped in a brown paper bag, she stumbled into a chair and then slumped back against the wall and laughed.

"Julie, are you drunk?" Ed asked, as naturally as if he were asking her if she were well that morning.

"Bin celebrating," Julie replied. Ten minutes later she told us, thick-tongued and angry, that she had been celebrating the return of her stepfather from prison, the same stepfather who had been sexually molesting her for years. Her mother blamed her for this and for the time he'd spent in prison; but hoping to ingratiate herself, Julie had helped her mother with the party preparations and had eaten and drunk with the rest of them. Then, afraid of being raped again, she had left the apartment and had ridden the subways all night, drinking, until West Side opened up in the morning.

By then I thought I had managed to accept that, like an insect's vision, things that once seemed static became more and more dynamic the closer you came to them; but the only thing I ever managed to do after one of these occasions was to go home and take to bed. It was something I did regularly anyway: crashed out each day after getting back from school and writing my notes, not because my life was so very tiring but because it was the only way I knew to bridge the gap between the two worlds I was inhabiting—the exaggerated and warped version of my own hyperactive youth and the infinitely calmer, sturdy(ish) domesticity of my comfortable present.

3

MAURICE JENSON SMITH was eighteen when I met him that first day at West Side. Then he became twenty, then seventeen, and then eighteen again before he ever got around to being nineteen. I've never been sure, but I think now that he was actually seventeen, if only because it was the age he most vehemently denied. It took me some six weeks to finally sort out that he lived in the same residential center for emotionally disturbed teenagers as Lucille. That was what gave him away, in fact—he told me with a wink that he lived with Lucille, and when I said that I thought she lived in Williamson's there was nothing he could do but grin sheepishly and shrug. Before that he had told me that he lived variously in his own apartment on the Upper East Side, a job he had dispatching messengers at twenty-four dollars an hour providing him with rent money; in the Bronx; with his mother, sister, and little brother in Park Slope, Brooklyn; and in a small studio in Queens, which he shared with a "brother" from the Ninety-second Street Mosque.

And he had been to China, too. One afternoon in McDonald's he spent close to half an hour telling me about the trip. By then I was used to his stories and listened happily as he explained that he had traveled the length of the Great Wall with the Harlem Boys Choir. It had been magnificent and strange seeing all those temples and meeting all those people and singing for them in his gold-and-red robes, he told me, though after a while the trip had become tiring because they'd had to travel everywhere by bicycle and he'd become a little bored of eating rice three times a day, even at breakfast. He had also been to Europe, he added, with the cool finesse of a limp-wristed socialite, "crossed it side to side." Besides which he had visited Minnesota, Texas, Boston, and Chicago.

Here is one version of his childhood: Born in Bellevue Hospital in Manhattan in November 1975, Maurice was taken to live with his grandmother in a small house on Bell Avenue in Kingston, Jamaica, and didn't return to New York until he was eight years old. Once here, he moved in with his mother on the Lower East Side, stayed there a year, and then moved to Park Slope in Brooklyn.

Here is another: Maurice had lived since his birth in 1976 with both parents in a spacious ranch house on Staten Island until he was seven, when his father died. "Big Maurice," as Maurice's father was known, had been a famous drug dealer there. He was six foot nine and had zero percent body fat, so he'd been easy to recognize, and he used to make cocaine and heroin and angel dust in his apartment. He had as much money as anyone could ever want. Times were fine. Then a gunman burst into the kitchen and shot him: "Four times—twice in the back and once in the neck." Big Maurice returned fire until the police and the ambulance arrived, and then he managed to hold on for three months in the intensive-care unit. Against his mother's wishes, Little Maurice snuck in every day and hugged and kissed his father and asked him please not to die, but to no avail.

Or this: Maurice's father was a successful painter; he spent most of his time in front of his easel and was scared of his son from a very young age. In this version, Maurice was a karate expert by the time he was six, a tae kwon do black belt by the time he was eight, and he knew how to throw a knife. One day, when the family was living in Queens—Maurice was three foot eleven at the time and weighed just ninety pounds—he heard his mother shouting for help. Maurice walked down the corridor holding his knife in the correct Oriental throwing position, peeked his head around the door, and saw his father beating his mother. Enraged but calm, he threw the knife. It missed—just. The blade came close enough for Maurice's father to think twice about hurting anyone in the family again.

Or: Maurice was born in 1976 to a student-of-communications mother and an artist father, a mural painter famous in all five boroughs. His father was just nineteen at the time of Maurice's birth but already had samples of his work all over the city. By the time Maurice was school-aged his father had made enough money to send him to a private Catholic school where he had to wear a little suit and a purple tie, and to put him in a cab every day to take him there and bring him home, too.

None of these stories were necessarily true, of course. Maurice lived at Williamson's for a reason, and if it was natural to exaggerate, beautify, or even distort your life when someone was interested, Maurice took the process to an entirely different level by creating hundreds of alternate realities in and out of which he could jump at any given time. He wasn't deluded. He knew perfectly well what was real and what was not. And he didn't seem to mind if everyone else did too. It was the process of creation he was hooked on, not the convincing of others, so he lied about everything: what he had for breakfast, how many cigarettes he smoked, and who he had spent the previous evening with, as well as about the larger issues of his childhood and his father.

It took me a while to understand all this, and longer to accept it. For the first few weeks I dutifully wrote everything down, nervously trying to ignore the obvious factual errors as I copied out my notes onto the computer in the afternoons. But after a while they became impossible to ignore, and I finally confronted him about it in Family Group. I pointed out that he couldn't have been born in two different cities at two different times to two different fathers. And it was when he simply covered up the inconsistencies with the lumpy wallpaper of yet another version of his childhood that I realized I had little choice but to go along with his fantasies. Everyone else did—Rasheem, Shadi, Lucille, and anyone who just happened to be around tended to accept his tales verbatim, and sometimes even took part in the fantasy, so that Rasheem would veer from Maurice's "man" to "cousin" to "brother" ("Blood brother?" "Full blood brother, Tina. Word.") before reverting back to "friend" or, more ominously, "associate."

All of which goes at least partway to explaining why I never found out where Maurice was born or where he grew up or what happened to his father. Initially, all I was certain of was that he had once attacked a principal seriously enough for Ed to be constantly aware of it, and that he found his way to West Side through Williamson's, where he'd been living for years and which would have sent him home long ago if, as one of his counselors told me, it wasn't for "his horrific home situation."

"Before I was at Williamson's I was previously upstate and the address was the juvenile correction center," Maurice told me once I had finally cornered him about where he lived. "My mother felt that if I would have stayed in the city most likely I would have been in trouble or I would have done something stupid, so she moved me upstate."

"Don't you have to commit some kind of crime to go to a correctional facility upstate?" I asked.

"You do," he admitted. "And my crime was assault, which was false because my principal had attacked me. See, I was suspended. I had hit a kid with my book bag and cracked his head open, so I was not allowed in the school for a time, but I just went back to get some of my friends. I went upstairs and the principal saw me. He got real mad and started to escort me downstairs again. Thing was, while he was doing that he assaulted me—punched me in the stomach—so I had an altercation with him."

"You punched him?"

"I did more than punch him: I punched him and then I pushed him down the stairs—a flight of stairs from the fifth floor to the fourth. At the bottom I kicked him a few times and ran.

"There was also a small gun charge," he said a few moments later, making sure to lean up close to my cheap little tape recorder.

The Williamson Center is tucked away close to the edge of Central Park, just a few blocks north of one of the city's most exclusive residential neighborhoods: the upper east side. They are the blocks, however, that take you from the green canopies and doormen-polished brass entrances of wealthy apartment houses to an area where landlords find it more profitable to burn down their buildings or simply let them sit there, abandoned and crumbling and waiting to rot. But the center itself was privately run, forward looking, and more than adequately funded. With one counselor for every five residents, health services on the premises, and even a school, it was a good place for troubled teenagers to end up. Perhaps as a result of the highly individualized care he had been receiving there, Maurice had passed all the required high school Regents Competency Tests (RCTs) and needed just four credits to graduate. This fall, he had registered for a reasonable combination of writing, economics, American history, science, math, and weight training, but none of the classes was particularly taxing, and he could come and go as he pleased without ever seriously affecting his work. That still didn't leave him enough time for the girls. In all of his life this was the thing that kept Maurice focused. More than his musical talents or his mother and his occasional stints as a drug kingpin out on the street, girls were what kept him going from day to day. And if anything was certain about Maurice, it was that girls adored him right back. It wasn't his looks that attracted them, I don't think, though he is tall, dark, and quirkily handsome, with big eyes and sensuous mouth. It was the force of his character—the overwhelming assurance of a con man edged with just a touch of the deranged—that women couldn't help but respond to.

It hadn't always been that way. Up until he was sixteen he swears that no matter what he did, however he wore his clothes or did his hair, or whether he modeled his walk on the suddenly formidable presence of his two older half-brothers, he could never get a girl to go out on a date with him. He was so small back then, in fact, that once a girl even beat him up in front of everyone in his school cafeteria and wouldn't stop hitting him until he apologized for whatever it was he had said and audibly begged for her forgiveness. Now that he had grown he was getting his revenge. He often brought girls back to Williamson's just so he could tell them to leave once they had made their desire for him clear, and when a woman approached him at school or on the street or the subway—something I witnessed a number of times—and smilingly introduced herself before asking for his number, his usual response was to grin and say something like, "What you want my number for, girl? I'm busy." He wasn't being cruel when he said this, either. For once he was just being practical, because Maurice was busy. Too busy for another casual girlfriend anyway.

He had seven or eight of them already, besides his "wife," the thirteen-year-old Lucille Andrews, and if that wasn't enough he had also recently taken to spending his lunch hour with a West Side student named Suzie—a situation made more complicated by the fact that Suzie, by anyone's standards, was deeply disturbed."

Short and stocky and with the wide-set eyes of a mongoloid, Suzie tripped over herself as she spoke, or interrupted herself, or repeated the same phrases over and over until she forgot what she wanted to say. But she was seventeen and attractive and aware enough of her sexuality to dress in tight clothes, black jeans mostly and brightly colored, clingy mohair sweaters, and to prop herself up against the edge of a door, crack a knee, and smile whenever Maurice was near. She told me that she liked Maurice so much because he took her around the back of Madison Square Garden most afternoons, and sometimes sang to her there. There was something about the oblique innocence with which she told me this that made me nervous. Maurice was no child. However much he liked to sing he had better things to be doing in back of Madison Square Garden with someone like Suzie. Even Rasheem, his orange-dressed sidekick, was worried about it. "Suzie—oooh, she a confused young girl," he told me once. "That's the way I see her. I think there might be something wrong with her as far as mentally. She's on the verge of breaking. I don't know what Maurice see in her, but if that was me—if I was in that kind of situation, I wouldn't—Well, you know."

Though she wasn't in Ed's Family Group and was scheduled for special-education classes most of the day, Suzie spent enough time roaming the corridors and sitting in the pleather seats out in the lobby for Lucille to wish she'd stay away from Maurice.

"I don't see what Maurice see in her," Lucille said of Suzie.

"I don't like her. She be buggin' for no reason," Suzie said of Lucille.

"The reason they are mad at each other is because Lucille likes me and Suzie likes me too," Maurice said with a smile. "It happens a lot. Females like me. It's just something I have to deal with. It's kind of hard actually because a lot of them are very attractive, but you can't be with too many girls or eventually you get caught, and then they want to fight each other and you have to be the peacemaker when in actuality you are the one that started everything. Usually what I do is just leave it to dry. By which I mean that I give the girl that is upset a little bit of space until I feel it's time for me to talk to her and make her feel good again."

He had been doing that with Lucille for months by then. And perhaps because she had started going to school with him now and so saw more than she should, she was on the verge of having had enough. Besides, as another resident of Williamson's, Lucille clearly had her own set of problems to deal with as well. Born in Grand Cayman, she had moved to the city with her mother when she was six and her childhood had been appallingly twisted ever since. She didn't like to talk about it much and usually brushed aside questions with a wave of her hand before rattling off a list of abuses as though she was bored even with the anger such memories still evoked: "Crackhead mother. Drunkard father. Abused. Mother too (same man). Ran away." By the time she arrived at Williamson's she had been sexually abused by one of her "fathers" for five years and been beaten so many times that individual incidents blurred into such generalizations as, "My mother never missed, she had excellent aim."

But she was daunted by West Side sometimes, and because she found it difficult to make friends with anyone outside of Maurice's orbit we ended up spending a fair amount of time with each other, before Family Group mostly, up in the empty lunchroom on the tenth floor. We'd share cups of hot chocolate since, like most thirteen-year-olds, she hadn't yet developed a taste for coffee or tea.

Thirteen. One year more than twelve. Three years less than "sweet sixteen." I was still eating the daffodils that the principal of my school kept on her desk before assembly every morning and then giggling about it with my friends, when I was thirteen. A whole group of us were obsessed with the musical *Annie*, and with *Godspell*, and in the evenings we used to spend hours in my room with the plastic speakers of the stereo my mother had bought me for my birthday pushed right up next to our ears, crying to Cat Stevens's *Tea for the Tillerman* album. I had never smoked a cigarette, kissed a boy, or had a drink, and it would still be a full year before I would wear my first pair of high-heeled shoes, which gave me the corn I have to this day on the longest toe of my left foot. Thirteen, then, I had to keep reminding myself, was amazingly young. But Lucille was thirteen—it was hard to imagine that so much callous indifference could be inflicted on someone so young.

"Did your mother work?" I asked her one afternoon.

"No. She stayed home. Or hung around outside. Came back. Drunk. High. The usual."

"She looked after you as best she could, or what?"

"Sometimes. All depend on her mood. Up and down like that. When I was young—like six?—I'd be bad to see what she'd do. I'd go outside and not come back until five-thirty in the morning. I'd be sitting outside."

"Just sitting outside by yourself?"

"Umm-hmm. On the steps. If my mother really cared she would care for where I was and come for me."

"Did she sometimes?"

"Nah. She'd just stay right there in the house and go to sleep."

Thirteen years old. She had lived in all five boroughs, and had run away from all five boroughs too. Each time, she had lived alone out on the streets and bought food with whatever money she had been able to take with her, until loneliness drove her back, first to her mother and then to whichever foster or group home she had most recently been placed in.

But now, at Williamson's, Lucille was getting some help. She sometimes talked about her hopes of being adopted by a nice lady somewhere, perhaps out in Brooklyn, by the sea. She concentrated mostly, however, on becoming what she called "a woman of the nineties," by which she meant somebody with some sense, somebody who knows what she is doing and why. She told me this one evening when I got permission to take her out to McDonald's, on the condition I bring her back by seven. "But I can get discouraged," she said. "You look for honesty and you look for people that's going to appreciate you for you, appreciate what you do for them. And then you bump into someone like Maurice and you get depressed because you do for them, and you do for yourself, and you try to make them and you happy, and you end up getting hurt for the simple fact that people like Maurice don't know how to be honest. They going to pretend that they are looking out for both of you but on the down low—like on the side?—they playing games with you which you are just too blind to see."

Earlier that same night Lucille had been sitting with Maurice in the lounge of Unit 2, on the third floor of Williamson's, when the phone had rung. Maurice had gone to pick it up and Lucille knew that it must be a girl on the other end of the line because of the way he had laughed, and because he turned away when he started to talk. Then she'd heard him say, "'Course I love you, Suzie. Word, baby." Lucille had made a big deal earlier that day that I couldn't take her out to dinner unless we brought back a couple of cheeseburgers or a Big Mac with an order of supersized fries for Maurice, but when I reminded her of this as we got up to leave she just turned and stared at me like I was from Mars and stormed out of the brightly lit restaurant into the street, mumbling something about the shoddiness of my car and the embarrassment she would suffer if anyone she knew ever saw her in it.

She was still furious the following morning. She marched into Family Group and, without saying a word to me or Ed or anyone else, sat down in a chair in the corner of the room and buried all but one eye in her arms on the desk. Like an iguana she swiveled that one eye over to me when I said hi and then swiveled it back across the room to Maurice. As far as I could tell she never blinked once. She certainly didn't move the rest of her body, and for the entire length of Family Group she sat slumped over her desk, her one visible eye focused so unflinchingly on Maurice that, confused by such single-minded persecution, he couldn't even pull on his brand-new, blue Polar jacket, and got it so twisted and turned inside out that he left the room still struggling to put it on.

They must have made up later that day, though, because sometime around eleven, in the middle of fourth period, I saw them waltz into the stairwell together, Maurice's arm resting comfortably on Lucille's shoulder, his lips hovering near her ear. Suzie was coming down from the tenth floor at just the same moment. She often went wandering at this time of day, but she generally waited for the elevator because her physical coordination was such that she had to concentrate as she went down the stairs. Holding the handrail and watching her feet as though willing them to do the job right, she trotted down toward Maurice and Lucille, oblivious to everything but the regular rhythm of her wooden-soled sandals on the stairs and the traces of a tune she was humming to it.

"Why did you call me a bitch on the phone last night, Suzie?" Lucille asked, all concerned innocence.

"I didn't," Suzie said, reaching the landing and coming to a stop.

"You did. Maurice said you called me a bitch."

"What do you mean I called her a bitch?" Suzie asked Maurice, who took a step backward, crossed his arms over his chest, and said nothing.

"You did. He told me you did."

"I didn't." Suzie was getting confused. "I didn't!"

"He said you did, last night, he told me as soon as he got off the phone, and he laughed about it too."

"?---?---?"

"Why, Suzie," Lucille said, impatiently.

"I didn't, Lucille—I didn't. You're my friend. I didn't call you a bitch. Why would you lie, Maurice? Lucille's my friend." But faced with Maurice's blank look and then with the thin slits of Lucille's eyes, all lids suddenly, all she could do was turn and start trotting down the stairs to the street. As Suzie fled, hand tightly gripping the rail, the beat of her footsteps echoed now not by a tune but by the refrain "Why, Maurice, why?," Lucille burst out laughing.

"I love it when I can do that," she said. Out of the corner of my eye I saw Maurice smile.

4

MAURICE, LUCILLE and Suzie were not the kind of students to thrive in traditional school settings. Marginalized by both economic and social shortcomings, they had visited the full spectrum of educational options in the city before coming to West Side. They were either too bright, too bored, or, in Maurice's case, too disturbed to have learned much more than how to exert some level of control over their peers. But at West Side most of the staff members were adamant that if nobody else wanted them, it wasn't because they were irredeemable. Some no longer even used the term "dropout" to describe kids who hadn't made it in a traditional school setting. Arguing that it was often the school, not the student, that was at fault, they preferred the term "pushout" and operated under the belief that traditional schools were no longer working for many students and that a different approach needed to be tried.

Initially West Side didn't have a mandate to serve this type of student population. Twenty-two years before, it had opened in a fanfare of public support for community-controlled education that many hoped would help stem the tide of middle-class flight from the public schools. By the mid-seventies the perception that New York's educational system was the best in the world had become a distant, increasingly mythic memory. Urban areas were in decline across the country as job bases and middle-class workforces shifted to the suburbs, and inner-city schools that had once been predominantly white were becoming increasingly black and Latino. As the de facto segregation continued to worsen, parents of the students who remained in the schools began to demand changes in the system. In step with the radicalized tenor of the time, newly empowered community groups came together in New York and insisted that members of their own community could better teach their children than those chosen by representatives of the centralized and predominantly white Board of Education. When the board did nothing, parents started to boycott local schools. Teachers in many communities staged walkouts. Two years of turmoil ensued, but it wasn't until after the infamous teachers' strike of 1968, during which schools across the city closed for as much as seven months, that community groups finally wrested control of the city's elementary schools from the centralized board.

The city's high schools, however, were a different matter. Citing the need for standardized testing and required levels of achievement, the board retained control. It wasn't until a year later, when the educational reformer Harvey Scribner was elected New York City's first independent school chancellor, that the board announced it would charter a handful of local community-based, experimental high schools. On the Upper West Side a local activist named Doris Rosenblum gathered together a group of educators, teachers, and parents to draft a proposal for a more intimate, ethnically integrated learning community in School District 3. When their proposal was approved they spent the next seven months drawing up plans, designing curricula, hiring staff, and canvasing local junior high schools for students. They chose high-minded ninth graders, typical seventies kids mostly, buoyant with notions of broad-based, student-controlled education, and by the beginning of the summer the only thing they lacked was a building.

Months passed with nothing forthcoming from the board. By July some on the West Side team had begun to give up hope. Then the board came up with some space in the top two floors of an old primary school on West End Avenue, and the problem seemed to have been solved. That fall, two young and eager full-time teachers, a part-time instructor, and their one hundred students—one-third African American, one-third Latino, and one-third white, just as they had outlined in their proposal—marched into the building. Expecting to take part in a school where, as one student of the time told me, "kids would sit out in the corridors devouring books and accumulating knowledge just because they wanted to," they were confronted instead with a badly lit, crumbling old building already partially inhabited by a school for emotionally disturbed and violent young men. Lost in a huge old building with unlocked fire exits open to the street, unlit stairways, and long, dark corridors, West Side's student body made perfect victims for the building's other tenants. The school's proud belief in open learning soon had to take a back seat to the more immediate problems of danger and fear. According to Rosenblum, not a single day passed without one of her students being jumped, beaten up, or intimidated in some way.

Rosenblum spent easily half of her day breaking up fights and the rest complaining to the board. Stolid even back then, the board did nothing. More interested in the experiment of community schools as a political salve than as the beginning of a real commitment to alternative education, most members of the centralized bureaucracy had tired of Scribner's radical ideas, and his influence there was already on the wane. West Side was told there was no other space for them. They were welcome to close, but if they wanted to stay open they would have to make do.

By January, however, the situation had become so bad that the board finally agreed to lease a renovated ballet school ten blocks north, on West Ninety-third Street. West Side had lost close to 60 percent of their student body by then, including most of the middle-class kids it had tried so desperately to attract. At the same time the district's zoned schools were becoming increasingly overcrowded. Interpreting West Side's alternative philosophies as an invitation for students who couldn't make it in the regular system, many zoned-school counselors saw West Side as the perfect place to deposit students with discipline problems or behavioral difficulties. West Side quickly became known as a dumping ground. By the time Ed showed up, four years later in March 1975, the school had hit rock bottom.

Ed was certainly no disciplinarian. Nor was he a toughened old-timer with his own hard-won belief in the educational system. In fact, he might just be the only principal ever to have served in New York City on a temporary junior high school science teacher's license. Pressed to pinpoint the exact reason he got into education in the first place, he admits that it was at least in part because of the draft exemption you earned by teaching in a hard-luck neighborhood. Still, his work with drug-addicted teens in New Jersey had prepared him for difficult situations, and three months after he arrived attendance had picked up and discipline problems had been reduced, or at least muffled, enough for the board to keep West Side afloat.

By then it had also become clear that life was easier in the regular neighborhood schools if they could place their difficult students elsewhere. Year after year West Side continued to grow as a result of the transfers, and it soon needed more space. Once again the school was shunted north, this time to a much larger, once grand Victorian elementary school building in the Douglass housing project on 102nd Street and Amsterdam Avenue. Five stories tall and festooned with turrets and spires and copper-roofed pediments of terra cotta and glass, the building had a gym, a nursery, and a full-sized auditorium, as well as a lunchroom with its own, fully functioning kitchen. Ed loved the place. Renaming it Château West Side, he drew up a list of much-needed renovations. The board approved them all with the warning that it could be years before the bulk of the work was implemented. In the meantime they had to make do with a leaky roof, fire-damaged walls, and cracked and broken windows, through which the wind whistled. Then on February 12, 1989, the weekend before renovation, Ed got a phone call. A roof had fallen in on a school designed by the same fanciful architect, and a team of engineers had found the same structural flaw in his own building.

At first Ed insisted the board correct the structural problems and continue with their plans for renovation. The board wouldn't even consider it, but when it became clear that Ed was not going to leave they offered him a new building instead, right there on the grounds of the old Château. He was suspicious at first. A new building would cost millions, and though the board was flush with cash at the time, it was only when they began to draw up plans for the new building, that Ed agreed to evacuate the site.

West Side would have been the first alternative school to have its own, brand-new building. And because for once it seemed that the board was acknowledging the good work his staff was doing, Ed didn't mind too much that renovations to the temporarily leased office space in midtown Manhattan were sloppy and cheap. It was better than the other space they had been offered—an underground and windowless facility that had stalactites growing from the ceiling as a result of chemical seepage from the sidewalk above. But even he was taken aback when, six months after they had moved, the board changed its mind and decided that money for construction of the new school was not to be forthcoming after all. Construction costs had been removed from the capital budget, he was told matter-of-factly, and without any further explanation the matter was dropped.

"It's disgusting," Ed said in an uncharacteristic burst of anger one afternoon. "We came down here to what they call 'swing space,' so they could build a new school for us, and the fact that we don't get the new building is just part of the disrespect we are treated with. Last year we had no blackboards, we had no desks. The blackboards finally came in December. The desks I basically begged. In this system you are related to the kids you deal with. I've said this before, I know, but if you teach in Bronx Science or you teach in Stuyvesant everybody looks at you like you must be the cream of the crop. If not. . . ."

When Ramón C. Cortines came into power in September 1993, Ed had no expectation that West Side would get more attention than it had in the past. Cortines had been hired to replace the previous chancellor, Joseph A. Fernandez, who was ousted after a series of highly political battles over the liberal, multicultural curriculum known as Children of the Rainbow. Fernandez's persona had been larger than life. He had single-handedly turned around Miami's troubled public school system before coming to New York, and his arrival had created huge expectations. Cortines, in contrast, was a quiet, bookish insider who was chosen as chancellor by the mayor's conservative allies on the board. But Rudolph Giuliani and he had shared a surprisingly strained relationship ever since. The strain arose, Giuliani aides insisted, after a meeting in which the mayor asked Cortines to assess the effectiveness of the school bureaucracy. According to Giuliani, Cortines told the mayor that the problem was far worse than anyone could imagine and pledged to dismiss thousands of employees, only to change his mind at their next meeting, when he drastically reduced the number of workers he was willing to let go. Cortines always declined to discuss these events. But their feuding became increasingly public over the next few months and culminated in a battle over school spending that prompted Cortines to resign for two days, a state of affairs that was patched up only after then Governor Mario Cuomo intervened.

It is virtually a New York tradition for the mayor and the chancellor to battle this way (a battle made all the more inevitable when the city has a $2.3 billion deficit, as it did that year). While the city contributes about 40 percent of the schools' annual $8.84 billion budget, it has no say over how the board of education decides to spend it. To Giuliani the solution had always seemed simple: the mayor, he argued, and not the chancellor, should be in control of the board. In the upcoming months he would even start to call publicly for Cortines's resignation. "The Giuliani administration hopes to dissuade him from staying by forcing him to consider whether he wants constant strife from City Hall," an aide was quoted as saying. And though, for his part, the chancellor had most education experts and the majority of the board on his side, it became increasingly clear that if he was going to keep them there he had to present himself as an apolitical, "kids-first" coalition builder.

In an attempt to get his down-to-earth image across, Cortines started his term by taking what was portrayed as a good, hard look at the schools under his control. He made unannounced visits to schools all over the city and studied charts and statistics and measures of attendance and grades and reading and mathematics scores. After a few months he even came up with a report that would be sure to garner some media attention and show that he was aggressively taking on his job. It was a list of the sixteen worst schools in the city. "Academic failures" he called them, and West Side was one of them.

Ed had been the principal at West Side for close to twenty years by then, and he knew things like this tended to happen when a new chancellor arrived. In their eagerness to define themselves, nearly every one of them had made one dramatic pronouncement or another—the results of which were perhaps in part responsible for the chaotic state of education in the city and for the fact that in the past ten years New York has had seven new chancellors. And while this was just the latest in a long string of humiliations Ed had suffered at the hands of the board, it was particularly vexing this time because the main factor leading to the school's inclusion on what became known as the "underachieving-schools list" was not that 84 percent of his students had already failed at two high schools before arriving at West Side, or that

46 percent of them stayed less than a year, or even that nearly a quarter of the student body were learning-impaired in some way. The main reason he was seeing the name of his school printed next to the city's worst educational failures was clerical error.

Eighteen years before, someone at the Board of Education had decided that West Side could not keep students from different grades in the same Family Group. When Ed had asked why, he was told only that it ran contrary to the board's best interest. Knowing better than to argue with that kind of logic but determined to keep Family Groups integrated, Ed decided that the easiest way around the ruling was to quietly register his entire student body as eleventh graders. Because West Side didn't operate on a grade-based system, this didn't affect the day-to-day running of the school at all, and no one even knew about it for years.

Then Cortines arrived and decided to judge the city's high schools on the reading scores of their eleventh graders, the logic being that by then the typical student had been at their high school long enough for the school to take either the credit or the blame for their academic performance. Thus the test included West Side's entire student body even though half of Ed's kids didn't have enough credits to place them in the tenth grade, if anyone cared to notice. Still, West Side had been diagnosed as a failure. It was right there on the list printed up in the *New York Post* and the *Daily News* and the *Times* and in three colors in *New York Newsday*, all of which left Ed sitting at the receptionist's desk after everyone else had gone home one afternoon, newspaper clippings in hand, as close as he ever gets to being despondent.

Why was it, he asked, doodling over the large capital W of West Side on one of the published lists, that education was the only field in which the professionals who take on the most difficult cases are condemned? Even without the ridiculous blunder over the eleventh grade his school would never do well in a direct comparison with one of the city's choice schools—how could it when he worked with the toughest kids? But while a heart surgeon who performs the most intricate and minuscule operations on the sickest of patients is respected even if his patients have a higher mortality rate, a school that tries to help the most difficult kids, and that does its best to keep those kids coming every day, and that even manages to graduate 74 percent of them every year, is viewed as second-rate—not as a real school at all, but as a messy attempt at one.

"The Sloan-Kettering cancer hospital would change its specialty if its mortality rates were compared to those of a general hospital," Ed said, without even the slightest pretense of outrage. "I try to laugh about it, truthfully, but it is deeply discouraging because we are here all day doing our best for the dissed of this world, by whom I mean the disenfranchised, the disadvantaged, the disrespected, the dissatisfied—and the disabled and disturbed sometimes too—and even our own leaders condemn us."

That was another thing the test had not taken into account. The problems many West Side students dealt with were more nebulous and ephemeral than state specifications could ever outline with an intelligence test or a Rorschach blot, and just as many successful lives were bolstered at West Side as confused ones were straightened out. It was true, however, that with 17 percent of its student body classified as having special educational needs, West Side had come to have more than its fair share of mentally and emotionally needy students as well.

Ed believed in giving such kids the chance to go to a normal school, and he ended up taking students who many believed should have been placed in a more protective environment. The kids from Williamson's were an example of this, and Maurice's part-time girlfriend, Suzie, had been grating on so many people's nerves that her advisor and special education counselor were spending hours every week looking for another school in which to place her. For the most part though, West Side's special-education department could deal with anything. Unlike so many regular zoned schools, which section students with special needs off into separate classrooms, floors, or, in some cases, even buildings, West Side tried to involve special-ed kids to the point that often even a teacher didn't know who in their class was special-ed and who was not. Sometimes, of course, this led to problems. Undifferentiated expectations can become overwhelming to kids with special needs, especially if they have trouble with reading or writing. But most students flourished under the increased expectations, both social and academic, and grew in both skills and interest far more quickly than if they'd been kept in a segregated world.

None of which is to say that extra help, when given correctly, wasn't often needed. I had spent several hours with Janina, the special-education teacher, and had watched as morning after morning she cloaked her students with an intimacy and personal care that stood more than effective guard against the confusion that surrounds so many kids with special needs and allowed them to actually think.

One morning she drew little oval shapes in green around the sentence "Who Am I?" and then added lines jutting out of it like porcupine quills, next to which she asked the kids to write whatever came into their minds, words or phrases—anything. After ten minutes or so a pretty girl, delighted with the newfound knowledge that she could start a new line whenever she wanted if she called what she was writing a poem, came up with the following:

I am a girl
I am in tetligen sumart
and I'm a girl who fighting
to have hight school
and go to collage
I want to became important
and educated
I am a person who fighting
For everything I wanted to be.

Another time I went with Esther, the art teacher, and a group she had been preparing for over a month, to the Museum of Modern Art. In the velvety quiet of the museum I watched as the art-viewing public turned pale and gasped when an inspired student stormed by them on his way to a painting by Dalí. The mostly middle-aged, mostly white crowd had literally stepped back as we passed, as if wanting to protect themselves from this six-and-a-half-foot-tall black boy striding across the carpeted floors, waving his arms and exclaiming in excitement. There was a time, not long before, when I too might have retreated, I had to keep reminding myself. But familiarity allowed me to see now that the boy charging around the museum, the straps of his overalls flying out behind him as he flung his hands dangerously close to priceless works of art, was having a moment of exhilarating enlightenment. Exclaiming in delight or disgust or wonderment as we flew past Brancusis and Giacomettis, Tony Phillips, a boy listed as being both mentally and emotionally disturbed, had wanted to see some paintings by Dalí ever since he had seen a slide of some melting clocks in one of Esther's rigorous preparation classes. "Artistry," he exclaimed when we finally found the right room. "Look at this! Two people praying, woman growing, love here, look—love and death and insects and corn, life! You know! Life! All of it, he just draws you in. That's why I love his work, man, it's multidimensional."

The art so excited him that we were the last ones out of the museum and had to rush to join the rest of the group at the subway station. An old man was playing an accordion just down the platform from us, and as Tony pulled an apple from a pocket in his multicolored cotton jacket and took a huge bite from it, he tapped his foot in double time to the tune. Searching the ads and the movie posters on the platform as intensely as he had the art on the walls of the museum, he took another bite from the apple, then another. After consuming the core in the same way, he reached into his pocket and pulled out another. Then something in him snapped, and he stuffed the half-eaten apple back into his pocket, leapt toward me, and, picking me up, carried me along with him until I realized that what he wanted was to lead me in a tango down the platform. We danced the entire length of the station and did a great dipping turn at the end, much to the approval of the rest of the class and of the accordionist, too, I think. And as we danced our way back again, out of the corner of my eye I could see a blur of skirt suits and pants suits and briefcases, folded newspapers and clocks—not melting, but the solid kind, ticking—and for the first time I not only felt at home at West Side but downright exultant: consciously, startlingly happy to be dancing with Tony instead of checking and marking and measuring and criticizing with all the other harried professionals waiting for a train.

But when I tried to tell all this to Ed the stories fell flat. It wasn't his students that got to him, he told me. He was proud of his kids and of what his school sometimes managed to do for them, and he'd had experiences like that a thousand times over. It was just that stories like the ones I'd just told—experiences and achievements and enlightenments like that—weren't what the Board of Education was looking for. They were looking for statistical achievements, numbers that West Side wasn't able to provide, and as a result the school was on Cortines's list and there was nothing anyone could do about it. Sitting on the desk next to him now, flicking tentatively through the newspaper clippings, I asked Ed what being on the underachieving-schools list meant in real terms. Would someone come by and try to tell him how to change the way he ran his school? Ed gathered up his papers and laughed.

"No one's going to do that here," he said. "The last person we had come evaluate us was from upstate. Strong, his name was. He was so scared of the kids that he didn't even want to go into the hallways, let alone the classrooms, and decided to do his studies from paperwork. So no. No one is going to come in here and change anything." Nonetheless, however much time Ed spent on the phone reassuring parents and supporters and private sources of funding that he had nurtured over the years, the school was starting the year in trouble. And after a half hour of letting off steam, sitting there behind the light-blue desk and the sign that read "Welcome to West Side High School" in the kind of rounded gold letters that are usually strung from the ceiling at a children's birthday party, Ed simply shrugged, gathered up the paper clippings, and daintily dropped them into the garbage can at his feet. "Oh—who cares? How do I feel about being on the list? Really? Who cares?" he said. "It makes no difference in the end, we'll still be here tomorrow morning."

5

SANDRA AND CRISTY had been coming into Family Group wearing strings of colored beads around their necks for weeks. Cristy seemed to prefer plain yellows and whites, while Sandra experimented with blues and purples. From across the room I listened as they discussed new combinations of colors and the additions of the gaudily Catholic doodads they sometimes hung from the ends: a crucifix, a sacred heart, a raised, pressed-plastic portrait of the Virgin. The beads were of all shapes and ranged in size from a grape to a grape seed. As time progressed, their morning debates became more and more heated. Once Cristy even stormed out of the room with a fistful of pastel-colored, pea-sized beads, close to tears, before Sandra brought an end to it all one day by pulling out a thick necklace of purple and clear hexagonal beads tipped with a large, transparent Plexiglas cross, placing it defiantly on Cristy's desk, and saying: "I've decided. These is the colors."

"Ay Sandra! I thought I told you I don't like the cross! Everyone wears crosses—why can't we just be different and be ourselves?" Cristy said, whining slightly.

"We having the cross, Cristy," Sandra replied. "It's like a weight to keep the beads down." For a few minutes Cristy sat and looked at the rope of tightly strung beads. She ran her perfectly polished nails along the edges of the transparent cross, scrunching up her lips until they made a perfect O right in the center of her face. She bounced the cross up and down in her palm a couple of times, twisted the beads so they caught the light, counted them, and then acquiesced.

"OK. We having the cross. But I still think that a pretty, light mauve would be better for the girls than this purple, Ma," she said in a more conciliatory tone. Then, noticing that I had been watching her, she walked across the room to where I was sitting, placed a dainty finger up against her shining lips, and said, "Shhh. Don't tell no one. R3—that's the name of our family, but we don't want Ed to know."

Sandra and Cristy had been impregnable up until then. Perhaps because they shared the same most-popular-girl-in-the-class arrogance that had always attracted me when I'd been a teenager arriving in yet another new school, I had been trying to win them over since my first day at West Side. But it had been hard. They were inseparable. Best friends who had seen each other every single day for the past two years, they were referred to as "the twins" or simply as "those two" by teachers who had to deal with them sitting in the back of their classes, willfully ignoring whatever it was they were trying to teach. Mostly they gossiped about neighborhood things or applied layers of makeup to their pretty, neat-featured faces. And though they enjoyed art and weight-lifting, they seemed to have only the vaguest interest in the rest of their classes. Most mornings they ended up leaving school sometime around eleven o'clock.

I hadn't known much about "families" before then. Aside from the Mafia, the Colombian cartels, and the Chinatown tongs, I didn't think there were such things as "gangs" in New York. And until Cristy told me about R3 that morning I'd had no idea that their constantly changing necklaces were anything other than fashionable ornamentation. In fact they were *collares,* the identifiable signature of their own particular group, and an important element in the newly styled youth gangs that had been growing dramatically across the country for a couple of years. The importance of those *collares* was pretty much the only thing on which experts on the subject could agree. Otherwise there was little consensus over such basic issues as how to define a gang or even what gang-related criminal activity might be. In New York, wars fought out block by block for the sake of turf were no longer relevant. Even less so were the horrors we read about in the tabloids or watch on lurid, real-life TV shows or even see, occasionally, in some of the hipper photography galleries—those black-and-white images of prepubescent gang kids on the West Coast cleaning guns and smoking dope and laughing on their way to their first drive-by shooting. Such gangs do exist, of course. In Los Angeles the Crips and the Bloods were judged to be responsible for 40 percent of all homicides in 1996, and even New York has groups such as the Wild Cowboys, a $16 million-a-year drug ring who were responsible for ten killings over the past few years and who have been tied by investigators to twenty more. But these are well-organized criminal enterprises ruled by and created to profit from drug sales. The majority of New York's youth gangs are something else. Small, loosely organized, and often short-lived, they are more like surrogate families than criminal organizations. Once Sandra and Cristy decided to accept me into their confidence, it didn't take me long to realize just how much they both needed that kind of support.

Sandra had been dangerously out of control since she'd first started junior high school. Her mother had been a teenager herself when Sandra was born and had spent the past seven or eight years studying, first to get her GED and then to become a nurse. A couple of years earlier she had encouraged her daughter to drop out of school so that she could look after her baby half-brother at home. This arrangement lasted a year, until Sandra disappeared for several days with her grandmother's gun. She never used it, except to shoot up into the air from a neighbor's rooftop, just to see how it felt. But her mother had been so shaken by the episode that she'd placed Sandra under court supervision, and ever since, whenever she stayed out late, or spent the night at a friend's, she had to answer to a Family Court judge.

Sandra and her father hadn't really been in contact over the past decade. He had spent the last couple of years languishing in a prison in the Southwest, where he had been held ever since the police arrested him for driving through the state in a stolen car full of grade-one felony drugs that Sandra insisted were planted. Not that she cared, she said: he was a crackhead who was frequently violent when he was around. And though she would never have romanticized his effect on her upbringing, she did credit him with teaching her how to fight and was proud of her well-honed skills. Her mother had long since learned how to pop her daughter's knuckles back into place after they were dislocated in a fight, and at seventeen Sandra had already had three restraining orders taken out on her by girls who had crossed her. Mostly she fought over boys. Though shorter than average, she weighed close to 150 pounds and made an impressively hulking figure when she was riled. She had sent one girl home from her junior high school prom half-naked, after scraping the girl's face against the wall, throwing her repeatedly to the floor, and ripping her dress down to the waist. Another girl moved back to her native Santo Domingo after Sandra beat her up so badly that "she looked like she had just finished fighting Mike Tyson. One of her teeth? I pushed it back, all the way back. Her eyes? I put my fingers inside her eyes. I wanted to take her eyes out, so they were all bloody and scratched. Her nose was cracked. She ended up in the hospital."

This had happened repeatedly as far as I knew, which might have explained her swagger as she walked into the Family Group room and the thin but prevalent layer of disdain she had for those of us who never dared live our lives so brazenly. It might also explain why, when I finally summoned up the courage to overcome the adolescent insecurities the two of them brought out in me, it was Cristy, rather than Sandra, I sat next to in Family Group.

Cristy was also a large girl, and she was proud of her size and worked hard to maintain it. In the weight room I had seen her leg-press 385 pounds with an injured knee while Sandra lounged about in a designer jogging suit, eyeing the boys who paraded around the tiny, windowless room with their shirts off, muscles pumped and glistening with sweat. Less confident than Sandra and still not comfortable with her slight Central American accent, Cristy was clearly determined to be louder and brasher and bolder than any other girl in the school. But however much she cut the softness of her natural roll down the corridor by stamping each foot as it landed and by holding her arms out, flexed, by her waist like an overdeveloped bodybuilder, however loud she shouted, and however convincingly she sneered, she never quite managed to hide the fact that she was neither as outgoing as Sandra nor as tough and that she was really a well-brought-up, shy girl from El Salvador whose personal manners were delicate to the point of being prim.

Almost every morning I would watch her delicately sip cups of hot chocolate while eating the carrot-cake wedges she got free from the school lunch counter, bite by tiny bite without ever smudging, cracking, or even blurring the sheen from the fluorescent lipstick she always wore. One morning, careful to sit in the chair on the other side of the one she usually reserved for Sandra, I asked if she painted some kind of varnish over the color to keep it on—some kind of setting gel for the lips? Cristy glanced at me sidelong. "It's lipstick, Tina," she said, as though she were talking to a five-year-old. "You know? Lipstick?"

Cristy moved to the States when she was nine. Her mother's sister was already here, living successfully from the profits of an off-the-books business she had established in Washington Heights. So though Cristy's mother arrived illegally and with no knowledge of English, it had been relatively easy to settle in. She had always been paid at least enough money to afford a nice-sized, well-furnished apartment. Her hours were long and irregular, though, which left Cristy alone most of the time with her brother, a sometime drug addict she told me, who became violent when he drank. Like Sandra, Cristy could hold her own in a fight, and it wasn't rare for her to send him out of their pink-walled apartment crying in defeat. But when he was drunk or high enough he would attack their mother too, and that Cristy wouldn't stand for. Once she had to beat the back of his head with a cane to stop him from throwing their mother out of a third-story window. Despite this, and despite his long absences and his constant thieving and abuse, Cristy's brother still held a position of respect in the household that all of her cooking and cleaning and washing and folding and ironing of clothes would never topple. He was her mother's eldest son, and when he was around she was expected to wait on him hand and foot, no matter what, and even get out of the shower whenever he asked her to.

In R3, though, everything was different. With a series of beeps any one of them could summon a group of fellow members to help dump an abusive stepfather's possessions out on the street, look for a missing sibling, or hold a drug-addicted mother down in the house while she went cold turkey. It was an essential service for kids like Sandra and Cristy, who had nowhere else to turn and who were blindly determined to at least try to create some kind of order in their lives. And though much of their time with R3 was spent sprawled across "their" benches in the park across from McDonald's on Dyckman Street, complaining about cops and parents and brothers and sisters while drinking from paper-bag-covered bottles of Zima and forty-ounce bottles of beer, they spent an equal amount of time planning meetings, too, dreaming up complex hierarchies and militaristic titles, and outlining (in duplicate) specific punishments for specific infractions. They wrote laws and bylaws and oaths, and evening after evening compiled lists of beeper numbers and gang names and birthdates and codes in case of emergencies. They even collected money from their members every week in order to distribute it again according to need.

It was true that discipline was rigid, and that occasionally infractions were punished by beatings, and yet at a time when New York City had slashed after-school programs and almost all extracurricular activities within the schools as well, even a supervisor in NYPD's Gang Intelligence Unit, a burly blond detective sergeant named Matthiessen, admitted that many youth gangs actually did manage to have a positive impact on their members. It was rare of course, he hastened to add. Re-emphasizing the facts that, like Sandra and Cristy, most youth gang members came from violently destructive homes and already cut classes and got in trouble with the law, he nonetheless concluded that criminal activity wasn't an organized or coordinated part of most familes' routines. If the truth be told, he said, the presence of youth gangs usually led neither to an increase nor a decrease in crime. Most often the only noticeable change was that "the drug dealer and the thief and the small-time stick-up artist who were always there start wearing the same colored necklaces."

It was true that Sandra and Cristy were missing more school than ever now, and that they ran out of West Side almost every other day after receiving a beep from one of "their girls" needing help. But the new sense of security that the group lent them was palpable, and when in school they seemed more focused and calm than they had before. Sandra took the lead, of course, and you could feel her new sense of purpose just looking at her. But even Cristy started to relax and open up after a time. In school her accent made her uncomfortable speaking out or voicing her opinions, except in those short, flat, aggressive-sounding haikus that had so bewildered me when I first met her. But in R3, all members were Spanish speaking, and with no reason to feel self-conscious, she began moving beyond her old confines and started to make real friends.

About a month into the school year she even found a boyfriend. A Puerto Rican named Jonell, he was her exact equal. They were both second in command, she of the girls and he of the boys. Standing in the art room one afternoon, her stretched canvas balanced between the metal legs of a chair upturned on a table, she taped the shooting red stripes in her abstract painting to make sure the edges stayed straight while she painted in the background, and admitted that she might even love him. "He treats me good. Different, you know?" she said. "Not like a girlfriend but more like a friend? Last week I slapped him during one of our play fights, just to test him. . . ." She pursed her lips, leaned in close to her painting, and applied one, two, three careful strokes of thick black gloss before adding in utter disbelief: "And you know what, Tina? He didn't even hit me back."

It was close to eleven then, and the art room was packed. Esther, the teacher, had spent most of the morning trying to show at least some of her students how to use a linocut knife, but two of her students had already run the curved edges of their blades into their thumbs. The cuts were not serious, but a few drops of one boy's blood had spilled onto the fresh cream of his new Guess sweatshirt. Esther was trying to get out the stains with a variety of concoctions she kept expressly for the purpose in empty yogurt tubs under the sink, so she didn't even notice when Sandra burst through the door, stormed into the classroom, and pulled her right sleeve up to her elbow to show a bruise.

"Yo, yo Cristy! Wait until you hear what happened to me last night, yo!" she screeched. "Tha's from the handcuffs, man! I was walking home and this cop, this little white-nigger-rookie, smiles at me and does like this." She stuck out her tongue and wiggled it and then described in minute and exuberant detail how the cop became infuriated when Sandra refused to flirt with him and how, in the end, he had lost his temper, pushed her hard against the fence, and handcuffed her. When he searched her pockets and found several strands of her R3 beads, she told him that they weren't hers, that she didn't know anything about them, and she was just about to be let go when a passing squad car pulled up for a look.

"R3," the cops in the car said when they saw the purple and clear beads. "That's the new crew round here."

"Uh-uh, R3 wear blue and white," Sandra said then, desperately trying to hide her pride in the fact that they had finally been recognized. "The kids who hang out on Two hundred and fourth Street"? she added. "R3? I know them—they wear blue and white." The police were confused but interested. It wasn't often that kids started talking about gangs, and Sandra answered their questions about this fictitious R3 for the next few minutes, until she was feeling so good that when the rookie finally uncuffed her and handed her a ticket for disturbing the peace she tore it up in his face.

"If you are going to give me a ticket—give it to my PO," she told us in the art room she'd told him. Then she'd asked for his name and number, saying that she would lodge a harassment complaint with her parole officer as soon as she got home. A harassment suit was actually justified, since he'd not only stopped a woman walking quietly along the street, alone, without probable cause, but had not called out a "lady cop," as Sandra put it, to search her.

This is a problem that often occurs up in Washington Heights, the northern Manhattan community where both she and Cristy lived. Unlike many impoverished neighborhoods in the city, Washington Heights was not so much in decline as on the verge of exploding. In recent years, New York immigrants from the Dominican Republic have outstripped those from any other country, and most of the new arrivals have settled here, joining family members already established in the area. This population boom has led to grossly overcrowded schools, packed apartment buildings, a breakdown in already tenuous social services, and one of the highest unemployment rates in the city. The resulting chaos has also fostered a thriving underground economy, in which drugs play a dominant role. Easy access to supplier nations, along with the absence of an effective extradition treaty, optimize conditions for the illicit trade. People in the neighborhood complain not only about the shootings and violence associated with drug dealing but also about the volume of traffic that comes in from New Jersey, across the George Washington Bridge, to buy cocaine and heroin. For residents of the area, parking spaces were all but impossible to find.

The excesses of drug peddling had engulfed the local police in scandal as well. In 1994, thirty-four members of the 30th Precinct were arrested for crimes ranging from perjury and civil rights violations to stealing cash and drugs from drug dealers. The effects of this were so wide-reaching that more recently, Judge Harold Baer, Jr., the U.S. District Court Judge for the Southern District of New York, denied the admission of seventy-five pounds of cocaine as evidence in a case, because, he said, although police officers testified to seeing the three suspects running away from the trunk of the car as they approached, this was not suspicious behavior, and thus did not provide sufficient grounds for a search. "The residents of this neighborhood," the judge wrote, "tended to regard police officers as corrupt, abusive, and violent. Had the men not run when the cops began to stare at them, it would have been unusual."

Under political pressure reaching all the way up to the White House, Judge Baer later reversed this decision. Nonetheless, the incident offered ample proof that relations between the police and residents in the area were shaky at best. Many blamed the tension on the differences in language and culture between the majority of the population and the police force, a gulf that was only increased by the overburdened, underperforming educational system and social services in the area. It is at least in part in response to this combination of poverty, chaos, and perceived institutional racism that, in an attempt to carve out some space for themselves, so many teenagers have joined youth gangs in the past five years.

According to law enforcement officials, the United States now has some 1,439 gangs and some 120,630 gang members nationwide. The phenomenon isn't confined to the inner cities either: gangs are cropping up in even the most bucolic suburban communities. In New York, however, membership has increased particularly rapidly. Once I started paying attention, I quickly became aware of the variations in color and style of the groups' different *collares*. The gold and black beads of the Almighty Latin King Nation, the most notoriously violent gang in the city, were easy to spot in downtown Manhattan. Unknown on the East Coast five years before, they now boasted 2,000 members citywide. They had a large chapter down on Delancey Street, and there was one too, I was almost sure, over at Fiftieth Street on the West Side, because almost every time I visited the area I saw four or five Kings hanging around the red-brick steps of the Zeckendorf public garden there. The next largest group, the Netas, who wear black, white, and red beads, seemed to have some kind of headquarters slightly farther south, on Thirty-fourth Street between Sixth and Eighth Avenues, ironically enough right opposite a police station, though I have often seen a group of them calmly sitting on the steps of a famous Episcopal church on Fifth Avenue as well. In Brooklyn I have seen both Latin Kings and Netas in the Polish and Mexican and now artsy neighborhood of Williamsburg. There is a large outpost in Bushwick and in Red Hook, too. And on the subway, regardless of the line or the station, there is almost always a smattering of the blue and red beads of La Familia, or the engraved maps of Africa worn by members of the Zulu Nation. Once I was standing pressed between two young men in the evening rush hour and flinched so visibly when I saw the intricately strung beads of the DPs—a rival group to one I had been spending time with—hanging from their necks that I thought it best to get off the train at the next stop.

Most Manhattanites notice none of this. If they see the beads at all, they dismiss them as just one more intimidating accoutrement brandished by the already too intimidating inner-city teenagers. But many cops on the beat, at least those who are interested enough to seek out information and advice on such matters, have been warned to look out for these strings of beads. Many have been advised not to touch them. There is a theory going around that gang members believe their beads have sacred powers. The tradition has been co-opted from Santeria, the syncretic Caribbean religion whose followers wear the brightly beaded necklaces of their individual gods for protection. Many Santeria devotees believe these necklaces will spontaneously break apart in warning of danger and have been instructed to protect them from the contaminating touch of nonbelievers. Similarly, gang beads are supposed to possess strong powers of protection, and police officers have been told that if they try to break, remove, or even touch them, they will be risking a violent response.

R3, of course, wasn't quite in this league. Ed did not allow gang beads to be worn openly in the school, and neither Sandra nor Cristy seemed to mind tucking them under their sweatshirts when they walked into the building. They were proud of their beads, and after a time also started to thread bracelets and earrings in the same purple and clear pattern. But they had no qualms about taking them off and handing them to other kids in Family Group to inspect in the mornings. Power came from recognition, they knew, recognition from numbers, and they felt more strongly about getting the word out than they did about the supernatural power of beads they had bought themselves just a few weeks before.

Bit by bit their reputation grew. Sandra started to wear her beads openly on 180th Street, even when she was on her own. Once or twice she and a few other family members had banded together and slouched their way down Dyckman too, their beads prominently displayed around their necks as they refused to move out of anyone's way. They knew that the police had noticed them, which, according to Sandra, was "all good." But in the thrill of their mounting notoriety they had never thought of getting the official "green light" to wear colors from some of the more established groups in the area. And when one of their parties was invaded by a group of Latin Kings one night, no one knew what it was about at first.

Cristy thought it had been the sight of string after string of purple and clear beads that had so irritated the Kings. But Sandra believed they had known all along that R3 was holding a party and that that was why they had turned up in the first place, seven of them, all armed, at around three in the morning. Their very presence in the room was a direct challenge to R3, and the situation would have exploded quickly if a lieutenant in the Latin Kings' cousin organization, the Netas, hadn't arrived and been able to convince the Kings to step outside, down onto the street, to talk things through. R3 was not really a gang, he told them, not really a threat. They were just a bunch of kids, and to prove it, the Kings could go right back upstairs and collect every R3 *collare* they saw, if they wanted. They would encounter no resistance, he promised, cousin to cousin.

Grudgingly, the Latin Kings agreed, and after months of establishing trust in the kind of close-knit protection they had promised each other, the members of R3 were forced to line up in Jonell's carpeted living room and hand over their precious crucifix-tipped purple and clear beads to the seven armed Latin Kings. Getting stripped of your beads that way almost always means the end for a fledgling organization. It's the equivalent of a victorious army's taking of the flag after battle, and once you have lost face that way there is just no coming back. It happened all the time, Detective Matthiessen had told me: destroying the smaller gangs in the city was one way the larger groups recruited good people—a street version of a corporate takeover. And true to form, all talk of R3 stopped dead after that. In fact, it was less than a week before Sandra and Cristy turned up at West Side in the black, white, and red beads of El Asociación Neta.

With close to two thousand members citywide, the Netas were second in size only to the Latin Kings. Even the balding director of West Side security did a double take when he first noticed them striding through the door with the telltale black, red, and white beads hanging from their necks. Panicked, he hauled me into his office, pulled open a drawer of his desk, and rifled around the hairbrush and hair gel and comb to find a sheath of papers for me about gangs and their dangers. He had been in a gang when he was a kid, he told me. Hadn't realized what it was doing to him until he left them for the "biggest gang in the nation—the US Army," and now he had no patience with those who did the same thing. They were losers, he said, desperadoes, especially the new recruits and the girls who were out to prove something, and I'd do better to keep well away.

But despite what he told me, Sandra and Cristy were insistently, innocently proud of their newfound allegiance. They seemed to have been converted as legitimately as if they had taken up religion. As part of their "probation" period they were required to stay out of trouble, to go to school every day, and to complete all their homework; they also had to memorize the Neta rule book and study the numerous selected histories of the group, at least as hard as any catechist studies the catechism. Teachers were amazed to notice them suddenly coming to school on time, going to classes, and even responding every now and then to a class discussion, and Ed couldn't believe it when he saw them hurriedly completing homework during Family Group.

Though it would be months before they were made full-fledged members, just wearing the beads meant they could travel anywhere in the city and find stalwart friends. They were invited for meals, taken to parties, and escorted to their destinations by strangers they'd just met on the train who wore the same colors. Even the coffee shop around the corner from West Side had two or three Netas who dropped in regularly for donuts and coffee and who now greeted Sandra and Cristy like long-lost cousins, enveloping them in bear hugs before touching hands in a strange kind of finger-flicking ritual and then sharing a booming *"Corazón!"*—"With heart!"

"Some people just consider the Netas a gang because they really don't know what we're here for and they just say oh if there is one bad apple in the bunch," Sandra told me one afternoon in the coffee shop. "They think that then the whole bunch is ruined. But that's not true. Instead of living negatively you can live positively, like go to school. Or if you don't go to school you have to have a job, you can't just stay home. They won't allow that. You gotta go to school. And you can't steal and you can't lie, you can't betray nobody, you gotta take care of one another and there is no back stabbing. We are here to stop abuse everywhere. Worldwide. It's a whole new way of life," she said, taking a sip of tea thick with sugar. "A new way of living."

"She even getting married," Cristy interjected then.

"Married?" I asked.

"Yup. On Saturday, to the head of the local Neta chapter. The head from the floor—right, Ma?"

Sandra smiled and wriggled girlishly as she pulled out a photo of her husband-to-be and then looked over my shoulder at the image of her skinny-looking, pale Puerto Rican boy with green eyes sprawled shirtless across a sofa. His Neta beads, tipped with a heavy white plastic crucifix, hung down to his belly button. I had seen Sandra's enthusiasm for boys before. West Side's block was filled with what she called "handsome little courier boys," and she often used to stroll around the corner to leer and smile and pout and wink at one or another of them. Once I saw her stare so intently at a good-looking young man with a thin, ribbony beard that he actually stopped loading his truck, straightened himself up, put his hand on his hip, and then cracked a knee, so that up there on his flatbed, he looked like a girl modeling a swimsuit in a second-rate beauty competition.

"What's all this for?" he asked coyly.

"I can look, can't l?" Sandra retorted and then, all suggestive smiles and swinging hips, she walked away in a cloud of laughter so deep and throaty and downright elemental it was enough to make any man faint.

But this one was different, she assured me now. That was why she was marrying him. His name was Rankin Rodriguez and she had known him for three weeks—though he had asked her to marry him just five days after they met, she said. Her mother didn't know, of course—she had never even met the boy, didn't even know her daughter had a steady boyfriend because so many boys called her at home. Though Sandra had started to wear her new fiancé's ring, she had always worn a big gold ring on her wedding finger, big enough to have heart shapes cut out of it, and her mother hadn't noticed the difference.

Besides, there was really no need for her mother to know because they were not having a civil wedding but a Neta one. Not that the contract wasn't binding, Sandra added. In fact, it was "very much legal for the simple fact that it's better" than a state-sanctioned wedding. "Everyone knows you can get divorced from a regular wedding but for a Neta it's a commitment for life."

In the Netas, she told me, if your husband plays around he gets a *universal*, or a serious beating, at the next citywide meeting, where there are maybe two hundred young men willing to help with the task. It's the same for a wife who strays, though she is most often beaten by girls. As for the interloper, she gets what's called a *sesión*: "That's when they take a big wooden stick—you know, the ones they play croquet with," Sandra said, "and then beat her at least fifty times with it across her back."

For all that the Neta wedding ceremony is a simple one, though it makes for a good weekend—a ceremony and a prayer and a party with everyone all dressed up, their beads as binding as any family name: white for peace and harmony; black for the mourning of their founder, Carlos Torres Illiarte; and red for the blood shed, or willing to be shed by an *hermanito,* or "little brother," as members of the Netas are known. Cristy and Sandra's cousin Nikole were the bridesmaids. And though she spent a full week insisting that she would wear jeans and a sweatshirt, perhaps a new pair of sneakers, for the ceremony, in the end Cristy admitted to wearing a skirt that matched Sandra's short summer dress. The whole Neta chapter had gathered at Rankin's apartment. At around eleven the "head" arrived. He read the bride and groom each an excerpt from the Bible before asking them privately if they were sure of what they were going to do.

"Then he took us both into the living room, where everybody was like in a circle," Sandra told me the following Monday. "It was like twenty people, and they were all in a circle and we stood in the middle, whatever, facing each other, and he read the Scriptures and it was about love, saying, like, that we have to have the same love and respect that Jesus Christ had for us whatever-whatever. And then he gave us a blessing and we traded rings. We traded colors. And then we kissed. Everybody came and hugged us and jumped us! And everybody—all the girls—wanted to cry, especially Cristy, who was moaning, 'O-o-o-ohh! She got married! She got married!' whatever-whatever. Him? Him they gave a beat down."

6

BY THE SECOND week of October the fruit flies were all over the seventh floor of West Side: in the empty garbage cans that were left in the corridors by the students in charge of the schoolwide recycling program; in the chalk holders under the blackboards, in books, squashed into replicas of themselves like childish ink drawings, and in every cranny of every wire-reinforced window on the floor. Ed had so many in his already chaotic office that he gave up trying to name them. Rochelle, the English teacher who liked to keep her room open so students could eat their lunch there, had to ban eating in her classroom, and Esther had to stop using flour-and-water paste for making the brightly colored papier-mâché piñatas that hung like lanterns across the length of the art room. They were tiny little things, the flies, not really bothersome unless in a swarm, but they seemed resistant to fly spray and, like any infestation, they were demoralizing. The kids had been grumbling about them all week, and perhaps to cheer himself up after a staff meeting where they were again the main topic of discussion, Ed began his Family Group that Monday by reading a column by Michael Daley of the *Daily News* about a young financier who spent $8,500 on dinner at a restaurant named Le Cirque the night before.

The story was leaked by one of the financier's bodyguards who had shared his boss's meal. He was a retired police officer not used to the luxuries afforded by such a place, and he spoke with wonder—no, awe—of sitting down at the restaurant's most prestigious center table, surrounded by ten eager waiters, and drinking not one but two bottles of 1929 Château Ausone, which sold for $1,500 a bottle, out of a wine glass that could have "fit a gold fish from Coney Island inside—you know, the kind that you win at the stands."

Ed loves good food, good food served by great restaurants, and though he rarely manages to visit them he keeps avid track of the latest restaurant openings in the city. But even more than that, he loves incongruity, especially when it means that the good guy ends up winning for once, and it was clear that he was as much delighted with the image of a retired cop being pampered in the best restaurant in the city as he was disheartened by the discrepancies of a life where in the same edition of the same paper there was a photograph of fifty-six kindergartners crammed into one tiny classroom as a result of budget cuts.

"Now, at a moment when he had two sons out working the desperate streets as cops, Gates took a sip of the Château Ausone," Ed read. "'I'm waiting for buzzers to go off,' Gates remembers. 'I guess the connoisseur would be able to explain it. Maybe I tasted it wrong.'" Ed chuckled at the notion and then couldn't resist reading it again, this time acting out the motion of swirling one of Le Cirque's oversized wine glasses in his hand. "'Maybe I tasted it wrong,'" he said again.

Maurice was unimpressed and insisted that even if he had that kind of money he would never spend it on dinner. Bobby Peaks, a boy with a floppy black sun hat and slurred speech, disagreed. I had first seen Bobby the previous May when I had made some introductory visits to the school. He had been carrying a basketball then, one of the few things that are simply not allowed in a classroom at West Side. Ed had asked for it, and Bobby had been reluctant to hand it over. "It's my acorn, man! I gotta have my acorn." I hadn't seen him since, but he was the type of kid you couldn't forget; staff members who knew him called him "The Mayor" because of the way he worked the floor as if he were campaigning. But after three years of trying and testing and placating and encouraging, Ed placed him in that small percentage of his students for whom he no longer held out much hope. It wasn't simply that he sold drugs. Several did. It was more that "he has absolutely no sense of being a fifteen-year-old. Everyone likes him, of course—how could you not? But really he is one of the few hopeless cases that we have."

Earlier that morning Bobby had shuffled across the room in his trademark black sun hat and his huge black jacket and outsized black pants, and, as though being there was the most natural thing in the world, he'd sat down next to a friend in the corner with his back to the wall. Animated now by visions of absolute wealth, he rambled out loud, lisping through a permanently stoned haze, the words never quite making it past the rim of his lips, about what he would do if he had the money that the millionaire at Le Cirque seemed to have. "—And I would have solid-gold french fries and a salt shaker that shook out diamonds instead of salt and chocolate cake, yeah, chocolate cake from scratch with crumbs of gold and silver on the top."

Ed is not one who believes in minimizing the gross inequities in life. He doesn't see the point. Especially as most of the students at West Side exaggerated rather than diminished the gulf that separated them from mainstream society. Existing in such exotic contrast to the limited possibilities of their own lives, many seemed to barely even believe in the possibilities and hopes and options that most of America takes for granted. If they thought of middle-class life at all it was usually in the grotesquely stylized images of afternoon soap operas, and they tended to cast it either as a glittering sequence of untold wealth or as a uniformly bigoted, greedy, and repressive world that wouldn't let them in even if they did have straight As and a clean nose. They saw it as the "white world"—separate, unattainable, and so distant from their own tightly bounded reality as to seem as unreal as *Star Trek,* or *Little House on the Prairie,* or any of the other worlds portrayed on television.

So it was perhaps in an attempt to keep porous the boundaries that the city has created, and the kids themselves maintain, that Ed frequently brought in articles like this one about Le Cirque, or about Bill Gates, or discussed the average wages of corporate lawyers, advertising executives and the typical Harvard graduate.

"Anyone know where Harvard is?" he asked later that same morning. One boy, his face partially hidden by an army-green hoody ragged with wear, motioned with his arm as though pointing to heaven and said: "Up there somewhere?"

"Upstate?" someone guessed.

"New Jersey?"

"Cambridge, Massachusetts," Ed told them finally. "It's the best school in the country and it costs nearly thirty thousand dollars a year to go there, folks, so you better start saving."

"Why spend one hundred and twenty grand over four years to go to college when you just gonna end up without a job, hanging round the apartment high the whole time, begging people for a couple of dollars to get by?" Bobby mumbled. "And anyway, what happens if you get wounded and then it was all for nothing?

"Can you imagine that?" he asked, looking down at his desk, an ephemeral smile dancing from one side of his mouth to the other. "Four years and all those thousands and thousands and thousands of dollars. And they could throw you out too. I heard that if they catch you smoking weed up there in one of them dormitories they have in college they just throw you out." When Ed assured him that the way he was going he would get thrown out of West Side even without all of those dollars, I'm almost sure something in Bobby changed gear, though it was always hard to tell with Bobby because his grin hovered long after the impulse died.

"Oh come on, now," he said, almost bashfully. "Everyone knows it's better to hustle than to go to college, Ed, 'cause then you can have a good time and have nice clothes and a nice apartment. It's true that you always do end up in the joint in the end though," he added without changing either expression or tone. "I know because tha's what happened to my brother."

Serious now, Ed leaned forward in his chair and, ignoring the rising chatter from the rest of the room, focused exclusively and entirely on Bobby. "You have a bleak picture of the world, Bobby, did you know that?" he asked. "The way you see it, there's no way out. If you go to college you drop out. If you don't, you end up dead or in jail."

"Yup." Bobby nodded, and, looking directly at Ed for the first time that morning, he smiled broadly, as if pleased to have summed up the situation so nicely.

It was this clear, concise, wrongheaded summary of what one could expect out of life that drove me home to bed so often during my year at West Side. Perhaps because I grew up the child of a mother who told me how lovely the world was and how gracious and caring and giving and warm and decent most people were, I was convinced, for the longest time, that their state of mind was only temporary—the result, predominantly, of adolescent alienation like my own. And perhaps, partially anyway, it was. The problem was that the finite image many students at West Side held of themselves was continually supported by society around them. All day, every day, television, films, even advertisements reinforced the idea that if you were poor and African American or Latino your expectations better be humble. But much more damaging than these prefabricated images was the real-life reinforcement they received every day, through countless encounters with people from outside of their world—shop clerks, pedestrians, fellow subway travelers, policemen, taxi drivers—otherwise perfectly normal people who stared or sped past or shuffled away from them on their way down to midtown and school in the mornings. What Ed was trying to do at West Side was counter the weight of all this by guiding them down an alternate route to the one society expected them to follow. By encouraging them to believe sufficiently in the possibilities offered by mainstream society he hoped to help them shift course and begin to pursue the straighter, narrower path of consistent achievement and hard work.

My problem was that this wasn't a route I had ever stuck to. I'd never excelled at school, and I'd been far more delighted with disruption than any kind of positive investigation. Nonetheless, I was ten years older now and could see more clearly. Clearly enough to understand that West Side students were not given second chances all that often and that one mistake was usually enough to have them seriously hurt or thrown in jail for long enough to ruin them once and for all. If I wanted to help, I realized, I would have to guide them down a path that I had spent most of my own life rejecting. As a result, I lied to the kids constantly about myself. When they asked me if I smoked pot, I said that I didn't; I also told them I didn't drink much, though back then I was knocking back two or three stiff glasses of whiskey a night. And I never told anyone at West Side that I had turned my hand to drug dealing when I was a teenager either because—well, what good would it do?

My drug dealing had been strictly a middle-class affair, of course. Nothing like the operation managed by Bobby Peaks on the Upper East Side or even like the businesses run out of squats in central London, where tattooed hippies, aging skin hanging in sun-worn folds from their bare chests and stomachs, used to sell twenty-pound bags to kids like me in the evenings. I kept my stash in the blue leather briefcase my father had bought me when I was fifteen, after I'd admired it in France in a shop window. After a time I stopped buying from the hippies and bought in bulk instead, from a friend who swore it was pure sinsemilla flown in straight from Jamaica. I found out years later that it was grown in Bristol, in a student's bedroom under growing lamps, but I believed in its quality myself so much that no one ever complained. Besides, I was generous with my measure—I never did get around to buying a scale—and on the whole, sales were brisk. I had a little moped, a sky-blue 50 cc, and delivered free of charge, which helped as well. Even when it was cold out I enjoyed dodging traffic with my illicit bundles and would have continued with it, I think, if my friend and partner hadn't smoked her half of our last bulk purchase and left me without even a penny profit.

Of course, I could do all that back then because, unlike Bobby, I had no idea of the consequences if I got caught—literally no idea even that I might be caught or that I was really even a drug dealer in the first place. I had never yet found myself in a situation so severe that a little quick thinking couldn't get me out of it; the only time I'd had a run-in with the law, it had gone relatively well. I had been stopped by a policeman at a local London fair, a fair for people who lived in a great Georgian square with its own private park in the middle of it. My friends and I had to scale the sharp-tipped, black iron railings to get in, and before we went on any rides we wanted to get stoned. Passing a man who raised his eyebrows and smiled, I invited him to join us under an overhanging bush. Turned out he was a plainclothes policeman. When he saw what we were doing he escorted me back out onto the street, made me pour my bag of grass down a drain outside the park gates, and let me off with a warning. The same thing happened to many of my friends too. I'm sure it still does: stern warnings issued to middle-class kids on the mutual understanding that dealing was more of an experimentation than a permanent career choice and that the phase would pass.

At West Side, on the other hand, people were clear about what they were doing and about just what it made them, too. I never met anyone who, when I asked about their drug dealing, didn't shift around uneasily and scrape their feet and shuffle—barely repressing their urge to run. They were all more than aware of the risks they were taking.

Stories of gang rapes in jail, of becoming someone's "girlfriend" if you didn't "represent yourself" and "keep it real" were common. Everyone knew—fifteen-year-olds knew—about the need to stuff a two- or three-inch box-cutting blade deep into your anus for protection if you were going to Rikers Island or Spofford, the juvenile detention center in the Bronx where offenders under the age of sixteen are sent. First you tape the edges of the blade with wide black electrical tape—it is important that this be done carefully, because the thickness of the tape blunts the sharpness of the blade, and any slippage around the edges can cause serious injury. Next you wrap it tightly with toilet paper until it is roughly the diameter of an Italian sausage. You then slip the covered blade into a plastic bag or a rubber condom, tie a knot, grease it, and literally stuff it inside. According to Carlos, a sometime member of Ed's Family Group, whom I spoke to on his first day after being released from Rikers, guards hardly ever find "stuffed" blades because it is rare during a strip search for them to do anything more than ask you to bend over and cough. It was essential anyway to risk it, because without protection in prison these days you are anyone's toy.

Having thoroughly understood all this, Bobby still believed that it was better to hustle than to sit at home and do nothing. Looking around at the projects in the South Bronx, where he lived, at the block after block of deserted wasteland and at the burnt-out buildings and garbage incinerators, he knew of only one other alternative—the "chump's choice" of taking the drugs yourself. The way he saw it, "Money's money. To me it's like, you making yours, you just getting paid. I never knock it. As long as you not slouching off like a broke bum you ah-ight. You making yours, you chillin'." When I asked if he didn't feel in any way responsible for the state of his customers, the response he gave offered a surprising echo of what most Americans would say about him: "It's like they doing it to theyselves," he said. "Just like what I do to myself is look strong and this and that, doing drugs is what they want. They want to be like that. That's the way I see it. Like damn! Fools wanna be like that."

In his quieter moments though, even Bobby occasionally admitted to the dream of one day saving enough money to leave the city and buy himself a "nice house" out in a "quiet little town somewheres and kick back and chill." But he never really believed it would happen. He couldn't name even one drug dealer who'd made it big enough to quit. And as for other, more reputable ways to progress out of the confines of his life, there simply weren't many examples to follow. Not enough, really, even to understand what the shape of that progress should look like. It was a common problem at West Side.

"The working class," an English teacher up on the tenth floor asked her students one afternoon in an attempt to help them better understand a poem, "what kind of people would we normally put in the working class?"

"Doctors and lawyers and stuff?" a girl suggested

"No, that would be more the middle class," the teacher said, drawing two lines down the blackboard and in the middle column writing *doctors, lawyers,* and *teachers*. "What about the upper class? The ones with real money?" she asked.

"Drug dealers?" someone suggested.

7

"I GET LOVE from my family; we're real close and I don't want to have to leave them and have to go off to jail. I'm done with all that selling drugs—I am never going to Brooklyn again. And I never did it every day neither. It was just easy money. Not easy money, but I mean . . . see, I don't need it anymore—I already got my clothes," Emanuel Martinez told me abruptly one morning and then looked down at his fingertips.

Manny was a handsome and delicate fifteen-year-old, the kind Greeks used to fetishize, with olive skin, a moon-shaped face, and huge, almond-shaped, dark-brown eyes, velvet-deep with what looked like innocence. He was the most beautiful boy at West Side a lot of the girls agreed, but he was quiet too, shy and reluctant and reduced too often to hiding deep beneath the layers of Ralph Lauren Polo clothes that he loved so much and spent all his money on: his thirty-five-dollar socks and fifteen-dollar underpants—which I never saw, of course, but which he insisted he wore every day—and his bright red Polo hat emblazoned with the letters USA and his jean jacket with the slash-cut sleeves and the bold American flag stamped across the back. So many of his clothes sported these national emblems that I asked him once if he was proud of being American. His wide eyes stretched even wider, and they never left my face as he replied, "Made-in-the-USA, kid! Tha's quality kid!" in such a way that you could tell he was talking about himself as much as the sweatshirt he was holding. He'd been confident then, and he'd had money in his pocket, which always made him cocky, but that morning in the corridor, after he'd been arrested for the second time in less than ten months, he wasn't feeling so sure of anything. "I'm kind of depressed," he said, pulling the beak of his hat down just a little bit lower. "And I'm stressing, you know, Tina? Stressing quite bad now 'cause I just don't want to have to go away."

Manny was the type of student who would sit near the back of a classroom next to a window and stare out of it for the entire duration of his class, even though the glass was intentionally smoked and showed nothing but a creamy stretch of soft, white light. He was so quiet, in fact, that though I had been going to the class nearly every day for months I hadn't even noticed him until the teacher, Rochelle, pointed him out and asked me to tutor him, one on one, for a while.

Rochelle was a stringent teacher, an old-school type who maintained a certain professional distance between herself and her students. She insisted on punctuality, good manners, and hard work; she gave homework every day, and made it clear that any student who didn't complete all their assignments would fail. Perched on the edge of her desk in front of the class, her stainless-steel chalk holder in her left hand, she told students that she understood her standards might be hard to maintain, but explained firmly that life was hard too, and that college was harder than most of them could possibly imagine and wouldn't she be doing them a disservice if she didn't at least teach them how to write? Besides, her kids were the best in the school, and she never gave them anything that she didn't know they could do; they were a smart bunch, she told them, over and over, until most of them started to believe her and struggled to hand in the story she'd assigned the day before at the beginning of class.

Rochelle said she had twenty thousand titles for these stories running in a continuous loop through her head on any given day, and it was true that in a year of attending her class I never heard her give the same title twice. She liked the built-in structure of suspense, and most of them run something like "*Blank* woke up and screamed in horror," or "*Blank* had never felt that way toward anyone until now." The title she had given the day in early October when she had first asked me to sit with Manny was "*Blank* turned around and saw. . . ." Mostly the kids wrote realistic sketches of their everyday life, which, as a believer in the innate therapy of self-expression, Rochelle encouraged. At the beginning of the year she had even jokingly promised that she would never report anything she learned in their stories to the police. But Manny had written about waking up in a strange forest and realizing, moment by moment, that he had been changed into a grizzly bear. He hadn't had any paper or a pen—he didn't have a book bag to put them in, he explained apologetically—but Rochelle always kept a supply on her desk, and once he had the empty sheet in front of him he had started to write and hadn't paused until both sides of the paper were covered.

The story opened with his character noticing a hairy paw where his hand should have been, and a description of the lumbering sensation he felt when he tried to stretch was followed by a long paragraph depicting his panic when he leaned over a nearby stream to drink and he saw his reflection. It was then that he "turned around and saw . . ." a shining little man in a neon-green belt pointing and laughing at him. The story wasn't finished by the time the class ended, and Manny promised to take it home and finish it and then bring it in the next day. But he didn't come in the next day, or the day after that, and by the time he did come back the sheet of paper was lost. He'd been in Brooklyn, he explained half to me and half to Rochelle the following Friday, and he must have forgotten to watch out for it. He gave his pockets one last search and then grimaced guiltily. "I can write you another one, I think I can pretty much remember it," he said, eyes peering up from under his hat. "You got some paper I could use?"

He'd had one of Rochelle's stories in his pocket the afternoon he'd been arrested for selling twenty dime bags of heroin, too. He'd been out with the other underage dealers on Knickerbocker Avenue in Bushwick, Brooklyn, on the corner of Putnam Street, just outside of the bright yellow deli there, where he always stood, when someone gave the signal that TNT had pulled around the corner. TNT—the Tactical Narcotics Team—was an undercover, mobile, antidrug squad with an impressively high arrest rate. But anyone who has been out on the street awhile can spot them easily, Manny said. They always ride in white vans or Toyota Camrys, new models mostly, and they pack four to a car; when they get out they don't look sleepy enough and their noses aren't red enough and their arms and necks aren't pocked with the pussy scabs of infected track marks the way the arms and necks of real junkies are. Or else they give themselves away when they approach a "shorty" (as the youngest dealers are known) by saying things like: "Hi shorty, what you got?" when every kid on the street knows a junky has no time for such pleasantries and will simply demand the brand they want by name.

Manny had seen their little acts time and time again. And though he had fallen for it once and had sold to one of them and been arrested on the spot, he was convinced he would never be fooled again. Nonetheless, their presence there on Knickerbocker was enough to bring work to a close. Manny reached up and took his two bags of heroin out of the hole in the wall where he kept them, put one up his sleeve and, as he turned and started to walk away from the corner, tucked the other in his pocket. Never one to swagger, he was particularly conscious right then of keeping his stride to a casual stroll, and though he knew he'd made a mistake in putting that second bundle in his pocket it was too late to move it now—with TNT behind him there was nothing to do but focus his eyes somewhere about two feet ahead of him on the ground and keep walking. He was three blocks away by the time the cops stopped him. They found the heroin in his pocket immediately, and then, later, when they got to the Eighty-third Precinct building on Knickerbocker Avenue, just off Bleeker, they found the bag in his sleeve and his story too. It was titled "Life Is the Luck of the Draw."

"It was just another day in Brooklyn, when I saw her. I knew she was not from the neighborhood because she was black," he had started to write that morning in Rochelle's class. "But she was beautiful—I decided to stay on the corner for another couple of hours and then ask her out. I never dreamed I would get arrested that day—"

"Hah! This one even writes about getting arrested!" the TNT undercover mocked. "This your homework, kid? This what they teach in school these days?!" And then, no doubt puffed with the pride of a bust, the undercover agent read Manny's never finished story out loud to anyone in the station who wanted to hear it, while Manny sat there in the waiting room, handcuffed to the water pipe, wishing he had never started writing those damn stories for Rochelle and me in the first place.

His hearing had been scheduled for late in October and when he'd asked if I would accompany him there I had agreed to meet him outside the courthouse at 8:30 A.M., half an hour before the doors opened—"Better to be early," he'd said. On the day, however, Manny still hadn't shown up by 9:15, and after I'd been standing around outside for an hour, the chill of the crisp fall day had begun to sink into my bones. To get my circulation pumping again I had begun to stamp my feet and clap my hands together like a ridiculous windup toy, so I didn't notice Manny and his father making their way up the line to the door until they were standing right next to me and Manny was formally introducing me as his tutor.

At first glance Manny and his father looked just alike: the same height, the same face, even the same birthmark under the same eye, and they had the same name too—Emanuel Martinez. But at thirty-five Manny Sr. was bulkier than his son, which made him look shorter. His eyes were flatter, too, at once more certain and less hopeful, and looking at him I was overwhelmed for a moment by the sensation that I was looking at Manny in twenty years' time, at the same beauty smoothed away now into the bland shape of a generically poor Puerto Rican man in generic jeans and a generic thin, gray sweatshirt pulled tight against the cold.

Because of the rigid security system, which had been in place ever since a man in a divorce case had pulled out a gun and shot his soon-to-be ex-wife along with a couple of security guards, it took us close to forty minutes to get into the building. The line started thirty yards down the street, stretched through the atrium, and then bent and folded to the far edge of the main room, where a twin set of metal detectors stood. On the wall of this room were two murals—one of a mother leaning over a sickly baby, the other of an almost saintly trinity: mother, father, and child bent over an open book, helping one another learn. In some kind of unwitting parody of this image, Manny Sr. put his arm around his son's shoulders as we approached the metal detectors and whispered: "Give me the knife, Manny, that way they'll think it's mine."

Without hesitating, Manny pulled a three-inch brass-and-stainless-steel blade out of his pocket and passed it to his father. Two minutes later his father handed it to the policeman. The blade was irregularly serrated down one side like a jagged piranha's jaw, and the policeman raised an eyebrow but said nothing as Manny Sr. signed a receipt slip—to be returned on his way out of the building in exchange for the knife.

Brooklyn Family Court is used for divorce cases and child-custody battles as well as for juvenile-delinquency cases, so there were all types milling around the large beige-and-brown room we had been sent to wait in: middle-class professionals with cellular phones and suits and an irritated air, harried social workers with groups of ten or fifteen tiny children, patient grandmothers, single fathers, lonely shuffling children, and a handful of young teenagers like Manny, cowed by the thought of being sent away. This was not Manny's first time in court. He already had been convicted for selling to the TNT agent, and though he had lied to his arresting officer, he was sure they would discover he was still on probation, and was half convinced he would be whisked away as soon as anyone recognized him. But the room was packed; there were no numbers to take or any other system for checking in or identification, and nothing for us to do but find a seat on a bench that had the high backs and curved edges of church pews. "A lot of worried people here," Manny commented. "Sad people," he said.

Manny's father had taken one look at the room and decided to wait outside in the corridor, where there was more space. Other parents might have done the same, but it was striking that nearly all the other young teenagers seemed to be there alone. Propped up against the walls, staring at fixed points in the middle distance, they desperately tried to keep their faces blank and their postures relaxed. So many of their clothes were embossed with the stars and stripes or with the rounded black letters USA that they looked more like a junior Olympic team gathered for a meet than a group of juvenile delinquents. Whereas middle-class kids tend to rebel against the deadening control and safety of their childhood homes by dressing down, these kids responded to the unpredictability and humiliation of poverty by dressing neatly and well. And looking now at the group of young men draped in the pseudo-sloppy solids of Nike and the fall country colors of Timberland and the bright yellows and reds of Guess and Tommy Hilfiger, I guessed that each of them had spent misguided, pathetically clueless hours earlier that morning trying to choose the outfits that would best "represent" them to the judge. Manny, anyway, had suffered through days of indecision before settling on a disarmingly incongruous yachting outfit: a crisply ironed Polo wind breaker, a plain navy cotton Polo T-shirt, brand-new white Polo trousers (which he had been saving for the occasion and was surprised to find uncomfortable and sweaty), Polo socks, Polo underwear, and a new pair of white top-siders.

Even as he was sitting there in that overcrowded pew, stressing at the thought of being sent away, the outfit lent Manny an almost patrician air. It was an integral part of his image, that understated but determined detachment. It went with his politeness and his charm and with his work ethic too, because unlike so many kids in the city, Manny would never dream of boosting, or stealing, his clothes. He worked for every penny he spent on them and that was the point. It was the Liza Doolittle phenomenon, a misguided attempt at self-improvement which Manny took so seriously that he believed it has to be studied to be mastered. "Learning to dress," he called it. And he had been studying, he admitted, ever since the fourth or fifth grade, under the watchful eye of his favorite uncle and his mentor, Paco.

Two years ago, when Manny was just thirteen, Paco had been "the Man," Manny told me once. He had not only a car and stylish clothes ("mad Polo stuff; mad stuff"), but a beautiful wife who cooked for him and stroked his hair and put the CD player on low whenever he walked through the door, two adoring kids, and all the money he ever seemed to need. He was kind and generous and funny too—and attentive to Manny, so when Paco first asked for some help down on the "the Ave" Manny never even hesitated.

For close to a year and a half Manny watched for police, held packets of drugs and money, bagged heroin, cooked crack, and ran errands for his larger-than-life uncle in Bushwick. Paco was "the Man" down on the Ave too. He had been around for as long as anyone could remember and had a reputation for being crazy and unpredictably violent. This probably helped Manny in the long run because people knew they were close and treated him well. Certainly no one objected when he eventually branched out on his own as an independent "shorty" on Knickerbocker. Nowadays Manny rarely had a problem getting rid of a "bomb," or one hundred small bags of heroin a day. He handled several brands, each with their own devoted following and each with a printed insignia on the package too. Ironically, Homicide, Undertaker, and Grave Digger were the most popular around his way, though Manny pushed One Love the hardest because he was friendly with the supplier and so took 30 percent instead of the usual 20 percent commission on each bag sold.

Still, contrary to public opinion, Manny wasn't getting rich out on Knickerbocker Avenue, though he could make as much as two hundred dollars a day if he worked from 11 A.M. to 11 P.M. For each $10 bag he sold; for each customer he watched straggle up the street, trying to tell by the way they looked if they were an undercover cop or a psychopath or a bona fide junky; for each time he took their money and stashed it before reaching into a hole in the wall or the underside of a parked car's tire for his bundle, he earned just two dollars. Not exactly the big time. Not even enough to cover his round-trip journey to Brooklyn. But Manny didn't mind. If it took twelve hours to sell a "bundle" of ten bags, then he would work twelve hours, never complaining or losing concentration, never attracting attention to himself either because that would only draw looks from the other shorties on the Ave, or from the older dealers. Looks had to be responded to, which was dangerous because there was never any way of knowing when play would turn to anger, and he still hadn't learned how to tell who was "strapped" and who was not. Besides, he had a true capitalist's faith that in time his percentage would grow, and as long as he had the occasional two-hundred-dollar day, he was happy to work hard and risk being sent to Spofford one hundred times a day so he could buy himself his clothes. Besides food and video games and laundry, they were all he spent his money on.

But unlike Bobby, Manny was terrified of being sent to a juvenile-detention center—petrified of the crazed teenage boys with overdeveloped muscles and razor blades he imagined there. "Tough kids," he called them, "crazy kids," and every time a guard came into the huge brown waiting room to pin an extension to the list of cases scheduled to be heard that day, Manny would wipe the sweat from his palms, walk to the board at the front of the room, and, lifting the visor of his hat a little, lean in close to look for his name. But it was never there, and after checking four or five times he would come back to our pew, puzzled, unsure whether it was good news or bad that no one seemed to know he was there.

He got nervous too every time a cluster of people dressed in suits came in through a wooden door at the side, carrying awkward piles of manila folders and long sheets of shiny white fax paper. These were the assistant district attorneys and legal aid lawyers and they strolled through the room from the front to the back reading off the names of their clients with the detached, flat tone of bingo announcers: "Fernandez—Fernandez," "Benson—Benson," "Robertson—Robertson." Occasionally someone raised their hand in response or lifted themselves from the sea of people by standing up in a half crouch, but most of the time no one responded at all. The place was just too chaotic. Listening for your name was like trying to interpret the mangled vowels that squawk out of a speaker on the subway platform—the harder you listen, the more impossible it becomes to hear anything—and most often the lawyers ended up tucking the file back under the bottom of the pile and calling another name. By midday Manny's cool was starting to wilt. He started promising that he would never go back to selling, that it was dumb, a loser's game, and that what he really needed was a good education. He just didn't want to be sent away, he started to tell me. That's all he knew. He just didn't want to be sent away. And however hard he tried to distract himself by printing neat inventories of his clothes in the back of my notebook or making doodles of himself out on the Ave surrounded by scowling friends and expensive cars, he couldn't shake the notion that he wouldn't be going back home that night, that he would be taken out to Spofford instead through one of the ominous doors at the front of the room, numbered 264 on the right and 267 on the left, both covered with signs, stuck on with long-brittle tape, that read: DON'T ENTER. DON'T KNOCK.

So it was a relief when a guard announced that the court would be cleared for lunch recess. Manny's father had been standing in the same spot in the corridor outside all morning because he could smoke there and because he was an active type of person, he said, who couldn't bear sitting still hour after hour. Almost as soon as we joined him, he patted his pockets impatiently and asked: "You got any money, Manny?"

"Yeah. But we gotta go to Brooklyn after to get the rest," Manny said, handing his father five one-dollar bills, carefully unfolding them, one by one, from a very thin wad—a ten and a couple of leftover ones in his hand.

"You were supposed to get that yesterday."

"I know."

"Well, your clothes are going to be all stunk out. I spent twenty-five dollars on washing clothes yesterday and yours are still all in a pile," Manny Sr. said. As we stepped out onto the street he raised his hand in a half wave and started walking away.

"Where are you going?" Manny asked.

"To see some old friends round here," his father replied without turning around.

"Be back here at one, Pa? One o'clock the court opens again, OK? —Damn!" Manny said almost under his breath as his father turned the corner. It makes a big impression on a judge when a parent shows up in court with their child. It can mean the difference between being locked up and being let go, and the thought of his father disappearing now clearly made Manny jittery.

"He been in a methadone program for a couple of years," he said as though trying to reassure himself. "He don't get sick so often now."

"Your father is a heroin addict?"

"Umhmm."

"And you sell heroin?"

Manny nodded.

"So what do you do when your father does get 'sick,'" I asked then. "Do you ever give him some of your stash? Do you sell to him?"

Manny shook his head no but then added, "Like if he don't get his meth and he needs one I give him one cause he goes through a bad sickness. See, dope is the worst drug you could really get on," he explained patiently. "When you get on that and you try to stop, you can't because it hurts. You start crying and you start feeling like you going to die, so you gonna get a bag to straighten yourself out, you know? It's bad. I heard so much stories about it and I'm glad, I'm glad I heard them all and seened it too, because once you've seened it you gotta be stupid to try it."

Manny resolutely refused to mention his father again. But after a long, silent, mournful meal at a Blimpies in the nearby Fulton Mall, his anxiety started to get the better of him and he couldn't stop himself from scanning the crowds and looking back over his shoulder as we made out way back to the courtroom. As we waited in line on Adams Street he stood on his tiptoes and tried to peer over the heads of the people in front of us. Once or twice he even left the line to stand out by the street's edge, from where he could see for several blocks in either direction. But it wasn't until we'd passed through the metal detectors and turned to walk up the stairs, back to the second-floor waiting room, that Manny finally spotted his father coming in the door at the tail of the line.

"Go on ahead!" Manny Sr. said, waving an arm over the sea of people between us, clearly proud to have beaten expectations and come back. "Go on! Go on up ahead." Manny was so relieved that back in the waiting room he walked through the swinging door to the ladies room by mistake and was chased out by an angry older woman, which made everyone already sitting in their pews again laugh, and Manny flush with anger and embarrassment. Two hours later, almost five hours and forty-five minutes after we had first come into the building, a middle-aged woman in a blue skirt suit and an airline stewardess's kerchief finally called Manny's name. "Martinez, Emanuel. Emanuel Martinez," Manny panicked. He shot up from the bench and because he looked like he was on the verge of making a run for it, I held his arm and walked him over to where the assistant district attorney was standing. She had Manny's file with her. It was so thin it looked empty. When she reached out her hand to shake Manny's the file flopped open, and a single sheet of xeroxed paper floated to the floor as she explained politely that all the evidence had not been gathered for his case yet, that there were still samples to have analyzed and witnesses to be questioned and that as a result his hearing had been put off until the middle of November. She had Manny sign a sheet saying he would return on that date and had his father co-sign it. Then she warned Manny to stay away from the scene of the crime, wished us all a good weekend, and said we were free to leave. Manny was giddy, literally dizzy with relief. "I'm so lucky, I'm so lucky," he kept saying. His father was so pleased that he just smiled politely when the policeman who was holding Manny's knife said: "Bring anything like that back here again and you'll never get it back."

"Anything you say, sir," he said.

8

ONLY A COUPLE of generations earlier there was a clearer path to success for kids like Manny: then, even if he'd never managed to graduate from high school, he would still have been able to find a job where the finer skills of reading and writing were not essential. This was how so many newly arrived immigrants with no knowledge of English had managed to haul themselves out of poverty. But with the shift over the last three decades from a manufacturing to a service-based economy, the jobs that had been the leg up for the unskilled were fewer and farther between, and were now often found only in the suburbs, far from the crime and high rents and taxes of the inner city. Those people that could leave did. And increasingly that is what happened: those who, despite the sluggish economy and the still significant barriers of race, had found purchase on the ladder moved on and out of the city, leaving places like East Harlem and the South Bronx with some of the highest concentrations of poor in the nation.

In an increasingly segregated world, this gradual but incessant decline in the living standards of the poor continues. And while many people have grown terse on the subject, few deny that over generations a culture of despair has evolved from which it has become ever more difficult to escape. Through extraordinary acts of courage and will and bloody-minded determination, some young people do manage to break through. Their stories are frequently so inspiring that the media broadcasts them night after night on the local news. But many other, often more normal, less imaginative, less daring teenagers like Manny, end up looking around themselves at their crumbling neighborhoods and the increasing crime and find it hard to believe that anything different lies in store for them.

Waking up on the couch with her mother and sister sleeping in the next room, another sister with her baby behind the thin walls of the elevator shaft, a girl in Ed's Family Group named Isis may have been only vaguely aware of the recent 50 percent cuts in after-school programs, nutrition allowances, job training, summer youth employment, and the low-income heating and energy-assistance program. But after two generations and close to thirty years of increasing poverty in her family, a sense of futility had cloaked her life almost from the minute she was born. Even James, one of the most polite and gentle of the boys in Ed's Family Group, had been toppled by the pressure of spending his early teenage years at home, looking after his twin half-brothers while his mother went out to work during the day and to school at night; he had finally broken down and was sent away after getting busted as the leader of a juvenile mugging ring he had created to bring home extra housekeeping money. His mother had wanted to stay home to prevent this kind of thing from happening, but under the Aid to Families with Dependent Children (AFDC) guidelines she would have been eligible for just three hundred eighty dollars a month, nowhere near enough to support herself and her two children.

Other families self-destructed even before they had a chance to form. A student named Danny Figuera had been deserted by his family altogether when he was four and had been living in group and foster homes ever since. Shaping himself against the impersonal boundaries of federal state and city mandates, he'd been twelve when he was first arrested and just sixteen when he committed the crime that earned him nine months in Rikers Island. Just five years ago Danny would have received counseling, special education, and job training, as well as placement for up to a year as a juvenile parolee, but recent cuts in the criminal-justice system had reduced juvenile care to a ten-minute interview every two weeks. The system was so overburdened that upon his release from jail no one even tried to stop him from being placed in a homeless shelter directly opposite the Brooklyn House of Detention. The detention center was taller than most buildings in the area, and the prisoners' only exercise was taken in a fenced-in courtyard on the roof. From almost every window in his building Richard could see these specters of his future, languidly dangling the tips of their fingers through the diamond-shaped crisscross of wire, staring down at the street, watching the trucks and the cars and the buses pass by on their way to somewhere else.

And yet despite this, he still woke up at seven in the morning and made the one-hour trek to midtown Manhattan and school every day. It was true that he might not always have attacked the challenges placed before him in the way that kids from more stable backgrounds might. But considering the gaping distance between the chaos of his life and the ordered world of school, the fact he showed up at all, and that West Side had an attendance rate of close to 70%, came to seem increasingly miraculous.

All the students had heard, of course, that if they wanted even the tiniest chance of escaping the lives they'd been born to, education was their ticket, no matter how worn. Every teacher and store owner, every social worker and counselor and city charity worker had always told them so. When asked, they were all quick to rattle off learned phrases swallowed whole: "I gotta get my education," "I gotta chase my education," "I need to finish my education." Even West Side's wildest students rolled their eyes and said "yea-ahh" when an adult asked if they planned to go to college. That they said it in the tone most people use when asked if they would like to be a millionaire gave away the fact that to most of them a college education remained a fantasy—more akin to becoming a top-gun navy pilot or a spaceman or the president of the United States than an attainable, sustainable goal.

Almost no one at West Side came from a family with a college-educated member, and many would be the first in their families to graduate from high school, if they managed to stick it out. This made even a completed high school education an extraordinary achievement—one only partially tarnished by the long understood fact that a high school diploma wasn't much good for anything anymore beyond gaining access to an occasional low-level service job that barely paid minimum wage. But if many students secretly believed that sooner or later they would give way to the pressures of the status quo and drop out, even the most brazen of them felt the need to act out the motions of going to school, however occasionally. Like agnostics in modern-day America, even the oldest of these kids was still too young to completely close the door on the possibility of salvation.

West Side, of course, did everything it could to encourage these visits. Despite the constant budget shortfalls, staff members were adamant about keeping as many extracurricular activities open to their kids as possible. Marie, the health teacher, was tempting young mothers to take part in a parenting program sponsored by the Children's Museum uptown by plastering the elevator and the corridors with brightly colored signs. Esther was holding a portfolio-creation course for those serious about developing their art skills and was pointing kids with any signs of real talent to the after-school and Saturday classes offered free to those who qualified by Parsons School of Design and Pratt Institute. On the eleventh floor, a teacher named Susan had started a student-run radio program that aired on two local radio stations in the city and that provided invaluable experience in the field of journalism and broadcasting. A basketball team for boys and a volleyball team for girls were already competing; there was a community-service program; a part-time-jobs program, as well as the interschool job service, which Ed spent a far larger percentage of his budget on than anyone knew. And then there was West Side's showcase, the trip to the Middle East, which was just getting under way again. A twenty-year veteran science teacher named Stewart took fourteen students, seven boys and seven girls, on a ten-week trip to Israel and Egypt every year. He had started a nonprofit organization called Youthworks to help fund it and had even built himself a tiny little office to work from up on the eleventh floor. Because of the lengthy application process, Stewart had already begun to give slide presentations, and almost every day staff members received reminders to have their students fill out the forms and get the application sheets in.

One girl in Ed's Family Group responded immediately. Propelled by the example of her sister, a teen mother who "just sits at home and takes her checks and does nothing," Michelle was a compulsive overachiever. Since arriving at West Side she had managed to maintain a straight A average. She also attended night school and worked in a factory near the school from one to five on the weekdays and from eight in the morning on the weekends. So it seemed natural that she might want to add one more activity to her already overfull schedule, and one morning, after seeing the slides that Stewart showed of kids working in a kibbutz, picking fruit from an orange grove, or simply lying in a field of poppies, the red dramatically, breathtakingly beautiful against the green of the long meadow grass, she approached Ed quietly and, swaying slightly from the hips in embarrassment, asked him to write a reference for her. "Don't forget, Ed, right? You not going to forget?"

But the photographs that Stewart showed, and the meetings he held, left most of Ed's other advisees unmoved. And though almost every day Ed read out a list of new extracurricular opportunities from his mimeographed sheet, their most frequent response was to shrug and look vaguely bored. Even the ones with the most to gain, like Rasheem, whose drawings were extraordinary and who could clearly have benefited from serious art classes, didn't seem interested in the offer from Pratt. Not that he didn't love to draw. He carried a worn, black, hardcover sketchbook with him wherever he went. Mostly it was filled with unfinished cartoon sketches: comic-book faces, eyes and jaws and windswept hair, fragments of arms punching or blocking lethal-looking laser beams, bits of invented superhero costumes, bizarre land-scapes. There was one finished image: a portrait of an African American Mickey Mouse, a homeboy who slouched against the whiteness of the page in a pair of sagging jeans and an oversized sweatshirt. Nonchalant and sexy, this Mickey pointed out at the viewer and chuckled as though at our surprise. It was dazzling. And though whenever anybody asked him what he wanted to do Rasheem would say "draw," he couldn't be persuaded to enroll even in a lunchtime portfolio-creation class with Esther, because, he said, there was too much else he wanted to do with his time—like go to A&S Plaza and hang out in the food court.

Much of this reluctance had to do with the fact that they were teen-agers, of course. Almost all adolescents rebel against the reality they are faced with and, in America, anyway, most announce their rejec-tion as loudly as they can. Without lingering consequences many spend their high school years as Deadheads or metal heads, art freaks, druggies, slackers, or freaks. At West Side this refusal to accept inher-ited wisdom was only magnified by the fact that so many kids lived with no normative regulations at all. Besides, many had become so accustomed to the harshness of their own realities that, adolescent re-bellion aside, they would never have considered taking on additional, unnecessary risks. It was as if, Ed said, he were laying out a table of sumptuous delicacies—jellied candies and truffles and rich meats with sauces and sorbets, only to have his kids turn their backs on it all, saying they were full. With his usual wryness Ed labeled them academic anorexics. One morning in Family Group he even wrote the term on the board and spent the rest of the class explaining it.

The situation was made more disheartening by the fact that a lot of students came to school so late that they missed Family Group altogether, and so didn't hear about many of the opportunities in the first place. In fact, as the fall wore on and the weather got colder, more and more kids were using the distance between school and their homes as an excuse for straggling in late, and the already curtailed school day began to shrink. Cristy still usually made it in for at least half of Family Group, but, even in her new incarnation of overachieving Neta, it was rare for Sandra to stride in earlier than five minutes before the end of class. James swung between half an hour early and a whole hour late, depending on whether he had to drop the twins off at school or not; Bobby would usually arrive sometime during the middle of third period, and although Manny hardly ever came to school regularly, some kind of unconscious attempt to drag himself back into a mainstream life led him down to West Side at least once a week. Even then he was almost always late. If he arrived a few minutes before Family Group ended, at 9:32, he felt pleased because that way he could at least apologize to his adviser, a gentle Colombian named John, and promise to do better.

It was a habit students traditionally slipped into, and it never seemed to have been a problem until the middle of the fall that year, when Charyl, West Side's new dean, got a bee in her bonnet about punctuality. She had been in the position only since September, and even a casual stroll past her office at the edge of the central lobby on the seventh floor showed she was still adjusting. But it was clear she felt a sense of mission in her new job. As if solely responsible for dragging the school back from the underachieving-schools list, she was simultaneously reshaping the school's admissions policy; taking charge of schoolwide discipline, covering each individual dismissal; and, driven crazy by the steady trickle of kids sloping into school at 9:30, 9:45, even 10:00 in the morning, initiating an antilateness drive, which kept her outside on the street for at least half an hour each morning.

Charyl was the only staff person to have a walkie-talkie, aside from the school's security team, and she wore it with the mouthpiece clipped up against her chest and the bulky battery pack slung across her hip, like some kind of small-town sheriff. Short but broad-shouldered and strong, she had the tendency to lean forward from the hips when she spoke to a tardy student and to bark like a shorter than average sergeant major while she told them that she was not Mother Teresa, that West Side was no charitable institution, and that if they wanted to improve their lot they should at least make an effort to get to school by nine in accordance with the school's new policy.

"That's right, *new* policy. Nine-fifteen isn't an acceptable time to be arriving at school anymore," she explained in the curt tone of an empowered official. "You turn up at this kind of time in the morning, you sign this form here. Yes, I know it's a transfer sheet, because that's what you'll be doing next time you wander in past nine o'clock; you'll be picking up this transfer sheet and be taking it back to your zoned school. Do you understand?" she would say, leaning forward on the balls of her tiny feet, staring up into her students' faces, her eyes tiny slits, her chin jutting forward so that her bottom row of teeth stuck out, bracing herself for the moment when the kids' initial disbelief would turn to anger and then outrage.

It was a performance, of course; no one could keep up such levels of anger hour after hour, and if you watched her long enough you realized that it was a gleefully operatic and self-conscious performance as well—she even turned her back on students every now and then to chuckle or wink at a passing staff member. And though she seemed to enjoy nothing more than playing the outraged dean, she occasionally forgot to mask herself in fury and slipped into her more natural chiding but nurturing self. Still, if you were a West Side student who happened to be late, her great barreling force and her promise to have you transferred were pretty convincing. For a lot of West Side kids, who knew there was no other place that would have them, it was a pretty dire set of circumstances.

Once, on a freakishly cold morning that forced her inside the cracked and peeling gray-painted entranceway two weeks or so into her campaign, a tall, bulky boy in army fatigues and an olive-green sweatshirt weighed down with a huge gold St. Lazarus pendant encrusted with diamonds pulled a fifty-dollar bill from his front right pocket and slid it across the table toward Charyl. He then suggested that it would be replicated weekly if Charyl would only leave him alone and let him pass unmolested into the school at whatever time he pleased. Genuinely outraged, Charyl glared down at the fifty-dollar bill and demanded his school ID. The boy squeezed the top ends of his fingers into the too tight edges of each of his pockets, and when he finally handed over a credit-card-sized picture of his girlfriend instead Charyl nearly lost her temper. Very quietly, icily, she told the boy he would be suspended if he didn't fill in the transfer sheet and then get out of her sight, at which point, the kid—shocked, I think—filled in the form. On his way to the elevator, though, I saw him pull a brass and silver-colored bullet about an inch long out of his pocket, hold it upright between his thumb and forefinger, and point over to Charyl, grinning. She wasn't getting any more popular for her efforts.

Nor was she improving the statistics on promptness much either. Whatever she did, however much she stood outside and screamed and postured and jutted her chin, those kids who wanted to be late, or who didn't care about being on time, or whose lives were so chaotic that the clean-cut efficiency of being prompt was merely a wavering mirage on the horizon of their lives continued to arrive as erratically as before. The biggest problem with her method was that the smart ones skipped school altogether on the days they saw Charyl in front of the school. I watched eight or nine kids do it every day—stroll up out of the subway station, see Charyl guarding the front door, and simply turn around and go back home again. Not everyone was quiet about it either. "Oh come on now, Charyl! I gotta be mad jus' 'cause you're mad? I gotta be serious 'cause you're serious? You got menopause?" a girl who arrived at 9:25 said one morning when confronted with a stack of transfer sheets. "You can't be throwing people out 'cause they late twice. You having menopause, girl! I'm goin' to talk to the Board of Ed about this—word." Then she spun around and flounced back out the door and down the stairs, into the subway and anonymity again.

There were other ways around the problem too. Sandra used to get into the school through the office building's front entrance on Eighth Avenue, take the elevator up to the ninth floor, and then walk two floors down to West Side on the seventh. Others waited around the corner in the coffee shop or in McDonald's until nine forty-five, when Charyl left the corridor for her other duties in her office upstairs. And though some students did become so panicked that they genuinely tried to change their ways, the school became increasingly divided over the wisdom of Charyl's newest policy.

Even the teachers were more or less evenly divided. Many believed that their students should be forced to arrive at school on time and were convinced that they would shift their schedules and the patterns of their routines once they understood the consequences if they didn't. Being loose and pliable enough to adjust to the needs of kids was one of the things that separated West Side from neighborhood zoned schools, however, and others argued that strict rules and rigid discipline were more likely to drive students away than improve their behavior. This was why students were allowed six absences every two months without it affecting their grade at West Side and why the school operated on a cycle-based system instead of traditional semesters: dividing the school year into six cycles and two minicycles meant a student was able to start entirely afresh eight times a year. Besides, Ed, for one, simply wasn't prepared to expel a student from the school for being late twice in a cycle, or even three or four times, for that matter. Their students were used to being threatened, he argued. The idea of punishment was one they were already familiar with. More interesting to them, he hoped, and ultimately maybe intriguing enough to become appealing, was a gentler approach of individualized care.

By the end of the month the two sides had reached a stalemate. However much they tried to keep their disagreements confined to the staff room, their bickering soon leaked into the rest of the school. Within days the students were roiling with the controversy and it soon reached the point when Marie, the health teacher, had to give over a series of classes to discussion of the trauma.

The kids in her class were always engaged and verbally active—how could it be otherwise when her main topics were relationships, sex, and drugs and when there were sometimes even huge line drawings of vaginas or penises propped up against the blackboard? Now, though, her students were up in arms not from sexual tensions but from genuinely felt outrage. As the big kid with the Lazarus pendant had said downstairs when he was eating a fried-egg sandwich before he tried to bribe Charyl: "We got rights."

"If I meet her in the street I'm gonna yoke her, man, and take her money for being so nosy! I'm serious!" a boy in the back was saying at the same time as a girl next to me flatly insisted that it was her own business if she wanted to ruin her chances of getting an education. Jasela, a girl from Ed's Family Group who spent most of her time aimlessly drifting around the corridors of the tenth floor, was so traumatized by a recent run-in with Charyl that she could do nothing other than grin wanly and try to accept the fact that she would soon be transferred. Marie tried to reassure her, telling her that Charyl was just trying to scare her, but by then a rumor that eighteen students had already been transferred was in circulation and no one believed her. One girl, Jo Anne, had become so incensed that she had even written a petition and had had a friend type it up during Family Group. In the past few hours she had gathered 180 student signatures. Carefully she pulled it out from her notebook and read:

"We the students of West Side High School appreciate Charyl's efforts to get us here on time so that we can get educated. However we suggest a compromise to the current rule. We should be able to come in uninterrupted by 9:15 A.M. due to the responsibilities that students have such as taking their children to day care and baby sitters. We face transit difficulties every morning. We are humans and it is possible for us to be late, not at all times, but having two times and being neglected from our education is unfair."

Most of the staff were impressed. It was rare for the kids to organize themselves this way, even in opposition to something, and many thought that the proposal of 9:15 should be considered as a reasonable compromise. Charyl, however, would not be swayed. Convinced that it would be fatal go give up now, she persisted in storming downstairs every morning at a quarter to nine with her manila folder full of transfer forms and her walkie-talkie until all that standing around by the open door made her lose her voice. When the wind picked up and the temperature dropped, her cold turned to flu, and she was finally confined to bed for two weeks with a heavy dose of walking pneumonia.

By then, though, a compromise had already been reached: students would be expected to be at school no later than nine, but being late would never, in and of itself, lead to expulsion.

The day after the meeting Ed passed out the new stipulations in Family Group and read them out loud: the first time a student was late they would be asked to sign a transfer form; the second time their parent or guardian would be called; and the third a teacher-parent conference would be scheduled to discuss how best to improve the situation. No one would ever be sent away from West Side as a result of being late, he said, "school policy. Fact." But Bobby Peaks was unimpressed. Constantly late himself, he had been bickering about Charyl for months by then. It had become a habit that, like most, was hard to give up. And no matter what Ed was saying now Bobby still thought Charyl should be stripped of the title of dean.

"Number one, Charyl is a lady and ladies get mad when they don't get what they want," he said, circling the room with a soft, dust-clogged broom. When Ed upbraided him for disrespecting a woman lying sick in bed because of what she tried to do for kids like him, he said: "Yeah. Well, what go around come around, baby."

9

MAURICE AND LUCILLE were leading lives so sedately regimented by Williamson's that they were almost always at West Side by 8:00. Most mornings they would both be waiting for me, Maurice leaning against the post of the school door, taking care to avoid the dark stains left there by homeless men the night before; Lucille, closer to the subway, practicing dance steps on the sidewalk. She would watch me struggle up the stairs, tired usually and harried after the long, rush-hour packed trip in from Brooklyn, and then assail me about my already and freely admitted lack of clothing sense: "Tina, oh come on, girl! How can you do this to yourself? Gray and brown? Uh-uh, that ain't going to do. You too young to let yourself slide—you need help," at which point I would either smile or tell her to shut up and then take them both to the corner for coffee or tea or, most often, hot chocolate and a couple of honey-glazed donuts.

Williamson's gave them breakfast, of course, and made sure they woke up and left every day with their homework done in plenty of time to make it to school. It was not a punitive but a protective center, a good, well-funded foster home for kids who were too troubled to be elsewhere. The first time I visited I was surprised that there was no sign on the door announcing anything untoward, no visible security systems or barbed-wire-topped fences surrounding the building. Past the fire-engine-red entrance doors, the lobby was quietly ordered and officially cheery too; high-gloss, primary colors decorated the counter where I was asked to sign in and show proof of ID by a friendly young staff member, and the notice boards and display cases were similarly covered with bright notices of upcoming group trips and sporting and music events. Upstairs, in Unit 2, where both Maurice and Lucille lived, there was a kitchen and a living room, complete with comfortable sofas and a bookshelf filled with encyclopedias, reference books, and paperbacks that looked random enough to have actually been read. There was a computer room too, spray-painted by an old staff member in a dazzling array of blues and golds. In the evenings a tape machine in here usually played bassy rap loudly. The place was as close to normal as one could hope an institution to be. But there were rules too. One of the most strictly upheld was that there be no sexual relationships between residents. So though they "lived together," as Maurice had first told me, I soon learned that at Williamson's itself, neither Maurice nor Lucille paid even the slightest attention to each other. As Rasheem later told me: "In there they don't have nothing. Nothing—Maurice can't go near her. It's not allowed."

Like all teenagers, of course, they thrived on a touch of the forbidden. I had noticed them furtively glancing at each other when they thought no one was looking, and smiling and occasionally even winking, though Maurice was more adept at this than Lucille. But though gestures like these might have been romantic early on, as the months passed the forced surreptitiousness began to lose its allure, and a crimping frustration settled in its place. It was a frustration that could only have been increased by the fact that, no matter how nicely it was camouflaged, they were in a lockdown situation at Williamson's. Each time I visited, the young counselors had to jangle their way through large rings of keys and unlock the door from the stairwell to even let me into Unit 2. More disturbingly, they always locked the door behind me too. There was something about the metal-on-metal scrape of the key in the lock that chilled me every time I heard it; its effect was a little like the instant need to pee that always used to overtake me when I played hide-and-seek as a child, or the reflexive passion of a jilted lover—they don't want you, so you need them; they lock you in, you have to get out. And though Maurice and Lucille both insisted they were used to it and didn't notice it at all anymore, I always thought of it when I saw them hanging out on the street in the mornings, an unlockable place where they could share some time, staking out their spaces together to greet friends as they straggled in later in the day.

But one morning in November when I arrived late to the staff meeting, Maurice was in no mood to welcome anyone. He was jittery and nervous and didn't even greet me except to take a short, violent drag on his cigarette, scan the street as he exhaled, and say, "Hi." I looked at Lucille for an explanation, but she just rolled her eyes and asked for a raisin roll from the coffee shop on the corner. Maurice escorted us there and still didn't bother to mention the fact that he had been beaten up the night before. Ten minutes later in Family Group, however, he quickly settled into a tight-lipped telling of the story: he'd been jumped the night before, at around seven in the evening, outside of Williamson's, he said. A group of twenty or thirty Puerto Ricans had appeared out of nowhere and had started to harass a small skinny boy from Aichorn who had never won a fight in his life. Maurice had had no choice but to step up and defend him and had managed to floor four or five of them before finally being knocked to the ground himself with the broad end of a splintered plank of wood. The girls in Family Group were dizzily impressed, and under their admiration Maurice started to relax and grow more expansive. But some of the boys were less susceptible, and when a few of the more skeptical began to look doubtful, he unbuttoned his shirt to reveal a huge bruise stretching like a shadow from the base of his neck all the way down his right side to his waist—a deep, black, unnatural-looking bruise pricked with tiny bursts of exploding purple.

I'd assumed that Lucille had heard all of this earlier, but maybe she hadn't. Maybe they hadn't had a chance to talk on the subway downtown, or Maurice hadn't wanted to worry her, or had simply been so embarrassed to have lost a fight that he hadn't been able to admit to it until challenged. Certainly his side looked battered enough for Williamson's to have sent him to the doctor if they'd known, I thought, and there was a bashful anger about Maurice now that made me think he felt overexposed. Whatever the case, Lucille was about as interested in her boyfriend's narration as she was in the educational magazines that Ed sometimes handed out in Family Group, and just as Ed lifted the phone to speak to the nurse she turned to me, tapped me hard on my forearm, and whispered, "I'm worried about something."

There were several days like this at West Side. Days where, following weeks of teenage standoffishness and bravado and wrongheaded independence, a handful of kids simultaneously decided to reveal their greatest secret and most intimate needs. It was almost as if the kids were psychologically synchronized, bottling up their anxieties until they all burst out together in a great rushing cacophony. And because I didn't have the knowledge, or the training, or the innate grace to deal with more than one catastrophe at a time, it almost always made for a terrible set of incomplete conversations and bruised egos. Irritated by the interruption more than anything, I turned to Lucille and asked her what was wrong. She mouthed a two-syllable word that I couldn't make out. Emphasizing its urgency, she threw the inner edges of her eyebrows down to the bridge of her nose.

"Parent?" I guessed. "Pretrial?"

"Pregnant," she said, finally audible. "I think I'm pregnant." Then she stared at me, unblinking, until I looked away.

It was the first time I had ever seen Lucille at a loss for words. Usually she talked for as long as anyone would listen. Just a few days before, after eating three large chunks of chocolate from a box of McDonald's-sponsored charity candy that Ed had given her, she had taken over Family Group entirely by performing an incredible, spontaneous monologue right from her chair. Flicking her arms and wrists out to the sides as she spoke, she turned her head and twisted her neck in such a way that if you started looking at her too closely you lost touch with exactly what she was saying because the movements themselves became the narrative:

"You always hear that the man did this and that the man did that, that the man act devious and hurt you and all. But I tell you that women do this, and do that, and play that head game better than ever a man could," she began, her voice pitched a bit higher than usual. "And just because I got feelings for you and you got feelings for me don't mean I gonna have my heart broke, because I be playing the mind game with you and making you think I gone, and acting like I gone, and talking like I gone, but I ain't gone. I'll play you. And you'll get hurt just as bad as I get hurt cause I might be weak physically, but I crazy strong here—crazy strong mentally—and I can play you cause *I* in control. Nobody don't have no control over me. I could just be standing there with my homegirls and a bunch of guys come by, and I notice one of them and think he looks crazy good cause he stand out from the crowd, and then he catch my number and I catch his number and maybe we go out and get an ice cream or a soda, and then maybe we be talking later on the phone, but I don't have to be having no sex with him, if I don't want to be, when I say no I mean no, I say no right then and the way I'll say it I mean it, no ifs, ands, or buts about it because those are my boundaries and I'll protect them. Like my mother—take my mother for example, she crazy strong for a black woman and I don't mean physically neither, woman is weak physically but strong mentally, it's only when you strong mentally you can be weak physically, and my mother was both, nobody never liked her, she stabbed a girl once right through the eye with a silver nail file on the school bus when she was young, that girl been giving her problems more than two years until my mother did that, same day she pulled another girl up and held her upside down over a garbage pail that she had set on fire; they'd killed her dog, see, burnt it because they didn't like my mother much, she weren't too crazy about none of them neither, so she just held this girl like that over the flames to teach her a lesson, she was crazy tough my mom and she knew how to play . . ."

And on and on, rapid-fire and without a pause, absolutely without a pause, not even for a breath, so that the veins in her neck began to inflate and stick out and a girl sitting next to her felt the need to tap her on the shoulder: "Lucille, Lucille, Lucille! Take a breath!" James, the basketball player, was clapping his hands every now and then, saying, "Yeah!" as if he were saying "Amen!" Maurice hid his eyes, initially, embarrassed to be associated with her, and then began to slide his chair away from hers, so that she was all alone in the corner of the room. Ed just stared, his normally bulging blue eyes now nearly bursting from their sockets. And when she finally took a breath and all of a sudden was done, and was left sitting there, pert and upright and flushed but sheepish now, the room—in awe at the deeper, darker, more usually hidden place that her barrage had come from—burst into applause.

I could only guess that her words had been directed in Maurice's direction. She never looked at him or referred to him by name, but it wasn't difficult to see that their relationship was tumultuous and that when it came to any kind of intimate, personal honesty they were not the best communicators. Like most teenagers they tended to flounder when it came to emotional intimacy of any kind, and because they had both spent the bulk of their lives presenting pictures of complete strength to the world, any gropings outside of this were bound to be tentative and awkward. Maurice, I was beginning to realize, layered his reality until it was presentably fictionalized; Lucille desensitized with dramatics. And I think it was because neither of them had ever known anyone with whom they felt completely safe that they saved their greatest moments of revelation for a public place, where the very lack of intimacy somehow made them feel protected.

Many kids at West Side had the same impulse, and I had frequently seen Family Group serve as a forum for them to air feelings that, in a perfect world, might have been better served in a quieter, more intimate space. Ed had spent years perfecting the balance of formlessness and shape that allowed this to happen, I knew, and though it seemed haphazard, any one of his advisees could expose themselves there without fear of unwarranted attention from their peers. Usually, of course, there were two or three conversations going on simultaneously, which helped, and a handful of students finishing up homework or flipping through magazines as well. It was extremely rare for someone to claim the center of the room's attention the way Lucille had done that day, and she had gained a certain notoriety for it.

But she didn't want to attract anybody's attention now. She wanted to be invisible or, barring that, to be a little girl again, the little girl that she still was, in fact, but hadn't paid much attention to for years. Even as Maurice's scenarios became wilder—the number of kids that attacked him growing to fifty or more and the wooden plank becoming an uprooted street sign—Lucille rocked gently back and forth, tracing the pattern of wood grain across her desk with her well-filed nails, blinking back tears. She didn't even seem to notice when Ed finally managed to convince Maurice to visit the nurse. And half an hour later, when Lucille and I walked toward the same nurse's office on the tenth floor, she was surprised to see Rasheem in the corridor outside, sketching in his pocket-sized notebook while slumped in a chair with a broken back and only one arm. Determined to take a pregnancy test, she barely greeted him, didn't ask after Maurice, and walked right into the nurse's room. It wasn't until I closed the door behind us that she became a little girl again and, smiling and twisting from the waist, admitted to me, in a shy child's singsong voice, that she didn't really know what to say. The nurse was sitting at her desk, reading a magazine, and to get her attention, I told her that Lucille had something she wanted to discuss in private.

"Not in private but—I want to take a pregnancy test," Lucille said.

"How old are you?" the middle-aged woman asked, without removing her finger from her place in an article.

"Thirteen."

"Then we need a consent form," she said flatly, and her harshness seemed to snag on the edge of Lucille's girlish persona and drag her back into adulthood again. Straightening up, she calmly explained that she had hoped to discuss the situation with her family once she knew for sure that there was a situation. "We still need a consent form," the nurse repeated as she reached behind her and, without even looking, lifted the top sheets from several piles of papers lying there. Explaining that they had to be filled in by her parent or guardian but that there was nothing on them about pregnancy tests, she presented them to Lucille. Serious still, and mature, Lucille took them and tucked them carefully in her bag.

"I'll be back tomorrow then," she said, struggling to be upbeat.

"Just as long as the forms are signed," the nurse sighed, already reading her magazine.

As we stepped into the corridor from the nurse's office, the physician's assistant, close to panic, was storming out of the examination room next door. "We have got to see Ed," she shouted over her shoulder to the nurse. "We need to go to the emergency room right now. This kid Maurice may have a number of broken ribs and doesn't live at home—doesn't seem to have a family at all." Surprised, Rasheem leapt to his feet. Maurice, as close as I've ever seen him to shaken, came out of the examination room still buttoning up his shirt with his one good hand and then followed the nurse downstairs. Lucille must have been more bound up in the nerve it took to ask for a pregnancy test than I thought because she barely noticed the activity at all, and later, when I asked her how she felt about Maurice's being hurried off to the hospital, she was surprised and asked when it had happened and how I knew.

Although no one seemed to believe the roving Puerto Ricans story, few of Maurice's friends were surprised that he had been beaten up by *somebody*. Rasheem told me that the way Maurice mouthed off, he was bound to end up dead one day. He confessed that his friend was so completely incautious about who he chose to receive his lippy belligerence that it often felt dangerous just standing next to him. Within a day rumors started to multiply: It was drug related—Maurice had sold some addicts a bag of clotted detergent for the fun of it (only they didn't think it was so funny); it was cop related; it was a case of mistaken identity, or of racist vigilantes, or of revenge for an incident the week before when a friend of Maurice's from Williamson's had been jumped by a group of "crackheads" just as Maurice was walking by and Maurice had shooed them off. This started to seem the most likely scenario to me: plenty of addicts roomed in the hotel down the street from Williamson's, the one painted blue with a sign reading CHEAP RATES. COLOR TVS. Besides, even Maurice admitted that crackheads weren't particularly difficult to scare and he wouldn't have had to do much more than simply appear to frighten them away.

Whatever the case, Maurice was confined to bed for two days after his dramatic exit with the physician's assistant. And Lucille, the only one who might have learned what had really happened, knew nothing. Williamson's rule that residents of different sexes not be in each other's rooms was steadfast, and too intent on getting the health clinic permission slips signed to risk getting in trouble, Lucille stayed away. Like all underage girls, Lucille was terrified by even the possibility that she might be pregnant; and at thirteen, the almost mythic fear of what her future might hold, the impending responsibilities and isolation, and the crippling realization that with one act, she may have changed the entire path of her life had started to paralyze her. The idea of speaking to the father of her child never crossed her mind, and, girding herself for what she began to see as her ultimate downfall, she waited for word of West Side's consent form, alone. Her caution won her nothing in the end, though; after looking over the papers Williamson's told her that they were legally responsible for her medical health and that there was no way they could revoke that responsibility with a child of her age.

"I won't have an abortion. I don't believe in that. My mother didn't kill me. Why am I going to kill my child?" she announced the next day, leaning back against the door to Ed's office while we waited to go in. "It's strange, though. I'm surprised. Because I'm not really active. There are some kids that are like, 'yes, yes, yes,' every day, but that's not me. I was raped from when I was six to when I was ten, but they say that doesn't count because I didn't give my willing consent. Which means I've only really had sex once. And no. No, Tina. I know what you are thinking but it was not with Maurice. Most definitely not," she said and then cricked her neck and stared at me hard.

I'm still not sure when Lucille decided to ask Ed for help, but she seemed relatively calm waiting to go into his office that afternoon and didn't falter when she told him she might be pregnant. After sitting herself down and waiting for him to finish signing some papers, answer the phone, twice, and then look for, find, and finally hand over a tiny box of computer equipment to a teacher named Nancy, she said simply: "I think I might be pregnant, Ed."

For the briefest instant Ed's expression collapsed and he leaned forward slightly as though he'd been punched in the stomach. "You need a test, Lucille, or you've already taken one?" he asked gently, and after listening to Lucille's explanation, he picked up the phone, and as casually as he could bypassed the nurse and asked to be transferred to the physician's assistant upstairs. But it was illegal for her to hand out a pregnancy test to an underage girl without consent, she said—utterly and completely and supremely illegal. She would lose her job. Not to a girl that age. Not without at least some kind of consent form. Ed waited patiently for her to finish and then asked if she could give the test to a girl in her twenties. The PA answered that of course she could, and Ed nodded at me and said, "OK, I'll send up Tina Rathbone then and you can give it to her."

"Now you tell me what happens," he said to Lucille as we left. "Don't leave me hanging, OK?"

The PA ushered us into the examination room, handed me a small brown grocery bag folded over several times from the top, told me to remember five drops, not the four suggested on the package, and then shooed us out of her office to the nearest student bathroom. Lucille's hands were shaking as she transferred each droplet of urine from the pipette to the tester, naming each one as it fell: "one" shake shake, "two" shake shake, "three . . ." Then we waited. She put the diamond-shaped white plastic tester on a shelf by one of the two sinks and stared at it from above as though it were a captured animal that might escape. A pink triangle would appear at its center when the results were final. A blue band would designate a negative response; a blue check or a blue check and a band, a positive one. Lucille didn't move. Balanced on her tiptoes, staring down at the white plastic diamond, she stood as if frozen. After what seemed like an eternity, she span around, wide-eyed with panic, convinced that she had a faulty tester because all this time had gone by and still nothing was happening. Thirty-five seconds had passed by then. The tester took four minutes to work. We waited.

The smell of cigarettes was overwhelming; the graffiti, dull. To pass the time I asked Lucille how she had done on her science test. She had just scraped through the first test of the year with a 65, and it had so bothered her that she had managed to pull her score on the next test way up into the 80s. Without moving a muscle she replied, "Thirty-six," and then glared at a girl who had come in to fix her hair. Science was her favorite subject, and I knew that at any other time it would have humiliated her to have done so badly, though now it didn't even distract her. Three hovering, swamp-silent minutes passed. The girl finished her hair and then left. Another came in and walked straight into a stall. She peed. Then, finally, the blue band started to emerge. "Blue band, negative, right? Blue check or blue check and blue band positive," Lucille repeated, holding the tester in her hands now, leaning back against the radiator, staring at the blue line as it slowly gained substance. Maybe five seconds later, the pink triangle appeared. She was not pregnant. For a moment she was utterly still. Then she moved just her eyes, slid them silently up from the diamond with its pink and blue shapes to me.

"I was nearly ready to cry waiting for that thing to work," she said, in utter disbelief at the level of sentimentality to which she sometimes still sank. And then, as if all the tension that had been trapped in the shell of her impervious self-control released itself suddenly into pure screaming energy, she ran out of the bathroom and headed for the stairs. "No worries now, I'm free!" she shouted. "I'm so happy. I'm so happy—I can be a young little buck again. Now I can worry about Maurice."

She didn't have much to worry about, it turned out. Though Williamson's had taken a series of photographs of his shoulder as part of an ongoing investigation into the incident, the X-rays showed no fractures. The doctor had given him a course of pain killers, the effects of which he clearly enjoyed, and aside from wearing a thin cotton sling that made his elbow look awkward and his hand dangle oddly, there was very little to be done to help the healing. He was back at school the day after Lucille took her pregnancy test, and though he still didn't know of her scare, he seemed oddly distant as he sat down next to her in Family Group and ignored her for the first twenty minutes of the class.

The lottery jackpot had reached fifty million dollars the night before, and Nino, the lawyer's assistant who had been fired for forging checks, had bought thirty tickets. He was so convinced he would win that he was offering to buy his classmates whatever they wanted. Cristy had asked for a house, Sandra for a country. But Lucille wasn't interested. As if in celebration of her newly diagnosed noncondition she had had her hair done the night before. With it neatly slicked against the sides of her head in thousands of tiny wavelets, she looked like a flapper from the twenties, sophisticated and old. Every now and then she ran her fingers over her hair, squeezing a ridge here, smoothing a gully there, but otherwise she did nothing. It was almost as if she was shy of Maurice suddenly. Once I even saw her turn to him and smile, saccharine sweet and girlish, which confused him I think, as he just smiled right back and continued telling Rasheem "the real" reason why he was jumped. He was the secret head of a drug-dealing operation named "the Foundation," he said, cupping his good hand in front of his mouth so nobody else would hear. The kids who jumped him had become jealous of his success and had attacked him in an attempt to build their own reputations. Rasheem looked nervous. Kids had surrounded Maurice earlier that morning, wanting to take revenge for his beating, and though he was fairly sure that Maurice's stories were fantasies, a friend had to stick close at times like this, and there could be trouble. He fidgeted nervously with the cinnamon bagel he'd ordered from the coffee shop downstairs and methodically poured sugar on top of each toasted and buttered half from a pile of small packets on the table beside him.

Tired and obviously worn out, Maurice slumped back in his chair and, with a sigh, added more loudly now that "the Foundation" was in turn affiliated with the uptown mosque at Ninety-second Street and that if they ever found out that Maurice had been jumped "the matter would be out of my hands, because disrespecting me is disrespecting them."

No one but Lucille heard him, though. Ed was talking now about the odds of winning the lottery—"Less than being in an airplane crash," he said. "Less than being wounded by a terrorist bomb."

"Nah, nah, nah, nah, nah—don't jinx me now, Ed—don't be jinxing me," Nino protested, and just as James was about to join in, Lucille unzipped her book bag and pulled a single piece of paper from it. "Ed? Ed? Can I read this prayer, please?" she asked. "Everyone always accuse me of not showing any emotion, Ed, and I want to prove them wrong." Ed waved his hand to say that it would be fine and, cocking her head to the side, the fresh sheet of paper held carefully with both hands in front of her, she started to read:

"To that Big Diamond in the sky sitting on his throne and my mother on the right-hand side," she began, not able to repress a quick glance over toward Maurice to make sure he was paying attention. He wasn't, of course. He seemed incredibly interested all of a sudden in the way the sugar was melting into the pools of butter on Rasheem's toasted bagel and was redistributing it with the edge of a coffee stirrer. Lucille looked back at Ed and carried on: "Heavenly Father, my mother always related the message that you were my friend but if that's so why do I feel loneliness within? Where were you when I fell in love and had questions about things that weren't quite right? I still put up a fight, because I'm sure loneliness is something we all feel quite frequently. I know I do. But falling in and out of love I just give up. I can't face the pain anymore. It hurts too much.

"So, Father, can you tell me who there is to talk to when people seem deaf? How is there a river overflow when there's no tears? How is there fear when there's no emotion? How are you a victim with no crime? There is no response. Just dead silence. It's a dead-end street, God. Where do I turn when loneliness is near? Will the answer appear or will I have to just keep on searching?"

There was no moment of silence when she finished this time. Other students had been chatting quietly all along, but when she stopped reading Maurice looked up and, nervous that there was more to come, laughed approvingly. Smiling back at him, she folded her prayer in two, put it back in her book bag, crossed her arms up under her chest, and waited for a groupwide response. Apart from Ed, the only person who responded was Nicole, the girl who brought sliced pickles in for breakfast and who had grown up in a crack house. For some reason, Lucille's prayer infuriated her. Frantically flicking through the file she always carried with her, she finally found a poem that she had written and then thrust it toward Ed.

"Here. Read this out loud, Ed," she said. "It's nothing like hers. Hers just asks questions. Mine answers them."

10

RASHEEM WAS ONE of the most obviously talented of all of Ed's Family Group. Lanky and tall and elegantly handsome despite his corked teeth, he could almost always be found in the far right-hand corner of the room, studying comic-book instruction manuals and longing for colors so obscure as to not really exist outside of the comic-book world, colors like ochre and indigo. He had been an A student a few years before, and a promising young track star too, but he was shy and awkward and embarrassed around girls, which may have been the main reason why he so willingly served as one of Maurice's acolytes at West Side. Along with Shadi, a Yemenite shopkeeper's son who could hardly speak English and who Maurice spent time with only because he always had a twenty-dollar bill in his pocket, Rasheem had been so overshadowed by Maurice for the past couple of months that though I had spent hours in his company and shared coffee with him every morning—draining off half the cup before handing it over to him to add four or five sugars, depending on his mood—I barely knew him.

He was bright, I knew, and nurtured a carefully tailored eccentricity that everything else about him seemed geared to. He often made light of his awkwardness around girls by saying that his estranged father, an immigrant from Camaroon, had so many children that it put Rasheem in a constant state of anxiety, lest he end up kissing a sister by mistake. This was not very likely. If Rasheem had a relationship with girls at all at West Side, it was in the role of pesky little brother. I often passed him in the morning only to have to turn back and rescue him from a mob of childishly, awkwardly flirting girls—one poking him with her umbrella, another punching him hard on the arm, and a third tickling him. "He's a yapping little puppy," I heard one of them say. "More like a burning hemorrhoid," the other shot back before hitting him again.

On the rare occasions that he did burst out of the small slither of space allowed him by Maurice and take center stage, he got the same reaction. Once, when I was sitting with him and Maurice in the corner of Family Group, he burst into song. I didn't know what he was doing at first, when he took in a deep breath and cocked his head to one side like a sparrow. But I was transfixed by his quiet, high, quavering voice. It was so delicate that it sounded almost Oriental, an impression only heightened when he started to twist his wrists like a Burmese shadow dancer and extend his long fingers, so that their tips pointed to the ceiling when he hit the really high notes. It was an extraordinarily pure voice, piercing and clear, but when he had finished the three girls around him just laughed.

"What would you do if you saw him out on the street?" Sandra asked Lucille. "I mean if you just ran into him in the street just like that?"

"Singing one of them songs from *The Lion King*? I'd ignore him; I couldn't let people see me with him," she said. "Mmm-nmm. Not on my block." Rasheem leaned back in his chair and allowed his orange sunglasses to slide down his nose. This was just the sort of reaction he seemed most pleased with. It was what his penchant for orange was all about, as well as his peculiarly elaborate patterns of speech and even the often-repeated fact that his uncle made a living by customizing car alarms so they spoke in foreign languages. "And I mean foreign languages—Swedish, Japanese, Russian—I lie to you not. If you ever hear that, a car talking Swedish, my uncle did it." The fact was, that even if he was little more than Maurice's sidekick, Rasheem didn't want to be like everyone else. "I like to stand out from the crowd," he told me once. "I do not lie—how many kids you know who wear orange every day?"

Ever since he could remember, he told me, he'd been able to smell the color. Or to detect it at least with a sense that has no name, so that when he walks into a store he knows which way to go to find it. He had been wearing the color almost exclusively since the third grade, and even though his mother didn't like it, he intended to go on wearing it. "She thinks I'm overly obsessed with it and that I should try to get into other colors," he said. "But I did, I tried. But the only two colors I like is orange and yellow, that's it—I tried green and it nearly stuck, then it just fell. I *do* like lime, that's one of my favorite colors—lime and lemon yellow, not counting orange, that's my colors." Still, it was hard, he said, to find a orange coat, or even a lemon yellow or a lime one, for that matter. Trousers and T-shirts were easy, and even shirts weren't that bad but, aside from shoes, which he'd had to give up on long ago, coats were the hardest to find, and the thin orange jacket he'd been wearing since the first day of school had seemed like a rare stroke of luck when he'd found it one afternoon, hanging in the window of a discount sportswear store.

He had worn it every day since then. And because he cared for his clothes well, and always looked fresh and different enough to be immune to the rigorously demanding dress code of inner-city fashion, people seemed to accept this otherwise inexcusable lack of variety and settled in to calling him Orange. "Yo Orange, s'up?" they'd say. But it was starting to get cold out now, and the jacket was cut from thin summer cotton. While other students delighted in the change in temperature and started to pull out their Polar specials, Rasheem simply drew his jacket tightly closed around him and, hunching over a little, struggled on in his one pair of orange jeans and the pair of green and white pseudocamouflage sneakers that had originally belonged to Shadi and were three or four sizes too big for him. So that though he did genuinely seem to like the color orange, I began to suspect that it was a screen for his poverty more than anything else.

Because Rasheem was poor, even by West Side standards, and homeless too. He had come to West Side because he and his mother and sister had been shifted from one shelter to another for so long that it had been hard for him to amass credits in a school that ran on full semesters. Rasheem never told anyone this, not even Maurice, though everyone must have suspected as much. You couldn't help but notice the hovering nervousness that came over him whenever Ed gave out travel passes or the quiet way he'd fill them in with yet another new address. And although he often talked in Family Group about the apartments his mother was thinking of moving into, and he frequently took days off "to move" and even sometimes referred to his nomadic status, the reference was always oblique and was always dressed up as the flighty indecision on the part of his mother, who he portrayed as a woman "having some problems, you know?" No one ever teased him about any of this. He might have been the class clown and an open target for just about anything, but poverty was not something that was ever mocked at West Side. Except in the most glib generalizations or vicious put-downs, it remained hidden behind screens that were readily and uniformly believed in.

But if poverty can be hidden by bravado, it is difficult to conceal its effects and however original an orange jacket might be, it simply wasn't heavy enough for the brisk New York autumn. One morning in November after a particularly cold stretch, Rasheem came staggering into school with a fever of 104. I ran into him in the elevator and offered him a sip of my coffee. "I, I can't right now," he said, and when I asked him why he spun around in the opposite direction, trying to locate my voice. That was when I noticed that his eyes were unnaturally wide, as though his morning had been tremendously, outrageously surprising. He looked scared, in fact. And confused: simultaneously manic and vacant, like a rabbit trapped in a passing car's headlights. So when I reached out to feel his forehead I wasn't surprised to find it burning hot. The nurse couldn't understand how he had ever managed to get to school in the first place with a fever like that. "This boy has got to get home. He has to get home and get to a doctor as quickly as possible," she told Charyl. "To the emergency room if necessary. He has a fever of one hundred and four!"

"Don't breathe in my office then," Charyl joked, and for just a split second I saw Rasheem take a deep breath of air and clamp his lips closed. His day had been dreamlike from the minute he had woken up, and nothing could shock him anymore: faces had twisted and bent on the train as he past them, shadows smothered him, and noises had echoed and bounced and leapt and turned, so that he had had to sit down when the first train came barreling into the station. Even now he was hearing friends calling for him, though no one was there.

"What's your mother's phone number, hon?" Charyl asked gently. Rasheem shook his head and told her that his mother didn't have a phone. She asked for the neighbor's number, and then the super's. Rasheem shook his head again. "Nope" he said, and then "nope" again to his grandmother's and his aunt's and his guardian's. "She don't like being bothered," he said at one point, reminding me of the time he'd explained why his mother had refused to come down to West Side when he'd first registered for the school. But otherwise he pursed his lips and kept quiet. Even with a fever of 104 there was no way on earth he was going to tell Charyl or me or anyone else who might be around, lounging on the chairs outside across from the elevator or passing by in the corridor, that he lived in a homeless shelter. Charyl slumped back in her seat and fumed. Misinterpreting Rasheem's embarrassment for stubborn belligerence, she tried to explain that it was illegal for a school to send a sick student home without contacting a family member first. He could pass out on the subway, anything could happen; and without someone at home being informed there was simply no way they could take that risk. He'd have to go back upstairs and make himself as comfortable as he could until the end of the school day, she said. Rasheem simply shrugged.

I suggested that maybe I could take Rasheem home. Charyl agreed, but only on the condition that I escort Rasheem right up to the front door and make sure he got in safely.

"Right into the building? No no no no. She don't want to do that," Rasheem protested with sudden and surprising energy.

"Into the building," Charyl repeated.

"Can't she just drop me off outside?"

"You don't promise me that you will escort him right up to his door, he doesn't go anywhere except right back upstairs to the nurse's room," Charyl said. So I did. "I promise," I said, and, trying to be as casual about it as possible, on our way out the front door I asked him:

"So where do you live, Rasheem?"

"Where do I live? Where do I live? I lived in the Bronx and in the South Bronx, I lived down Baruch, lived in Rochedale and in Corona and in Elmhurst. I lived on Staten Island. One reason I'm behind is because my mother been bouncing around from place to place"—he exploded suddenly in a fit of fevered frustration—"I bin to one, two, three, four, five, six, seven high schools," he said. "And this is in one state—it's a whole other story when I was living in Jersey, but here in the city? Seven high schools. Lehman, JFK, Flushing, Norman Thomas, John Adams, been to them all," he said. "We going to my aunt's house now, though. It's closer." Realizing that nothing I could say would change his mind, we boarded the downtown A train, changed at West Fourth for the F, and ended up walking six long blocks from the F train stop on Second Avenue and Houston Street to the projects on Avenue D where his aunt lived. It was cold and raining by then, an unusually wintry day for the middle of November, and Rasheem, in his orange cotton T-shirt and thin orange jacket, shivered all the way.

11

MAYOR RUDOLPH GIULIANI announced the latest in his series of spending cuts at the beginning of November. On top of the $1.1 billion that had already been cut the previous summer, an unanticipated gap in the city budget now had to be closed with further reductions. Combined, these cuts would be the largest since the fiscal crisis of the 1970s, when the federal government had been forced to intervene to help bail the city out. Although Wall Street was beginning to warm up to the boom that a few years later would translate into a tax-revenue surplus (showing that at least one segment of society would be doing better than ever), the city's economy as a whole continued to lag. Saying that the budgetary steps would be difficult but necessary to keep the city on course to full recovery, Giuliani cut almost every government service, from sanitation and hospitals to school programs and food programs for the elderly.

As was usual, though, the poor suffered most from these reductions in city services, and poor kids most of all. For high school students planning to graduate in January, a $7 million midyear budget cut to the City University of New York system would lead to the deferred admission of 15,300 community-college students. All city funding of soup kitchens would be phased out, as would 1,900 places in day-care centers. In the already grotesquely overcrowded prison system, Giuliani's budget would also lay off 800 correction officers and would further reduce recreational, educational, and counseling services for inmates, a move that the head of the correction officers union said would "push city jails into the danger zone." And, as was becoming increasingly common under the Giuliani administration, the Board of Education was again singled out for the biggest reduction of funds: $190 million on top of the $360 million that the mayor had pushed through the previous July.

The crusade had come to seem almost personal for Giuliani. Obsessed with the notion of reducing what he was now calling "the bloat," he insisted his education cuts could be made without increasing the size of a single class in the city. He wanted to target the bureaucracy, he said over and over, not the students themselves, and he often cited a report which showed that while spending per student was higher in the city than in the rest of the state, less and less of that money was reaching students in the classroom. This was true, and, impressed with his tough talk, most New Yorkers thought he seemed to have a point.

But the reasons for the imbalance between classroom spending and total costs were more complex than the mayor was prepared to admit. Certainly, it was not too difficult to understand why the city's school budget was proportionally larger than those in outlying areas and upstate. Simple plant costs were one reason: it was more expensive to own and operate a building in the city than practically anywhere else in the world. Another was transportation: the city relied mostly on public transportation and had to pay for hundreds of thousands of subway fares every day. Then there were the special needs of the urban, and often poor, public-school population: the huge cost of security—a cost not usually figuring in suburban-school budgets—and of bilingual, remedial, and special-education classes, which, because of higher immigration and poverty rates, occurred in the city at a greater rate than elsewhere in the state. So although there was reason enough to be dismayed by the seemingly small percentage of money that actually reached the classroom, shifting the balance was not going to be easy. In a city as complex as New York, change would not come overnight. What was a required was a delicate, diplomatic pruning; the mayor was calling for amputation.

But after months of public squabbling, Cortines was in no position to tackle the increasingly popular mayor and was forced to clear his calendar for ten days to look into possible ways around the deadlock. In the end he did come up with several suggestions to help implement the cuts. Aside from raising the price of school breakfasts and lunches and reducing the amount of overtime a teacher could charge for, these included placing advertising on school buses to raise revenue, scrapping many school sports programs (including all of the alternative-school leagues), and ordering single chapters instead of complete books for use in classes.

Of course, at West Side, with their unfinished library, too thin walls, temporary plumbing, only vaguely warm lunches (which were brought in every day because of the lack of kitchen facilities), and fifty-square-foot, windowless weight room, the citywide debates seemed distant and irrelevant. Ed was no great admirer of the Board of Education, but neither was he convinced that even a vast reduction in its staff would lead to an increase in money for students. After nearly twenty years, he was used to promises being broken and to budget-balancing platitudes disguised as concern. Besides, there was nothing about Giuliani that made Ed think he was genuinely sympathetic to the plight of public-school children in the city. The mayor's own son attended a private school that offered the small classes, extracurricular activities, and language labs that public schools had long only been able to dream about. And, as Edward Costikiyan, an education adviser to Giuliani, was quoted as saying in *New York Newsday,* the mayor didn't have to worry about cutting public education too much because "most of his constituents don't have kids in public schools. They go to parochial schools and say 'Thank God he didn't raise my taxes.' The public school parents are weakest and don't vote in large numbers."

But however dismissive local government and the city at large were becoming about the quality of life of its poorer teenagers, and however pompous the mayor was as he inflicted this latest round of cuts, West Side kids always seemed to keep their equilibrium. They understood that their reality was becoming increasingly marginalized; by simply looking around they could see that. But rather than give up, their response was tough and brazen and witty—that's what I most admired. And it was elegant too, in its own brassy way. They expected the worst, and when they got it they played with it, distancing themselves from their pulpish cores and surrounding themselves with what looked to me like a well-burnished armor of humor.

Even Halloween for West Side kids had little to do with the cute masquerade parties and endearing strings of children trailing from door to door that I read about in the *New Yorker* late that fall. Instead, those who went out at all had to spend the day dodging sinks and other kitchen appliances thrown from their neighborhood rooftops, avoiding storms of rotten eggs, and keeping as far away as possible from large groups of angry, antsy cops, quick with their nightsticks. But the following day trippingly upbeat accounts of horrors evaded blended with the darker humor of stories of friends-of-friends who had not been so lucky. Perhaps because many of them had never known anything else, they didn't complain about any of this. They didn't complain either about the rodent infestations in many of their homes or the nonfunctioning elevators in the tall buildings they lived in, or the way the buildings smelled, though Rasheem always insisted that no one should ever touch the walls of one except to push the button because "you never know what's splashed against these walls." Even when police stopped them and asked for their train passes when no one was doing anything more than hanging out in the corner, they made a joke out of it.

They made a joke out of everything: being harassed by shopkeepers anxious for them to leave; emptying out the subway cars when more than four of them boarded at one time; even being beat up. And when I heard a guard accosting a female student at 10:30 one morning—"Where are you going?" "Home." "Home? Why?" "'Cause I got a backache from having sex all night"—I began to understand that by way of protection most of the kids were buying into what older people suspected them of being anyway, and then in a wild twist of imagination and self-confidence they were throwing the images laughingly back in our faces. So that Nino expressed his fondness for Marie, the health teacher, by putting his arm over her shoulder, guiding her to the corner of the room, and telling her with a completely straight face, "You know you crazy cool. You so cool that if you were ever to come into my neighborhood—even in the middle of the night, even if you came alone in the middle of the night—I still wouldn't jump you." Only the wink he gave as he left the room a few seconds later hinted at multiple realities, multiple dialects, multiple poses all unreadable to anyone over the age of twenty. And only semiconsciously I started to long for the grace they showed everyday.

Soon and idiotically I found myself spending whole afternoons browsing in stores, longing for a pollen-yellow sweatshirt or a bright pair of red-red trousers, as though just by dressing the way they did I would somehow assume their aura. Turning the dial to Hot 97, I started to listen to more hip-hop too, and sometimes when I got home I would change into a pair of too-big jeans and a Texas baseball hat—bright red with a blue-edged T for Tina on the front, or a black one emblazoned with a white CR (for the Colorado Rockies, Crazy Ricans, or Cristina Rathbone, depending on where your priorities lay). I even began to get lax about my notes. Sitting at home I would look back on my day at school, think that nothing really important had happened, and turn the TV on instead, making sure to keep the volume on low so that my boyfriend, working in the second bedroom, wouldn't know. After taking lengthy advice from Maurice, who for some reason I felt to be a reliable salesman, I bought myself a beeper too. I hid it deep in my satchel when I went to school and only once got caught, by Ann, when I forgot to turn its setting to vibrate and it went off in the middle of her history class.

But for the same reasons I lied to the kids about my own past, I didn't want them to see just how much of an effect they were having on me. If I had a role at West Side, it was to act as a buffer to all of their freewheeling bluster, to contain it by confronting it with alternative responses, and I couldn't do that if I was seen to be emulating them. So every morning I would dress in my corduroys and sweater and sensible shoes, pull my hair back into a sagging ponytail, and let the kids continue to think of me as a hopelessly irredeemable nerd. One Monday morning Sandra asked me what was wrong, and when I said that I was just tired, that I'd had a wild weekend, she sneered and said: "What, you forgot to take your vitamins?" Her comment stung me as much as if I had been eighteen, which for all my dancing round the edges I was becoming increasingly glad I wasn't.

Their self-sufficiency had its costs, of course. However much they seemed impervious, the kids at West Side knew where they stood in the general scheme of things. And although the incredibly scintillating, brisk, and charming exteriors they developed allowed them to survive the casual blows of day-to-day life, many kids ended up suffocating in the tiny emotional space they allowed themselves to hold onto. This is one reason why psychic breaks almost always occurred when adolescents reached their late teens, Linda, one of the social workers, told me. She was always on the lookout for symptoms: the taut withdrawal, quick flashes of anger, and prolonged depressions that signaled the beginning of a breakdown. But even the most stable of students exhibited some signs of stress and negative internalization.

In history class one morning, Ann was trying to negotiate the always tricky subject of race and class identity. As an exercise she asked her students to describe how West Siders were seen by the rest of the city: "dangerous," "lazy," "dropouts," "pregnant," "Puerto Rican sluts," and "kids who can't make it in the real world because they are too dumb and angry," were just some of the answers they gave. These stood in stark contrast to the kinds of responses that a national poll Ed handed out the following morning was looking for. It had been created by the Boy Scouts of America in an attempt to get an up-to-date, nationwide portrait of contemporary teenagers, and it asked questions like: "When you look out of your window at home what do you see? Forest? Trees and grass? Farmland? Ocean? Or mostly apartments?"

Typically, the kids didn't take it too seriously. I watched as Maurice and Sandra filled out answers more or less randomly: they had never considered joining a gang, they wrote; had often thought of becoming a Boy or Girl Scout, and had never been harassed in school. Among other extracurricular clubs they might be interested in joining they included a religious group, a group that focused mainly on community service, and a marching band. Ed, though, was so irritated by most of the questions that he ended up telling them to put it aside and performed his own, informal survey in the room. That was when I found out that of the twenty-five kids in Family Group that day, only four had never been thrown out of their apartments by their parents. Lucille had been the youngest: she was eight when her mother had told her that she was sick of Lucille hanging around so much and asked her to leave. Maurice was twelve when his mother first kicked him out. Nicole had been ten; Nino waved his hand back and forth as though there was no point in him even trying to remember how old he'd been or how often it had happened since, and Cristy said that she was still thrown out at least once a year, when her mother suffered from severe PMS. By the time Ed got to Sandra she was laughing. She was thrown out the house four or five times a year, she said, adding that she would feel bad if her mother stopped doing it. "It makes me feel wanted," she said. "It's fun."

"Fun?" Ed asked.

"Yeah, it's like comedy, Ed," Cristy said.

For many of the kids it seemed there was no alternative to making the best of a bad situation by at least trying to see the humor in it, and I continued to be filled with admiration, even awe, at the courage and resourcefulness they displayed in keeping up their nimble dance, however exhausting it became.

Just how draining it must have been, in fact, was suggested by the lives of their parents, who presumably had started out just as buoyant as their kids were now. While I hadn't met many of them, I would soon get the opportunity at an upcoming parent-teachers meeting, and stories like the ones I'd just heard made me apprehensive.

Although West Side had been created in order to give parents more say over how their children were educated, parental involvement had already waned by the time Ed became principal. When the school was still on 102nd and Amsterdam, right in the heart of the Frederick Douglass Houses, where many West Side families lived, it hadn't been difficult to bring even the most reluctant parents to the school at least once a year. But the school's eviction from the building had erased that connection. Distance, however (as well as the not insignificant $3 round trip train fare) was only the most concrete barrier facing West Side parents. Working two jobs or working during the day and studying at night, many simply didn't have the energy to come down to school; others lived such marginalized, impoverished lives that simple survival had to take precedence; and still others had so little contact with their kids that they never even knew about the school's invitations to visit.

Besides, many parents (and many of the best ones, too) had spent lives so invaded by city institutions that they felt threatened and nervous at even the thought of talking to a teacher. Institutions like welfare had accustomed many to be distrustful of anyone in authority. Paperwork always came first: employment offices offered no employment; housing authorities came bristling with lists that regulated everything from overnight stays to what kind of day care was acceptable; and child-welfare agents, with their own lists, snooped and pried, intimating by their very presence that their "clients" were unworthy or unfit parents. So an invitation from yet another institution, albeit one from a school, was not always welcome, and those parents who did come often arrived cowed. Once, when I went down to the superintendent's office one cold winter's morning, I shared the waiting room with a group of mothers and grandmothers. Many of them had been there for quite some time, but still bundled in their coats and scarves and woolen hats, they were doing their best to ignore the pot of steaming hot coffee on the opposite table. It was a scene that embodied more than I hope I ever know of the distrust and enforced humility that had taken lifetimes to learn. For a full half hour they sat there, until, finally, one woman stood up and quietly asked the receptionist if the coffee was on the house, and when she nodded the whole group breathed a collective sigh of relief and rose to pour cups for themselves.

Still, West Side hadn't given up. Telephone contact was maintained by most advisers when a student had a phone, and letters were frequently sent to update parents on the current status of both their child and the school. West Side threw parties and open houses too, and whenever they could they made festivals out of otherwise intimidating events, like the upcoming parent-teachers meeting. In an attempt to attract more parents this year, Ed even offered dinner.

It took a lot of work, but on the day of the meeting the lunchroom looked wonderful. Esther's art students had frantically scrambled to finish their paintings in time to have them hung. Sandra's *Lovers in a Storm,* which she managed to take from just started to absolutely finished in one period, and two examples of Cristy's geometric designs were hung, along with an almost abstract naked woman by a talented boy who, Esther told me, had never painted before. Computer students had printed a large "Welcome to West Side High School" sign, and the school clean-up crew had done their best to cover up the graffiti. It had been hard to match the bluish color of the walls, though. They'd found that their brushstrokes left blotches when the color wasn't exactly right, and in the end they had decided to cover the tags with bold geometric shapes instead—diamonds and circles and squares in lighter shades of green and pink.

By four, a double table outside the room was covered with the food that Anne's culinary arts students had prepared. They hadn't been able to provide hot food, but they proudly displayed cold cuts arranged in floral and star shapes and macaroni and potato salad, and they had put out family-sized bottles of Coke and cherry and raspberry ginger ale. Inside the room itself the teachers were seated along the lunch-table benches. Each had a paper plate filled with food and a drink and a pile of xeroxed information about their students. Those who were organized had everything alphabetized and stapled and ordered neatly; the less organized had soft black canvas bags slung over their shoulders or resting next to them, filled with haphazard collections of files. Each was responsible for escorting the parents of their advisees around the room and for introducing them to their teachers. But however hard they had worked, the teachers remained in the majority throughout the evening. Parents entered in a steady but thin trickle between five and eight, and there were never more than five or six of them in the room at any time. Over the course of the entire evening only seventy-five parents showed up. One in ten.

Lucille didn't have a mother alive anymore or a father. But her counselors from Williamson's had been planning to come. They had even called and asked for a new list of all of their clients' teachers so that they could be sure not to miss any. This fact had Lucille very worried. Earlier that day, she had waited to speak to Ed through the entire third and fourth periods, to ask him please not to tell them that she had been skipping out on her third-period class. She had seven absences, she told him, and they would restrict her if they found out, or take her out of West Side altogether. She'd only been missing so many classes because her younger sister had taken to running away from her group home downtown and visiting Lucille in school, often frantic and in tears. What was she to do, Lucille had asked, "Leave my sister to wander round on the street by herself?"

"How old is she?" Ed asked.

"Twelve."

"And where do you take her?"

"Oh, around. I make sure she gets back OK. Make sure she gets some food. Sometimes I take her to my aunt and beg and plead that she won't tell anyone and won't make her go back to the home until she is ready to go back."

"So you are, in fact, being responsible with your time?" Ed asked, a glint in his eye.

"I am, Ed," Lucille said, and patting her on the shoulder, Ed had promised he would try to make the counselors see that. He had a good relationship with Williamson's; of all the schools in the city, his was the only one that took their clients, and they appreciated that. So early in the evening, when Ed guided them around Lucille's third-period teacher, waving him aside as if what he had to say would nor be important, they didn't question him. Luckily, perhaps, they had left by the time Maurice's mother arrived.

He had insisted she would be there and had spent a fair deal of time in Family Group bragging that she would be the only "executive" in the school that evening. She was in charge of programming for the Fox network, he insisted, which meant that everything we saw on channel 5 we saw because she had chosen it. *The Simpsons, Beverly Hills 90210, Melrose Place* and *America's Most Wanted* were on the air only because his mother liked them, he said. No one believed him, naturally, though most of us sat back and raised our eyebrows and enjoyed imagining that it might be true. Nevertheless Maurice walked out of the elevator with a regal, elegant woman in her fifties. Wearing a designer suit and designer green-framed glasses and with her whitening hair braided and pulled back into a soft ponytail held with a scrunchie, she immediately stood out from the handful of more humbly dressed parents there.

But Maurice's mother had a crisp, cold air to her, too. It was her first time at the school, and it was clear she wanted the experience to be over as quickly as possible. Maurice was all dressed up in a suit and a tie, but next to her he looked wide-eyed and younger than he usually did, almost timorous. Walking half a pace behind her, he followed her to the door of the dining room, which she entered without even glancing at the table laid out with food. Because Ed was talking to another parent I introduced myself, telling her that I had become a close friend of Maurice's and that I thought he was quite extraordinary. Tight-lipped and defensive and without ever turning to face me, she replied: "I think he is a young man with a certain potential, yes. But he is clinging to things that will pull him down, and as I tell him over and over, he isn't pulling me down with him."

I didn't dare look at Maurice then. Of all the students at West Side, he relied most on appearances, and for his carefully constructed image to be trampled this way must have been overwhelming. I turned my attention instead to a small woman who had just come out of the elevator and who was buzzing around the food table like an insect, an effect heightened by her huge tortoiseshell glasses, the kind that fade from mud brown to clear across the surface of the lenses. For ten minutes or so I watched as she walked from one teacher to another, and was struck by her odd disconnection to what was happening around her. It wasn't that she didn't react; she became appropriately angry as she traveled from one of her son's teachers to another, hearing the same descriptions of the negative and passive way he struggled through his days at West Side. It was just that there was a showy edge to her anger, as though she felt she should be seen to be angry in the face of all this absenteeism and distance and that simultaneously she should be charming and polite too. One minute she would be fuming and shaking her head and tut-tutting and the next she would be smiling and chattering as gaily as if she were at a cocktail party. When I introduced myself she took a step back, put her hand on her chest, gasped and then promptly invited me for dinner. I think she fancied me for a daughter-in-law, but I can't be sure. "Are you a friend of Api?" she asked, looking me up and down. "I didn't know he had friends like you!"

There were many parents like this there that evening—nervous, jittery men and women who had made the long trek down to West Side despite the clear anguish it set in them. Confronting parts of their children's lives they had at least subconsciously hoped someone else was tackling was a difficult hurdle for many to overcome, especially publicly. Dayna's father was one of these. From the way she used to speak about her boyfriend, a man in his fifties who bought her whatever she wanted, whenever she wanted it, I had always assumed that she lived alone. Now I realized that it was just that her father was hardly ever at home, and not because he was irresponsible, but because he was too responsible. In order to keep a roof over their heads he had to work two jobs, he told me apologetically, and he had night-college classes too, four times a week and the occasional stint as a security guard over the weekends, so by the time he got home he could usually do little more than lie down on the sofa and go to sleep. He had always known he should be around more for his daughter. He felt bad that at sixteen "Dayna is forced to take on certain responsibilities in the home," he said. But until then he'd had no idea just how far Dayna had slipped at school. "She tells me a different story than I am hearing here. I never realized she was so behind. . . ."

Another father became so upset when a math teacher told him his daughter, Ylaria, had been absent twice since the beginning of the school year that he threatened to beat her black and blue when they got back home. He had worked hard all his life in two jobs, sometimes three, he said in a clipped English edged with the precise consonants of a Mexican accent; he had suffered his whole life in order that his children could grow up in America, and this was how they repaid him, by betraying him. There was only one other parent in the room at that moment, so he had the teachers' attention. In an attempt to calm him down Stewart made his way over to the man, a soothing smile fixed to his face, and spoke enthusiastically about the possibility of Ylaria traveling to Israel with him that spring. But this did nothing to assuage the man's rage. He couldn't see any reason why he should be giving anyone a dime to take his daughter to Israel (*"Israel,"* he said, as if it were a leper colony) when she had so repeatedly and single-mindedly lied to him. Ylaria had disappeared by then and his wife, a diminutive woman who spoke no English, looked as scared by her husband's anger as she was embarrassed that he was unleashing it here. Sensing this, one of the English teachers escorted both the man and his wife out of the lunchroom and into a quiet corner in the corridor outside where she gently reminded him that a lot of good things had been said about his daughter that night. Why, Ylaria was an A student in her class, she said, pulling out her grade book to prove it. Besides, she was just sixteen and was bound to make some mistakes, and if he wanted a sustainable relationship with her later in life he should remember that now. "But she lied to me, she must be punished," the father replied, seething, quietly stoking his rage. "She must be punished and she will be punished just as soon as we get home."

That man made me think of Manny's father. Manny had told me he used his extra bulk to beat him up every now and then, when the pressures of under- rather than over-employment became overwhelming, or when his methadone ran out, or when he felt too tightly bounded by the walls of his increasingly clean apartment. I had spent a fair deal of time with Manny Sr. by then and didn't expect him to show up that night. He was too distanced from even the most general aspects of Manny's education, and I could imagine him opening the envelope with the celebratory red invitation: "What's this, Manny, a parent-teachers meeting? You think I have to go?" "Nah," Manny would have said with a shrug, and it would have been stuck to the refrigerator with tape and then forgotten about.

In fact, hardly any of the kids I was by now referring to as "mine" had parents at the meeting that evening. I had met Rasheem's mother accidentally when I had been walking down Ninth Avenue with him a few nights before and had finally seen that she was a wild, woolly-haired lady, the kind with several skirts and too much makeup who stands up and rants on the sidewalks during afternoon rush hour. Sandra's mother worked too hard as a nurse's assistant and then at school to have the time; James said his mother wasn't going to come because she had no one to look after the twins. Nicole's mother was in the hospital with a drug-related illness, and her foster mother had too much else on her mind to waste time down at school, she said. Even Shadi smiled blandly and shook his head in a vaguely reassuring way when Ed asked him if anyone would be visiting from his family. His father ran a late-night cigarette, beer, and magazine store around the corner from Williamson's, and though Shadi helped out there most nights he was still too young to be left in charge all alone. When, earlier that week, Ed had asked Cristy if she thought her mother might come she pursed her lips, cracked her knee, and said "Ed, how long you know me? Two years? How often you seen my mother? How often you spoke to her even?"

But Michelle's mother was different. Whenever Ed had asked his advisees how many of them thought their parents would be coming, Michelle had always screwed her face sideways and raised her hand. Michelle's mother worked nine to five as a communications technician, and she was supposed to come straight from work, so I was surprised when she hadn't arrived by seven. Fifteen minutes later, however, she rushed from the elevator, explaining that there'd been trouble on the trains and she'd been held up. Like Maurice's mother, she was elegantly dressed in an above-the-knee skirt suit, but she had none of the former's taut erectness, and, smiling as she piled samples of the turkey and ham and cheese and salad on her plate, she seemed pleased to be there. She had reason to be, too. Michelle had maintained straight As in all her classes since September, and for the next twenty minutes Ed and Rochelle both positively gushed and Stewart almost went so far as to tell her that Michelle would be chosen for the trip to Israel: "I've heard so many good things about her that it is impossible to ignore it all," he said, at which point Michelle got shy and twisted the ball of her foot against the newly polished floor and then reached out to limply slap Stewart. "Oh come on!" she said in just the same tone she used with Dayna. "Come off it, Stew!"

The stream of parents had slowed to a trickle by then. Trying not to look at their watches too obviously, the teachers relaxed as they rearranged themselves into more natural social groups in preparation for wrapping up the meeting. The evening had been run-of-the-mill for the most part. Only one woman had lost control entirely and had sat and sobbed on the bench next to Ed, and apart from the irate Mexican father, whom no one remembered seeing before, the same parents had showed up that always showed up. There were some surprises, of course —no one had expected Bobby Peaks's father to come, for example. A soft-spoken, gentlemanly fellow who must have been seventy, he'd made the long trip from the South Bronx because he wanted to apologize for his son and the way he was sure Bobby behaved at school. Dressed in a thickly woven three-piece suit and bent over a cane, he told Ed that he appreciated his patience and all the effort he made. He had made the same effort himself, he said, shaking his head. He'd done all he could for the boy, but there was just no changing him, and at his age, he no longer had the strength to even try. Bobby was running him ragged, he confessed while Ed listened and nodded his head in sympathetic agreement. A little later Ed made the old man laugh by telling him how the teachers referred to his son as "the Mayor." Then, placing a hand under his arm, Ed guided him around the now litter-strewn lunchroom, stopping only at teachers who might have something good to say about the boy.

12

SANDRA AND CRISTY had not been doing well at West Side of late. Despite the Netas' insistence on regular attendance and passing grades, the girls had quickly discovered that, as an organization with a questionable reputation, the Netas were easier to fool than even a careless mother. It was hardly possible for a *primero* to come down to the school to check on an *hermanita*'s progress, after all, and though Sandra's attendance had always been erratic, by November even Cristy had started to stay away for whole weeks at a time. Teachers at West Side had always worried that by emulating Sandra's attitude toward schoolwork Cristy was asking for trouble, because while everyone agreed that Sandra was perhaps bright enough to get away with it, the general consensus was that Cristy was not. With her still imperfect English, she had trouble writing and, as Ann, her history teacher, said, "The essence of her problem is that she won't accept she has a problem, and until she does that, she won't even start to improve."

But if Cristy followed Sandra in most things, the impulse to cut classes for an occasional week or so was genuinely her own. All through the school year she would periodically disappear, entomb herself in her apartment, and take to bed. It was impossible to reach her when she did this. She would stay resolutely off the telephone and spend all day lying in her room, watching TV, getting up only to eat. At times like these, she turned all her outer strength inward in a piercing and accurate assessment of her situation. So after a while I stopped paying attention to her brash affectations and noticed a tendency toward depression instead. At school, whenever her moods started to tumble, she would sit stock-still in her chair, and when I would ask what was wrong she would say, without moving, only "Tired."

Her boyfriend, "Jonell-from-R3," didn't help. Even aside from the distance he seemed to have been placing between himself and Cristy since R3 had folded, he spent most of his time with her complaining about his ex-wife. He was so obsessed by her that at times his frustration would crescendo into very real threats that he would kill the woman. Then it would take Cristy all night to persuade him that he shouldn't—that murder would only land him back in jail and that he should take his ex-wife to court instead. Needless to say, Cristy never came to school after a night like that. Instead she would spend her afternoons planning ways for him to make enough money to win custody of his child legally and to finally rid himself of his ex-wife—a woman whom Cristy was rapidly growing to hate.

Whether the plan she eventually came up with was ever entirely workable or not, I'm not sure, but Cristy certainly believed in its easy effectiveness. She never told me the details, but the way she rolled her eyes when I asked her to be more specific left the implication clear. "I tell him, 'You won't get caught, you don't even have to carry it yourself, you just find somebody to carry it,' but he's a hardheaded man, and he doesn't do it," she told me one morning in Family Group when she came in exhausted and frustrated and so harried that she hadn't bothered to do anything more with her hair than scrape it back into an uneven ponytail. "He could make five thousand dollars in a week, Tina, ten thousand—and I tell him it's what he got to do. I tell him: 'You're not working, you need this money to solve your problems and then that's it, you stay out of it.' Because first of all he needs money as a fund; second he needs money for him to buy himself some clothes; third he needs it for his daughter. And he would be able to deal with his wife too. I keep telling him, 'Whatever you agree with her, that's your problem. I can't get between it, and I don't want to take her place. I don't want to take nothing. But I'm getting tired of chasing a shadow.'

"I tell you," she said then. "If I run into her on the street I wouldn't let my mouth off, out of respect, you know? But if she were ever to raise her fist to me—ooooohhh I'd wipe her out, Tina. I'd trash her ass."

One way of getting Jonell's attention, Cristy was sure, was to have his baby. Almost every week she would come into Family Group gleefully announcing that this time, *this time,* she was sure she was pregnant: because she had felt sick in the morning; because her hair was becoming straighter, her fingernails thicker; or because she had just weighed herself and noticed she had put on four pounds in one week and everyone knew that that was what happened in the early stages of pregnancy, especially if the baby was a boy. One morning, though, she came into Family Group looking tense and worried and told me that she thought one of her ovaries was hung upside down. Jonell's cousin had made the diagnosis, and it would explain why she hadn't been able to get pregnant. "An upside-down ovary produces no eggs," she explained. Jonell's cousin had no medical training and had only come up with the suggestion when a neighbor had been similarly diagnosed. But the notion stuck in Cristy's mind for weeks and perhaps because a visit to the gynecologist was out of the question—"Jonell wouldn't like it"—nothing I could do or say would dispel her fear.

Many kids at West Side shared both Cristy's belief in the sanctity of motherhood and her vague, superstitious approach toward pregnancy. And for all the talk of contraception and planned families that went on Washington, there was little that Marie, the health teacher, could do about it either. Not that she didn't try. Week after week she discussed every kind of birth control, from the pill to dental dams, the often fruit-flavored sheets of thin rubber latex that originated in the dentist's chair and that evolved primarily as an AIDS-prevention tool for use between gay women. She discussed AIDS and gonorrhea and herpes and syphilis, and had a series of gruesome slides that were almost enough to put anyone off sex for decades. A few years before, she had even made a video about day-to-day life with a baby, but it never gained distribution through the Board of Education because it was deemed to be too depressing. Whatever she said, though, however much she told the kids that it was hard, that a child took over your life and that it often ruined it too, the deeply ingrained sense of womanhood that being a mother entailed—especially for the Latin girls—overrode everything, and a willful veil of ignorance prevailed.

One morning I sat in Marie's class as a nineteen-year-old boy and father of two asked whether sleeping with a pregnant lady might not hurt the baby's head. You could tell that most kids in the class had been worried about that as well, because a momentary hush fell across the room while Marie gave her answer. A pregnant girl in the back was concerned that if she slept with a man other than her fetus's father, the fetus would inherit the lover's characteristics. "Would it affect the baby's complexion?" she asked. Another wanted to know whether a man ejaculating inside her would give her unborn child birthmarks, and a third was worried that because her child had been born with the birth sack over his face he would grow up seeing ghosts.

"Marie, Marie, where the glow come from?" a girl asked then. "You know how people say you glow when you pregnant? What causes that?" When Marie started to explain that it came from feeling healthy and happy, Sandra, who until then had been sitting in the back row reading a magazine, grew impatient and interrupted: "Like if you ever had good sex and you all smiling and feeling good when you come into school and people is saying, 'I know what you been up to,' tha's what the glow is like, only longer."

Since getting "married" Sandra had stopped talking to me about such intimacies, though I knew through Cristy that she and Rankin were also trying to get pregnant and that she was convinced her first child would be a girl. "Umm-hmm. We'll be needing even more clothes then," Cristy had said. But she did speak to me, incessantly, about her association with the Netas. Both she and Cristy had made it through their probation period and were now on "observation." Perhaps in an attempt to reduce her time in this limbo land of the not-quite-member, Sandra had started volunteering as a member of the security team at a primary school on 181st Street, where her local Neta chapter was based. The building was kept open after school hours, she couldn't help boasting, through funds from the highly successful Beacon Project, a program set up during former Mayor David Dinkins's administration to provide community-based organizations with a place to operate, which had miraculously escaped Giuliani's most recent rounds of cuts. Everything from basketball to sculpture to GED courses to English as a second language was offered, free, to anyone who cared to participate. The project was run locally by the Alianza Dominicana, and the local chapter of the Netas was providing security in exchange for the use of the auditorium on Friday nights for their meetings.

Sandra knew she shouldn't talk too much about any of this at school, but one rare morning when she made it in on time for Family Group she couldn't resist letting Ed know that she at least had a job.

"Yo, Ed, you got one of them work-credit sheets?" she asked him, referring to the forms that must be filled out by an employer if a student wished to receive high school credit for working. Then she sat back in her chair in amused anticipation of his response. For once, though, Ed said nothing. One of the reasons he had been glad to have West Side relocated to midtown was that the area afforded opportunities for work and internships. He had been pleased when Sandra and Cristy had shown an interest the previous summer and had quickly found them two places with a jewelry manufacturer just a couple of blocks from the school. The job was simple enough—threading beads onto cords of nylon and then attaching a stainless-steel clasp—but Sandra hated it, hated the hours and the dullness and the uncomfortable stool she had to sit on. When her boss finally lost his patience with her and threatened to kick both her and Cristy out if they didn't stop chattering and improve the percentage of salable necklaces they turned out, Sandra shouted right back—she wasn't going to be dissed like that—and then Cristy had stood up next to her and the owner had felt threatened. Ed hadn't heard the end of it for weeks. It was the only time he came close to losing the cooperation of a participant in the program. So now, after a couple of minutes, Ed simply raised his eyebrows.

"Are you working?" he asked, trying not to sound too surprised.

"I bin working already for weeks," she told him. "Security."

"Security?"

"Yeah. Security for a school round my way, through the Alianza Dominicana," she said. "School security Ed—at PS One forty-three."

Up until then it had been impossible for me to attend a Neta meeting. Secrecy was one of the first oaths a Neta initiate took, and having told me even as much as they had could be grounds for both Sandra and Cristy's expulsion. Besides, I was a writer, Cristy had pointed out one morning. "Yea-aah," Sandra had agreed, chewing gum. "From the media." Rummaging in her bag, she had pulled out a new flyer that had started to appear on lampposts and mailboxes uptown. "A MESSAGE TO THE LATIN KINGS, ZULU NATION, NETA AND ANY OTHER ORGANIZATION STRIVING FOR POSITIVITY!" it read.

> Be on the look out for two of the biggest gangs in the city <u>THE POLICE DEPARTMENT</u> and <u>THE MEDIA.</u> WHO ARE THE REAL ENEMIES? WHO IS STARTING THE VIOLENCE? WHO IS DIVIDING AND

CONQUERING US? WHO IS OPPRESSING YOU? WHO IS DECEIVING YOU, AND MAKING YOU THINK THE ANSWER IS YOUR OWN BROTHER? The answer is simply in front of your eyes, so open them. THE NYPD, THE MEDIA and their followers and supporters. Look at your true enemy and REALIZE . . .

Just a few days before I had read about PS 143 in the *New York Times,* and now that I knew that the Netas were involved with the Beacon Project there I could approach them from a background wholly unattached to either Sandra or Cristy. The school formed a small part of a story about how crime was on a downturn in Washington Heights, and I had torn it out and had been carrying it around in my bag, hoping for a chance to show it to them, because in the middle of it was a quote by a man named Ramón Garcia, who was described as being "the leader of the Netas gang in Washington Heights." I pulled it out now and showed Sandra the relevant section.

"That's Ramón!" Sandra screamed when she saw the quote. "That's him! That's El León!" She was so proud to see her leader's name in the newspaper that I went down to the store and made a copy of the article for her before she left.

Ramón Garcia, a.k.a. El León, turned out to be a twenty-six-year-old, broad-foreheaded, white Puerto Rican with a lot of thick, straight hair swept back who, except for a thick black beard, could pass for a young Marlon Brando. He had been hit by a car just before I met him, a hit-and-run, he said, and was in a wheelchair. His left leg, broken in three places, was up on a leg rest, and great half-inch stitches barely held together fleshy clumps of his left palm. Less visibly, his right shoulder was dislocated, and his collarbone was broken. I knew where he would be both from the newspaper article and from the countless stories Sandra had told me about her duties in the school, and I met him in the lobby of the building, just in front of the receptionist's desk, where he was sitting in his wheelchair flanked by two younger Netas, to whom he referred as his "legs."

Convinced and dogmatic and proud and probably a finagler all at once, El León was less defensive than I had imagined he might be. It was true that he flinched when I mentioned the *New York Times* article and that Mickey, the second in command, laughed and said, "You made a big mistake mentioning that round here." But once we got past that and established that only two years before I had been in a hair-raising automobile accident myself and had ended up spending six months in a wheelchair, after we had compared details of our mutually smashed tibias and fibulas and complained about the trials of extended hospitalization, Ramón began to relax.

He said that he would rather not speak too much about his prison experience, or the crime that got him there, though he flatly denied that it was murder, as the *Times* had reported. But he did acknowledge that he had become a Neta in prison, and that he had spent the best part of the last six years behind bars, and not for one crime but for several: he'd go in, then come out, then go in again, he explained. Now, with a whole month out on the street, it was as though he'd just realized that crime didn't pay, and he was full of phrases like "the dark path of crime" and "the light path of empowering employment." He was sincere too, as far as I could tell, and casually powerful almost to the point of being regal, so that when he announced, "In this community we need more lawyers and doctors, not hangers-around," I felt a strong urge to click to attention and carry out his orders at once—an urge not altogether diminished when he added somewhat ingenuously: "That's what I think anyway. But I'm not so smart."

We spent the next few hours sitting out there in the linoleum hallway, and I soon discovered that despite the Netas' secrecy rules, El León liked to talk. El Asociación Neta began in 1979 in the prisons of Puerto Rico, he told me proudly. They had fought for increased prisoner rights, for better food, and for more time out of their cells and had won all three concessions. From there they spread to institutions on the mainland, to Ithaca, Rikers Island, and Sing-Sing, where black Muslim prisoners ran the show and Latin inmates needed protection. Just a month before our meeting the Latin Kings and the Netas had engineered a successful "no work, no food" strike at Rikers, where their demands included better treatment of visitors and the rejection of a proposed early lockup time. And although many people suggested that, simply for protection, inmates no longer had any choice but to join a gang in prison, Ramón insisted it had been the organization's discipline and fierce cultural pride that had attracted him, and he credited his membership in the Netas with his move away from the revolving door of prison.

Mickey was more careful. He refused to discuss his membership in the Netas or how or where he'd joined, and he only shrugged when I asked him if he'd ever been in prison. He seemed most comfortable asking me questions, and whenever Ramón started to get too specific about certain Neta histories he coughed into his hand and nodded his head down the corridor and asked me to leave them alone for a moment or two. But he was usually smiling by the time I came back, and after another couple of hours of sitting out there in the hallway even he seemed comfortable with the idea of me attending some of their meetings.

In accordance with this newfound acceptance he even ordered two lowly *hermanitos* to escort me back home at the end of the evening. "Not only to the station but onto the train as well," he admonished. They couldn't have been older than fifteen, either of my escorts, and they were skinny, and shy with me; only the Neta beads hung proudly around their necks allowed them to overcome their awkwardness with a gentle swagger and a heightened sense of macho protocol. They insisted that I enter the train first and then sit down, while they stood on either side, tall and serious and filled with the importance of their mission, like members of the president's Secret Service team. Glowing myself then—with some kind of feminine pride, I suppose—I remembered my trip up to the school earlier that evening, the way the train had emptied out, and the nearly three-block walk down an almost entirely deserted street to the school, and I knew then, as the train swayed its way back downtown, that even if the worst I had heard about youth gangs was true, even if many of the Netas had had less than salubrious pasts and had been recruited in prison, and even if the organization really was responsible for a murder in Connecticut, as the papers said it was, that if I were a sixteen-year-old girl from Washington Heights, nothing in the world could have stopped me from joining the Netas.

The night of my first meeting, however, things weren't quite so welcoming. Neta guards had been stationed outside the front door to the school, at either end of the reception table inside the lobby, and at the top of the stairs. Each guard wore the same puffy, black jacket that ballooned down to their knees, and there was something about their uniformity and the evenness of the black and white beads tipped with red that I found profoundly intimidating. This, I'm sure, was exactly the point. Ragged-looking kids with scars, stares that could kill, and swaggers that permitted just one of them to walk down the wide curving stairs at a time scowled as they passed by me on the way to a rigorous weapons search that had been established by the entrance to the auditorium downstairs. Both males and females were spread-eagled and patted down before they were allowed in.

The meeting had been slated to begin at 7:00. According to Ramón, sixty-three *hermanitos* were supposed to be in attendance, but by 7:30 only twenty-seven had arrived. Cristy was one of the absentees. She had told me she might not be able to make it and had only shrugged, rolled her soft shoulders up to the base of her ears, and pursed her well-painted lips when I had asked her why. Sandra walked into the auditorium just minutes after I did, but now she was so involved in an intense conversation with Mickey, who she was making laugh up in the second row from the front, that I don't think she even noticed me sitting quietly in the back. After five minutes or so Ramón took his seat on top of a high metal stool and stared at the assembled teenagers as his wheelchair was folded up and placed out of the way by the third in command, a beefy-looking giant named Felipe.

"Damn man, look at this," he said, glancing across the rows of empty seats. From then on, he declared, anyone turning up later than 7:15 would not be allowed into the meeting and would "have to bear the consequences." It was a phrase he liked a lot, I already knew: "bear the consequences," "take the consequences," "suffer the consequences." He had used them over and over the first time I'd met him—because it sounded suitably ominous, I'd thought, without making him have to be too specific about just what he meant.

"Corazón!" he boomed as he thumped his right fist hard against his heart twice and then thrust it into the air.

"Corazón!" the auditorium echoed, and the meeting was begun. Still nervous, I reached over and picked up a white sheet of paper lying on the seat next to me. Mickey had been handing them out to the

hermanitos earlier, and I wanted to see what it said. It was printed on both sides, Spanish on one, English on the other, and was headed with a neat little address:

> Asociación Neta
> Capítulo #6,
> High Bridge.

The English side read:

> RULES TO BE FOLLOWED
> 1) As far as all the meetings are concerned there will be no talking, no hats, no walk-mans, no gum chewing and all beepers must be turned off.
> 2) In order to speak you must raise your hand and wait your turn.
> 3) Leaving the meeting is not allowed at any time. In order to leave the meeting there must be an emergency and there must be permission granted.
> 4) Everyone must be seated at all times.
> 5) Dues have to be paid at all meetings.
> 6) No talking to your Brothers and Sisters while another person is talking.
> 7) No one can enter the building while intoxicated, this includes the meetings.
> 8) No weapons allowed into the building.
> 9) No alcohol or drugs allowed into the building.
> 10) Everyone will be searched at the entrance.
> EVERYONE WHO BREAKS ONE OF THESE RULES WILL SUFFER THE CONSEQUENCES.

It wasn't the kind of hard-nosed gang's oath of allegiance I'd been expecting, though when Ramón opened the floor up to questions, point number 8 seemed to cause the most trouble. Many of the younger boys were particularly confused.

"Can we bring like a box cutter or something?" one of them asked.

"It's right there, number eight, *hermano*. 'No weapons allowed in the building.'"

"I ain't coming if I can't be strapped," another young Neta pouted.

"What to you need a gun here for? To shoot me?" Ramón asked. "I'm in a wheelchair here. Leave your guns and whatever at home."

"But what about for protection?"

"You don't need them in here, *hermanito*."

"But what about for getting to here though?"

"Mira," he said—"Look." *"No hay ninguna razón para venir aqui preparado."*—"There is no need to come in here prepared"—and there was something about the sudden switch to Spanish that ended all further discussion.

Still, if there really was no reason to be "prepared," I couldn't help wondering why there were four Neta security guards posted in the room: one on each side of the stage and one guarding each of the doors in the back—all of them with walkie-talkies. Relaxing a little, I told myself that if they really were setting out to "end all abuse everywhere, worldwide," then they needed to look at least as if they might be forces to reckon with. And as if to prove me right, Mickey stood up then and announced that the "theme of the day" would be Neta history.

They had even arranged outside speakers for the evening. Two excons, one who had been released just the day before and one who had been out for a couple of weeks, stood when they were introduced and then perched on high stools in the front, just to the left of Ramón and Mickey. For the next hour and a half they gave historical lectures and fielded questions from the floor in the measured and authoritative way of accepted experts. Lengthy speeches were given about the Puerto Rican Independistas, and diagrams of the flag the group designed for an independent Puerto Rico were distributed before talk turned to the more pressing issues of Neta historical fact.

And that was it, really. After all those hours of built-up nerves, that was the gang meeting: a handful of troubled-looking teenagers sitting quietly in an auditorium too large for them, discussing historical minutiae like a huddle of retired clerks turned local village historians. Politely but enthusiastically they debated the exact date of the death of their founder, Carlos Torres Illiarte—was it the twenty-eighth of March 1981, or the thirtieth? Holding scraps of paper above their heads as they waited to be called upon, they argued over where he had been buried and whether he was killed in his cell at Soblanco prison or in the exercise yard, as some of the pamphlets said, when he had only a rolled-up copy of *La Vida* newspaper to defend himself with. As time wore on even the guards onstage began to look younger and less and less threatening as they passed the time by nibbling at their radios' rubber antennas and flicking the royal-blue curtains draped at the sides of the stage back and forth and round and round with their feet.

It was a young man named Oscar Ramos who had brought Capítulo Seis—Chapter 6 of the Netas—in from the cold to the school's auditorium at PS 143. He was the head of security for Alianza Dominicana, and although he was only twenty-four he had an aura of adulthood about him that might have come from having supported a son since he was a senior in high school. He had grown up in El Barrio, to the east of where we were now, and though he'd known about the Netas since he was a kid and had watched Capítulo Seis as they joined in their traditional circle, week after week in the small park opposite the school, it had still been a risk bringing in a gang to watch over the toddlers and old people and nonaligned teenagers that streamed in and out of the building every night. But since they had started volunteering, he told me, they'd done their job better than any other volunteer group he had tried—turning up more regularly and, when there, behaving with an efficiency and a quiet discipline that anyone who had ever worked with teenagers could only admire.

Oscar was there that night, sitting quietly but attentively in the back, occasionally jotting down notes on a large yellow legal pad. Listening to the speakers cajoling their audience, I recalled his hesitant explanation for the growth of the Netas outside of the prison system. In all the years of the organization's existence in Puerto Rico, not one street chapter had ever evolved; perhaps, he offered, it was simply an expression of the very North American desire to expose and share our most secret failures and desires that they were doing so well here. Listening to one of the ex-cons berate himself for the mistakes of his past, I understood what he meant and thought that anyone familiar with the traditions and growth of the AA movement would have had no difficulty in understanding their appeal.

Every year 120,000 prisoners are released nationwide. Disoriented and with little chance of finding legal employment, many need a kind of AA of their own, a PA, prisoners anonymous, or IA, inmates anonymous. On the street, this is pretty much what the Netas initially tried to provide: a judgment-free group where ex-inmates could gather and boost one another's spirits with shared tales of troubles overcome and temptations, for the most part, hopefully, resisted. From there, of course, kids who'd never been to prison became interested in these characters who wandered around their neighborhoods with their jail ripe muscles, black and white beads, and a certain and communally tough sense of restraint. And so, ever eager for an increased membership ("numbers are strength and strength is power," they say), the Netas bloomed. They were, however, still adapting to their new cultural surroundings, and many of the rules listed in their primary rule book bore little relation to life on the street—especially if you happened to be seventeen years old and female, like Sandra and Cristy. Rule number 7, for example, reads: "Street beef is street beef. In jail it is dead"; number 11: "Respect the rules of silence: an inmate's sleep is sacred"; and most particularly number 3: "Don't look at your brother as a woman—unless he feels like one."

This last, suggestive hint at multiculturalism reverberated later that evening when, after the earnest question-and-answer session had been going on for close to two hours, an older *hermanito* with a shaved head and a nervous, feminine manner raised his hand and asked if it was true that Carlito's right-hand man, William Rivera Rivera, had been a homosexual. The guards onstage stopped twisting the gold curtain cords and looked toward the ex-con. The ex-con looked down at his feet. In the sudden silence he took a deep breath, rolled the page with the day's rules on it into a tightly wound scroll, and then curtly nodded his head. "*Sí.* Yes. *Sí—Sí.* William Rivera Rivera *era homosexual.*"

The auditorium fell silent. A few *hermanitas* and *hermanitos* looked into their laps, others slid down a little in their chairs while Ramón scanned the audience, his eyes just a little too wide to be absolutely calm. Most of them must have known about this already. It was right there in their initiation pack and had been one of the first things Cristy had told me about. In a voice hushed like an incredulous little girl's, she'd said: "We accept homosexuals, you know. Latin Kings do not accept homosexuals, but we do. We have some and we have to accept them as our peoples because they the weakest ones; they the ones that get picked on more easier in and out of jail because of the simple fact that they're homosexuals, they get beat up and they even get raped and stuff too."

But for it to be out in the open like this was another matter. Up at the front of the room the Neta speakers bristled. "Everything is different on the inside," the one who had been a Neta for twelve years was telling them now. "Everything, and on *La Isla*," he said, referring to Puerto Rico, "the gays took the place of the women inside. Let everyone understand what most people already know—homosexuals make superb warriors. However"—and this, he emphasized, was a very important point—"gay members of El Asociación in *La Isla* were given *ni voz, ni voto*—neither voice not vote." They were like the women, he said. Neither got a say in how the organization was run. "Like politics in the real world, that is left up to the men."

Sandra had been sitting quietly up until then, the perfect example of a Neta novitiate, but now she spoke up. "Excuse me," she said, seething visibly, but not forgetting to raise her hand in the Neta salute in accordance with rule number 2. "Excuse me. I am a person who believes my voice is as good and as strong as anybody's. I may be a female, but if being a Neta is really a way of life, if it's really about more than a string of beads and an attitude, then what is to stop me from doing as well as you? I can live the life and have the mind of a Neta as well as anyone," she said and then, exhaling loudly, dropped heavily back into her seat.

"Corazón!" shouted the girl seated near her, and then some of the other girls as well. Joining the chorus, a group of the younger boys thrust their fists into the air, smiling now, pleased at a bit of excitement. Ramón quieted them with a great bellow of a *Corazón!* The visiting speaker, the one who had just been released from prison, smiled nervously. After glancing at Ramón, he said that it wasn't him that made the rules, that it was the elders in *La Isla*, and that of course he agreed with Sandra that all people were equal.

Sensing that the response was not quite satisfactory Ramón sat still and stared at the back of the room.

"This is all good. All good," he said after a time, nodding his head like a ponderously wise old monk once the room was quiet. "Remember, *hermanitos: Somos guerreros hasta la muerte. Pero somos guerreros humildes. Guerreros humildes,*" he added again for emphasis—"Humble warriors. Better solve it with words than with action." With a slanting glance across the auditorium he brought the discussion to a close.

It was this very emphasis on intellectual discussion that supposedly distinguished groups like Chapter 6 not only from other youth gangs but from other chapters within the Neta organization itself, Oscar had explained. It had been an unspoken condition of their coming into the school, and he used the long hours of security work during the week to talk to Ramón, Mickey and the other members of the group's governing "junta" about the forthcoming meeting's agenda. Oscar insisted that the junta themselves came up with the issues to be discussed and that he just helped out with the structure, but Cristy was convinced that Chapter 6 had changed beyond recognition over the past month. To tell the truth, the long elegies to Puerto Rican revolutionaries held very little appeal to a first-generation Honduran. And though I would often run into her up in the lunchroom in the early afternoons reading and rereading one of the Netas's several official texts, underlining them with a highlighter and folding down the edges of important pages, she never mustered the confidence necessary to take the final test to become a fully fledged *hermanita.*

"Ay, I don't know, Tina," she said one day. "The Netas is for real and they is good to me and all that but there is so much to learn and they ask you questions up there in front of everybody and if you don't know the answer to any one of them you fail. It could be embarrassing." At one point she started talking about a boot camp that Chapter 6 was thinking of sending her to, for training in the basic philosophies and history, but she seemed to lose the last threads of her interest when, halfway through November, Jonell left her to go back to his wife. When she found a job at the end of the month, the final ties were cut.

It happened by chance, she said. She'd been in bed with the blues, thinking, "It's time to get serious," when a friend she had met in Esther's class called and told her that there was an opening at a movie theater in midtown. Cristy hadn't cared. She didn't want a job, she said. She didn't want a boyfriend and she didn't want to join the Netas. She just wanted to rest. Her girlfriend was persistent, though. She called again that afternoon and then a third time, and Cristy finally decided to give it a try. She got up and bathed and did her hair and then she went down for an interview. It was easier than she'd thought it would be. The questionnaire was short—asking only for former work experience and educational background—and because the manager was a young man, it didn't take her long to make friends. She was hired that same day to work behind the candy and popcorn counter. She would work thirty hours a week and would take home $125 after tax.

It was the first official, legal, and above-board job she had ever had, and not only was it in a movie house—a top-of-the-line job for high school students in the city—she got to wear a uniform too, a black trouser suit, white shirt, and a bow tie that she kept in the shoulder bag bought expressly for the purpose and placed on the seat to the left of her now, on her first day back at school in a week. All dressed up and with her hair straightened and oiled and pulled back into a gently curved avocado-shaped bunch at the back, she rested both her legs on the table in front of her. I asked to see the bow tie but, flushing with pride, she said no.

I asked again.

"No, no, no, no, no."

"But I must see it. I have to see it," I begged, until, beaming, she finally pulled it out of the bag, where it had been neatly folded under the crisp, white collar of her shirt. It was dark gray with marbleized streaks of hot silver running through it. She had worn it loose around her neck the night before, she said, so that the pretied bow hung down like a Neta necklace, and the manager hadn't seemed to mind. "I think it's kind of cool-looking that way," she said. But her feet hurt so much, she told me then as she refolded the tie and put it away; she had to stand up all night! By herself! All night, by herself, behind that candy and popcorn counter *and with nowhere to sit down!* She looked at the clock, which read 11:45, and asked me if it was right because she had promised to wait for Sandra but the theater opened its doors at one and she didn't want to be late.

I hadn't seen Sandra since the meeting uptown a week before, and I couldn't believe she would show up now. She had gained a following among the younger girls since her outburst at the meeting, and though there was already a head for the Chapter 6 girls, she was hardly ever around, and a movement was brewing to nominate Sandra as a replacement. Of course, Sandra would still have to pass the test and become a full-fledged *hermanita* first. But while Cristy drifted further and further from the group, Sandra was busy making a name for herself as a strong young *hermanita* in waiting, and for now, anyway, West Side had fallen by the wayside. Cristy sighed, checked the clock again, then patted her thighs once with the palms of her hands and slowly heaved her feet off the table as if she had been doing this for years and was long resigned to the exhaustion. "Neta. Neta. Neta—I guess she's kind of busy these days. Me, I really don't got time for none of that no more," she said, trying to sound mournful but ultimately failing to repress a grin. "Well, I gotta go to work now—it's not all of us that get to hang around in school all day."

13

THE DAY IN November that a schoolwide war was narrowly avoided started usually enough. I was standing with Bobby Peaks, the boy with the floppy black hat and slurred speech, who was close to finishing a pencil outline of his painting for Esther's third-period oil-painting class. The painting was titled *My Neighborhood,* and the main figure, god-like, was a giant named Fuck the World. He was wearing a sweatshirt with his initials, F.T.W., scrawled across the front and was standing at center frame with his legs apart and his arms raised to flex his biceps. Beneath him and on a different scale altogether sprawled a landscape of cramped housing-project buildings. Over on the right was a posse of fifteen tiny stick figures wearing hooded sweatshirts and shooting clunky-looking, oversized pistols at two other characters, who were draped in ghostlike capes and hoods.

"Ku Klux Klan niggers," Bobby explained as a tall black kid—six foot five, maybe—came into the room and walked across its length to a stocky boy named Julio, a member of the Almighty Latin King Nation, who was mixing some colors over by the sink.

There was something about the purposefulness of his walk, the focused stride so different from the usual student shuffle toward a new paintbrush or a fresh pot of paint, that made Esther look up and, in a tone not at all like her own, ask him to leave. I had never seen the boy before and someone that tall was not easy to miss, but she knew his name—Paul—and when he ignored her she asked again, still calm but edgy now, with a higher pitch and a quaver to her voice.

"Paul, would you leave the room now please? What are you doing? Paul?"

"You got beef with my man?" Paul asked Julio, ignoring Esther entirely.

"Yeah," Julio said, looking scornfully across the room to Bobby, who everyone seemed to know was Paul's "man." "I don't like him."

The room froze. Paint dripped from brushes held in the air. Of all of New York's youth gangs, the Latin Kings had the toughest reputation, and everyone in the room right then knew better than to challenge a King to his face.

"You only speaking so tough because you a King," Paul said, jutting his chin toward Julio's gold-and-black beaded *collare*.

"You think I need this?" Julio said as he started to unwind his beads from his neck. "I don't need these. I don't need nothing. I'll use my hands." For a moment the two of them stood still, Julio short but broad, Paul towering over him and peering down, so that they looked almost like a poster advertising an Arnold Schwarzenegger– Danny DeVito movie. Then Paul smiled. But it was not an expression of happiness, nor of anger, nor loathing, nor even of contempt. Instead it was a pragmatic, slow peeling back of the lips to reveal a razor blade clenched between his teeth. Julio didn't move. The rest of us were silent, trapped in our seats and about as capable of having any kind of effect on the performance in front of us as an audience has on the movie they are watching. Esther was on the phone to security by then, but between the two boys there was silence so profound it seemed impossible that either of them could hear her.

"Later," Paul said suddenly, turning from Julio as he tucked the blade back behind his molars and sauntered out of the room. Julio stayed right where he was, shoulders tense and square, hands clenched down by his thighs. The art-room door clanged shut, and through it we could hear one of the security guards confronting Paul, telling him to get out of the school now before he had him arrested. Looking around I noticed for the first time that Bobby Peaks was no longer in the room. I glanced across to the other side of the table to find an explanation, and when no one else would meet my gaze I realized for the first time how fine the separation was between life in the school and life on the street. The confrontation between Julio and Paul was all it had taken to polarize the entire room. Latin versus black. Within an hour the word that a black kid had threatened a Latin King had spread across the school, and by lunchtime nerves were beginning to fray.

Things rarely got so out of control at West Side. The only cardinal rule at the school was "No physical or verbal abuse of any kind by anyone to anyone." For the most part it worked. Relieved to at least partially drop their guard for a time, most students viewed West Side as a sanctuary, a castle complete with moat and retractable drawbridge which protected them from the often anarchic circumstances that were the rest of their lives. And though during the year I was there fights would occasionally break out, the careful accountability and intensely personal relationships established between students and their advisers often circumvented the problems before they became unmanageable. That was why Ed placed such supreme importance on respect for others, on tolerance, and even on maintaining a dependable good humor. It wasn't that he didn't approve of an emphasis on academics. In an ideal world, or even a marginally better one, where socialization and care were provided by the family and society at large, the ancient Greek idyll of students pondering the meaning of eternity or death would be as appealing to Ed as to anyone else. But the reality was that modern day society wanted nothing to do with his wayward black and Latin teenagers, and he simply didn't have the time.

"You know as well as I do that the issues here are not academic, the issues are social and emotional and mental and spiritual," Ed told me once. Perhaps because it had always been that way, because kids now were suffering from the same kinds of emotional deprivation that they had been ever since he had first taken control of West Side, almost twenty years ago, he sighed a little as he said it. He had been my age exactly, just a few months over thirty when he had walked into the converted ballet school on West Ninety-third Street. Now he was fifty, and even though there may have been more failures than successes, and even if his successes had been largely unspecific and vague—happiness and security and a sense of self-worth not being as measurable as graduation rates—he had somehow managed to keep the island that was West Side afloat with the caring and humor and constancy he had established on his very first day at the school.

But today, on another street in another world and another time, the sheer weight and force of another generation of kids had made a mockery of the protection he had so carefully established. There was nothing Ed could do but hope that some remnants of the more or less tranquil sanity he had spent so much of his life implementing would pay off. These kinds of crises had happened before. Once, after a party he'd allowed the kids to throw, he had found himself balanced on top of a Dumpster wailing and crying for the crowd of students below him to stop fighting. Now he was standing in the entranceway to the school, quieter than he had been before but just as desperate. "I just hope and pray that we've convinced at least some of the kids who have some influence with others that it behooves them— That this is not the right place for it—" he said, giving up simultaneously both on trying to express himself and on waiting for any inspired peacemaking to rise up out of the muck of rumor and fear and aggression. Standing in the lobby, Ed picked up the phone from the box by the door. As much as he hated to, he requested police assistance.

"Fuck the Kings and their muscle" I heard a usually placid and well-behaved young black man mutter then. It was just a few minutes before lunch, and kids were everywhere. They shuffled out of the elevator and came sauntering down the stairs and onto the street. I hadn't seen so many kids together since my first day of school. Outside, small groups walked up to the corner and back again, a distance of maybe twenty yards, or leaned against the cars and the double-parked trucks that were always there, their drivers loading and unloading great rolls of fabrics, or hung from the railings of the two subway entrances, lighting cigarettes and drinking soda from brown paper bags. They clustered around anyone who they thought might have seen something across the street, or heard something in the elevator or in the coffee shop or the hallway or the McDonald's around the corner. Over on the opposite side of the street Latin kids started to congregate. A crowd formed. Black heads were turning toward Paul, who was still lingering on the school side of the sidewalk. Both crowds grew. Panicked security guards marched up and down the street waving their arms, telling everyone to disperse: "Just get off the block—off!" Meanwhile a petite white woman in an argyle sweater struggling with several Macy's shopping bags hurried past, and an ancient Chinese man, tiptoeing somewhere with a brown paper lunch bag balanced precariously on top of a thin white cardboard plate in front of him, wove his way through the crowd. Even the men that pushed the clothes racks, three or four together sometimes, one piled on top of another and all sagging with furs or suits or sequined dresses in plastic wraps, kept their eyes steadfastly on the ground as they passed. Some of them even stopped halfway down the block and waited.

The police arrived within minutes. Their sirens were not on, but their lights were flashing, the reds bouncing off shop windows and the whites seeming to shoot straight up into the air. Four policemen unfolded themselves from a packed patrol car, and ten more leapt out of a blue-and-white transport van. They looked very young, all of them, and very pale, if rosy-cheeked and, in comparison to the crowds around them, very short. Even their uniforms looked a childish shade of light sky blue. And they were scared, it was clear, not so much by what could be starting to happen but by where: right in the middle of the garment district at half past twelve on a weekday. Clenching their nightsticks firmly, they formed a cordon across Thirty-fifth Street where it met Eighth Avenue. This packed the already tight corner of Latin kids even tighter and when a line of policemen started to walk toward the school from the other side of the street they heedlessly herded black kids there from every direction too.

"Whose street is this anyway? This a school—why can't we be outside of it? It's not our fault if the damn school moved down to where white people work!" Tony Phillips, the boy who'd taken me tangoing down the subway platform, was saying from the relative safety of the school entrance. A few minutes later a neat white policeman mistook me for a student and pushed me back toward the door with his nightstick. It took all of my control to stop myself from telling him what he could do with that unnaturally heavy, smooth stick of his and, seeing this, Tony laughed. But the crowd of students kept its cool amazingly well. The group on the near corner had spilled out onto the street when it had become clear that the whole block had been shut off. And despite the police presence, there was still an intensity between the two, now more integrated, groups of kids. When a short, skinny, prettily dressed girl named Justine started to shout at a cop who had pushed her, two officers threw her against a wall and pulled her arms behind her back to cuff her. Ed pushed past some students to reach her, but a cop laid the edge of his nightstick across his belly.

"I'm the principal," Ed calmly explained.

"Yeah? Well, you lost control," he was told.

Reluctantly Ed stepped back and started shooing the kids down into the subway station, telling them to go home, that he'd see them all tomorrow, to just go home and relax and try to enjoy life. To begin with he had little success, but sensing a potentially dangerous shift in mood when two more vans packed with officers screeched to a halt on Eighth Avenue just south of Thirty-fifth Street, the kids started to disperse. Oddly languorous suddenly, they loped down off the street to the subway station, or sauntered around the corner onto Eighth or down to the other end of the block, to Ninth Avenue. In five minutes the street outside West Side was empty.

"They don't want to be around when the popping starts," I heard Ed say to no one in particular. A few minutes later Jim, the teacher who had been dean before Charyl, came to the door to check on the status of the girl who had been arrested. He and Ed decided to walk the two blocks to the precinct together. Watching their backs sway down toward Eighth Avenue, Ed big and fat, Jim tall and a long gray ponytail hanging down his back, and both of them with their hands in their front pockets, a student was prompted to philosophize.

"Ed's getting old, man," he said, shaking his head as he leaned against the school's doorjamb. "No doubt about it—he getting slow."

Doris Rosenblum, the founder of West Side, had said the same thing to me just the day before during an interview she'd been giving me about the school's history. I looked down the street again and noticed that Ed was limping. I wasn't surprised. It had been an exhausting day, and he often developed a limp when he was tired. Instead of charging up and down the corridors in between classes he would roll slightly and hold himself unnaturally over the left leg so that he looked like a wounded veteran of some kind. He was doing it again now, that rolling, vertical jerk that peaked over his left foot and dipped and slid over his right. It didn't affect his speed. In fact, when I followed him around the school, I often had to break into a half jog to keep up with him, and he was half a pace or so in front of Jim now too. But he would be out of breath, I knew, and sweating, and in a short time he would be panting, the way he did when he climbed the stairs between the seventh floor and the tenth. Perhaps the student was right and Ed was getting old.

Just a few days before I had even seen him sitting at a table in the empty teachers' room during class time with his face in his hands as if he were praying. He stayed that way for only a few seconds and immediately came to himself when he realized I was there. But it wasn't the first time I'd seen him like that, and each time I saw it, it looked more like a miniature collapse, a momentary sinking into nothingness and away from the constant and exhaustingly multiple reality that consumed him every day. It had to wear him down sooner or later, because the way Ed worked was extraordinary. From a quarter to seven in the morning to five at night he held no corner of himself back. It wasn't the most efficient way to get things done, of course. Existing in such intimate interaction with one student after another, Ed had no chance to compartmentalize or organize or even to prioritize. His office was in such a state of disarray by this point in the year that he never went in it except to deposit another milk crate's worth of unsorted papers on a pile. And I often saw members of the staff storming out of the teachers' room, in despair that even the most basic administrative system would ever be established at the school. But Ed's approach toward his work had nothing to do with efficiency, or even with a conscious desire to give his all or do his best. It was far more passionate and essential than that, elemental even. And when I'd found him slumped over his hands at the head of a table in the empty teachers' room, I half-saw that it came as a natural response to the heightened understanding he had not asked to receive, but had received nonetheless at the moment that his son, Javier, died.

Ed wasn't his son's biological father, or his stepfather or foster father or even adoptive father. In fact, Ed didn't meet Javier until he was four years old and a pupil in his ex-wife's Head Start program. He had arrived in class with badly burned hands, the result of his mother's rage when she suspected him of stealing her money, and had spent the first few days hiding under the piano, threatening to hurt anyone who came near. Ed's wife at the time, Karen, had a habit of taking kids on trips when they seemed to be having particular difficulty in adjusting to her class, and Ed had loved Javier, adored him, from the first time they took him to the Central Park Zoo and he'd pointed to the bear and said, very clearly, "Dat's Ed." He suffered from numerous learning disabilities, which was why he couldn't speak properly. Taking the lackadaisical evaluation skills of the child-welfare agency into account, it also wasn't impossible that Javier suffered from some undetected retardation over and above the consequences of the abuse he suffered at the hands of his mother. After all, it was as a result of the investigation into his burned hands that the agency had mandated Javier's presence in Head Start in the first place, and though the agency must have known who was responsible for the boy's mutilation, they never made the slightest suggestion that he be removed from his mother's care.

Soon Ed was spending great stretches of time with the boy. He enrolled Javier in private school and made sure he got help from the best tutors available. He even had him to stay in his apartment regularly, once even getting him for eight months when his mother's apartment building burned down. But he never made any legal moves to adopt the boy. Javier's mother didn't seem to mind Ed's interest in her son as long as Ed didn't threaten to take him away from her. She needed the child-support money from welfare too much to allow that to happen, and because Ed was wary of removing any child from his mother ("After all, who was I?" he says now), Javier grew up with two homes, one in Stuyvesant Town with Ed and his wife and one on the Lower East Side with his mother, an older sister who had been born a deaf-mute, a younger sister, and a cousin whom the child-welfare agency had given his mother custody of even though at the time she was a hopeless heroin addict.

For years Ed would go down to pick up Javier, whom he referred to by then as his son, and take him to his apartment, or to the house in the mountains upstate that he had then. Once he was nearly knocked over by one of Javier's cousins, who fled out of the apartment building with Javier hot on his heels. The cousin and a friend had been bullying Javier terribly for years, but that morning Javier had grabbed a stick and was chasing the two bigger boys down the street toward Avenue D in such an apparent state of rage that he struck out at every car he passed—hitting the fenders and headlights and windshields as he ran by, screaming all the time. The older boys, their eyes wide with panic, were running flat out by the time Ed regained his balance. Knowing that his son was prone to violent fits of rage, Ed started shouting for him to come back, but Javier kept screaming and slamming and chasing until his tormentors rounded the corner and vanished from sight. Then he turned toward Ed and sauntered up to him, grinning. "Sometimes you just gotta make them think that you're crazy," he whispered. Victoriously throwing the stick to the side of the road, he took Ed's hand and they walked off together as calmly as if nothing had ever happened. Javier was nine at the time and Ed, of course, was dazzled.

But his son's rage wasn't always a show. Whatever Ed did, however much he cloaked the boy in love and care and watchfulness, Javier would still erupt every now and then, and lash out. Even when he finally moved in with Ed at the age of eleven, and started to lead the quietly ordered life of an only child, he still felt most comfortable expressing himself violently. For years Ed did everything he could to help soothe the boy. But shortly after he graduated from West Side, and for reasons that Ed still doesn't entirely understand, Javier left his care and moved back in with his mother, ravaged by then by her heroin habit.

Ed has never been quite sure of all the details. Javier didn't discuss them with him. All he really knew is that his son developed a drug habit himself, crack and powder cocaine, Ed thinks, and that he ended up finding himself work as "an enforcer" for a crack crew down on the Lower East Side. An enforcer isn't a kind thing to be: it's the heavy, the policeman, the bully—the guy who makes sure debts are paid and theft is punished. Eventually Javier found himself serving a seven-month sentence for, "Well, it ended up being a weapons charge, but it was for a lot of things really," Ed said. By then, his son had become so careless with, and detached from, his own humanity that the other inmates named him Pit, short for Pit Bull.

Nonetheless, Ed went to visit him every week. He still remembers the interminable bus rides followed by impossible lines, the guards searching his mustache for drugs and the waistline and hem of his pants for weapons, and all the other intricate and ritualized humiliations relatives of the incarcerated are routinely and efficiently subjected to. And perhaps because of the transformation that Ed saw taking place in Javier while he was in prison, the completion of a mutation that had started in his early childhood but that came to maturity there, Ed swore that when his son got out he himself would never set foot in a prison again. He stuck to it, too. The only time I ever saw him refuse a favor to a student was when a young man named Pedro, a Latin King, as a matter of fact, came to our Family Group to say good-bye before going off to serve a one-year sentence at Rikers Island. Pedro suggested, more than asked, that Ed might come and see him there sometime. I didn't know about Javier then and was surprised when Ed shook his head and said that he couldn't, that he had made a vow he never would and that his memories of the place were still so strong that he didn't dare break it.

Eventually Javier got out. He went to the Bronx where Ed had moved, which was about as far away from his old neighborhood as it was possible to get. Ed found him a job, which he quit after seven days. There was a brief hiatus, and then Ed found him another, which lasted for seventeen. One afternoon shortly after that Javier called Ed to ask if he had had any luck with a third position for him. Ed told him that he was working on it but that he hadn't managed to find one yet. "I am not a patient person! I'm leaving," Javier raged.

"You know, I always thought when he said that he was just going to leave and go off somewhere again—I didn't think it was the big leave," Ed told me. Ed went out that night and had dinner with his ex-wife, and then returned to his house to find Javier hanging from the ceiling, dead at the end of one of Ed's belts.

He hadn't left a note; he had such trouble writing that he wouldn't have. Instead he had gathered all his baseball cards up and left them in a neatly stacked pile beneath him for Ed to find.

Ed still cries when he remembers this detail, or when he speaks of it, at least, because he remembers it every day, I am convinced. (He doesn't sob, and he doesn't take his eyes away from you either; he just lets them well up and stares right at you with the unwavering humanity of his round, sky-blue eyes and says: "Yup, yup. That's Javier.") The experience was what allowed him his generosity and his passion, I think—not guilt over his son's death, but acceptance both of the reality of cruelty and of the impossibility of ever hauling anyone clear of it. It was what made his commitment to the possible and to kindness and respect so strong.

The elevator operator was looking nervous when I arrived at school the morning after the confrontation between Paul and the Latin King. "It's too quiet," he said. "Something always happens when it's this quiet.

Last time it was this quiet I warned Ed about it, and something did end up happening too." Fred was always the first to notice a shift in the mood at West Side. And looking down at Ed's message to the school on top of the day's mimeographed notices, in the teachers' meeting, I realized that Ed must have been thinking the same thing too:

> Yesterday we had a potentially dangerous situation pass without anyone being hurt. Thanks to the help of our security and staff and police no violence occurred! West Side High School is not the STREETS. We live by a different set of rules. If we were not different, what would be the purpose of trying to educate you? In the street the vulnerable are attacked, matters are settled by use of weapons and beatings and people do what they want without regard for anyone else. Here in school the vulnerable are protected, matters are settled by dialogue and there is one rule for everyone: NO PHYSICAL OR VERBAL ATTACK OF ANYONE BY ANYONE.

Ed's message seemed as much a plea for continued calm as a thank-you. A plea that was necessary because though everything seemed calm that morning, the hush was more muted than peaceful, and I soon discovered that even a short stroll through the corridors left a shimmering trail of tension behind. A glance, a whisper, even the depth of the quiet itself seemed ominous. Clocks ticked, the phone rang, classes began and ended just as they always did, but something else was at work, too. An expectation, perhaps. A fear. A sixth sense, still raw, which blanched at even the most mundane actions: a girl's sneeze, a hand reached out to you in greeting, a foot disappearing behind a door. Five minutes into third period I found out that underneath all that taut, gagged quiet lurked the now persistent rumor of a gun. It was Ed who told me. Quietly and without even stopping as he charged down the corridor he just said it flat out: "gun." I was stunned. There was a gun somewhere here. Someone, somewhere had a gun. This was what brought out the sixth sense: the vagueness of the someone and the fact of the gun. I walked past a group of kids. Someone had a gun. I chatted with a student, went to the bathroom, drank some coffee bought from the café upstairs, but someone still had a gun. It had gotten stuck, the phrase: A gun. A gun. A gun.

The school security team was dealing with it by making noise. Storming back and forth along the seventh floor, talking uselessly into their walkie-talkies, they filled up the already bursting silence with antenna crackle and half-finished words until a unit from the office of school safety's special task force arrived. Their sergeant had just returned from a conference on gangs, it turned out, and he felt he should warn us that if a Latin King had decided on a specific course of action—"Violent action," he said—then that action "would be carried out" even if the school had ten teams from the special task force and a whole platoon of cops. "TOS," he said then, leaning back in his chair and smoothing out the pair of handcuffs that hung from his belt. "Have you heard that phrase at all? TOS? Means terminate on sight. If you hear anyone saying anything like that—duck."

Ed didn't flinch. There was something almost wry in the way he dealt with this brash young sergeant. But I'd started to feel the kind of frosty, rising fear that, until then, I'd only experienced in dreams; the kind of fear that makes things around you somehow lose their solidity, and with it their ability to reassure. The edge of a wall, a corner, a door became impediments now, because anything could happen behind them, and it wasn't only me who sensed this either. When Bobby Peaks came sauntering onto the seventh floor, cheerily denying rumors that he had been expelled, two members of the special task force grabbed him and frog-marched him to the bathroom to be searched. There, a zealously dutiful guard rummaged through the garbage can. He found a piece of metal pipe and wielded it around victoriously—a weapon!—until he realized it was just a broken towel rail from above the sink. "Typical Board of Ed," he said as he sheepishly tried to replace it.

But Bobby wasn't armed, and after he was escorted back out of the building the heavy, deadening, crimping silence descended again. I wanted to leave. Kids were shot in schools—if not frequently, then at least every now and then, and teachers got shot too, and so did passersby and strangers. That year alone, a total of 1,502 weapons had been seized from schools in New York City, among them 45 handguns, and although I had known all this before I'd started attending West Side, since then I'd had no more experience with it than if I had been writing a book about suburban gardening. Up until that day I'd still only half-believed in the possibility of any kind of real violence happening to me—I mean gun violence and death. When you've watched kids struggle with a two-paragraph history paper or a math problem or paint childish sketches, when you've spent hours reading their essays about first love and turning into a bear in the woods because of a magic spell cast by a glowing dwarf, it seems impossible that the same kids could ever shoot and kill anyone. I knew that life outside of the school was a completely separate reality from the sort of quiet control that permeated West Side, but I don't think I ever really appreciated the depth of sanctuary Ed had managed to create until that day, when the two realities began to be drawn together as though by the focus knob on a sharpshooter's rifle sight. Wandering around the seventh floor, trying desperately hard to look normal, I was starting to have trouble breathing.

I watched as pumped-up security guards shoved a student who said he was on the way to the bathroom back into his classroom, and as girls were herded out of bathrooms and escorted back to theirs—because who knew who was a Latin Queen and "girlfriends can be used as scouts and can also 'carry' for the Kings," the special task force sergeant had told us. That was one reality. But there was another reality too, one that I was aware of only in the dimmest way, of classes and teaching and the reading of science texts and poems and history books. By chance there was even a crew from CBS in the school. They were there to film the second of Stewart's Israel meetings and had no idea about any of this. Realities seemed to be multiplying. There was the surface and then there was the fact that the school had officially been in a state of high alert for two days, which informed all the rest.

Only Ed managed to bind them all together. The two most senior security guards had been following him since the Bobby incident, begging him to allow them to round up the kids suspected of being involved. They talked to his back as he barreled down the corridor, to his arm as he filled in for the receptionist on a break, and to his leg as he stood on a chair and changed a light bulb that had been out for weeks, and still he wouldn't agree to it. It was as if the complete disjuncture between his physical and mental activities allowed him to think through the situation uninterrupted, or the whole group of situations actually, because from the outside, from the point of view of people who didn't know, people like the CBS crew, or many of the teachers even, there was no tension, and so no threat or potential violence. By fixing light bulbs and answering the phone Ed seemed to be trying to straddle both realities and measure them against each other: Which was true, the razor-edge tension or the calm school day?

But the guards were more like me. Panicked and edgy, they had no idea how to find a way out of the situation that had been re-creating itself for some time by then, feeding off the tension that in turn fed off it. New York public schools had established methods for dealing with situations involving both firearms and gangs and even without Ed's permission, guards soon started to haul suspected gang members and their girlfriends out of classes, marching them down to the teacher's lounge, where they would be interrogated and searched for weapons. Ed had asked the task force to maintain as low a profile as possible, so they had gathered there to oversee the interrogations, and with five of them and four regular members of school security, the room was a sea of blue. Tension soon turned to anger. Unsuspecting teachers spluttered with rage at having their classes interrupted, and students, seeing themselves disrespected, were flipping out in the corridors, shouting and cursing as they were escorted out of the building one by one. By the time Ed showed up in the teachers' lounge, forty-five minutes later, tired looking but calm, Julio, the Latin King who'd been threatened in the art class, and a friend of his named Rafael were standing next to the center table, refusing to sit down, furiously demanding lawyers, and insisting that they didn't have to talk to anyone and that they knew their rights.

Ed pulled up a chair and sat down at the table. Very calmly and quietly he apologized to the boys for having them taken out of their classes and reiterated the fact that he and everyone in the room knew Julio had been the victim yesterday and not the aggressor.

"Fuck these fucking cops, man," Julio said then. Ed didn't blink. As if he might be able to burn away the dross with his ability to care and get to the truth of the matter, he locked eyes with Julio and again praised the boy's self-control and again apologized for the possibility that he himself may have overreacted. That was the center of his internal debate, I was to realize: Had the overwhelming police presence yesterday and the task force today been responsible for preventing anything from happening, or had all the tension and fear and worry been created by their presence in the first place? Because nothing had happened it was tempting to blame the cops, but it was impossible to say.

Ed widened the field of his debate to include the Latin Kings now sitting across the table from him. He started talking more generally about the vagaries of prevention—the extent to which it was possible to alter the outcome of an event, and the complexities inherent in trying to balance the achievement of a nonevent with the possibility that the nonevent would occur on its own. I couldn't help thinking of something he had told me about Javier once. "In some ways I think of his suicide as a gift to me. He had so much rage and it was always directed outwards, and I thought if he was going to do anything he would end up mowing down eighty people before he went down in a blaze of glory. That would have made much more sense to me than his killing himself. He didn't care, you see, he just didn't care. So what I'm trying to say, I guess, is I don't know what he would have been had he not met us."

Ed, it seemed, had lived in this amorphous world of possibility and prevention and almost always thankless negation for quite some time. I realized then that this was what he had been trying to achieve for the last twenty years—a negation of all the madness and violence in his kids' lives; and that because it was impossible to prove a negative there was no way anyone, even Ed himself, could ever be certain he'd achieved it. If he didn't prevent a suicide in Javier's case, did he at least prevent a slaughter? And if so, how many crimes and moments of despair and isolation and hopelessness had never happened because of his or West Side's intervention? Who could tell. It is not the way the world works—especially the parallel but separate world that lives and breathes and dies by counting and judging achievements. Ed didn't live in that world though. And neither did most of his kids. They lived in a world where simply surviving was an achievement—amorphous and indirect but real nonetheless. It was almost as if they were starting from a negative point and were struggling constantly and with superhuman effort to drag that point up to the calm lake of zero.

The Latin Kings were more relaxed now. With the shift in conversation from the specifics of weaponry to generalized philosophy their emotions had been soothed by their intellects. The guards, however, were still jittering around the edges of the room, adrenaline pumping. Bobby had been officially expelled by then, and his friend Paul arrested for criminal trespass. But these were the Latin Kings right here in front of them: these were the dangerous ones, the ones who killed each other for breaking childish rules and who ran drugs and had $5 million war chests. Here was the enemy and here was Ed, this sagging white man who couldn't possibly understand any of this, talking to them as if they were plausible human beings, diffusing what had once been a clear-cut situation into a hazy forum for deliberation and discussion. Unable to control himself any longer, one of the guards made a move toward Julio's jacket, snatched it up, and started to talk frantically into his walkie-talkie as he groped at its lining. Without even looking at him Julio slipped his hand into a pocket of his jeans and then carefully placed what looked like a metal pen onto the table. "The only thing I got is this, Ed, which I bought off Esther a year ago for a dollar." Frantic now, the guard picked it up and unscrewed the lid to reveal a very thin, scalpel-like art knife.

"Could slice through skin with ease," the guard said out of the corner of his mouth as he handed it to Ed. Ed only nodded. He thanked Julio, and for a moment they sat there, both of them straight and proud and mutually irritated by the interruption. Then they returned to the conversation at hand. They couldn't be sure Ed had been right in calling in the police yesterday, or the task squad today, Julio said, speaking for both himself and his friend. But then again he couldn't deny the fact that nothing had happened downstairs on the street either, despite the fact that almost the entire student body had been waiting for some kind of action. As long as Bobby Peaks wouldn't be strutting around the corridors, smugly victorious, then it seemed the problem had been resolved, he said. No harm had been done, and it would stay that way. He would guarantee it. Ed rolled the penknife between the tips of the fingers of both hands, nodding with what could only have been relief. Then they shook hands, Julio and Ed, in the same space now, that flip-side mirror world where just as much happens as does in the lighter, smoother, more monied space of the positive. Creators now of their own set of options, the two Latin Kings rose from the table and, thanking Ed, left the room.

And that was it. It was over. Admittedly there were five cops by the front door, and all of the task force and the regular security outside, but by lunchtime their adrenaline levels had dropped to somewhere close to normal and people flowed and moved and that awful, suffocating tension was gone. Upstairs CBS was still obliviously tap-ing Stewart's Israel meeting, and the promise of multiple future broadcasts went at least partway to explaining why there were over sixty kids crammed into the radio room on the eleventh floor, all dressed up in their best clothes, lipstick shining, hats pulled down low over their eyes.

Ed popped his head into the room, looking the way a high school principal should in a jacket and freshly ironed shirt. When he noticed a set of Latin King beads hanging openly around a boy's neck he lightheartedly pointed to them and mimed tucking them under his collar. The boy grinned back, caught in an act no more serious than being absentminded, and put them inside his shirt. Ed tapped me on the shoulder. "This," he whispered as he closed the door, "is a miracle."

14

MANNY DIDN'T HAVE any truck with gangs or their members and thought that all their pronounced toughness was just so much posturing. "They shoulda left all that stuff back in the seventies," he told me once. "All that gangsta-trying-to-be-too-down stuff is old. They is out to make trouble or start a fight just to make a reputation. Me, I don't need a rep. Once people get to know me they know that I'm cool. I don't need to be cursing or going wild. I'm just myself. Nowadays you just gotta be cool. You know, open up and let people get to know who you really are."

Over the past month or so I had been spending a lot of time with Manny, and almost every time I saw him he would make some kind of attempt at self-definition like this. They would usually occur in transitional moments—on the subway going from school out to Brooklyn, or in a McDonald's, where his stomach always cramped after eating a $2.99 double-cheeseburger Happy Meal. It was as if he needed those times to remind himself of who he was, because of all the kids at West Side I had come to see that Manny was the one with the least understanding of what he was doing and where he was trying to go.

He spent most of his time on "the Ave" in Bushwick, and was coming to school so sporadically by then that I was used to not seeing him for days at a time. But I knew he liked the sense of invisible normalcy that arriving at school occasionally lent him, and when he didn't show up for eleven days in a row I dragged myself up to his apartment in the Wagner housing projects on East 123rd Street to make sure he was still alive and not in jail. Like many kids at West Side he had no phone, but I had been to his apartment before and thought I could remember which building he lived in. I passed certain landmarks I recognized—the little, green-lawned park edged by a decorative grave, nine or ten feet long, with a single stone marker which read only "CRACK," and the tiny playground for toddlers where adolescents now lolled, curved over the jungle gym, or draped over the swings—but I couldn't find my bearings. Every building was identical: tall, too skinny columns of dry red brick. If Manny's father hadn't come bounding around the corner I'm not sure I would ever have found the right one.

I had seen him earlier, halfway between the subway station and the projects, but I hadn't stopped to greet him because he'd been shadowboxing a lamppost at the time. It was not a warm day—ice even coated the sidewalk in parts—but he was dripping with sweat as he dodged and parried, and there was something so unplayful about his bout with the gray metal pole that I pretended not to see him, crossed the road, and headed straight for the projects instead. Now he came flying past me, ran through the door of the building closest to me and into the lobby, where he swooped down on the elevator button like a famous basketball star, spun around hissing out of the side of his mouth as though imitating the applause at Madison Square Garden after a particularly magnificent dunk, and then reared backward when he saw me and said: "Hi-hi-hi-hi-hi!"

"Hello," I said.

"Hi-hi-hi. How you doing? I don't know where Manny is. He supposed to be in school, I know—he hasn't been going? Hasn't gone today but he should be in school. He's out somewhere with his mother today—he helping her with some errands . . .

"Did you see that black girl lying in my bed?" he asked me suddenly. "I decided it's time to get back on track—back in the game! I don't pay attention to color, and I don't pay attention to shape or size of the body—I don't look at the face—just as long as they got something in here," he said, tapping his temple, by which time the elevator had arrived. Giving me a wink, he invited me in. I checked again to see if Manny might be upstairs, and when Manny Sr. grinned and said that he hoped he wasn't, he'd just made the girl a present of his yellow Polo sweater, I left him with a note instead, writing down my telephone number and asking for him to please call.

I knew by then that Manny's mother had run off with an African American bus driver three years before. Manny Sr. had been addicted to heroin for years by the time this happened, but he loved his wife, and was so crushed by her desertion that he got far worse when she left. For months afterward he would chase any city bus that passed him, frantically screaming and crying and threatening with a brick or a stick or whatever was closest at hand, in a futile attempt to get at the black, bus-driving, fancy-car-loving man who had taken his wife away. Manny was eleven and thought this was funny the first time it had happened. But after a while it grew tiresome and then embarrassing, and he soon started inventing excuses so he wouldn't have to go outside with his father at all.

It had always been Manny's mother who had kept track of the bills and paid them too, with money she earned from a night job cleaning offices in midtown Manhattan. And although Manny Sr. had worked many jobs since dropping out of high school, everything from flower delivery to construction, he was no longer capable of performing appropriately at even the most simple of regular jobs. After a couple of months they lost their apartment and Manny and his sister and their father moved into the shelter system. The first place they stayed was nice enough. The three of them had their own room as well as the use of a kitchen. But their stay there came to an abrupt end when Manny Sr. was caught with a woman, or a bottle of liquor, or a bag of smack—Manny couldn't remember which now, because the same thing happened in each of the shelters that followed. After a year, during which they had stayed in places so filthy that Manny had resolutely refused to step into the shower stall, they moved in with Manny Sr.'s little brother, Paco, which was when Manny reinvented himself out on the Ave.

Things had improved since then, of course. They had even moved into their own apartment again. But Manny's home life was still inverted and unpredictable and constantly unsettling. It wasn't that his father didn't try. He was always very polite with me, and respectful, and he showed a genuine concern for his kids, too. With nothing else to do but wait for the methadone clinic to open and sip coffee out on the corner with some friends, he cooked every day for Manny and his sister and was compulsive about keeping their two-bedroom apartment clean. Every time I visited, the stools in the kitchen were up on the counter, the floor shimmering beneath them with a fresh layer of lemon-scented rinse. It was just that he had no clue about how best to raise his kids, and lacking any real grasp of the rigors demanded by a constant reality, he more or less let things drift. One result of this was that nine people were now living in their two-bedroom apartment, not counting the rotating string of "womens" he brought home with him.

Manny, his sister, his father, and his little cousin Lazarus, who had been living with them ever since he had run away from a juvenile-detention center upstate, shared one room. Manny's uncle and his new girlfriend shared the other, and because there was nowhere else for them to go, her three teenage kids slept out in the living room: the oldest on a couple of chairs pulled together, the daughter on the hard wooden sofa, and the youngest curled up on the coffee table. They had been there for months, and since none of them were even enrolled in school they hardly ever left the house, and they looked waxen from the lack of fresh air. It drove Manny crazy having them in the house. Especially as the oldest one had started borrowing his clothes and had once taken a brand-new, sunshine-yellow Polo jacket from one of Manny's sagging wire hangers and had then spilled ketchup on it. Manny had waited for him in the corridor when he'd noticed the stain and had beaten him up when he'd stepped out the door—so he told me, anyway. I believed him, too. Not only because the boy disappeared whenever Manny walked into the apartment but because I knew by then that the steady accumulation of fine, couture clothes was the only thing that focused Manny through the fog of the rest of his life.

I could never be sure Manny got the note I left for him that day, or the two or three others I left at various times on the kitchen counter or on top of the TV, or in the hand of one of his "cousins." Even if he had, school was such a distant and hazy thing in Manny's life that even a momentary lapse of concentration erased its image altogether. The strange thing was that when he did come in, he frequently had no notion of how long he'd been away. He would be genuinely amazed when he was told he had been absent for ten days, or seven or four. "That long? Dang—it didn't feel like that long," he would say, as though mourning the loss of all that time to blurred confusion.

His position at West Side was so tenuous by then that he wasn't even officially enrolled in the school. I discovered this one afternoon when I went to the office to make a copy of his transcript. Cathy, the woman in charge of student paperwork, had looked first in one filing cabinet, then in another and then cross-referenced his name in the computer before taking in an asthmatic breath, shrugging, and telling me that there was no file under the name Emanuel Martinez, no reference to his name, nothing.

"As far as I'm concerned, he doesn't go to school here, hon," she told me. "You'd better talk to his adviser about this."

But his adviser, John, already knew. He knew too that if Manny applied for an official enrollment now, when his attendance rate was hovering at around 15 percent, he would almost certainly be transferred. Because that would do Manny no good with his probation officer, John kept him in his Family Group unofficially, warning Manny that it couldn't stay that way forever, telling him every time he saw him that he had to come more often, that he had to start buckling down. Manny always listened politely to these injunctions and invariably (and seemingly sincerely) agreed that his life was veering off track, and that he had to start coming to school. Then his eyebrows would shoot down toward the center of his face and his mouth would go rigid and he would go to every class he had been assigned that day, write down homework assignments on random scraps of paper, and finally leave the building at 12:20, determined to come back the next day with a notebook and a pen and all his work done.

But he never came back the next day. And hardly ever on the day after that, so I wasn't surprised to learn that apart from John and Rochelle, barely anyone was aware of Manny's presence at the school. Even Ed shook his head, furrowed his brow and held a finger up to his lips before asking, "Manny Martinez? No. We have a Miguel Martinez and a Cristina Martinez, but I can't think of an Emanuel Martinez, no."

Manny did have one friend at the school, though, a strange and vaguely frightening-looking boy named Api, the son, it turned out, of the buzzing, disaffected woman at the parent-teachers meeting. They had met in the lunchroom one morning during orientation when they'd both first arrived. And though theirs was a friendship based more on mutual need than attraction, so that at some basic level it really didn't matter what the other one was like, Api seemed to be the perfect foil for Manny and helped him forget the fragility and frustration of his life out on the Ave.

Api was intelligent but distant and quiet almost to the point of being reclusive. Admitted to West Side after a prolonged stay in the hospital for depression, he enjoyed building model airplanes and cars at home and then painting them and arranging them neatly on his bedroom shelf. He loved to read too, and was indiscriminate about what he read—anything from the Danielle Steel novels his mother passed on, to histories of the IRA and a treatise on the possible origins of Stonehenge. Anything that kept him off the Bronx street where he lived, a street that he avoided because he was scared. "I just keep away," he told me. "If you know there's a trouble spot somewhere, you're not going to go to it. If I did hang out a lot I'd just be—Well, I know I'd get in trouble."

Until he'd met Manny, Api had never had a friend outside of his family, while Manny, for his part, felt most comfortable with kids like Api. Green and unsuspecting and easy to impress, they were a relief after the tougher standards out on the Ave. Besides, Manny had been like Api himself before his mother had run off—not quite as morose, perhaps, but an "apartment nerd" nonetheless who left home only to go to school. And perhaps because he insisted that he spent most of his time thinking about the street back then—"about outside—going outside, doing this, doing that"—he now felt duty-bound to help unlock the door for others.

Little Lazarus, his roommate-cousin, had been the first he'd taken pity on. He'd been a "corny weed-smoking kid who never did nothing to improve himself or his situation in life" when Manny first met him. Just as Paco had done for him, Manny had patiently taught Lazarus how to dress and how to make conversation before taking him out to the Ave. Step by detailed step, he'd taught Lazarus everything he needed to know—not only how to hold and count and sell the drugs, and how to spot an undercover TNT agent, but the more abstract yet equally essential dictate of "keeping true to the game" as well. Now, perhaps because the thought of replicating such a friendship was at least subconsciously appealing to Manny, he offered to take Api out to the Ave with him, one afternoon, and show him the ropes.

Api was amazed. For a couple of minutes he just smiled, unable to make up his mind if Manny was joking or not. As he dipped lukewarm french fries into a small tub of bar-b-que sauce he grinned and said, "Yeah?" and then, "Nah!" By the time he'd finished his french fries though, he could no longer resist the temptation and said "Sure."

Api had never been to Brooklyn before and was surprised by the scale of the place and then by the roughness of Manny's friends: kids like Jam, HiLow, and Antoine, who were their age and worked with Manny on the same side; not to mention the older guys, who were eighteen or nineteen probably, and sold on the other side; or the gang of girl dealers who worked kitty-corner across from them. Manny didn't introduce Api to the girls that day, but he'd heard all about them from his friend back at school. They had been there for years, Manny had told him, and they were tough, tougher than most of the boys, and in case someone might doubt it, they spent a fair deal of time chatting with Chono and Rock, the "old men" from down the block on Cornelia Street, who every shorty worth their salt knew not to mess with.

Api couldn't stop staring at the four girls when Manny disappeared to go buy his day's supply from an apartment half a block down the road. He knew better than to do it openly, knew better than to do it at all, in fact, but he just couldn't help himself. Every few seconds he could feel his eyeballs slide over to the left and blink it all in: the huge solid-gold earrings and the expensive jackets, all red, and the jeans and the lipstick and magical hairdos, kept up God knew how. When one of the girls turned toward him and pinched her eyes into slits as though trying to see him more clearly, he nearly turned and ran. But he just wanted to see how it was, he reminded himself, just wanted to do it one time so that he would know how it felt, and he forced himself to stay.

After what seemed like hours Manny came back down to the corner and casually handed him a few small plastic packages of heroin. At Manny's instruction Api pushed them into his jacket's inner pocket, because TNT never searched there, and then moved a little away from his friend, and waited. To begin with he didn't really think about anything as he stood on the street outside of the bright yellow deli whose windows were entirely pasted over with long past special offers. He just wanted to keep cool and not look too suspicious or too nervous or too interested even. Api had an unusually immobile face, which must have helped, but he didn't have the clothes to really look the part. His jacket was army surplus, as were his pants; even his shoes were no-name discount specials, and apart from a cheap green terry-cloth band around his head embossed with a large yellow A, for the Oakland Athletics, he had not a designer's logo on him. He stuck out, he knew. And although Manny had introduced him when he first arrived, every now and then a shorty would pass by and look at Api in a way that could only be interpreted as a challenge, and he would just rock back on his heels and glance over to Manny and hope that it was all going well and that they could hurry up and get out of there.

Every time a customer walked by it got worse. They were ragged, strung-out, skinny user types, too pathetic to frighten even Api, but he still didn't like being near them. It was the image of his mother that frightened him the most, he said, the look he imagined would be on her face when she came to get him out of the precinct building or the prison or wherever Api became certain he would be by the end of the day. Manny, on the other hand, seemed to be in his element. He called to the customers along with all the other sellers on the block, and if one of them selected him he would talk to them for a couple of minutes. Some would walk away, disgruntled for some reason, but others would hand money over to Manny, who would then call to Api and lift one, two, or three fingers, indicating how many bags he was to give to them. Transactions didn't happen very often, Api couldn't help noticing, and as the day wore on he felt increasingly exposed standing out on the street with what must have been at least ten bags of heroin in his jacket's inner pocket. The windows across the street started to seem like the ideal place for cameras to be hidden, every passing car seemed obviously filled with policemen, and almost every time a woman came along the avenue, a "family-type" woman with a coat buttoned up against the wind and a hand-held cart for her shopping, he would try to hide his face, just in case she might be a friend of his mother's or his aunt's or one of his uncle's.

But Api didn't end up being recognized or getting arrested that day. He was saved from even holding the bags a little after five by one of Manny's middle-aged female suppliers from the apartment upstairs. When she heard that Manny had him out there holding the heroin she stormed down onto the street, furious that Manny had a "new Jack" holding his gear. "He just got here," Api remembers her telling Manny right there in front of everybody. "If he gets busted, you know it will be his first time. He'll tell them everything he can." Embarrassed, Manny nodded and said, "Yeah, yeah, I know. Yeah, yeah, I know," until she left, at which point he motioned for Api to hand over the bags. One or two of the shorties on their side of the street—Jam and HiLow maybe, or HiLow and Antoine—snickered as Api rummaged through his pocket to make sure he had found them all, but at one look from Manny they shut up, and everyone ignored him the minute he crossed the street and walked up half a block to wait until Manny had finished for the day. Since he had arrived he had helped sell four bags of heroin, for a shared profit of eight dollars. Four dollars each, if Manny split it fifty-fifty. And although Manny had stopped working just a little while later and had then treated Api to McDonald's and even paid for his ride back to the city, Api shook his head and told him, "Nah, I got stuff to do," the next time Manny asked him if he wanted to "come out to Brooklyn."

15

THERE HAD BEEN trouble every year when Stewart made his final selection of the kids he would take with him to Israel. Teachers and advisers often became furious that a student they had encouraged to take the chance and apply hadn't been chosen. And no one was ever pleased about the way he announced the selection. After all, what good way was there to tell a student that he or she had not been chosen? In the past Stewart had tried printing lists of those accepted and posting them on the door of the Youthworks office. He had tried scheduling individual meetings and contacting applicants by telephone. This year he had stuffed nearly sixty long, whitish-gray envelopes with acceptance and rejection letters and was delivering them to every applicant via their Family Group advisers. Everyone knew they were to be distributed sometime in the first week of December, but Michelle didn't seem very interested in getting hers. She had been trying to ignore Stewart ever since her second interview because she didn't want to seem too keen, she said. And when he finally came into Ed's Family Group room, five minutes before the end of class, she looked intently down at her homework and pretended not to see him. Ed knew what the letter said, though, and once Stewart had left he lumbered out of his seat, walked over to where she was sitting, and smiled, waving the long envelope in front of her. Almost before she had a chance to look at it herself, Nicole read it out loud over her shoulder for the whole class to hear:

"Michelle—congratulations. You have been chosen to take part in the Israel trip!"

Michelle seemed nonplussed and embarrassed. She later explained that she had been convinced for so long that she wouldn't be picked that she had never even thought of the possibility of actually being chosen and was totally unprepared for the news. It would take some time, she said, before the excitement would begin to seep through. But there was something about the solemn way she folded up the sheet of paper, slipped it back into its official-looking envelope, and then tucked it neatly into the bottom of her pocketbook that made me think she was regretting ever having gotten involved in such a hare-brained scheme in the first place. Clicking the latch back into place, she looked almost as if she were going to cry.

Close to two and a half months of application sifting and interviewing had left Stewart looking more overwhelmed than excited, as well. The selection process had been grueling, and not least because more girls than ever had applied. They made up nearly three-quarters of the applicants, and because he was determined to take seven boys and seven girls, he felt awkward about the unfairness of the odds. Even his assistant, a young woman named Ayala, who was usually perfectly turned out—hair ironed, eyebrows plucked, base and then powder and blush all smoothly applied—was makeupless that morning and in jeans and a sweatshirt. Neither of them had slept much the night before, she told me when I went up to their office, and they'd been bickering all morning as they'd tried to brace themselves for the next kid to come in, crushed or angry with disappointment and shame. One boy in particular had upset them: an athletic nineteen-year-old named Dante had been so sure of gaining a place that he'd pretty much adopted their office as his hangout that fall, and the way he dealt with the rejection letter, the quiet, calm way he had walked into the office and thanked them for the opportunity to apply, had pretty much convinced them they'd made a mistake in not bringing him along. Pretending to be busy with paperwork the way Michelle had done earlier that morning, Stewart said, "You know, these are the kids who are always being told no and here was a chance for them, and the brave ones took that chance and here we are just saying no again." Ayala, with her back turned to him, nodded and blinked back tears.

Both of them were so worn-out with the guilt of rejection that the fact that there were fourteen kids wandering around the school, wide-eyed with not only the thought that they would be going to Israel in the spring but the idea that they had been chosen—recognized, favored—was all but lost on them. They had picked seven boys and seven girls, more or less evenly divided between African Americans and Latinos except for the surprising and last-minute decision to include Andro, one of the Philippine twins. By then Stewart had as good a feeling for creating a group as he did for the needs of specific individuals, and he thought that a lot could be learned by a little added cultural mingling.

Not that they wouldn't have been a varied bunch anyway. There was no set criteria for Youthworks participants, no minimum academic standard or behavioral requirement; even a criminal record didn't preclude a student's inclusion. In the past Stewart had taken a number of kids who had been involved with the criminal-justice system, and though now, after seven years, he was less inclined to take those sorts of risks, the group was still broadly representative of the school as a whole. Ranging in age from sixteen to nineteen, they came from all over the city: Washington Heights, Harlem, the South Bronx, East New York, Williamsburg, Jamaica, and Astoria. While some, like Michelle, represented the studious, older students at West Side, others were brash, or lacking in self-esteem. They represented such a broad spectrum, in fact, that two days later, when they were first brought together for an introductory and celebratory meeting in the library, they seemed to have little in common. Crammed into a too tight circle of chairs, tight jeans rubbed up against oversized ones, Nikes against loafers. And though one boy, a skinny, mop-headed nineteen-year-old named Fred, was wearing a roughly woven straw sun hat as if he were ready to leave right away, the others seemed nervous and strangely displaced in the tiny green library.

Even the rowdiest of the group, a short, round-faced African American boy named Reggie, was so nervous that he seemed to be doing everything in his power to be thrown out of the group and left to get on with the rest of his life. For the first fifteen minutes he chewed his way through a double order of sweet-and-sour chicken wings and interrupted Stewart constantly: "Stew, Stew, I heard there aren't any fast-food restaurants nearby where we going," he said in between mouthfuls. "Can I drink the water? How is the weather? What time would I have to get up in the morning to get to this dumb-ass job we going to be doing anyway?" The rest of the group was not so brash, but it was clear that they sympathized with his impulse, at least to the degree that they laughed loudly at his mouth-filled denouncements, and after half an hour a hip-looking kid named Kevin had joined in: "I heard they's no heating in the rooms and no cereal or milk at breakfast. Yo, I can't stand a cold room or an empty stomach, Stew, I'm serious! Is there any way we could get milk at breakfast? And is the milk—I heard it come straight from the cow over there?"

Stewart knew better than to rise to these tactics. After seven years he understood that the fear they had overcome to even apply for the trip was multiplying now as the slimmest of slim possibilities was suddenly an approaching reality. Like most West Side students, few in the group had traveled outside of the States before. Not counting a school trip to Washington, D.C., several had never even left New York City. Some were so isolated they weren't even sure that they believed in the rest of the world. Like a child shyly clinging to the concept of Santa Claus, a petite, angular girl named Carina had written in her application, "The main reason I am applying for this experience is because I want to see if there is really a world filled with different cultures out there." Because many felt completely comfortable only in their own tightly circumscribed neighborhoods, even a bus ride into an unfamiliar district or borough could sometimes cause panic. I had seen this happen once, when crossing the Manhattan Bridge into Brooklyn with the boys basketball team. We were due to play in the semifinals of the Alternative School League championship, and the team's spirits had been high as they piled into the bus outside West Side. For twenty minutes or so they dissected NBA maneuvers and discussed strategies and planned a victory party for themselves once they'd won. Then, as we started our approach to the bridge, a wave of silence spread from the back of the bus to the front. After a moment, the team's star center said flatly, but as if he were summoning up all of their childhood demons: "We headed for Brooklyn."

Almost under his breath someone replied: "Brooklyn. Yeah. I heard those kids is crazy," which prompted a few boys to nod and all of them to stare out of the window, as if out there, somewhere, they would learn the answer to an urgent and profound mystery that had been haunting them for years.

Imagine, then, the fears a trip to the Middle East could inspire. Airplane travel itself was so intimidating to some in the group that they couldn't get beyond it. For weeks Reggie would plague Stewart with questions about flight duration and wingspan and average traveling speed that he couldn't possibly answer. And if the mood in the library that first day seemed muted and lethargic, it was only because Israel was still an abstraction to them at that point, too distant to be imagined beyond the biblical and so not yet a proven cause for panic.

"I guess I'll see horses, ducks, chickens, camels, birds, lambs, cows, sheep," Ylaria wrote of her expectations. Michelle thought the country would be "dusty with small towns and homes and with grass in some areas, and many goats." Monica imagined it "looking like a flat plain or maybe have a lot of flowers all over and grass everywhere. I imagine small friendly towns with horses that maybe I can ride and camels and goats and cows." If they had any notions about Jews at all, as indicated by their responses to the application question "What are your impressions of Jewish people?" Kamilah's answer, "That they have curly things," was probably typical. A Puerto Rican named Melissa wrote, "A lot are very rude, the ones I've met at work anyway," and a girl named Naomi replied, "The basics. Along with: They killed Jesus, they stole land and they are closed minded."

Improving interracial relations, it seemed, was a significantly justified premise for the trip. So I was surprised to hear Stewart insist that it had had very little to do with the initial rationale for the program. Born in East New York, Stewart had spent almost all of his professional life teaching in the city and had realized early on that he achieved most when he took his students out of the classroom and broadened their horizons "through the challenge of hard work and the demands of cooperative living." Initially using vacant lots as campuses for the Tom Sawyer Crew, a group of kids who explored for insects, plants, and snakes, he slowly expanded the program by raising bees and selling honey futures to other teachers. Later, he developed a hiking club, a horticulture program, and a city-country project that allowed students to spend a week in the country. Ultimately he even took a group of kids to live on a thirty-seven-foot Coast Guard cutter on the Atlantic for a week, a program that was short-lived only because he paid for it himself and soon ran out of money.

It wasn't until he took a sabbatical in 1988 and spent four months on a kibbutz in northern Israel that he came up with the idea of taking a group of students to the Middle East. Impressed with the level of maturity and optimism in the young people he met there, Stewart thought the controlled atmosphere of a kibbutz would make a perfect classroom for his students. He encountered no resistance to the idea at the Bedford Stuyvesant Street Academy where he taught and set about writing fund-raising letters to business people he read about in the newspaper. He never received a reply, but he did get a one-thousand-dollar donation from a neighbor who had recently made it big in the stock market. Inspired, he approached an organization named the Jewish Community Relations Council and asked for ten thousand dollars. The president at the time put out his hand and said, "You've got it."

He had just enough to take his first group of students to a kibbutz, a trip he made in the spring of 1990. But discouraged by his fellow teachers' lack of enthusiasm for the project at the Street Academy, Stewart started to look for other schools as soon as he returned. Steve Phillips, the then Superintendent of Alternative Schools, suggested two: West Side and a school named Bronx Regional. Stewart approached them both and, to begin with anyway, both seemed pleased to have him on board.

Then the problems started. Though Stewart had been a teacher in the city for nearly twenty years, the suggestion that he take a group of mostly African-American students to Israel for ten weeks caused an uproar at Bronx Regional. Left-wing Jews, appalled that he would even think of taking students to an "oppressor nation," teamed up with radical Afro-centrists to oppose the trip, and between them they so riled up the rest of the staff that an outside mediator had to be called in. Despite the fact that by that time the children had already been selected for the trip, that their parents and guardians had given their consent, and that Stewart had once again managed to raise all the money, the matter was put to a vote. Inevitably, perhaps, the trip lost out; no child from Bronx Regional would travel to Israel. If they were to be taken anywhere, it would be to Africa. Because he felt like he had little choice, Stewart withdrew from the school and transferred to West Side, one of the few schools in the city, it seemed, where the staff cared less about where the kids were going than the fact that they were going anywhere at all.

Since then he'd taken groups of students to Israel and Egypt every year. He wasn't a great organizer, and maintaining funding was harder than he'd thought. But he scrounged money where he could, from business leaders and foundation board members, and because he felt that it was important to have the participants feel a sense of ownership, he insisted that each member of the group contribute a sum toward their trip as well. To that end Stewart and Ayala met with the parents or guardians of the fourteen participants and came up with figures to be paid that were appropriate to each family. With both parents working, Michelle may have paid more than any student before her, but others came from backgrounds as dire as any I had encountered and paid almost nothing at all. Monica had spent most of her childhood with her grandmother, the wife of the man who, she said, may also have been the father of her sister. She lived in the four bedroom apartment with thirteen other people, and until she was ten she was known only as "one of Doreen's girls," a phrase that she said almost everyone knew meant she was a failure—"a good-for-nothing no-hoper." In her case you could see the results: in a school where appearances were paramount, her clothes were often dirty, her hair was uncombed and unbraided, and she spent most of that first meeting slumped in her seat, unwilling even to speak. But the results of abuse and extreme poverty were far less visible for most of the rest of the group. Naomi was lithe and beautiful and well put together, and it took me weeks to find out that her father had done such terrible things to her sister that one evening she had thrown a pot of boiling oil across his back and they'd both ended up in foster care. A nineteen-year-old Cuban boy named Raul supported his family with the part-time salary he earned at the New York Public Library, and even Kenny, the tidy and polite Philippine boy, was so culturally confused that it made you dizzy just listening to him. He had grown up in Manila and had been brought to New York after his mother had established herself in the city. Bit by bit he had picked up elements of inner-city culture. Now he cursed without knowing it—"fucking damn cunt"—and otherwise kept quiet, nervously giggling whenever anyone asked him anything he didn't understand.

However extreme the circumstances, though, Stewart insisted that every family feel they had sacrificed something in order to send their child on the trip, if for no other reason than that it placed pressure on the kids, which was often essential to them seeing the journey through. Although they had been sifted from hundreds for their courage, resiliency and adaptability, he knew he could never underestimate his participants' fear, and experience had taught him that, without support and pressure from all sides, some of them would never even make it to the airport. Already the focus in the room was drifting as kids began to shut down emotionally. Fred was doodling on the piece of paper Stewart had handed out for notes, and looking over his shoulder I saw he had written the words "pyramid," "camels," and "Egypt" and was now busy crossing them out in a cloud of black pen. Reggie and Kevin were talking to each other, trying to look blasé, and I noticed that Kamilah's headphones were on under her hair. Michelle was sitting slumped over her chair, her chin in her hands, eyes fixed on nothing, and Kenny looked confused, less relaxed than he had when he'd first walked in. Calling for quiet, Stewart pulled a map of the Middle East from an easel at the side of the room. He told them that Israel was the size of Connecticut and then pointed out each of its neighboring countries in turn. But it wasn't until he mentioned the state of war between Israel and Syria that the kids finally fell silent.

Depressed but instantly resigned, Reggie asked if he wasn't right in thinking that the kibbutz they were going to was right next to Syria. Stewart said that it was.

"And you just said that Israel is at war with Syria?"

"Yes," Stewart said. It was as if the catch they had been expecting all along had suddenly revealed itself. The great meadows and tractors and smiling faces they'd seen in the slide shows had always seemed a little too perfect, and if they'd suspended disbelief for a while, they weren't surprised to see it all crumbling around them now. Here was the explanation for such a trip having been offered them in the first place—the country was at war! Nervous in a much more still, tense way than they had been when they had first walked into the library that afternoon, they only half-listened as Stewart tried to reassure them that very little fighting actually went on; that the kibbutz did have two large bomb shelters, but they hadn't been used for years; and that he could guarantee that they would feel safer on the kibbutz than they ever had here in the city. When Stewart wrapped up the meeting with another hearty congratulations I noticed that no one made eye contact with anyone else. Slumped in their seats, they stared at random points on the wall and, as if in rejection of all they had let themselves in for, they split up as soon as they stepped out of the library door and went their separate ways.

Back on the known territory of the seventh floor Michelle was met by Dayna. Dayna had been waiting for close to an hour and she smiled when she saw her friend. "How was it? How was it?" she asked. Michelle shrugged, turned down the edges of her mouth, shrugged again, and said, "OK, I guess. Oh, Dayna—I'm not sure I wanna go!"

16

WHEN MAURICE AND Lucille finally made love it came as a total surprise to both of them. For days afterward they were so dizzyingly passionate and bashful and shy with each other that their corner in Family Group exuded a palpable and treacly coyness which even Ed couldn't ignore.

It had started innocently enough with a neck massage in Lucille's aunt's house, where they often went to play video games straight after Family Group. Lucille had an ice cube in her hand and had started sliding it around the base of Maurice's neck as he played a game of cards in front of the TV with Rasheem.

"Rasheem got the message and left us alone, but I was surprised," Maurice said. "I was surprised, I tell you. We was both real surprised. You know how long we waited? Seven months! There was times we both thought we would, but it never happened and then—all of a sudden! But it was strange, B. It was funny, so together, almost like—synchronized. And it was everything. Strawberries and cream, everything. I wish you could have been there, I mean not been there—but it was just so cute." Maurice was standing outside the school, leaning against the door in his usual spot, smiling stupidly, his eyes wide with disbelief about the beauty of it all.

"I think she must have planned it," he said, finishing his cigarette. "She says she didn't. But it was all so perfect, the music, everything. It was totally and completely different than it's ever been before—totally."

As was usual with Maurice, though, this blind adoration didn't last long. After he'd drifted around the halls with Lucille for a week, mindlessly lovestruck and puppyish like a "herb man," his other girls, the ones he had carefully maintained and played off one another for months at a time, began to come back into focus. What he saw embarrassed him. Insulted by his recent lack of charm, they no longer flocked to him, eager and flirtatious. Instead, they stayed just as they were when he approached, leaning against a wall, arms crossed, mouths pursed. They might look at him for a second, but their expressions no longer shifted in the minute but distinctive and telltale ways that signified anticipated pleasure, and for the first time in years they turned back to their girlfriends—or worse, to their boyfriends—and continued their conversations without so much as acknowledging him. Maurice liked Lucille, but the situation was becoming intolerable. He had to get them back, and after a few days of consternation he figured out how. Sitting at one of West Side's computers, ostensibly to log in that week's stock movement in his economics class, he designed his own personal love certificate:

TO MY LOVE

You have been with me through thick and thin. You have stayed with me through good times and bad times. You have loved me when others didn't. You make my life worth living. This certificate is granted to you for being you. And loving me the way you do.

I OFFER YOU

MY

EVERLASTING LOVE

Love Maurice J. Smith

He printed eight copies. When I asked him who he was going to give them to he shrugged, and then smiled that demonic little boy's smile he had and said that he wasn't quite sure yet, that there were a few girls on the eleventh floor he was thinking of and one or two on the seventh. "If you want you can give one to Lucille for me," he told me as the last of them was being printed. "I'm not speaking to her for a while though—me or Rasheem."

I don't know if Lucille ever found out about those love certificates, but in the days building up to her fourteenth birthday she certainly lost the wide-eyed look she had shared with Maurice for the past month. True to his word, Maurice began to ignore her after distributing his leaflets, and in response she moved across the room in Family Group to sit with a large, truculent girl named Georgia who lived at Williamson's too and had recently been admitted to West Side. Georgia had originally been placed in a Family Group down on the seventh floor, but after threatening a couple of younger girls there, she had been transferred to Ed's room, where she had sat, isolated and angry, in a corner until Lucille adopted her. Georgia could look beautiful every now and then; once, when she turned up at school with her hair twisted into a pile of braids on the top of her head, she looked dramatically elegant. But most often she arrived in tight jeans and faded sweatshirts that looked like they had been balled up in a corner the night before, and then she sat, arms crossed in front of her, alternately scowling, glaring, and pouting at anyone who looked like they might try to approach. Maurice didn't like her. That was obvious, and though Sandra had been impressed with the force of her stoicism at first, Georgia had sneered in response to a joke she'd told, and Sandra felt she had no choice but to ignore her from then on. Lucille tried to make the best of it, but I often caught her stealing glances back across the room to Maurice and Rasheem. She and Georgia made such an unconvincing pair that even Ed made efforts to join the two in conversation across the room, and as Lucille's birthday approached he used the occasion to shower her with attention and small favors in addition to the birthday cake he bought for each of his advisees every year.

Good with numbers, Ed is the type of man who can do complicated calculations in his head, who remembers your phone number after hearing it once, and who can tell you the number of runs, baskets, or touchdowns scored by any New York team stretching back to September 8, 1952, when his father took him to his first Dodgers game at the Polo Grounds. So it wasn't hard for him to memorize the birth dates of his advisees, and a week or so before each he would ask them what kind of cake they would like. Most kids asked for a double chocolate sponge with chocolate fudge icing, which he could buy for ten dollars in a store around the corner, where they wrote personal inscriptions across the top for free. But back when Lucille and Maurice had been a heap of libidinous confusion in the corner, she had asked for a vanilla ice-cream cake topped with strawberries. Ed had dutifully gone looking for one, and when three different bakers told him they could never have one ready on time, Ed decided to make his own.

The morning of Lucille's birthday he brought in a cardboard box of dry ice that held the kind of deep, silver-foil cooking tray usually used for turkeys, into which he had pressed gallons of vanilla ice cream. In a plastic bag he had two family-sized yogurt tubs full of fresh sliced strawberries, a pile of decorated white plastic party plates, a bundle of plastic forks, and a packet of little white napkins with flowery borders. "For Lucille," he told me proudly as he deposited the various packages in front of me during the staff meeting. "I didn't want to disappoint her, so I made my own vanilla ice-cream and strawberry cake. Cost a fortune, but I figured she needed something special."

Lucille had had her hair braided the night before, and as she walked into Family Group that morning the hundreds of tiny braids were hanging loose around her face. Ed complimented her on her new look, sang her a bursting first line of "Happy Birthday," and then cut a square out from the flat tray of ice cream and added two large spoonfuls of the cut strawberries. Careful not to dirty or crease it, he picked up a napkin, balanced a fork on it, and then passed both over to me. I waltzed across to where Lucille had sat down next to Georgia, curtsied, and handed her the plate.

"What is this?" she said. "This ain't no ice-cream cake. This is just plain ice cream. Ice-cream cake has sponge. Ice-cream cake has icing. Ice-cream cake, Ed, has vanilla ice cream in between layers of sponge. I hate strawberries that ain't glazed. I can't eat this." Startled, Ed looked at her closely. "I won't eat this," she said again, staring hard at him. As he returned to silently cutting up the ice cream and spooning out the strawberries for his other advisees she added: "I'd throw up if I ate it."

Georgia got the giggles. It was the first time I had ever even seen her smile, and it was odd to watch her huge round shoulders shake now as Lucille glowered and the rest of the room sat in silence. Sandra looked disdainfully across at them and then met eyes with Rasheem and shared an "Oh my god, what is this" look. Cristy was outraged. Even Maurice was embarrassed. Picking up his fork, he shoveled his own slice into his mouth and, theatrically announcing that it was delicious, just what he liked to eat in the morning, he asked for some more.

But Ed didn't seem to hear. "Isn't it sad?" he asked me quietly a few moments later as he continued to cut up the ice cream. "I was certain that the vanilla was the most important thing." When I returned to pick up the next plate he continued: "I could have bought a pound cake and cut it in half and filled it with ice cream. I just didn't understand, I guess." Later still, when almost all the ice cream had been handed out and he was serving me, he said, "You know, once I made my sister a birthday cake when I was a kid. I made it from scratch and she refused to even try it." Then he shook his head and slid the nearly empty tray over to the neighboring table and wished Lucille a very happy fourteenth year. But Lucille was still in no mood to be civil.

"I don't like being fourteen," she replied. "Didn't want to be fourteen. Never asked to be no fourteen. Thirteen was better. But truthfully? Truthfully, I want to go back to eight," she said, burying her head in her arms on the desk.

However she felt, though, there was no way she could cancel her party at Williamson's later that evening. She had spent the past two days organizing it and had already distributed handwritten invitations and had chosen the food and the music too. About twenty kids were expected, and though she had pointedly not invited Maurice, she knew he'd be there because he lived on the same floor. She even had her hair redone for the occasion, adding multicolored shell-shaped plastic beads to the ends of her braids. I had promised to be the official photographer and to show up at seven-thirty sharp with my camera and two rolls of film. But by the time I made it past the reception desk and the ID check and then waited for one of the counselors to come down the stairs and escort me back up to the second floor, unlock the door, and lock it behind me, it was nearly eight. When she first saw me Lucille leapt out of her chair and shouted "Tina!" as though I was the last person she expected to see in the world. "You came! You came! I can't believe you came!"

Rasheem was there. He'd brought Lucille an orange balloon and tied it to the arm of a chair in the television lounge. It floated up over Georgia, who was staring at a silent cartoon on TV. I recognized another West Side student too; his name was Chris, and I'd first noticed him when he rolled up his sleeve to reveal a "C" burned into his forearm. He spent almost the entire evening bouncing to a tune he was listening to through headphones. But mostly the place was filled with kids I'd never met, acting like kids at parties everywhere, drifting in that slightly jittery, overly keen way, between the lounge and the computer room, where tables were laid out with baskets of fried chicken, corn bread, macaroni and cheese, and coleslaw. Some of the boys were even dancing, standing rooted to the floor, desperately posturing to the lyrics of rap tunes with the flat-handed gestures of hip-hop, like a group of deranged airport-control men. But though both rooms were decorated with streamers and birthday greetings, nothing seemed to be able to make up for the fact that no one—not one single member—of Lucille's family had called. The phone often rang, and Lucille was constantly being summoned by one of the smiling counselors and told there was someone on the line for her. The first few times she performed an anxious just-fourteen-year-old skip before running to the phone. But then she'd stopped. And though I'd started out asking her who it had been, after the third time she said "a social worker," I decided not to ask again.

It wasn't that she didn't enjoy herself. Many of the counselors, and even the director, had bought her carefully chosen and beautifully wrapped presents, and she adored them, adored receiving them, anyway: a book, a bottle of perfume, another book, a tape. And it was good to be the center of attention, and to have people dancing and eating and hanging out together on the sofa, in defiance of Williamson's rules, merely because it was her birthday. It was just that she didn't seem able to shake off the remnants of some other barely remembered, impossibly romanticized dream of home and family. A place where she wouldn't have to prepare a heaping plateful of chicken, coleslaw and macaroni and cheese for herself the way I saw her do, and then cover it with silver foil pulled from a huge industrial-sized roll, before checking that no one was watching, and carefully hiding it away in the microwave for later.

Maurice wasn't helping either. I didn't see them speak a word to each other all night, and there was no sense of conspiracy between them. In fact, since I'd arrived Maurice had been leaning up close to an older girl in a green dress who, suspiciously, was wearing the same style of braids as Lucille. Lucille did everything she could to attract his attention. But the more she shrieked and pranced and giggled and flirted, the closer Maurice moved to the girl in green. And though by 8:30 the lights had been dimmed and the music turned up and most of the kids had settled into the numbing semiconsciousness of being at a party, she couldn't help but notice him leave the room with the girl at one point, his arm casually draped around her ample hips. Furious and hurt and ashamed, Lucille spent the last hour of the party dancing with a skinny little boy from Georgia's unit upstairs. Like the elderly Caribbean women she must have seen growing up, she bent her arms back behind her and thrust her still barely formed bosoms out and from side to side as though wanting to shake them loose from her body. The following morning in Family Group, when I thanked her for the party, she said only, "I tell you this, Tina, if I ever make it to sixteen, I ain't going to have no damn whack sweet-sixteen party neither."

Perhaps it was because Lucille was so angry and upset and vulnerable still that she decided to punish Maurice by going with Georgia into what she must have known was a crack house up on 145th and Lenox the following afternoon. Or perhaps not. Perhaps it was just teenage boredom that led her up those stairs, or genuine curiosity, or some kind of need to revisit a scene she must have witnessed so often as a child. Perhaps it was even an expression of something she had tried to tell me about months before.

"When do you think you started leading an adult life?" I had asked her.

"When I was six," she'd replied. "Actually, I should say four. Doing dishes, the groceries, cleaning the house, doing laundry, making sure my hair was combed and that I had clothes to go to school. Ever since then I been in a rush," she had said. "I mean, since I didn't get a hundred percent of the attention that I needed then, I am in a rush to make up for it now. I'm trying to get all the attention I can get from anybody I can get it from."

Whatever it was, she wasn't particularly conscious of any motivation as she followed Georgia into the crumbling brick building, leaving Maurice and Rasheem out on the street, Maurice ridiculously laden with Lucille's book bag, which she had left in his care. They had only followed the girls up there when a belated sense of possessiveness had taken control of Maurice after he'd heard Georgia tell Lucille that she had someone she wanted her to meet up there, someone Maurice shouldn't know about. They had only been half welcome, and now they were stuck out on the sidewalk of 145th and Lenox Avenue, which wasn't the kind of place anyone wanted to be. In one of the worst neighborhoods in the city, this was one of the worst streets. Most of the buildings were burned out or boarded up. Strung-out hookers desperate for a hit from one of the crack houses on the block paced on the uneven sidewalks that looked as if an earthquake had torn them apart. Broken glass, bright plastic–lidded crack vials, and excrement cluttered the edges of the street. According to one of the counselors at Williamson's, "They will kill you there—or pull you into a crack house, get you high, have their way with you, and then throw you out like a lump of dead meat. It isn't a place for anyone to be hanging out."

After five minutes Rasheem wanted to leave. But Maurice wasn't going anywhere, not while Lucille was still inside, he said. They argued and then calmed down again. Maurice chain-smoked. A woman across the street who had gone bald except for two short tufts like a clown's on either side of her head argued with herself one moment and then made herself laugh. Maurice suggested they go in and try to find the girls. But they didn't know which apartment Lucille and Georgia were in, or even which floor, and anyway there were only two of them and who knew how many kids inside.

Two, then three hours passed. Every now and then they scanned the darkened windows of the buildings, though all they could see was the occasional scrap of cloth someone had hung up in a long-forgotten attempt at privacy. At one point Maurice became so desperate that he even called for Lucille, cupping his hands over his mouth and shouting for all he was worth. A few minutes after that Bobby Peaks, the boy who had been expelled from West Side, sauntered out of the building. Smiling, he approached Maurice and then said in that slurred, consonantless way he had: "Yo, your girl flyin' up there, yo. She foolin' with a whole bunch of niggers." For a second Maurice and Rasheem just stood there. "Just thought I'd let you know," Bobby said and then turned to walk back across the street. Without saying anything Maurice followed him. Rasheem shouted after him, but Maurice opened the door anyway and walked into the building and then up the first flight of stairs, to the second floor, where a bunch of kids strolled out of a darkened apartment, put a gun to the side of his head, and told him that if he didn't turn around and leave they would kill him.

Three seconds later Maurice was back on the street, where, for the first time in his life, he says, and to the complete surprise of both himself and Rasheem, he completely lost control. He started to shake and was somehow aware that he couldn't talk. At the same time he couldn't stop talking. He had no idea of what he was saying or even if he was making any sense, but he could tell something was going on because he could feel his mouth working and because he could vaguely hear his own voice coming from somewhere. This interested him for a couple of seconds at a time, but Rasheem was terrified. He tried to calm Maurice down and then to pull him off toward the subway station, but, bigger and stronger than his friend, Maurice refused to move. Then he started to cry.

"Five hours. I was crying five hours straight," he told me the next morning over the phone. "I was crying when I called Williamson's to tell them what was going on and to tell them where Lucille was. I was crying in the cab going back 'cause they said I was too emotionally unstable to take a subway. I was crying in my room in Williamson's. Five straight hours. I never cry. I lost it. I just lost it. I really lost it. Rasheem will tell you. I should have walked away, but I couldn't leave Lucille there—I could leave Georgia, I don't care about Georgia, but with Lucille it's different. When Bobby Peaks said that to me it was just a feeling I couldn't hold."

Lucille, for her part, swore that none of the men inside the apartment had touched her. "This guy told Maurice they had sex with me up there but that wasn't the case," she told me. "I wasn't even trying to play that. It never happened. That's the whole thing. I wish none of it ever happened. See, Georgia tried to hook me up with somebody else even though Maurice was there; she wanted me to ditch him and take my book bag and leave him, and I didn't want to do that. I left him with my book bag so he would know that at least he would see me again that day even if I didn't come back to Williamson's with him. If I was a little more aware and my eyes were a little more open I would've been all right. I should have been more aware when Georgia went into that room with one of the guys, even if what she did in there *is* her business. Later she did the same thing with another guy. But me? I just stood there smoking weed and drinking."

Whatever it was that went on up there in that apartment, Lucille readily admitted that by the time she left at nine that evening she was disoriented and depressed. Somehow she made her way to her aunt's house, where she was welcomed, and where she ate dinner and went to sleep for a time before returning to Williamson's. She felt like she had disrespected herself, she told me, that yet again she had been presented with a choice and had made the wrong one. But it wasn't until she learned that Maurice had waited for her outside on the street for all those hours, and that he had been threatened with a gun and had broken down completely under the strain of it and had needed hours of counseling, that she lost the last strands of her composure. In a flood of words thickened by that nasal-blocked, posttrauma voice that only comes after hours of sobbing, she told me:

"I felt fucked up this morning, real fucked up. I was at the point where I could have lost Maurice, because I mean, he waited for me all those hours. He didn't want to leave me by myself, and I thank him for that. At least now I know that he cares. But I mean, if me and him would have broke up . . . I told the staff that if they hadn't come into my room when they did it would have been all over."

She had woken up the following morning, she told me, desperate and depressed and convinced that everything was finished between her and Maurice—how could it not be? Thinking that she had very little choice, she found herself a razor blade and then settled into the corner of her baby-blue room and started to slice her left forearm and wrist. She managed to cut herself nine times. The cuts were not deep. She was building up to it slowly, testing each cut out, watching as the skin came apart and then bled as if it wasn't her body that was being hurt at all. Then a member of the Williamson's staff had found her and rushed her down to the infirmary, which is where she was when Maurice had called me earlier that morning.

"At least I finally got Maurice to believe me that nothing went on inside," she told me, crying openly now. "So now he can believe me . . ."

* * *

Lucille never came back to West Side. Her counselors decided she was still too immature to be out on the street by herself every day and that she would do better with closer supervision at the small school they ran themselves inside the building. I showed up on Williamson's steps often for the first few weeks after that. To begin with I brought chocolates and potato chips and french fries from McDonald's, but I was never allowed to see her. They thought it best to cut all ties, I think, and though I called she never came to the phone again either. I could never make up my mind, still haven't made up my mind, if this was her desire or Williamson's. I suppose that if she had really wanted to speak to me she would have found a way somehow or other. I also suppose that if I had really wanted to speak to her I would have found a way too. But I didn't and neither did she. Her mind was so sharp and unpredictable that she had always kind of frightened me, I had to admit, and though I would miss her, I often felt out of my depth when I was with her and was relieved to have any kind of responsibility for her taken out of my hands.

Maurice, however, did come back to West Side. He stayed away for over a week and then called and asked me to meet him in front of the school on his first day back. He said he'd be there by eight o'clock, but it was close to nine when he came out of the subway, and I was shocked to see him struggle so listlessly up the stairs to the street. It was a cold, gray day, raining slightly, but he was wearing only a shirt—no hat or sweater or jacket, just a striped button-down shirt and a pair of wrinkled jeans that needed a wash. Even the cigarette he was smoking looked pathetic somehow, soggy and bent in the rain. I asked him how he was and he shrugged and without looking at me said, "OK—I bin in better moods though." As we walked to the corner store he interrupted whatever it was I was saying with, "It was because she was worried about losing me that she cut herself that way."

"I know."

"She didn't want me to leave this morning but I said, 'I have to, I have to go to school.' But she was holding me and not letting me go, which is why I was late. She's worried I will leave her, that's why."

"Will you leave her?" I asked. And with more thought than I've ever seen him give anything he shrugged again and said, "I don't know," very quietly.

17

THE WHOLE SCHOOL was on a downward spiral by then. It always happened around this time of year, I was told. Thanksgiving had come and gone and Ed had thrown a characteristically festive and bountiful dinner, complete with a fresh roasted turkey and all the trimmings (the cost of which he mostly shouldered himself). It had been a fun party, but only a handful of kids had shown up, and it didn't really help shift the sense of drifting isolation that had settled, like damp fog, over West Side by the middle of the month. Nothing in particular had caused it. The school, on the surface of things anyway, seemed fine. If there was a sense of worn-down fatigue to many of the teachers, most were approaching the end of the year with a well-earned sense of achievement too. After months of frustration David had finally managed to convince even the most skeptical in his class of the validity of both positive and negative numbers. The history teacher, Ann, had managed to radicalize at least some of her students by teaching them about the nation's robber barons ("The history of labor in this country is the history of people dying"); and Rochelle had handed our her final literature paper with the proud announcement that the questions were the same as those she had been asked to answer in college. Even the boy's basketball team had made it to the finals. And though they lost in the end by over twenty points, they had been written about in the papers, which always boosted morale.

"You seen that kid Derrick play?" I heard one boy ask another in a packed elevator as they read an enlarged xeroxed copy of the tiny article. "That nigger jump to the moon."

"Yeah. That nigger float."

"The only reason that nigger not be known is he's not in regular school—if he went to regular school he'd be in all the damn papers."

"Yeah. I seen him. That nigger jump." For a second we all stood there, smiling, feeling good, proud to be part of West Side.

"Never seen him fight, though," the first boy added.

"True. True." Which brought us all down to reality again, face-to-face with the frequent realization that what could be seen in one way by most people could almost certainly be seen in another by West Side students.

Outside, of course, the city was gearing up for the year-end holidays of Christmas and Hanukkah. The Rockefeller Center tree had been cut somewhere out in the country and would soon be decorated in its traditional place above the tiny skating rink; the trees up Park Avenue had been dressed in lights, and illuminated snowflakes hung from the lampposts there, at least up to where the subway came above ground at Ninety-seventh Street, beyond which poor people started to live. Candy canes, giant menorahs, and toy soldiers several stories tall provided a backdrop for the countless Santas and Salvation Army collectors who stood on street corners in midtown Manhattan. And the smells of sugar-coated nuts and roasted chestnuts softened the edge of the cold winter air as shoppers spun out of department stores' revolving brass doors, or stopped to linger awhile outside the impressively festive window displays. But as the celebration and excited anticipation of the holidays increased out on the street, so things became more intricately dark inside the building of West Side.

Attendance had been in decline since the end of November, ever since Macy's put up their Christmas decorations. I'll never know for sure if this was just a coincidence, but many of the kids had to walk past the store on their way to school in the morning, and the boughs of elaborately lit pine and the spray snow and the red and gold ribbons drove some of them crazy because it wasn't for them, they knew. None of it was for them. Not the hearty good cheer, nor the spectacular decorations, or even the ads on the TV and the radio and billboards, which tantalizingly promised gifts proffered by smiling relatives in golden-lit living rooms most of them knew they should never even dream about having themselves. Even the students that did keep coming to school arrived brittle and angry. Isolated inside their puffy down jackets and their face-obscuring ski masks and hoods, many of them stayed so tightly wound that a slight which might have been ignored in October would most definitely lead to something now.

Once I saw Ed throw himself down onto his knees like a referee and count to ten, slamming his hand on the floor as he counted, warning the two clawing, scratching, hair-pulling girls beside him that if they didn't come apart by the time he finished he would have to ask them both to leave the school. Another time Suzie got into a fight with a large girl from the eleventh floor named Florinda. "You keep going like this and you going to get hit," Florinda had threatened, leaning into our Family Group room, where Suzie had come for her early-morning kiss from Maurice. Before I knew what was happening Suzie had leapt across the room and had prodded and pushed and poked at the far larger girl until Florinda finally lunged at her. I tried to get between them but Florinda was almost twice my size, and for the few dozen seconds before Chuck, the music teacher, came to my rescue, all I was aware of were the weight of her breasts, the glint of her huge, inflated-looking, hollow gold earrings, and the blur of Suzie's swinging, zipless, canvas bag.

Ed thought it best just to let the matter drop when he heard about it. After a barrage of tests, the Board of Education had finally found a more appropriate place for Suzie to go to school, and with her leaving on December 19 anyway, what was the point? Still, it frayed the nerves to start a day off like that. Especially when so many kids were falling apart under the strains of universal goodwill that Linda, the always overworked but now inundated social worker, had thought it necessary to put out an advisory sheet for Family Group advisers entitled "Holiday Depression."

"These suggestions are presented in response to the perceived need among our students," the sheet began. "You might initiate discussions by acknowledging the stress of the holidays. These stresses include unhappy family gatherings, troublesome financial situations, and the expectation of happy events versus the reality of the students' experiences. Don't assume that all students are spending their holiday with a parent or a loved one."

In fact, so many kids were showing symptoms of depression that members of the mental-health team at the school agreed it had become a "contagion." "A contagion of isolation and anger," one counselor called it, which had made even Ed deflate, sitting there in the tiny counseling room on the eleventh floor during what seemed to be turning into a much needed therapy session for the school's therapists. Rather haplessly he suggested that it might be nice to make decorations and give one to every kid in the school as a present for the holidays. When someone retorted that most kids didn't have anywhere to hang a decoration, Ed was left to look down to his hands in defeat.

"Well," he asked, "how do we address that?"

It was a question no one in the room had an answer for. Over the past two weeks in Ed's Family Group alone, Maurice had been threatened with a gun, Lucille had possibly been raped and had then been withdrawn and Rasheem had been kicked out of yet another shelter and had had to move to Jersey, where, still without a jacket, he'd fallen ill again. Another kid, Sean, had been admitted to the psychiatric ward of a hospital after he had smoked some grass that had sent him hallucinating for days; and James, trying to keep his headphones after being mugged on the subway, had been arrested, convicted of disturbing the peace, and sentenced to spend two full days with his attacker, scraping chewing gum off a subway platform.

Everyone in the room sat quietly, while a social worker named Barbara talked about being shouted at by a kid earlier that day and how tired she was of having them take their frustrations out on her. "I feel like a punching bag," she said. "And I feel like I've been punched until there's no more air in me." It was a common complaint. Two days before, I had watched as Rochelle tried to lighten the mood in her room by assigning a story titled "It Was a Very Special Day." But instead of the lighthearted response she'd been hoping for, a girl name Jeneena insisted that Rochelle read her story out loud for the class. Rochelle had had Jeneena as a pupil for the past three years, and she knew that her student often used stories as a place to express some of her more appalling childhood memories. She didn't want to read this one out loud. But Jeneena insisted. An eccentric, more influenced by downtown fashion than uptown, Jeneena's hair was pink. Sometimes she wore what she called grandma dresses with raggedy combat boots and zipper-covered, leather motorcycle jackets. Once she came to school dressed as Pocahontas. And because conformity was as important at

West Side as it is in every high school, she was generally regarded as being weird. But the rest of the class was intrigued now, and they wanted to hear whatever it was the girl had written. Exasperated and exhausted herself, Rochelle cocked her head sideways a little and again asked Jeneena if she was sure. Then, holding the pages at their edges as though frightened even to touch the words neatly written there, Rochelle began.

> It was a special day indeed. I was going to be ten years old. I had hair as straight as a silk blanket and a nose as cute as a button, a smile that would catch everyone's eye and eyes that had a shimmer as if I was going to cry.
>
> That day I decided to put my black and white dress on. It was my favorite. It had a collar with ruffles and long sleeves with cuffs. It was long. It would reach my ankles. It was my favorite one indeed.
>
> My mom woke up and saw me dressed up and knew it was my birthday. She said happy birthday and baked me a cake. It was three layers, with chocolate pudding in the middle of each layer and chocolate frosting with rainbow sprinkles. My mom and I had so much fun that day, but soon the day was over.
>
> As my mom and I were going to the store she met this guy. His name was Emilcar. I didn't like him one bit. He came over to chill and my mom started to go out with him. Here's when it all begins. Little by little my mom was changing. She wouldn't put that special smile for me like usual, and Emilcar became so irritable.
>
> It finally hit me! I waited till they thought I was asleep and spied on them. I saw my mom with a lighter, a glass tube and some sort of powder. This is how I described it as a kid. I didn't know what it was till now.
>
> She saw me and grabbed me by the arms and told me to watch. She would put the fire under the glass tube (a stem) and pour the powder in it (crack).
>
> She told me I had to learn so I could do it too. I knew it was bad because of the way it changed my mom. I ran off crying.
>
> After about a year in Far Rockaway, she began to abuse me as well as that asshole Emilcar. I mean on weekends I used to go

to my grandmother's house with bruises all over, a busted lip, my back all black and blue and eyes black and blue.

My grandmother noticed all of this and asked me what was going on. I wouldn't tell her because I was scared of what was going to happen to me if I did. Maybe they'll kill me or hurt me more, I don't want that so I stayed quiet.

I would go somedays without eating, and began looking like a bum. My mom cared less about me and more about her drugs.

One night my stepfather came to my room and began to play with me and I smacked him, because I knew it was wrong what he was doing. So he hit me real hard in my face and ripped off my clothes and hurt me. (Now I know what he did, he raped me.) I screamed for help, my mom was so high she didn't realize anything.

After he finished I curled up in a corner and cried for days. I decided at that moment I wasn't going to deal with it anymore. So I took some underwear, T-shirts, socks and of course my doll. I called my grandmother and told her I was coming to be aware and hung up.

When I got there I had blood all over my underwear and my grandmother asked me what was going on and I explained everything and started crying.

To make this long story short this is something I had to deal with for seven years, it is called ashamement. Now I live with my grandmother and am doing OK. I've learned how to cope with guilt and shame.

The response in Rochelle's room was so explosive that it transcended even the horrors of Jeneena's story. As if in revenge for all the Emilcars in this world, as well as, I couldn't help but feel, the great white lies that surrounded the students then too—the Santas in warm red suits chortling ho-ho-ho and the mannequins in store windows and the suited Manhattanites they saw on the train, laden with shopping bags and complaints about the few days remaining until Christmas—the class demanded to know were this molester Emilcar lived, what he looked like, where he hung out. They wanted to get him, to cut him, to kill him, they said while Jeneena sat there calmly, in her Raggedy

Ann dress and army boots, relieved at having spoken at last and pleased, it seemed, to have so many people express such concern.

I was exhausted too, by then, and was having a hard time avoiding the conclusion that the obstacles faced by kids who just happened to be born on the wrong side of some invisible line dividing the deserving from the disposable were simply insurmountable. Sometimes during those early days of December I would slink off home straight after Family Group, overwhelmed entirely by whatever it was that I had heard or seen. I was so flat, so closed off and shrunken, that I didn't pay much attention to the touting of the school's upcoming Kwanzaa celebration as a solution to West Side's end-of-the-year depression. Most teachers didn't. Created in 1972 by a black studies professor and heralded as a "nationally celebrated, indigenous, non-religious, non-heroic, non-political, African American holiday," Kwanzaa had been getting good play in the suddenly multicultural-conscious national media. Most white teachers, however, responded primarily to the celebration's vaguely separatist-sounding politics and were skeptical of the claim that it could be an effective antidote to all the anger and isolation that had built up by then.

Even if I had been more in tune, though, my opportunities to watch the academic preparations for the celebration were limited. It had always been up to individual teachers to allow me into their classrooms, and though an English teacher named Renee seemed to have no problem with my being around, Rosa, a history teacher, made it clear that she did. She was a fierce lion of a woman, protective and suspicious of any outsider, especially of writers—especially writers with English accents who didn't seem to know anything about anything—and the one time I tried to sit in on a class she told me in no uncertain terms to get out. She didn't like me, and that was fine, really. She didn't like a lot of people, and though she was in turn much disliked, there had never been any doubt in my mind that Rosa was an emotional and moral powerhouse at West Side, a driving force behind the lives of perhaps as many kids as Ed. She was angry, it was true, and perhaps she did overstep the mark of political objectivity when she got onto the subject of Africa in history, but she was passionate and involved in a way that a lot of the staff simply could not be.

"I am the single mother. I am the poor girl growing up in the projects. I am the welfare recipient. I am all that. I come from where you come from and I care. I am you," I heard her tell a student once. And like a fierce old-fashioned mother, always impatient with anything sloppy or lazy or stupid, during the weeks leading up to the celebration she chased and embarrassed her students into a sustained level of behavior and performance.

Piece by piece Esther's art room began to fill with African shields the shape of palm leaves, sheaves of paper reeds, papier-mâché masks and huge rolls of colored landscapes. These featured rural African scenes mostly, with two-dimensional grass huts receding into the distance and tall palm trees and ocean views. Some of the kids complained when they were forced to give up their own work in order to help with a landscape, say, or a shield or a mask, but a sense of impending achievement began to take hold that most students at West Side were drawn to.

I could see it in Ed's Family Group, too. At the beginning of the month, James had been furious about his unfair arrest, but now he was spending the mornings huddled in the corner with Dayna and Michelle, memorizing poems and writing character sketches and essays and stories following the patterns of traditional African storytelling. Even Maurice, who had been coming to Family Group regularly since the whole fiasco uptown, got involved by persuading Renee to allow him to sing a solo in one of the acts. And although he tended to leave after Family Group most days and go and sit and chain-smoke in the Blimpie's a couple of blocks away with Suzie—who was inordinately proud of her new status now that Lucille was out of the way, and who had swayed along the corridors with a confidence burgeoning on pride ever since she had heard she was going to a special kind of school anyway—he usually made it back in time for rehearsals after lunch.

The promise didn't extend to everyone, of course. Sandra and Cristy became increasingly disengaged with the school, and a boy named Emilio had been so bored by the preparation work he was assigned that he'd started a gambling circle in the stairwell. Because this had happened before, and because Emilio was a twenty-year-old drug dealer who was showing no signs of improvement, most staff members insisted he be transferred out of the school. But Ed couldn't give up on Emilio. He was smart and quick and funny and had a gentleness underneath all that charm that reminded Ed of Javier, so he insisted on taking him into his own Family Group instead. This action lit burners under the already simmering anger of many staff members, who saw it as the kind of typical and irrational sentimentality that kept West Side from ever getting anywhere. Tensions continued to increase until people became so tightly wound that statements like the following started to appear on the top of notices: "This is an annual holiday message to all of our students. It is a very difficult time to focus on school work. But when you signed up for WSHS you agreed that you would come, come on time, and do all the work assigned to the best of your ability whether you felt like it or not. We expect that to continue. If you cannot concentrate on your work, see me immediately. I'll arrange an extended holiday with your parents. We shall be conducting sweeps of different floors each period. Those who are found in the halls will have a phone call home made for them. Any questions see Ed Reynolds. Otherwise let's work together so we can leave on December 23 to enjoy a well-earned rest."

As was usual at this time of year, attendance rates fell for teachers as well as for students. On any given day up to ten staff members could be missing at a time. This meant that the teachers who did show up had to double their workloads. By the day Kwanzaa was to be celebrated, most people were utterly drained.

Renee especially was exhausted. She was as affected as everyone else by the-end-of-the-year blues, but now, up on the tenth floor and in the room where a complex sound system was being set up, she was trying hard to lead a huge group of kids in a raucous and not very organized dress rehearsal. To add to the chaos, the room was being transformed into an African village at the same time. Silhouettes of villagers had already been stuck around the columns and the walls, and tie-dyed flags and banners with African words painted across them were being hung. Kids were shuffling in and out of the room with still more decorations, others were frantically pinning costumes and practicing dance steps, and a whole group of girls were rehearsing monologues and historical skits out in the lobby.

"You may write me down in history/With your bitter, twisted lies, /You may trod me in the very dirt/ But still, like dust, I'll rise. /Does my sassiness upset you?/ Why are you beset with gloom? /'Cause I walk like I've got oil wells/ Pumping in my living room," one girl was reciting. She wasn't nervous at all and she swung her shoulders and flashed her eyes like a haughty flamenco dancer. A group of boys dressed as African elders in colorful drapes of fabric and white shorts and gold-strapped sandals were delighted by her performance, and just as they were starting to whoop, Renee started calling out for Maurice. I hadn't seen him all day; he hadn't even shown up for Family Group that morning. From the look on Renee's face, I could see how furious she would have been if she'd had the time. She had only given him the solo because he had seemed to need to be involved so much, and even then she'd made him promise that he wouldn't mess up. But now, halfway through the dress rehearsal, he'd disappeared. She had half-known he would; that was the problem with Maurice. After shouting for him one more time and asking the kids if anyone had seen him, she scrapped the scene altogether, finished the rehearsal as best she could, and turned her mind to the food that still needed to be unpacked, heated, and displayed: the *Morros y Cristianos,* fried chicken, corn bread, potato salad, green salad, meat pies, *picadillo, plátanos,* and the flaky *pastelitos,* which I couldn't resist tasting as I took them out of the industrial heater and which were sumptuous and sweet.

By four, the two dining tables were draped with brightly colored cloths, but the papier-mâché masks still needed to be hung and, three floors down, Esther was still playing with the tissue-paper floral table decorations. So you really couldn't blame Renee for panicking when she realized half an hour before the show was supposed to start that the knives and forks and plates and cups and sodas that Ed had promised had not arrived. Especially as no one seemed to know where Ed was. I looked all over the school but couldn't find him. Renee was just about to send a couple of kids out to buy emergency supplies when Esther told me he was asleep in his office and suggested I go down there and knock on his door to wake him up.

I knocked gently for a few minutes before Ed said, "Coming. Wait just one minute."

His office was such a confused mess that he had to pull the door hard to open it. The room was literally overflowing with boxes and piles of papers, files, books, and shopping bags filled with everything from sugar packets to new editions of suggested regulations from the Board of Education. There were two green metal pushcarts in a corner, along with a set of empty Apple computer boxes and cleaning utensils. A good year's worth of toilet paper had tumbled out of the cupboard on the other side, so that I couldn't help wondering how long it had taken him to clear the space at the foot of his desk for the folded blue padded blanket—the kind that movers use to wrap furniture in—which served as his mattress. He was in his undershirt when he opened the door. His hair was ruffled and his head was still foggy with sleep, and when I asked for the plates and the soda and silverware he said, "The soda! It's down in the car! It's all in my car!" as if he had just remembered that he'd left his child out on the street. From the way his eyes were bulging it was clear that he was still half-dreaming.

Still, by the time he arrived upstairs for the celebrations and took the microphone for an instant just to thank Rosa for her opening words—"I give you Ed Reynolds, the principal of West Side High School, and the only man who could ever give two hundred and ninety-nine percent of himself to all of his kids all of the time"—no one could ever have guessed that just ten minutes before he had been sound asleep on the floor of his office. The lunchroom was packed. The chairs that lined the walls were full and more people stood where they could. Over eighty people had come, students mostly and a few families, as well as two elderly and elegant representatives of the Black Panthers, who stood up and gave the power salute when they were introduced. The older of them, a dignified-looking man with cropped white hair and a white goatee, stood again a moment later to say that for all the schools he had visited he had never seen one like West Side. The celebrations had started with the black national anthem, "Lift Every Voice and Sing," ("We have come over a way that with tears has been watered. / We have come, treading our path through the blood of the slaughtered"), and he was amazed, he said, that there was a school in New York that would allow such a ceremony to take place.

His speech was followed by a presentation of the Kwanzaa symbols and principles and then by a troop of female dancers and a troop of male dancers, both accompanied by a trio of percussionists in costume. A series of skits involving African American and Latino historical figures came next, and the presentation of the Maya Angelou poem "Still I Rise" that I had heard earlier out in the corridor. That same girl had then stolen the show with her portrayal of Rosa Parks and had been followed by James, who played the role of Dr. Charles Drew—the man who'd invented a storage system for blood plasma and who, he said, later died after a car accident, because he was black and could not be taken to a white hospital due to segregation laws. James's performance was solid and straightforward, but he was completely eclipsed by a young man in thick cornrows and mirrored glasses who gave an incredibly impassioned revisionist account of the history of the New World. He traced its origins back to the fall of the Roman Empire, an event, he told the enthralled crowd, that was brought about by a group of ferocious black gladiators. It was turning into a radical evening, just the way it was supposed to, and although I couldn't help thinking that most of what I was hearing was absurd (how likely was it, after all, that the twelve tribes of Israel were made up of Cubans, Central Americans, Mexicans, Native Americans, and Peruvians?), it was a proud event too, and a harmonious one, where the kids suddenly looked like high school students anywhere—boisterous and carefree in delightedly expressing the tenets of their beliefs with the impassioned exclusivity of teenagers everywhere. "The-so-called-blacks-and-Latinos" was a phrase I heard a lot, and "Our-African-American-and-Puerto-Rican-brothers-and-sisters," and by the time a girl marched into the room chanting "Power to the people! Power to the people!" enough of a sense of communally shared oppression had been established for most of the audience to respond with appropriately thrust fists and deep *Ho!*s.

There was even an attempt at group chanting, though a lot of people had already left the lunchroom by then to mill around the tenth floor and to eat their meals on the tables that had been set up outside. And then, to finish the evening, there was the traditional libation, or sharing of drink.

"For the Motherland cradle of civilization./ For the ancestors and their indomitable spirit./ For the elders from whom we can learn much./ For the youth who represent the promise for tomorrow . . ." Whether I agreed with the overarching and fundamentally separatist politics involved, there was too much carefree ebullience on the tenth floor of West Side that night to deny that Renee and Rosa had been right, that the evening was far better than relying on a depressingly noneventful home Christmas to get through the holidays. Somehow, by carefully knitting together the strands of individual pride, cultural oppression, celebration, and just a hint of anger too, the students involved had achieved a unity that allowed them, for once, to be kids again. Engaged, domineering teenagers, just like they should always be. Maurice should have been there.

18

WHEN I WAS young, and for years when I was not quite so young as well, my mother used to shower us with presents at Christmas; the presents were ostensibly from Santa Claus, but my older brother and I had known they were from her ever since we'd stumbled across her hiding place under the bed one afternoon while playing war. It was never really the presents that made the holiday special, though; instead it was the routine, the classic and reliable inevitability of tradition. Every Christmas Eve, at about the same time and already changed into our nightclothes, my brothers and I offered performances in turn. My older brother usually played a tune on his recorder; my little brother always sang; and I read aloud from the Bible mostly—I remember because we have countless photos of me standing in a quilted dressing gown with a zipper up the front, my mouth open in the exaggerated gestures of someone still learning to read, my hands clenched around the hard cover of our illustrated Bible for children. Then, after due applause, we would gather on the sofa around my father, who read Clement Moore's "The Night Before Christmas," in exactly the same way each time—the same pauses in the same places, the same skewed emphasis on the same long words, and the same slow, deliberate acting out of "laying a finger aside of his nose,/ With a nod of his head,/ Up the chimney he rose." So magnetic were these evenings that I was twenty-six before I dared stay away from home for the holidays. Even after my parents divorced they were the magnet that drew us together and satisfied my most basic needs for familial reassurance.

That Christmas though, with only a few days off from school, I was once again staying in the States. A group of friends and I had decided to spend the holidays in the suburban house of another friend, who was herself leaving for her family home in the Midwest. Ever since making this plan I had been unable to decide whether to invite some of the kids from West Side to share the holiday with me. Sandra and Cristy each had family dinners to attend, and Sandra had plans to attend a Neta meeting too. And although I tried to remind myself of this whenever I started to feel guilty, I also knew that they were the lucky ones and that most kids in Ed's Family Group would have stingy, lonely, gray-tinged holidays at best. Maurice was staying in Williamson's for the entire holiday. Rasheem would be cooped up in a shelter with his mother and sister. Manny, I knew, hadn't celebrated Christmas at all since his mother had left. This year he'd at least had a tree in the apartment, bought on the spur of the moment by a visiting uncle. But no one had bothered to decorate it, and it had ended up getting in the way and had been shoved into a corner of the kitchen, where it had leaned against a wall until its fallen pine needles drove Manny's father out of his mind and he threw it out, four days before Christmas.

These were typical scenarios for kids at West Side, and Linda, the social worker, had spent years dreaming of a farmhouse in which she could deposit ten or twelve of the hardest-luck cases for the holidays. She often spoke of it, but when I asked her if she thought it would be a good idea for me to bring someone up to Connecticut she advised me against it. Three days in a friend's suburban home in Connecticut wasn't the same thing as having the run of a rambling farmhouse at all, she said. Besides, I was worn thin and needed a break, and unless I was prepared to give all of myself all of the time, a short trip like that could do more harm than good. Take a break, she told me. And I did.

There was snow on the ground when we arrived in Connecticut, at a big white clapboard house with a wreath on the door and fairy lights twisted round the pillars on the porch. I had never been to the house before and was nervous about having Christmas there, in the unfamiliar television world of up-market suburbia. But it was surprisingly easy to settle in. Soon we were making trips to the store to get turkey and stuffing and stale white bread for my favorite English bread sauce, or taking walks and flying kites and then passing the nights in a blur of strange music, drinking and wrapping one another's presents. On Christmas Eve, I stood up in front of the perfectly shaped Christmas tree our friend and her two children had decorated before leaving and sang a few Christmas carols. Then, kicking back into an overstuffed blue sofa, falling back onto it as surely as onto the bedrock of my own particular family ritual, I read "The Night Before Christmas" and tried not to think of the kids, whom I had left to flounder in the city, alone.

Rasheem had stopped thinking about Christmas at the age of five, when he'd asked his mother who Santa Claus was. "You want to know who Santa is?" his mother had answered. "I am. I am Santa Claus. I'm the one who brought you your tricycle and spent all the money and don't you ever forget it. You think I'd let a white guy like that come into my apartment? I'd shoot him first." Rasheem insisted that he'd been glad of the explanation at the time. "It opened me up to reality," he told me. But when I got back to West Side I would learn that this year he spent most of Christmas Day out on cold concrete subway platforms, waiting for hours for holiday reduced-schedule trains not because he had anywhere to go but just because it was a way of getting out of the small room he was sharing with his mother and his sister. I would also hear that two kids in Ed's Family Group spent Christmas Day in prison: one because he was caught driving a stolen car while he was still on probation, the other for doing nothing more than leaning against a wall outside of a local liquor store, one leg bent up under him, shades pulled up over his eyes, hood pulled down low—a pose threatening enough, he said, for a passing cop car to pick him up and then keep him in the precinct building for close to twenty-four hours without charging him. But didn't anyone in his family go looking for him, I asked, forgetting for a minute. Nah, he said, adding only that his mother was out at the time.

Manny would tell me later that he spent Christmas Day on a bus to Virginia's superior designer-clothing outlets, where, because he lived out of state, he was exempt from paying tax. He often did that, he said. Sometimes someone even managed to rustle up a car, but no one from the Ave had wanted to go this time, so he'd gone on his own, bought two "Polo Bear" knitted sweaters and then returned back to Brooklyn in time for a little night-shift work. But it was Nicole who spent the worst week of all. Long a ward of the state, she had been shifted from foster home to foster home for years, and had finally moved in with a friend of the family, a woman close enough to be called Aunty. Ever since she'd moved in though, the woman's attitude had changed. She was more than happy to cash the monthly foster-care checks that came in but she spent the money on partying instead of on food and expected Nicole to work for her upkeep, she said. Over the past few months Nicole had been having such a hard time that Linda had started the process of having her removed. There was talk of drug abuse and several instances of official neglect. But all that seemed inconsequential when a week before Christmas Nicole's foster mother informed her that she was taking her real children upstate to visit relatives for the holidays and that there wouldn't be room for her there. As a result the fourteen-year-old girl was left all alone in the city for the week with a ten-dollar bill and an empty refrigerator for company.

I didn't know any of this as I spent my afternoons up in Connecticut channel surfing through a seemingly endless string of cable stations and making soups and drinking wine with friends. Or rather, I didn't know the specifics, but I knew the kids; I'd spent the past three months with them so intensely that I probably could have guessed how their holidays would go. I had gained that much understanding at least. I knew that Maurice was disturbed, at times possibly dangerous, that Lucille was quick and vulnerable, and I knew more or less how they had come to be that way. I knew where Manny lived and how he worked and just what he had gone through to get there; that Rasheem was homeless; that one of Sandra's relatives was a big-time crack dealer; that Cristy's brother had tried to smother her when she was younger; and that Michelle would do anything to avoid ending up a single mother on welfare like her sister.

Even those who hadn't wanted me to uncover anything about them had revealed themselves in one way or another, however inadvertently. A boy with dental braces had collapsed right next to me in the corridor one afternoon, simply crumpled up and fallen down and had been forced to reveal a long-denied illness. A girl Ed had asked me to talk to after a fight had confessed that her boyfriend had just been thrown into prison for murder and that she was pregnant with his child. Even James, who had seemed so gentle and hardworking, confessed that he had tried to pull a gun on his stepfather. Even after finding the kind of equilibrium that allowed him to work three hours a day as a homework tutor for elementary school kids, he still couldn't control his temper, he said, and after watching him mistreat his mother for years he "ended up shooting him in the leg."

At the beginning of my visit to West Side these were precisely the kind of realities I had been trying to uncover. I had thought that if I could peel back the layers of bravado and charm and blanket aggression I would have achieved what I set out to do. But now, I was less sure there was any point to this process at all. To reveal wasn't enough, I realized; I also had to help. But if there was nothing I could do to remove the loneliness and humiliation so many of them had suffered in the past, and if my influence on the present was nebulous at best, I didn't see how I could even hope to have any effect on the future.

This was the thinking of a classic burnout, I realized later. Linda had told me about them before—the young idealists fresh out of college who rushed in to help the "underprivileged," and who then turned tail and ran when the last strands of exoticism were peeled away and they realized that the damage they saw there was real. It happened all the time, she told me, and the only way to prevent it was to downshift expectations. Even Ed had told me several times that he had realized five days after arriving at West Side that what he'd thought he could achieve in five years he wouldn't be able to do in five lifetimes. It was a favorite phrase of his, one I spent hours mulling, repeating it over and over, looking at it from every angle and examining it for cracks. But it was true. Simply knowing the truth was just the beginning, not the answer at all. Doing anything to change the truth was—well, an entirely more complex affair.

I knew by then that it was ridiculous to expect any kind of dramatic breakthrough, especially as the kids I'd naturally gravitated to were by and large the ones who had suffered the most and were more damaged as a result. But it was a strange and warring experience nonetheless to sit back and watch them make the wrong choices time after time, day after day, week after week, consciously destroying what little hope was left while simultaneously convincing themselves that what they were doing was, if not right, then at least in step with a pre-established life whose limits they were sure they knew. Kids like Manny, for example, who had pretty much stopped coming to school at all by then, and who, the last time I saw him, had left the court building straight after his hearing to go back to the Ave. Or Rasheem who had refused, simply refused, to sign up for the free art classes offered on Saturdays for talented young artists at Cooper Union because his mother had taught him to be wary of charity. Or like Cristy, who despite being so close to graduation had stopped coming to school so she could spend more time at her new job, and Sandra, who did the same thing for the Netas, and Lucille, who continued to put herself in harm's way because in her twisted world it was that kind of adventure that passed for a life.

There was a boy I'd heard about who'd even landed himself in jail because of some misguided notion of "keeping it real." Big Daddy had been renowned as the stud of his junior high school because he had experienced the "highest level of manhood." One evening he took a girl out on a date and then boasted about how he had taken her "doggy style." "Big Doggy Daddy," somebody had shouted, and he'd been renamed. For a few days he basked in the glory of his sudden notoriety, and no one noticed that the girl didn't come back to school. Then, two days later, she was found dead and raped on the floor of her apartment. Big Doggy Daddy was arrested and spent a year in jail before DNA samples finally proved it couldn't have been him who'd raped the girl that night. And in all that time, he never once volunteered the information that he hadn't even been in the girl's apartment—that in fact he had never slept with a girl in his life and that the night in question he had just walked her home and kissed her good-night on the cheek like a gentleman.

Driving past lawn after lawn, out of Stamford to the more humble neighborhoods of Glenbrook and Springdale, where the houses were smaller and the stores more generic, and then onto a bright, business-clogged thoroughfare where Taco Bell and McDonald's competed for space with huge supermarkets and car dealerships, I wondered what chance any of the kids in Ed's Family Group had of ever living like this. Having grown up in cities all my life, even I felt out of place in the pedestrianless repetition of strip mall after strip mall. But however ordered and pale and culturally isolated Connecticut seemed, at least it was safe. I passed young kids alone on bikes, groups of teens hanging out on their parent's car hoods or walking along the road to a nearby frozen pond or to a forested area with steep slopes for sledding. And my wonder at the normalcy of it all, at the friendly cops and the families making snowmen in their yards, helped me understand that the main difference between me and the kids at West Side was that while

I knew at least a portion of their reality, they knew not the first thing about this kind of place.

Even if I were to bring them all to my friend's big house in Connecticut, I wondered how long I would have to keep them here for them to actually believe they could share in a place where there was nothing to be afraid of except, perhaps, the occasional car driven by a festively tipsy dad just a little too quickly past the front of the house. It was all simply too foreign, I realized, too implausible. Because just as most middle-class people never consider the possibility of becoming welfare recipients, or homeless mothers or fathers trapped in a crime-ridden housing project, so many people in the inner cities never really believe they will be given the chance to stretch out and breathe in a white clapboard house with a picket fence, and a lawn edged with trees. To convince them even of its reality, let alone its accessibility, would take months, and understanding this for the first time, I drove myself back to the house, sat down on my friend's overstuffed blue sofa, and wrote a letter to Manny, desperately and ridiculously trying to convince him of the authenticity of a world where early death by gunfire was about as likely as winning the lottery.

> I remember you telling me once or twice that the corner out on Knickerbocker was all you have, that all of that other stuff might be nice for other kids, but that you, Emanuel Martinez, had only your corner—nothing else. Do you still believe that? If you got a job now you'd have plenty of money saved up for the summer and you could swim in the ocean with a beautiful woman, drive to the country on a moped you have bought legit, hang out, listen to music, drink good drinks, eat good food. . . . It's real, you know. Just as real as any other way of living. Hundreds of thousands of people do it all the time—millions of people do—so why shouldn't you?

But even as I was writing I knew that, like many other members of the "underclass," Manny had been so isolated from the very American mainstream whose viability I was so desperately trying to convince him of that he would be more likely to respond to the bland serenity of Connecticut with violence and theft and mindless destruction. Too much damage had been done, I told myself, folding up the letter and putting it away. Before we could expect anything else from them, kids like Manny had to be given the opportunity to claim for themselves a level of life that most of them could not even imagine right then.

But short of tearing down the inner cities, of permanently dispersing the poor among the rest of the population, I couldn't see any way of doing this. And when a successful computer programmer asked me later that week, "Yeah? So what's the solution?" when he heard I was writing a book on inner-city teenagers, I blushed, and then squirmed, and finally left the room, because after three months I had less of an answer than I'd had even before I'd started working on the book. Increased opportunities had to go hand in hand with an increased belief that the opportunities might indeed pan out, that was all I was sure of. And that belief could be nurtured only by bridging the divide between the bulk of Americans who lived comfortably and the minority that was poor. The sustained isolation of poverty damaged people in ways that were long-lasting and intractable—that's where we all had to start from. At the most simple, broadest level, nothing could be done until we all understood this.

"How can America as a nation just close their eyes to the obvious relationships between four hundred years of abuse and cultural murder and slavery and discrimination and low-performing adolescents? To ignore all that is criminal," Ed had said once when he was angered by a newspaper article blaming kids for their lack of educational success. It was a theme Stewart reiterated too, as did all of the best teachers at West Side. In order to have even the barest chance of success, you had to start from a position of reality.

19

ED'S APPROACH WAS to say that he looked at things on a different scale altogether, that he had long ago stopped seeking the gratification of the concrete and the immediate and the specific and that he now tried to see things over lifetimes. He told me a story once of three old West Side students who he had run into while waiting on line for a movie. They had been wild at West Side, rebellious and loud and obnoxious, but now they were in their late twenties and working, all three of them with families. They had come up to Ed to apologize for how they had behaved and to thank him too, for providing the support they had needed when no one else had been willing or able to be there for them. If Ed hadn't run into them that evening, he would have had no reason to think that anything he had done had made the slightest bit of difference in their lives. This was what he meant when he said he tried to look at the whole picture: it allowed a hard-nosed optimism that kept him coming into West Side ready to give all of himself the way he had done for the past twenty years.

Linda, the social worker, operated that way too, and like Ed she understood that the results of her work were rarely immediately visible. She planted seeds, she'd told me, and though she didn't often see the rewards of what she did, she had great faith that the seeds would root and that, in time, they would grow. For a long while I had believed her when she'd told me that the process of forming relationships with the kids, relationships that were real and complex and long-standing, was perhaps the most beneficial thing I could do while I was at the school. But I was having a hard time believing it anymore. I was there, after all, to listen and watch and report, and the distance that created simply starred to feel like it got in the way.

On the other hand, I knew I'd never be a teacher. I lacked the urge to discipline, to rein in. It was far more natural for me to see the school the way Ed did—as a comforting refuge primarily, instead of a rigorous academic establishment. That premise had informed my evolving role at the school, and throughout the time I'd been at West Side I had tried to remain available to the kids not as part of the school's already loose structure but as an independent, unbiased observer. Sometimes it had been difficult to walk the line between where teachers wanted me to be—helping them teach, basically—and where the kids wanted me to be—helping them cheat. But I'd more or less stayed my ground, and if the resulting balance had helped me get close to the kids, I had also started to flounder in its vagueness. So when the new year began and Rochelle and Ann asked me to help them tutor some of their kids in preparation for the statewide RCT exams, I was more than pleased to agree. Individual tutoring would provide a focus that I'd been lacking since I'd gotten back to school, and by trading in my vague sense of confusion for a more concrete and orderly progression, I thought it might allow me to feel useful for once too. Besides, Ed had already hauled in every extra tutor and counselor and high school mentor he could find and the kids needed all the help they could get.

First initiated in the seventies, RCTs, or Regents Competency Tests, were designed to ensure a minimum competency level for high school graduates. There are six of them: English, reading, math, science, global history, and American history, and all high school students in the state have to pass them in order to graduate. They are not very difficult. They are so easy, in fact, that Ed often told his students that anyone with a sound seventh-grade education should be able to pass them.

Nonetheless, they presented substantial obstacles to many students at West Side. The problem, of course, was that most of them had never received an adequate seventh-grade education, or sixth, or eighth either, for that matter. In response, West Side had come up with specially designed minicycles—two-and-a-half-week-long courses that served exclusively as cram-preparation classes for the exams. Not all teachers taught them. Some students had passed all their exams before ever transferring to West Side, and they needed to continue with the more abstract and general process of learning. But for the most part, teachers and students alike were exclusively focused on preparing for the exams during the early weeks of January.

I had always admired the teachers at West Side, the ones who worked hard every day, and who cared and who had the energy and the imagination to re-create their world anew time and time again in order to get their students excited. Theirs was more than a job, after all; it was a profession, one they had been trained in for years to be able to do well. They always worked hard, but it was amazing to see how the upcoming exams focused their professional instincts. It was as if out of the vast morass of absenteeism, failed grades, incomplete homework, lack of discipline, rudeness, irregular work habits, and impossible home lives, here, suddenly was a silvery thread that in and of itself offered at least the possibility of clear-cut success. Teachers were not going to let it slip by easily. These tests had to be passed. It was as clear and beautifully simple as that.

As if to emphasize this, teachers insisted that no student should ever try to impress the examiner, never respond to a question with an answer longer than absolutely necessary, and never be imaginative or cleverly elaborate. It simply wasn't worth risking the grammar and spelling mistakes that might arise as a result. This was advice that the thirty-two kids enrolled in Rochelle's prep class seemed to need, for most walked into the class with neither the grammar nor the spelling to stand a good chance of passing. Rochelle had teamed up with Jeff, another English teacher, to teach the course. As usual, they insisted on punctual attendance, sustained concentration, and completion of all homework, and they made it clear that if a student wasn't serious about passing the exam then they shouldn't bother enrolling in the first place. At the same time, of course, they began to buoy their students with steady and continual insistence that no one needed to fail, that if they followed instructions and kept a clear head they should all pass with a score at least 75. And sure enough, after a few days of making up lists, drawing charts, and copying sample responses word for word, comma for comma, the kids evolved into a well-trained army unit who saw a problem and responded without even thinking because they had done it so many times before.

Most of them did, anyway. There were one or two kids who had transferred into the school in January who had been overlooked all their educational lives and who were trying desperately hard now to almost no avail. Working on a sample business letter, one boy spent over half an hour on his own address. On the top line of his page he had written "500 Eath Avenue," and the "Eath" had been crossed out and underneath it was "Aith," crossed out, and then underneath that, "Iagth," and then "Eght," and "Eights," and "Aighth," in a long, wobbly column reaching almost a third of the way down the page. "I just don't know how to spell *Eighth,*" he said, giving up at last and putting down his pencil. When Jeff told him to pick another avenue, one with a number he felt more comfortable spelling, like "Sixth," perhaps, or "Third," the boy was so relieved that at first he couldn't believe it. "I can do that? For real?" he said.

Another student, the Latin King I'd come to know named Danny who had been housed in the homeless shelter opposite a jail, had even less chance of passing his RCT. Rochelle asked me to sit with him and help him through some exercises, and for a couple of days we struggled through a spelling drill she had given out. The test was simple enough. Neatly typed on a page were sentences using fifty hard-to-spell words written both correctly and incorrectly in parentheses. Students were instructed to circle the correct word. "I can't (believe, beleive) you" was the first. "I would like a (recommendation, reccommendation)" was the second. It was here that Danny stopped.

"I would like a recollection?" he guessed, panicked and embarrassed. "A relocation?" "A recharge?" Farther down the page "exaggeration" became "extermination," "pronunciation" "produce," "gradation" "graduation," and "discipline" "disciple." He had a particular problem with "advertisement," and even when I finally read it out for him he remained baffled.

"It's the long version of 'ad,'" I told him. "The things you see on TV for beer and cars."

"Hmm. That's not a word I use," he mused as he gently copied the word down into his notebook. I suggested we skip over the spelling and focus on the reading instead but, oddly composed even after all this failure, Danny insisted. "No, no, I've got to learn."

I was surprised when the same calm began to surround me as I crouched by his desk and continued to work through the sentences. It drifted down around us and united us there, over in the corner of Rochelle's classroom, so that time passed without either of us noticing. Soon Danny was spelling out the words, audibly tracing each syllable and waiting until he reached the end before leaping to a vaguely synonymic guess. We got to number 22 "Tom is a (villian, villain)" by the time the class finished.

Out in the corridor, though, the realities of his larger world came flooding back. When I asked him how his vacation had been he told me he had been thrown out of his shelter for arguing with the cook and that he'd spent over a week on the street before being forced back into a group home up in the Bronx. "I don't like the place neither. It reminds me of a jail facility," he told me.

"Why?" I asked.

"Because it reminds me of a jail facility."

"But why?"

"Because it does. I used to make nine hundred dollars a day!" he spat, his nose tilted over to the right as though suddenly unhinged the way it always did when he got angry. "Nine hundred dollars a day! That's the kind of kid I am—I used to have so much, and now I don't got nothing. Nothing! And all these people do is talk," he said then, making a sweeping gesture with his arm that encompassed teachers, counselors and students. "Talk talk talk talk talk."

I had seen Danny's anger before, and even an hour earlier would probably have responded with the same sympathy as I always had. But having just worked so intimately with him, I didn't feel my usual need to absorb it all. For a moment his anger seemed almost inappropriate, as if this was neither the place nor the time for it. And it was at that moment that I first understood the position teachers occupy in relation their students. By approaching the kids in strict thirty-eight-minute intervals, teachers like Rochelle managed to skirt the desperation that was on the verge of engulfing Danny right then and were able to focus instead on a finite but concrete attempt at improvement. If even a successful interaction didn't eradicate the conditions of his life, it meant that today at least Danny learned the meaning of the word "advertisement" and maybe felt a little better about reading and writing and spelling in general. It allowed Rochelle a sense of accomplishment too, I realized. Hope, that most elusive of qualities, was ever around the corner if you tailored your expectations to the reality at hand.

Besides, Danny was a particularly hard case. If there was only the slimmest of chances that he would ever pass his RCTs and graduate from high school, then there were plenty of other students who were beginning to show clear signs of progress. Rasheem had come back at the beginning of January lonely and worn but relieved that the pressure to be happy had lifted. At least now things were back to normal and he could be unhappy with immunity; he could even turn his dissatisfaction into an entertainment in West Side's own version of that always ominous question: What did you do over the holidays? He wasn't due to graduate that summer. He still had eighteen months at least, even at West Side's accelerated pace. But he was determined to pass his English RCT, and after spending the first few days of Rochelle's class griping and complaining and insisting that he had taken it before and passed, he buckled down and began working with impressive concentration. A week later, after he'd practiced on close to fourteen test papers, it became clear he would pass. Surprisingly, Michelle also had to take the English test. She had passed all her other RCTs before falling in with the wrong crowd at her previous school, and had even taken the more advanced Regents tests in both global and American history, tests that were not offered at West Side. But for some reason she had never taken her English. Rochelle was delighted to have Michelle in her preparation course and used her more as an assistant than anything else, having her quietly circle the room and help out other students with random spelling and grammar questions.

Even Cristy started coming to school more regularly when she realized she needed to pass American history in order to graduate in June. She still had her job in the movie theater, and she had almost no spare time. But the prospect of failing the exam terrified her. If she passed she would be the first in her family to complete high school and only her teacher Ann's rigorous insistence that she memorize a method of essay structure and lists of vocabulary words seemed to keep her calm and on track. Whenever I saw her she was holding a sheaf of American history fact sheets in the same way she used to carry round Neta handouts. I was as caught up in the drive to get kids through their exams as anyone, so I spent a fair amount of time with her, devising ways of memorizing concise definitions of terms like "amendment," "Constitution," and "Bill of Rights."

By the second week of school even Ed's Family Group began to seem like a tutorial. He bought himself a packet of colored chalk and took to drawing maps on the blackboard for the global exam, the most difficult of the six. Out of the blue he would pop questions to Emilio and James, who were due to take both global and American history; he would pose science questions to Nicole, and because his talent with numbers gave him the ability to do long strings of equations in his head, he peppered his math students with endless problems. The idea was to maintain the focus for as long as possible, both inside Family Group and throughout the school. Kids who didn't have classes were encouraged to stay home, and xeroxed tests from years gone by were scattered all over the desks in most classrooms, across the table in the seventh-floor lobby, and in the lunchroom. By the time the minicycle was halfway completed the kind of clear-minded enthusiasm that only a finite project can allow actually seemed to be spreading.

It was true that it was hard to keep things interesting. With less than three weeks to prepare, there was little room for diversion, and by the end of the second week the constant repetition of facts and methods and theories was starting to take its toll. It was grueling for Stewart to go over and over the process of photosynthesis and the balance of the inner ear when what he really wanted to do was take the kids out to an empty lot somewhere and show them what biology was really about. And even Rochelle and Ann started to long for the broader vistas of real knowledge. David was having less of a hard time, perhaps because his math classes were always more or less like an RCT prep, fast and jivey. He had even made up a rap song to keep his kids entertained: "I can't rap, I can't dance/ Put me with a fly girl and I don't stand a chance/ Go to Macy's but my clothes are whack/ I'm just a white boy who wants to be black/ I'm just a white boy who wants to be black." It was exactly the kind of thing that infuriated teachers like Rosa. But the kids loved it and loved him and, in part because they didn't want to disappoint him, they settled down to surprisingly sustained periods of work as the examination date approached.

There were some kids, of course, who didn't show up to the preparation classes with anything like regularity. Until now this might not have mattered so much, because any student who had showed even the slightest inclination to take an RCT had been encouraged to do so. But this year was to be different. The underperforming-schools list was on everyone's mind, and the open-door policy had been at least in part responsible for the school's abysmally low test scores. Besides, the low results of previous years had been depressing. They undermined the faith of those teachers who wanted to be able to rely on some empirical standards of success and failure, and this year teachers agreed to submit only the names of those students who had worked hard enough to have at least a small chance of passing.

Naturally, there were plenty of exceptions. In a meeting a week before the exams, staff members agreed that any student with enough credits to qualify as a senior should be eligible to take the test, whether or not they had turned up for their prep classes. And though there was also some question about whether students over the age of twenty should be allowed the same exemption, hours of meetings and sometimes quite heated debate produced a consensus that most of the staff could live with. In the end only the deadbeats, the chronically absent, and the downright destructive were not permitted to take the test.

Only Ed had argued that any kid who showed up willing to sit through two or three hours of test-taking deserved to be given the chance—even to fail. It wasn't that he didn't understand the teachers' point of view, he said. He agreed that procedure and policy were important, and he wanted West Side off the underperforming-schools list as much as anybody. But he couldn't understand a process that would reward a student who hauled himself to West Side to take a frightening and important exam by rejecting him. Because nothing anybody said seemed to change his mind, the teaching staff had spent days concocting projects that would take him uptown or to the Bronx or to Brooklyn while exams were being taken. But whether in childish ignorance of their desire or because of true determination to be there, Ed had always brushed their suggestions aside. On the day of the first exam he did so again; ignoring a last-minute request that he drive up to Columbia University to look into an offer of free computers, he took the elevator down to the lobby, and settled himself in at a table that had been specially set up in the corridor.

From an organizational point of view, Ed's presence there made the orderly progression of test-taking practically impossible. Faced with a student who wanted to take a test, he was simply incapable of sticking to the outlined procedure. After all, if he turned them away, where else would they have to go? "Walk-ins," he called them, and after listening to various excuses as to why they hadn't been able to show up before, he almost always wrote out a replica of the yellow cards that had already been handed out to those officially permitted to take the test. Then he assigned them to whichever room seemed to have the most space and wished them good luck.

As a result, the phone in the lobby started to ring off the hook with requests for more students in a room, or for less, for different proctors, more pencils, and more question-and-answer sheets. Charyl spent the next hour and a half traveling up and down in the elevator, bringing Ed frantic messages that room 709 was packed, that one of the proctors was having a temper tantrum, that room 1014 was empty, and that at least half of the kids were in rooms that they weren't supposed to be in. "Remember, their answer sheets are waiting for them in their assigned rooms, Ed, nowhere else," she reminded him when the next face presented itself in front of the table. "And no *one* else. You can't just let in every kid with a story, Ed. We talked about this. It was all agreed, remember?"

Ed nodded his head like an unconvinced but chastised schoolchild, and for a time he seriously set himself the task of turning the next ineligible student away. But it was hard for him to communicate with his students in the narrow, more objective field of teacher to student, and slipping into the far broader approach of one human being to another, he couldn't turn anyone away.

It was 9:30 or so before things finally started to settle down. By then the sheets Ed had been given were a mess. Room numbers had been moved and substituted, and names had been added and then crossed out and then added again underneath in an array of fruit-scented crayons that had somehow found their way onto the table. But upstairs I had never heard the school so quiet. On that first morning both American history and English were being taken, and by 9:45 most of the rooms on the seventh floor were filled with students hunched over their officially numbered answer sheets. Occasionally a teacher would tiptoe along a corridor with a fistful of newly sharpened pencils or accompany a student to the bathroom or replace a proctor who needed a break. Because no one was allowed to proctor a test in the subject they taught, a group of English and history teachers had gathered in the one empty classroom from which they could monitor the progress of their students through the open doors of their exam rooms.

For all their emphasis on a kind of measured professionalism, their anxiety for their students right then was clear. The atmosphere reminded me of a hospital, to tell the truth—an afternoon on a ward when an operation was taking place, each teacher concerned primarily for their own kids, but delicate and sensitive enough to inquire about other people's charges as well. English teachers politely read through the history exam, commenting on the essay subjects and clucking at some of the more difficult questions on the Constitution, while history teachers tried to console English teachers over the potential confusions they could see in section 2 of the exam. Gathered together, sipping coffee and speaking in lowered voices, they allowed themselves, this one time, the luxury of publically empathizing with the complete kid: there was talk of how a certain student's mother had just been sent away, of how another had run away from home and then had no place to study, and how a third was struggling with the effects of a recent abortion. On the corridor reserved for special-ed students, a teacher was trying not to even think about the circumstances surrounding two of her students whose homes had recently been burned down. Because of learning disabilities these students were allowed to spend as much time as they needed to take the test. Some spent all day in an exam room, returned home at 4:00, and then started again the next day. And as I sat in the seventh-floor lobby, waiting along with the teachers, I remembered that Ed's son Javier had done just that. It had taken him three days to complete his English RCT. It was one of his greatest triumphs, Ed had told me proudly, a supreme act of determination and control to return doggedly day after day, painstakingly spending the first seven-hour session writing a 250-word story, the second writing a business letter, and the third a simple, one-page essay. It was what allowed him to graduate at the age of nineteen, and I wondered then if any of the teachers knew the story and, if they did, how they resolved the questions it raised about the parameters of their professional roles and how much influence they could ultimately hope to have.

Rochelle, for one, understood that there was no way to stop the world from invading even the most protected and rigidly circumscribed classrooms. Back when she was still teaching elementary school she used to give out words for her students to fit into sentences, but she had stopped after one morning; she had chalked the word "bulletin" on the board, and a kid had written, "My friend Raffie got shot and died with a bulletin his heart." I made a mental note to ask Rochelle more about it later that day, but I was as nervous about how the kids had done as anyone and forgot until three anxious hours later, when the last of the students' exams had been collected. By then, and no doubt in an attempt to break the tension, the English department had set up long tables laden with bagels, cream cheese, crackers, cranberry juice, and even a chilled bottle of sparkling apple cider, in order to mark their papers.

All of the English teachers were there. Sitting around the tables pushed together in the center of the classroom, they were as focused on reading the exams as their students had been on writing them. By the time I arrived they must have done about fifty, and except for the borderline cases, which were read by two or three teachers, and the occasional groan of disappointment when a favorite pupil failed or yelp of victory when another passed, they mostly worked through their papers in silence.

The exams had been separated into three piles: the business letter, the essay, and the composition. Every now and then a teacher would straighten up a pile and read out a batch of scores so they could be entered on the official score sheets by Rochelle, who, as head of the English department, was in charge of recording the students' final grades. She nodded wordlessly when she heard that Michelle had scored a surprisingly mediocre 68 but slowly cheered up as it became clear that the majority of the students in her class had passed.

Slowly the bottle of cider emptied, and the plates of bagels and cheese thinned, and it wasn't until at least another hour had passed that Susan broke the calm quiet of orderly progression by succumbing to the exhaustion provoked by such a huge emotional chore. On the whole the kids in her RCT class had done fine. But she had been confronted with a series of surprising failures that afternoon as well. The first line of one of the papers she had read was, "The best think I learn and school." Another had been titled "Hight School and What It Done for Me." And when one student wrote, "I can do anything if I put all my mine to it," Susan crumbled.

"Why do we tell them that?" she burst out. "Why do we insist on telling them that everything and everyone turns out good in the end and that success is always possible. Why lie? You can't do anything in the world if you really put your *mine* to it. You can't." The rest of the room was silent. Perhaps she had let herself be too affected by the fact that only just over half of the kids who took the test had passed. I couldn't help thinking, though, as I looked around the room at the averted glances and wan grimaces, that the other teachers simply didn't want to consider the world behind the failures right then and that, at least predominantly successful for once, they wanted an afternoon to relish it. I thought of Javier again, and tried to imagine the path that in a matter of months led him from his greatest victory, graduation, to his greatest defeat. "Only put my mine to it," Susan said again as she straightened her pile of failed compositions. "The best think I learn and school."

20

AS AN OUTSIDER I hadn't been allowed to attend Sandra's final Neta "blessing" ceremony. But she promised to describe it in writing for me over the holidays, and the first time I saw her in January she handed me a neatly folded piece of lined paper almost completely covered with her large, rounded script.

> When I got blessed into the Association Neta I felt like if I was reborn. That I have a purpose in life and I stand out as a person who's fighting for something in life. I got blessed at 11:20 P.M. I will never forget that night. As my head or first stood in front of me reading a chapter from the Bible with my right hand on one side of the Bible and my beads on the other side, he kept reading. Then he recited the words of The Association with such grace, hope and pride, and with all the respect in the world I agreed to take the Neta association into my heart, my mind, life and home. So now when anybody asks me am I a Neta, I gladly say Yes, until I die,
>
> By Sandra Quintana, 100% de Corazón.

She had had no trouble learning the bylaws and prayers for her Neta test. She had studied for so long that she knew most of the group's prayers and historical incantations by heart, and she knew the history of their founder, Carlos Torres Illiarte, well enough to be versed not only in the facts but in the controversies too. American history was something else, though. She hadn't been coming to school much since the beginning of the new year and had made it to only two preparation classes. But she had shown up at school on the day of the RCT, and, finding Ed seated at the desk in front of his stacks of ready-to-use yellow cards, she had almost managed to sneak by. The test would go fine, she'd told him—wasn't he always saying the test was easy? Why didn't he ask her a question right then, any question. But just as Ed was thinking of one Charyl had arrived at his side again.

"How many credits do you have, young lady?" she'd asked.

"Seventeen."

Charyl hadn't bothered to respond. Sandra had at least two more years of school and with a sidelong glance at Ed, Charyl sent her away.

There had been a couple of other examples like that in Ed's Family Group. Saying he was sick, James hadn't shown up for his global history test and had failed his American history by just two points; Dayna had passed English but failed science, and Maria had failed everything. But most kids in Ed's Family Group had done well this time. Michelle's 68 in English had passed her, Rasheem had scraped by with 59, and though I had been sworn to secrecy until the results were validated by Albany, I couldn't resist telling Cristy that she had passed her American history. "Tha's it—tha's it, I'm outta here!" she yelled. "Just a few more months," I said. "Just a few more weeks!" she replied. It was a summation she seemed to take literally, because from then on her attendance dropped off to its former, sporadic level. At least she worked when she wasn't in school: her regular shift ran from 2:00 to 11:15 five nights a week, and they had recently started asking her to work double shifts over the weekends. That meant that she was at the theater an average of sixty hours a week. And perhaps because she needed only two more credits to graduate, Ed never gave her too much grief.

Cristy hardly ever saw Sandra these days and didn't have much news of her, except that despite all the ceremony and warnings and direfully serious oaths they had taken, her marriage to Rankin hadn't worked out. It was a case of lapsed good intentions, I think. Although Sandra and Rankin had the strongest desire to remain *hermanito* and *hermanita* together forever, she was simply too much for him to take, and no amount of promising was going to change that. I had spent a fair deal of time with the Chapter 6 Netas by then, so I wasn't surprised to learn that nothing happened, disciplinarily speaking, when the marriage collapsed. None of the beat downs or *sesións* or other "consequences" that Ramón had threatened before their marriage, or even any bead-stripping or public humiliation—nothing—especially not to Sandra, who had become such an active and central figure up at PS 143. "She one of the really strongest *hermanitas* we have up here—for real," El León had told me admiringly before a meeting one evening.

In fact everyone in the governing junta knew that Sandra had moved in with a new man from the Bronx soon after her "divorce." He was no more than a boy really, a fifteen-year-old name Jose, whom Sandra had chosen, she told me, because "although he's at that age where you start to experiment and make decisions and form your character, he's under my influence and is gonna make the decisions that please me."

When she wasn't with the Netas, Sandra seemed to be leading her life the way adoring housewives do everywhere: shopping, cleaning, and cooking for her man and his family, as well as—eternally, it seemed—washing and drying and folding his clothes. But she loved living away from it all, she said, way up there where she didn't know anyone and could go out to the deli, the pizzeria, or the video store (all right there on the block—she couldn't believe the luxury) in flip-flops and with her hair up, without having to worry if anyone would see her. Sandra was the first to admit that the apartment, the downstairs unit of a two-family house, was crowded, but it was a beautiful place, and it didn't bother her to have to share the sofa with Jose out in the living room while his mother and little sister slept in the bedroom next door. "His mother adores me too," she said. "First because I am eighteen and I got him back in the basketball team and off of the streets, and second because I know where he is twenty-four seven and I have all the phone numbers of all his friends and the clubs where he hangs out, and if anything is happening to him everyone knows to call me."

Shortly after moving in she'd even sorted out the problems the family had been having with the landlord. For years, he had been ignoring their complaints about leaking pipes that dripped down into their closet whenever it rained, ruining their clothes, as well as their requests for him to replace two broken windows, to fix the unreliable heater, and to bring in an exterminator. Once Sandra had moved in he had even started hinting threateningly about raising the rent, which terrified Jose's Spanish-speaking mother. Then, one afternoon when Sandra was in the bedroom folding laundry, she saw the landlord get out of his car and walk upstairs to his apartment with a well-dressed woman who wasn't his wife.

Sandra ran into the bathroom and put her ear to the pipes, which she already knew carried sound far more loudly than was comfortable for either tenant or landlord, and listened as grunts and groans and the steady thumping of a headboard reverberated through the metal. Five minutes later Jose's mother called Sandra back into the bedroom, almost out of her mind with the excitement of existing, suddenly, smack in the middle of a real-life soap opera. Pointing out the window, she clapped her hand over her mouth as they watched the landlord's wife climbing the stairs to the house. The other woman made it out the back door, pulling on her clothes as she went. But the next time the landlord came down to complain, Sandra took him aside and quietly told him that she knew what was gong on "up there with that other lady." If he continued to harass the Nuñez family, she went on, she would be forced to have a chat with his wife. He hadn't been down since—hadn't even called to complain when they'd had a party to celebrate Jose's sixteenth birthday a month or so later.

As far as Cristy was concerned, it was the move to the Bronx that had cut the remaining ties between her and Sandra. The apartment had no phone, and though Sandra still had her beeper, it was rare that she returned her messages and rarer still for her to initiate an attempt at communication. Cristy couldn't even rely on seeing her at West Side anymore because the trip to the school from Jose's apartment took an hour and a half: a walk, two buses, and a train. And when Sandra did come in to Family Group, Cristy was so often hurt at her friend's failure to return one of her beeps that she would end up pretending to be so involved with a piece of homework or a bottle of nail polish that she didn't even notice her.

For her part, Sandra insisted that it was Cristy who was too busy for friendship these days. "Cristy's changed," she once acknowledged. "She always busy with work." However proud Cristy was of her job and however happy she was to be working hard and to be able to help her mother our with the rent, which, at last, was beginning to have an impact on their relationship, Sandra didn't think much of the move. Perhaps she really was just jealous, the way Cristy said she was, but she only snorted when I mentioned the movie theater in her presence and every now and then added a drawn-out, unimpressed "Yeeah" before quickly changing the subject.

Whatever Sandra said, though, it was Cristy who beeped all the time, even from work when the movie was playing, and Sandra who only ever called back when she felt like it. Such an imbalanced friendship couldn't last, no matter how long its history, and unless it was an emergency, when she still believed Sandra would drop everything and be there, Cristy began to accept the fact that she could no longer count on her old friend. And when she met a man—a thirty-one-year-old, doe-eyed Puerto Rican named Ray who hated gangs and thought they were childish, things only became more complicated between her and Sandra.

"I tell you, Tina, we had so much fun before, it was like we were sisters, and now I don't got time and she don't got time and when I got time she don't got time and when she got time I don't got time," she said. Then, a little sadly, as if referring to an unwanted consolation prize, Cristy added, "See this?" And in the middle of Ann's history class Cristy pulled down a corner of her T-shirt to reveal a love bite on her neck. "My mother hates it. On the shoulders is OK, she said, but not on the neck—never on the neck—too tacky." As casual as could be, suddenly, she waved her fingers back and forth in front of her face so that the polish caught the light and, sighing slightly, told me she was exhausted. Completely exhausted, she said, adding that she wouldn't get any sleep that night either, because she was working until eleven and then had to go straight to her new boyfriend's house.

He was the first man she had been interested in since Jonell, and at thirty-one he was much older than she had been used to. "They teach you better," she said that day at lunch, a strange, new, uncharacteristically enigmatic smile playing across her lips. "He make me feel so good," she said. "He wants to see me all the time. He wants me like, right there. And it feels right lying with him. He don't make me feel bad or uncomfortable or anything and he tells me, 'Oh you so pretty, you so pretty,' every day—all the time—I get embarrassed!"

She had met him two weeks before at a cousin's baby shower, where they had sat next to each other in a circle while the mother-to-be had opened her gifts. Quick to laugh and extremely polite, Ray gave no hint to suggest that he could be violent. Several years before, however, he had nearly killed a man in a drunken fight and had been arrested and thrown in jail for almost five years. He still had nine years of parole to do. But for the past six months he had been a model parolee—staying sober and keeping quietly to himself most of the time, venturing out only for meals or small parties with his family. He had even found himself a job as a loading clerk on Thirty-seventh Street, where he was doing well and from which he could walk over at lunchtime and say hi to Cristy and sometimes, on a half day, take her home too.

Cristy was so impressed by him that she had already introduced him to her mother, who'd liked him so much that she'd actually stood up and kissed him good-bye. Shortly after that Ray arranged a party to introduce her to his family. They were walking along Thirty-fifth Street when he had told her this, right outside West Side. And as they passed a short red box-pleated skirt in the window of one of the wholesale stores opposite the school, he said, "You should wear something like that, Cristy, something ladylike and pretty. Sexy. But not too much, you know."

Ray didn't realize the fear he inspired in her at that moment. For all of her experiences up until then—the violence and insecurity that led her to leave Grand Cayman and the difficulties she had had in adjusting to life in New York, her brother's still childish fits of pique, and her mother, always working and never paying her much attention—for all of the difficulties she had overcome, she had never grown out of her deep and irrational fear of wearing a skirt. She had done it only twice before: once at Sandra's wedding and once at a cousin's first communion when she had been eleven. She didn't feel comfortable enough with Ray to tell him any of this, and trying to keep calm she smiled and kissed him good-bye and then walked into West Side only to duck out again once he'd left and beep Sandra. She waited ten minutes for a response, then gave up and went to Family Group and a math class before beeping again. Again she waited. She knew that if she added 911 to her beeper code Sandra would call her right back, but she couldn't bring herself to do it: 911 was for life-and-death situations, for if she were hurt or threatened or found herself in serious trouble with the law. Deflated and panicked and lonely, she walked back into West Side, where she turned to me in desperation and asked: "You wanna help me find a dress, Tina? I would ask Sandra to help but we growing apart, real growing apart like we miles away from each other. She don't even call me back when I beep her no more and that hurts, you know? And now I gotta find this dress. . . ."

The stores along Thirty-fifth Street are all the same, more or less. Wholesale outlets for second-rate clothing retailers, they specialize in cheap black lace, swirly gold evening dresses, and tight black stirrup pants, all covered in staticky dry-cleaning bags. They sell in bulk, mostly, so they have no changing facilities for customers, and the first store we went into wouldn't even show us anything unless we'd buy twelve of the same gown. Irritated and tight-lipped, the too skinny Latina in leopard-skin leggings and high strappy heels stretched her long fingernail to the sign on the window and shook her head: *"Solo ventas al por mayor"* she said, "wholesale only," and then, pressing a little button on the side of her desk, she made the door buzz and ushered us out. But the salesgirl in the second store we visited hadn't had a customer all day and was nice enough to bend the rules and let Cristy try on a black jumper with a matching white shirt in the back of the store, behind a rail of clothes that made a makeshift changing room. The shirtsleeves only just fit around the tops of Cristy's arms, and while she had managed to pull the dress on and even to do the zipper halfway up, it was clearly too tight. Looking at Cristy standing there, barefoot and stiff in front of the full-length mirror, vulnerable the way a girl is only when she is trying something on, both the salesgirl and I tried to be encouraging.

"It's not bad," I said.

"Umm-hmm. One size bigger and it would be perfect—it shows off your beautiful legs so good," the sales assistant agreed. "If you lost two or three more pounds it would be perfect." But the damage was already done. Pulling the clothes rack in front of her again, Cristy mumbled, "Oh, I don't want to go no more. It'd be nice but this mission is stressful. I'm too fat."

I had suggested earlier that we go to Macy's. " Macy's! Those clothes are crazy expensive," she had said, but after trying almost all of the stores on Thirty-fifth Street she finally agreed at least to look around. At first she seemed wary of touching the clothes that hung, unprotected, all around her and absolutely refused to take more than one piece of clothing into the changing room. "We don't even know if we are going to buy anything, Tina," she whispered, as though she were in a church. But she soon started to relax and first peered at the price tags and then lifted items off the rail, calling, "Tina, Tina look at this" when she liked the look of something or "What about it?" when she wasn't so sure. Less than five minutes later she had selected three shirts, all fitted, a black box-pleat skirt, a long, floral-print, soft-pleat skirt, and a short, black, vest-like dress with buttons up the front. All were size sixteen and all were on sale.

She looked good in the box pleat, but a little too much like a Catholic schoolgirl, I thought, because of the way her little tummy rounded out the top and her legs stuck out from the knee underneath; and although the long skirt looked womanly and elegant, it was the midthigh-length dress that transformed her. "I got fat arms. I really do got fat arms. I can't help it. But they look OK in this," Cristy said with a new buoyancy as she turned and twisted in front of the mirror. She smoothed down the sides of the dress, stretched out her arms, swiveled again, and then twisted a little to one side and smiled invitingly. "I like the buttons because then he . . . Well, you know what I'm saying."

That Saturday, the day of the party, she left her mother's house at midday and went straight to the beauty parlor, where she stayed for three hours—an hour and a half just under the dryer to set the ringlets she'd had put in her hair. Beauticians painted three shades of brown on her eyelids, and applied a deep-burgundy lipstick and blush. They even plucked and painted her eyebrows, and though Ray gasped when he saw her and then smiled, at first Cristy felt uncomfortable in her new incarnation. Ray had bought her some shoes as a gift, and they were gorgeous, she said, Italian, ankle-high leather. But their heels were higher than she was used to and the skirt prevented her from striding the way she usually did, jolting her leg back with its hem.

She'd felt awkward at the party too. People were friendly, but she was younger than anyone else and couldn't help but feel out of place. Then Ray introduced her to his oldest brother as his "lovely lady" and she started to relax. She would have counted the evening as one of her best if the worst snowstorm of the entire winter hadn't hit. Standing out on the sidewalk, shivering while Ray tried to talk a tired gypsy cab driver into taking them home, she tried to imagine walking the long blocks through snow and ice in her Italian high heels and her above-the-knee skirt with no stockings. But when Ray wrapped the edge of his not very new, not very insulated, nylon coat around as much of her as he could, she forgot about the chill that blew up her legs, past her waist to her armpits, even forgot about Sandra and the Netas and how she felt that they had never really wanted her there in the first place, and instead just loosened her grip on the world and relaxed. "Everything is going too good for me right now. So good," she told me. "But it's all going kind of quick. Swoosh, you know, like the cars going past on the highway? Swish swoosh swoosh?"

Sandra had not spoken to Cristy for weeks when Ray and she finally met, and Ray concluded almost immediately that Sandra was a bad influence. He could tell, he said, from her manner and her voice and even from her hair, which was hung with silver foil–tipped Neta bead braids at the time. Sandra talked nonstop about a rogue group of Dominican kids who had taken to hanging around outside PS 143. They called themselves DPs—which stood for Dominican Power, Dominican Pride, or Deep Pain, depending on who you spoke to—and wore incredibly intricate beaded *collares* representing the Dominican flag. They were young kids mostly, she said, fifteen or sixteen, poorly organized and thuggish enough to have taken to taunting Netas at the school. There had even been a few street fights, scuffles really, and though Sandra knew that she was giving a bad impression she was so pumped up about a recent clash she'd had with the sister of a DP that she couldn't stop talking about it. I knew what she was like when she got like that.

"Yo—I took off my earrings and ran across the street and I started knocking her," she'd told me once, vividly recalling a similar encounter. "I had a V-neck shirt on, though. A big one and when I went to slam her she held onto my shirt and pulled it off. All my girls were like covering me, whatever, and I'm still hitting her, but really I was trying to stop and put my shirt back on. The guys were like 'It doesn't matter if she fucking leaves you naked, kick her ass!' so I was like, 'Fine.' There I was hitting her: blam! blam! blam! blam! without my shirt: boom! Then my beeper fell and everybody's like 'Sandra your beeper, Sandra your beeper,' but she had me by the hands. They was like, 'wait wait wait—the beeper!' So we stopped, we took like a five-minute break. She picked up my beeper, checked it—it was fine—tunatunk! We started fighting again . . ."

"They didn't like each other and you could tell," Cristy told me after their meeting. "Simple as that. Sandra don't like Ray and Ray don't like Sandra. Ray don't want me to talk to her, you know, cause she is always getting jumped. He knows that if I'm next to her I am not going to let that happen, that I am going to get into it, and then they might hurt me instead of hurting her and that's what he don't want. Sandra don't like him because he don't let me hang out with her. Plain and simple. She think he jealous of her—like he don't want to share me or something."

Soon after that Sandra invited them both to the party she was throwing for Jose's sixteenth birthday up in the Bronx. She had been planning it for weeks. Almost all of the Netas from Capítulo Seis would be there, and some girls from West Side and from "round the way" too. Cristy had been looking forward to it for almost as long as Sandra had been planning it. But Ray didn't want her to go, and in the end she'd stayed in all night watching TV with him, hating her life. When I asked her if she was OK the following Monday, she spun around on her heel and said: "No, I am not OK. A friendship is breaking up here, Tina, and Ray don't care. And Sandra don't care. All she care about these days is the Netas. Netas-Netas-Netas-Netas-Netas! And then Ray! He don't let me go nowhere if it's not with him. He always thinking something bad of me and like I told him I don't accept that. It's like Sandra said, I'm not a player. I've never been known as a player. She's the one that's the player, not me. But still he thinks I'm going to go ahead and do it whenever he isn't around." Cristy's mood changed abruptly when a new friend of Sandra's named Graciella rounded the corner. A green-eyed mulatta with soft curling hair, Graciella had been to the party with her boyfriend, and now she was feigning concern. "Why weren't you at Jose's? I really-really thought I'd see you there?" she'd asked with an anticipatory frown. Cristy didn't say anything for a moment and then lied: "Bin too busy at work," she said. "But was it fun?"

21

THE SCHOOL WAS at its emptiest in late January. Sixty-seven students were due to graduate in February, and many of them were earning their last few credits through internships in offices and schools across the city. Others had moved or found work or had transferred to GED programs or night-school programs. Some, of course, had dropped out or had simply disappeared. In the intimate early-morning space of Ed's Family Group the crowd had visibly thinned. Lucille was gone; Nino, the boy who had been fired from his law office for forging checks, had left for California to hunt down the man who'd molested his five-year-old niece; Tawana, a skinny girl who had spent too much time with a boy who sold guns, had become pregnant and was staying away until the baby was born; Julio was back in Rikers; and Sean hadn't been back since smoking his tainted weed before Christmas.

"It's almost like a campaign. Like a war, " Ed told me once. "You know how you have a war and you fight a campaign and you start with X number of troops and by the end of the campaign—even if you meet your objective—you've gotten Y number killed and Z number wounded plus deserters and everything else? Well, in many ways the school year is like that. You start out and everybody is fresh with ideas and they really want to move on and Lucille is coming to school and she's all nervous about coming to high school and then she sees that she can carry on and then all of a sudden she's gone. Right, that's a Lucille. Then you have someone like James, who doesn't come at all at the beginning and somehow finds his courage on the battlefield and starts fighting round about now. I mean, I could go through the roll book—"

This population shift happened every year, and to fill the spaces West Side almost always ended up recruiting a hundred or so new students. In order to guarantee sustained funding levels, they had to fill the slots before February 10. There were always more applicants than there were spaces, but the constant budget cutting from city, state, and federal sources this year made every administrative decision more fraught. Schools with high-risk populations like West Side were under particular pressure, because under the new rules aid would be distributed not according to the number of students enrolled in a school, but on the basis of average daily attendance. At the beginning of the year 780 students had been registered and yet, with a 70 percent attendance rate, only 575 students routinely came to school. Only those 575 would count, and it made no difference that it wasn't the same 575 every day, or that one way or another every one of the 780 students turned up for an average of 3½ days a week. The tightness of funds meant the Board of Education was playing strictly by the rules: teachers' salaries would be allocated to reflect only the number of students actively participating in the school.

West Side had to take this issue seriously, and to rise to the situation Charyl implemented a series of modest restrictions in the admission policies of West Side. She firmed up the already unofficial minimum age limit of sixteen for any new incoming students and refused to admit any new kids from the Washington Heights and Inwood area because the school had so many kids from there already that they were likely to simply hang out with their friends. She also refused to admit any student over the age of eighteen who didn't have twenty-five credits and at least half of their RCTs already under their belt.

Considering that the vast majority of high school students complete high school when they are eighteen and that those Charyl was considering had only just over half the required 40 credits to graduate, these were not very strenuous restrictions. Even with all his RCTs passed, most schools in the city still wouldn't touch a twenty-year-old with only enough credits to place him at the start of his junior year. No one could argue that West Side wasn't still trying to take up the slack. But the move worried Ed. He couldn't bear the thought that even if they were not "creaming"—the secretive and almost universally denied but extremely common practice of skimming the best students from the top of a group—they were at least beginning to dump the worst kids. One morning I saw him storm down the corridor and accost Charyl right outside her office. Ed does not normally storm anywhere, and there was something incredibly intense about the way he charged, arms half-bent at the elbows, hands clenched, face thrust forward just ahead of his foremost foot, pounding down the hallway. He was holding a student's transcript, pointing and jabbing at it, saying, "Why didn't you let this kid in, Charyl? Look—at one time this boy was brilliant."

"Yes," said Charyl, quietly, her chin slowly rising as she glanced at his transcript. "You're right, Ed. In 1988 he was achieving nineties, but how many years ago are we talking? A lot of years, Ed. And now this particular young man has grown up. He has gone from a ninety to a forty-five. What has happened? Where has he been in the meantime?"

Ed was flabbergasted. He had always had an understanding with the school's previous deans that anyone he thought might benefit from West Side would be admitted, no questions asked. But when he mentioned this now Charyl just grinned. "Yes, but those were gentlemen's agreements, Ed," she said. "And I'm no gentleman. I'm a gentlewoman, and I'm not going for it."

This was just the kind of bureaucratic policy issue that Ed hated to deal with. The matter touched on the core of what West Side was now, as well as what it would become, and he didn't like the bind it put him in. After all, a good 50 percent of his own Family Group would not have been allowed to enter West Side under the new criteria. And while it might be true that Sandra, with only seventeen credits to her name, or Lucille, whose age would have been a problem, had not been succeeding in school, there were plenty of others in his Family Group who were exceeding expectations. Both Cristy and Rasheem had been showing signs of improvement recently, and even Emilio, the twenty-year-old drug dealer and chronic absentee Ed had taken in before Christmas, had started to come to school regularly. Driving down in his sensible, secondhand Honda, he arrived at Family Group right on time every day with a copy of the *Daily News* folded under his arm, and would greet me with the kind of crisp efficiency you would expect from a bank clerk—"Good morning, Tina"—before hitching up his trousers and taking a seat.

Of course, Emilio had been a some-time student at West Side for years, and, like him, most of the newcomers to Ed's Family Group were transfers from other Family Groups within the school. There were, however, some actual newcomers. Carlos, a still puppy fat–encased young Neta who'd been sent to West Side straight from Rikers, was so shy that he blushed whenever I sat anywhere near him and stammered whenever Sandra, his Neta superior, came into the room. Shortly after the RCTs Ed had also introduced a peculiar girl who wore bells around her ankles. From her very first day she had simmered with a visible distrust that her makeup, layers and layers of it, didn't hide. Because her clothes were so tight, her skirt so short, and her leather boots thigh-high, the girls had no choice but to stare at her, eyes thin slits of feminine challenge. The boys all thought it best to simply ignore her. Her name was Alana and her father was a hit man currently operating in Haiti, Ed told me, his eyebrows raised in that "Isn't life curious but I can take it all in my stride" way he had when things genuinely took him aback.

Like Sandra, Lucille, Emilio, and even Rasheem, Alana would never have made it through Charyl's new policy. She was at the school then only because Ed had registered her back in November, before she'd "left town" on a trip. She didn't even have a transcript, and she spent so little time in so many schools that the last three Ed contacted had no record of her at all. Not that there was any doubt that she needed West Side. Family Group might have been hostile, but Ed was welcoming, and she clung to his shadow, trailing around behind him, her ankles as vulnerable as an antelope's above her thin stiletto heels. She had plenty of money, Ed told me, because whenever her father went on a "trip" he left her enough to cover every conceivable emergency. The problem was that they never ended up staying in any one place very long. So as long as she enrolled in an English class, say, and art with Esther and perhaps a math class too, Ed thought he was probably doing her more good than harm by allowing her to drift to school whenever she felt the need for some relatively sane and community-minded company.

The question, though, was how much that kind of help was worth. Alana's life was so unsettled that it was unlikely she would ever rack up anything at West Side but a string of incompletes, and with an increasingly shrinking financial pie, schools that were even perceived to be failing didn't seem to have much of a future. If West Side wanted to continue to provide for anyone at all, it seemed they had to be able to demonstrate their viability in ways more objective than this: "What do we do?! What do we do?! Why don't you just come down here any morning and spend a few hours and see what we do—what miracles occur here," which Ed had screamed into the phone at an education official from upstate who'd called at the wrong moment and mentioned, just a little too blithely, the underperforming-schools list.

Of course, even the best of Charyl's new recruits were not A students; most weren't even average, and though many of them were very bright, they'd all had their share of trouble in the past and had attended at least one high school prior to arriving at West Side. In Ed's Family Group, anyway, Roland, the single new student Charyl had admitted, was certainly eccentric enough to fit in. He was a skinny boy with a dark complexion, and his long, serious face looked even longer because of the way he wore his hair, in dozens of tiny braids that stuck up from the top of his head like tiny palm fronds four or five inches high. Bright and curious and perhaps a little hyperactive as well, he soon became infamous for bringing live reptiles to school with him—iguanas, savannah monitors, and snakes that he kept in a shoe box carried under his arm.

I am terrified of snakes. Phobic about them. And although Roland told me that girls went into his room all the time, and that most of them didn't mind the reptiles as long as they didn't come too near, he had the same kind of sexual insecurities as Rasheem, and I couldn't help but think of them as some kind of evil charm used to scare off unwanted attention. He had dozens of snakes at home, it turned out, all kinds: pythons, boa constrictors, green-necked snakes, king snakes, scarlet snakes, milk snakes, rough green snakes, and garter snakes. The small ones he kept in glass-fronted cages; the big ones he draped over a six-foot-tall imitation tree that was a plastic pole really, with three branch extensions all covered with rope to imitate bark and several green plastic leaves. The snakes were free to slither off at any time. Sometimes when he woke in the morning one would be on the floor, one would be wrapped around the post of his bed, and one would be on the windowsill. Roland always swore that when he left the room they stayed there, wrapped round the tree at the foot of his bed until he came home and gave them the sign that they could move around.

I never believed him, of course, and never went anywhere near his house. Others did, though, and over the years he had developed a reputation as the Doctor Doolittle of the South Bronx. An old lady with a chihuahua had first put the word out that there was a genius living on 165th Street. The dog was having heart trouble, and after looking the animal over Roland had prescribed a monthlong diet of baby food, which had cured him. Since then he had learned how to press on a snake's stomach to feel for mites, how to tempt reptiles of all kinds who had lost their appetite by dipping live mice in castor oil before feeding time, how to more or less accurately tell the age of most animals, and how to bandage, splint, and even plaster broken bones in cats and dogs—all learned from on-the-spot training and the occasional visit to a well-stocked pet-care section of a Barnes & Noble in midtown Manhattan.

In some of his previous schools this obsession with animals had gotten him into trouble, and once he'd had to watch a snake of his, a ball python—so called because of the way it curls up into a ball and then buries its head in the center when it gets scared—being tortured and then killed by other kids at the school. At West Side, however, he quickly became a star. Out in the corridors two or three boys would stop him every day and ask for advice about their own reptiles or just beg to look at his snake, which, for a small fee, he would sometimes uncoil from its taut little knot in the shoe box and display like a crimped and bent plumber's wrench in the stairwell.

I tried my utmost to avoid these encounters, and yet I had to admit it was refreshing to see the way kids like Roland enlivened the school. Perhaps the energy in the place was just a result of the thrusting force of the new year, but I couldn't help thinking it was because of the new students that the elevator walls, bare usually but for a posting of the most recent Knicks scores, were now covered with notices announcing student leadership courses, after-school community-service programs, and even the creation of a Caribbean club. It was interesting to see the effect these new characters were having on the other kids too—even those who Charyl might have thought didn't stand a chance. In Ed's Family Group, Cristy had taken to spending time with a soft-spoken girl named Vicky, who was encouraging her to read a book, and even Rasheem was coming out of his shell enough to inspire some real optimism. While his transformation undoubtedly had more to do with the fact that after years of being shifted from one shelter to another he had finally moved into an apartment, it didn't hurt that in Roland he had suddenly found a friend who brought out the best in him.

Like everyone else coming into Ed's Family Group, Roland had been initially drawn to the crazy magnetism of Maurice. But he was too eccentric to be interested for long in Maurice's constant pursuit of women and eternal weed-smoking and had quickly shifted his attentions to Rasheem, whose nervous energy and wiry enthusiasm echoed his own. Not that their interests were the same. While Rasheem spent most of his time playing the fool, Roland actually enjoyed most of his classes and became a favorite of almost every teacher he had. But their friendship evolved quickly and soon they had staked out a corner in Family Group, where they pushed their desks up close, and chattered to each other for hours in a give-and-take that was unusual at West Side. When they weren't talking about snakes they discussed obscure Japanese comics, and they even invented story lines of their own, which Rasheem would sketch out in his book. These featured bizarre mutants who were able to transform themselves from superheroes to snarling reptiles, back and forth at will. Sometimes they would be so involved in their creation that they would still be talking as they left Family Group together. Stepping out into the hallway, they kept gesticulating wildly, prodding each other to leap from idea to idea as they walked down the corridor.

To cement their new friendship Rasheem asked Roland to accompany him down to his new apartment one afternoon. Rasheem had moved in just after the RCTs, and though he still never mentioned it, I knew this was the first private home his family had lived in for close to four years. It was brand-new, freshly painted, and by chance was located close to West Side, right between the school and the fashionable neighborhood of Chelsea. As the three of us walked toward it, down past the post office and Madison Square Garden and into a more run-down residential district, he spoke about the place as if it were a miracle. We didn't go in when we got there; he could never be sure when his mother would be home, and she forbid her children from bringing anyone around, Rasheem said. But as if to prove that he lived there, he opened the front door to the building with his key and showed us the fresh-looking mailboxes. Then we circled the tall, square-windowed, red-brick towers, taking care not to step on the grass and to stick to the paths. He tried to be as casual and nonchalant as possible, but Rasheem couldn't help boasting about the place every now and then. He simply couldn't believe the amount of space they now shared, he told us at one point, arching his eyebrows and stretching his grin so that he looked even more like one of his cartoon characters than he already did. And as we turned back to school he continued to wondrously comment on everything from the peacefulness of the block to the blue jay that nested in a tree just under his window.

Perhaps because he felt that as a normal boy living in a normal apartment he had to fulfill expectations far higher than those placed on a homeless kid with a half-crazy mother, Rasheem soon managed to find himself a job as well. Brimming with confidence, he simply walked into an art-supply store across the street from his apartment one Saturday morning, showed them his sketchbook, and told them that he would be starting school at FIT in the fall. Although he had only fast-food experience—a couple of weeks in a pizza restaurant and a ten-day stint at McDonald's—he had been hired on the spot and was now being paid thirty-three dollars a day. Up until then and ever since well before Christmas he had been walking around West Side with the same worn and fading orange baseball cap, bursting at the seams with the great clouds of loose hair he was waiting to have braided. So I wasn't surprised to see that the first thing he chose to spend his money on was a fancy new hairstyle—one he seemed to have created in homage to his new friend, Roland, who preferred twisties to braids and who liked to make a drooping palm frond with a pile of them on the back of his head.

Maurice didn't much approve of Rasheem's new hair, or his job. ("Tha's buggin', man," he'd said when Rasheem told Family Group about it. "What you do that for? Tha's not my scene.) He didn't much care for the new kids in the school either. Like Roland, they shared an independence that kept them out of his reach, and because they were older even the girls were harder to impress. Maurice still had an aura about him that held sway over most of the kids in Family Group, but ever since Lenox Avenue there was a hint of insecurity about him that his cavalier machismo couldn't quite hide. No matter what he did, no matter how he tried to woo his once-faithful sidekick Rasheem with promises of women and fly times, he never quite managed to mesmerize him the way he had done before. Even when Maurice took him to a recording studio up in Harlem, Rasheem had refused to be seduced and hadn't stayed long. It was as if, with the arrival of Roland, the joyous elegance of a new apartment, and the pride of a job, Rasheem was finally able to shrug off the burden of struggling under a character so much larger than himself and try to claim his own space instead. And from that day on I watched as strand by strand Rasheem deliberately unwound himself from the sphere of Maurice's influence.

Mostly the extrication process was not very grandiose. Once I saw him become frustrated in an art class because Maurice wouldn't stop talking. Rasheem had thrust his chin over to the other side of the room and said, "I'm sitting over there next time, damn!" And when Ed brought a college recruiter into Family Group a week or so later, Rasheem interrupted a long speech by Maurice to announce that he intended to go to one of three colleges the following September—the Fashion Institute of Technology, Parsons, or the School of Visual Arts—with enough conviction to impress even the recruiter, a jaded West African man in an ill-fitting suit who had about as much enthusiasm for high school students as an average meter maid does for car owners.

Saying, "I gotta get my priorities straight now. I can't be spending no more time with Maurice—he dangerous just to be around with—I got too much else going on," Rasheem even quietly withdrew himself from the Resource Room English and Sequential One Math classes that Maurice had chosen for both of them ("Easy credit, B!") and enrolled in the skill-appropriate classes preferred by Roland. And despite Maurice's increasingly frequent barbs that he was becoming a "herb B—just a no-good skinny-ass herb," Rasheem was suddenly adamant about attending all of his classes. He was excelling in art, of course, easily kept pace with Roland in math and science, and was even up to date with the extra-credit journal Ann had asked each of her Holocaust students to write.

The class was an interdisciplinary, double-period investigation into the causes and outcomes of the Holocaust. The history was taught by Ann and the literature by Rochelle. I had warned Rasheem that both teachers were ruthless about attendance and that if he slipped back into his old ways he would end up not with reduced credit but with no credit at all. He had gone ahead and registered anyway and a couple of weeks into the course Rasheem seemed to be doing fine. He still sat in the back row, and he still shied away from participating actively in discussions, but he kept up with his work and could always be counted on for a relevant fact should the need arise. In Rochelle's class he had even bought his own copy of the book they were studying: *Lord of the Flies.* Ever since she had started teaching, Rochelle had offered her students paperback copies of books at a discount, which she personally subsidized. Because it was usually a studious minority who bought copies, she was surprised when Rasheem raised his hand for one. Only slightly ostentatiously, he nodded his head when Rochelle double-checked that he wanted to spend the $2.50 required. "I hope you got some change, though," he said, letting himself slide back in his chair so that he was almost prone. "I haven't had time to make change from my pay package, and I got nothing but twenties—I lie to you not; twenty, twenty, twenty, twenty, twenty," he said.

The small Signet Classic edition of *Lord of the Flies* was the first nonillustrated book he had ever owned. And although he told me quietly one afternoon out in the corridor, where he was waiting for Roland to come out of his math class, that the book was incredibly boring (he couldn't really see how a group of "England boys—no offense, Tina—stuck on an island" could be anything but), he was steadily reading it anyway, paragraph by paragraph, page by page, chapter by chapter. In all his life, he confessed, this was the first book he had ever read. "I can't be messing up no more. I got no choice. I get along with everyone on the face of this earth when I want to, Tina, and I can get along with my teachers too," he said. Then he strolled downstairs to the street with his new friend Roland to sit on the blue metal pole that stretched across a delivery entrance to the nearby McDonald's. There, Roland would spend hours playing with his snakes while Rasheem flicked through a sample from his rapidly growing collection of comic books. Carefully holding a new issue with just the tips of his fingers lest he dirty it, he scrutinized each page, occasionally pointing something out to Roland before slipping it back into its plastic sleeve and, only half reluctantly, pulling out his copy of *Lord of the Flies*.

22

MANNY HAD NOT been allowed to take his English RCT in the end. Punctuation was his biggest problem, then spelling. With the help of Rochelle and Jeff's careful drilling he would have been capable of passing the test if he had turned up regularly and concentrated. But though he started off the minicycle well and had even attended class regularly for a time, he soon began to drift and seemed more interested in outlining the star-shaped points he had taken to drawing above his 'i's than in making any kind of progress. Giving up a few days before the exam, Rochelle had decided to withhold his yellow entrance card. "Why scrape by with a sixty now when you could get eighty in June?" she'd said, and Manny had looked straight up at her with no particular expression on his face and nodded.

He had been in only sporadically since, and I was on the verge of going up to his apartment to find him again when he shuffled into the back of Rochelle's room one morning, blank and distant and monotone. A while later when I went over to his desk I saw that he'd spent the first twenty minutes of class copying the same three vocabulary words over and over again, on top of themselves, until they became blurred and then unintelligible. Manny's adviser was still giving him a hard time about not being officially registered, and Charyl had gotten in on the act now as well, threatening to stop him from coming altogether if he didn't start to show up more regularly. But that didn't explain the distance Manny seemed to be placing between himself and everything at West Side that day, and when I finally decided to ask him what was wrong he looked up with that confused brow-bent look he had, smiled vaguely, and then returned to his task until, a few seconds later, the paper tore.

Patches of dry, white flaky skin outlined the corners of his mouth and the knuckles of his hand, and his T-shirt was wrinkled and gave off not the thick, sweet smell of prolonged wear but the rancid stink of fear or pain or panic. I asked him again what had happened. He turned and stared out of the fogged, wire-reinforced window, fiddled with a green tassel that hung down from the front pocket of his color-block Polo jacket, and then kicked the floor with the toe of one of his new Nike Uptown's before leaning over to me, intent suddenly, and saying, “Rich got killed yesterday—shot by a kid outside on the street.”

Rich had been like a father to him, Manny told me when Rochelle's class finally finished and we could get outside into the fresh air. His uncle Paco's best friend, he had helped raised Manny back when he was a kid living in shelters, and it had been he who had taught Manny how to use a knife, how to drive and how to steal cars, too. Rich stole every kind, though he preferred the luxury models, Manny said proudly—Lexuses, Jeeps, BMWs—and he had only stopped stealing them when his partner became the subject of a federal investigation. He'd had to lay low then and had spent most of his time at home with his common-law wife and their seven young children. Since Manny's own father had taken up with “the womens” again, rendering the bedroom in his own “crib” out of bounds much of the time, Manny had taken to dropping by Rich's place to spend some time relaxing with Maria and the kids, as he casually gathered tips on everything from picking up girls to hot-wiring Acuras. He often ended up staying for dinner.

Sitting in the coffee shop on the corner of Thirty-fifth Street and Eighth Ave, Manny periodically shook his head, and, in between long bouts of silence, said things like, “He was one crazy guy” or “He was the craziest of all of us niggers.” Once he said: “A lot of people used to test him, you know? When they heard his name?” I nodded and reached for his hand, but he pulled it away and then, as if to protect himself from any further advances, launched into a retelling of the story of Rich's death:

Rich no longer sold on the street. He was what Manny called a “connec” now—a wholesaler. After nearly ten years on the Ave, he'd had beefs with almost everyone out there except Paco and Manny. Recently, though, one man in particular had been agitating him. His name was Fidel, and rivalry between them was inevitable because Fidel sold crack and Rich sold heroin, and disputes always arose between crack dealers and dope dealers. Despite Rich's warnings, Fidel had opened a crack house right on Rich's block, opposite the house where his wife and his kids lived. Rich scoffed and snapped and glared at Fidel whenever he passed, and during an argument had finally punched him in the face in front of his crew. After that, Rich had been so sure of some kind of retribution that he'd given one of the boys who worked for him a walkie-talkie and posted him outside of his apartment, telling him to call as soon as he saw anyone from the crack house approach. But no one ever came. And though Manny had no proof, it seemed too handily coincidental for Rich to be shot dead two days later by a sixteen-year-old stranger. He'd been arrested just minutes after the murder, and word on the street was that the shooter was a gun for hire from the Lower East Side. "A low-life LES punk," Manny said, out for the quick bucks and the easy reputation.

Paco had promised to have the kid "taken care of" in Rikers, but nothing could make up for the fact that Rich was dead. "It was really the first time I ever seened Paco cry," Manny told me. And though he added "For myself, I'm not into crying," there were a couple of times when his nostrils quivered and his mouth trembled so much that he had to clench his top lip with his bottom to keep it still. It happened when he spoke about Rich's daughter, his seventh child, who had been born on Thanksgiving Day last year. "A beautiful child," he said. "And she had a beautiful little beauty spot too, right here under her ear just where Rich had his." When Api found us in the coffee shop it happened again. He'd brought a copy of the paper with a notice of the murder. There was no photograph, and the shooting had occurred so late in the day that the story had only managed to be squeezed into the "Daily Death Toll" column. But like an admirer looking at an ancient religious text or a hieroglyph in a museum, Manny kept his hands down by his side as he leaned over the spread-open paper on the table. Moving only to blink and to pull down the peak of his hat, he stayed like that for far longer than it could have taken him to read the paltry eight-line article.

> A 25-year-old Brooklyn man was shot twice in the head and killed on a Brooklyn street corner after he got into an argument with a 16-year-old Manhattan youth yesterday about noon, police said.

> Julio Delacourt of 222 West 20th Street was arrested and charged with second-degree murder in the shooting of Enrique Payano, who lived at 1936 Jefferson Street in Brooklyn. Payano died near the intersection of Jefferson and Knickerbocker Streets in the Bushwick section, where the two began to argue, police said. The shooting is under investigation.

"Nineteen thirty-six Jefferson—that's him," Manny said, reading out Rich's published address and then turning to stare out the window. "That's Rich—Enrique Payano." It was as if he'd never heard the name before and was rolling it around like a fine wine in his mouth, tasting it, testing it: "Enrique Payano."

Api was becoming embarrassed. Ever since he had come in with the paper he had been self-conscious and clumsy in the face of Manny's sorrow, which was almost palpable by then and strangely intimidating. Perhaps because he felt that the correct way to honor his friend's grief was to eulogize its object, he began to tell an uncharacteristically chatty story about how both Paco and Rich would have been millionaires soon and how they had planned to buy a big house. Big enough for their women and all their kids and three cars for themselves and Manny too.

It had all started with Paco's half-brother, Api went on, bouncing his knees up and down under the table. He still lived in Puerto Rico, and one night when he had been in Brooklyn on a visit, Paco had let him drive a recently stolen Mercedes. Everything had been fine until Paco pulled a gun from the waistband of his pants, wound down the window, and started saying how he was going to "spray some niggers." His half-brother panicked. Clinging hard to the steering wheel, he shouted at Paco to put the gun away, and when Paco started to laugh as they approached a group of shorties on the corner, his brother slammed his foot on the gas peddle, causing the car to lurch forward and Paco to slip and shoot his own leg, leaving him with a wound that would eventually develop gangrene, lead to the loss of his leg, and to a negligence case against the hospital so watertight that in an attempt to secure his case a firm of lawyers had already given him a down payment on his final settlement.

"And you can't even tell he's missing a leg nowadays, though," Api boasted. "His living room is all filled with weight machines like a gym and he's trained so hard that he walks normal now. All they had to do was wait for the money," he said, and then suddenly remembering where he was and what had happened, he looked across to Manny for some kind of acknowledgment. Manny didn't even nod. Bending and rebending a red-and-white-striped coffee stirrer against the tabletop, Manny said, "Rich died in the emergency room in the hospital, not out on the street. And he weren't shot in the head neither. It was body shots that got him." Then, after asking to borrow six dollars so that he could go see a movie and "distract myself from my thoughts," he wandered out to the subway, leaving me to sit there embarrassed at my impotence, like Api, I suppose, and stuck with the image of him slumped in Rochelle's class, attempting to copy down words from the blackboard: Thrust. Chortle. Pristine. . . .

Rich wasn't the first person Manny knew who had died in Bushwick, even since I had met him. One particularly harried day a few months before, I had run into him in the hallway and casually asked how he was, only to have him shrug, look away, and answer, "My friend died. Car crash. Skull peeled back and his brains poured out into his hoody." He had known ten people who had died violently, he said, or perhaps twenty, and walking around Bushwick with him a few days after Rich's death, I realized why. Though once a vibrant residential community, its tree-lined side streets now led onto dismal avenues whose most elaborate displays were the liquor-store signs lit by a series of alternately flashing light bulbs, half of which were out. There were bodegas with soot-dimmed yellow awnings and the occasional Chinese take-out place with two layers of bullet-proof glass between the server and the customer, but most of the other small stores were for sale or for rent. Instead of the billboards of even marginally better off neighborhoods—the bright green ads for Newport menthol cigarettes and the red-and-white Cop Shot alerts—elaborate murals eulogizing dead young men decorated practically every block. The homicide rate in the area was such that the neighborhood was almost colorful.

It had been Rich who had painted most of these murals, and we had come to take a tour of his work. Earlier in the day Manny had given me a lecture as to how to behave and, worried for my safety, he had focused mostly on what I should not do. This included trying to talk to any of those kids out there on the Ave about getting jobs and going to school, the way I did with him, because they were "bad kids" and wouldn't understand it the way he did. So I kept quiet as Manny thrust his hands into his pockets and clicked his removable gold caps up tight against his front four teeth and talked "shop" with the other kids out on Knickerbocker. Manny wore his mourning with a straight-backed formality, and as if in respect for his loss the chat was low-key and reverential. Rich's reputation was such that even the older dealers, who otherwise wouldn't have given Manny the time of day, sauntered over to the shorties' corner to express their condolences. When they turned to look at me questioningly, Manny's explanation that I was there to see Rich's work seemed to appease even the most suspicious of them. And soon we were on our way again, visiting one after another of Rich's murals.

Sprayed against metal doorways and brick walls and corrugated iron fences, there were all kinds around. Apart from the official memorials, there were more casual "Rich loves Maria 4 ever" and "MSD," scribbled in green spray paint, in just the same way as I had seen it painted on the elevator doors in Manny's building. But Rich seemed to favor great wall-sized paintings, and what struck me most about these exaggerated, brightly colored images was that, apart from one which read "He who done this must pay," they seemed utterly accepting of the wasteful deaths they were eulogizing. Though there was a sense of formality, and therefore of dignity about them, they seemed to laugh at death rather than suffer under it. We passed a garage door almost entirely covered by a blond-haired, potbellied angel with intricately feathered wings hovering over a corpse; holding out his hand to the viewer as if he were begging, he giggled. Another, on a cinder block wall, had the name Gordo (Fatty) emerging from the smoke of an exploded bomb. It wasn't a worryingly violent type of bomb, though, but the kind Buster Keaton used to run up against, or Charlie Chaplin—a round black ball with a curly string fuse sticking out of the top. They appeared in most of his murals I noticed, these bombs, though this was the only one I saw that had exploded, and only the words "Peace" and a bloody splat of "RIP" in the corner reminded the viewer of the somber finality of Gordo's end. Even the pair of praying hands wrapped around with a golden banner that read *"En las Manos de Dios"* were painted in an outrageous Porky Pig pink.

Walking past each of these murals, Manny remained resolutely stiff. Like a guard in an art museum or a visitor at a wake, he kept his hands clasped in front of him, his back straight, his pace measured. His muted sadness had struck me as an affectation at first, but I now began to realize that if the way he was acting was stilted and formal, then it was because he was imitating the only way he'd ever seen the emotion expressed before—in the overly mournful, restrained sadness of soaps on TV. And as we walked past Rich's irreverent eulogies, I began to sense that Manny was looking for other, more meaningful responses to adopt. He searched the patterns of spray-painted strokes, occasionally adding a name—"Yeah, that was Tootsie" or "Rafael Raffy—I remember him, he was MSD"—as if the recognition might summon up something more profound, or even distracting, than the empty finality of death. But despite all his training on the Ave, it was clear that Manny had not yet mastered the art of "keeping it real" to its conclusion, and was still unable to shrug off death the way Rich had so clearly advised. Like a man listening so hard for a punch line that he misses the joke all together, Manny ended up leaving most of Rich's murals empty-handed, even more confused than he had been before.

We finally stopped in front of the biggest mural we had seen so far. This was what Manny had really wanted me to see. Some of the kids on the Ave had combined their resources to raise the one thousand dollars needed to hire a professional artist from Manhattan to eulogize Rich. Parts of it were still wet. It took up half of a long block and was as elaborately whimsical as it was huge: African American angels with huge Afros and flowing pink robes danced across the Milky Way, past variously colored planets and huge glowing stars and the names of loved ones—Mom and Dad, Eddie, Paco—as the entire parade moved ineffably toward a giant floating red heart emblazoned with the words "Rich and Maria. Love is Forever." Just beyond this, at the end closest to us, was a vivid, biblically styled portrait of Rich's head on a platter of gold streaked with blood. His face was oval, framed like an acorn by tufts of black hair, and he wore a pencil mustache and a wavering, vaguely amused expression on his rather untrustworthy, rosebud lips. Above this floating face the word "Imagination" hung like a helmet, and above that was the legend "Within my stars I am still living! Nothing can stop me. Rich MSD. God bless."

As oblivious to the tongue-in-cheek jab at immortality as he had been to the more slapstick approach in Rich's own work, Manny stood beneath this mural as upright and erect as before. "I tell you though," he said somberly, after a time. "Rich kept it real all the way. His whole life he kept it real. He had fun and all that. He had kids. Damn." Then he turned and started to walk away, his hands in the pockets of his dirty Guess jeans, his T-shirt hanging out of the back of the same blue-and-gray checked jacket that he'd been wearing all week.

He didn't say another word until a homeless woman with a child in tow got on the train halfway back to Manhattan. She was standing at the opposite end of the car from us, asking for money and speaking theatrically about God and how she wasn't a crack addict but just a good Christian mother down on her luck. But even if she hadn't interrupted herself constantly to shout at her kid, Nat, it would have been clear that she was high on something from the way she scratched and picked and scraped at her face with her fingers. "Sit up straight, Nat!" she shouted down the car. "Nat, will you damn well sit up!"

Manny shook his head. "With the kid going up and down behind her?" he said quietly. "She should have left it home baby-sitted." Then, as if this little girl named Nat finally shook him free of his muted formality, he sat up in his seat and started to talk about a dog he had bought last summer, a puppy, a baby Rottweiler that he had dreamed of training and loving and being loved by in return. The whole experiment had failed, though, and he laughed now at his innocence in believing it could ever have been otherwise. "I tried to teach it, but that damn dog was so dumb I swear—every morning when I seened where he pissed I smackeded it hard across the face, smack smack so he could feel it. But he never learned," he said. "Never even learned to piss on that damn sheet of newspaper! All summer I had that mutt. All summer, and I ended up throwing it out, selling it for fifty dollars when he bit my Guess jeans, kid. Sold it, kid. Threw it away for fifty dollars for some dogfight round my way." He laughed again and then scanned the Brooklyn landscape for a couple of seconds before starting to talk about beating up women in general and his cousin Lazarus' sister in particular. She was out of control, he said, "Getting into this person's car and that person's car and sleeping around even though she's only thirteen. Lazo should have lumped her—she ready for it. I lumped my sister when she started giving me lip," he said. "Smack, just like with the mutt." Passengers in the train were squirming by then, looking down at the floor and trying their hardest not to listen, and perhaps to stop them from judging Manny, I told him that I thought he didn't really mean any of the things he was saying and that he was just expressing his anger over Rich's death. He looked surprised.

"Rich's death? Nah. That's got no effect on me. Maybe I'm gonna think about it a little for a couple more days but nothing really," he said.

23

IN MY NAÏVETÉ I had imagined that perhaps Rich's death might be the catalyst Manny needed to make the leap from the street to legitimate employment. If his mentor could die, then surely so could he. We had talked about it countless times, how he would be so much better off, emotionally as well as financially, if he had a regular job. There were times when Manny became convinced that a beautiful girl would only pay attention to a boy with a regular job and a car. Then, he even seemed keen about the choices he might have if he were only to go out and find them. Just after Christmas we had made a plan to go looking for a job for him together. He had talked for a while about how he would buy a motorbike with the money he earned and be able to leave work on it and pick up his girl and drive around with legal money weighing down his pocket, but somehow Rich's death put an end to the subject. Now whenever I suggested we go looking for a job together he'd say, "Nah nah nah, tha's just not for me," and when I asked him once if he would turn up for a job that I found for him myself, he grimaced and said: "I'm still young, Tina, you know? I should be out having some fun. And I really need a car—a Lexus, you know? But you don't gotta worry about me, though. I ain't no fool. I ain't a kid who's gonna try and make it all from selling all the time. Me and the boys got a scheme."

I had no interest in hearing about his scheme right then. However appalling and misguided it might be, there would be nothing I could do to stop it, and without being able to do anything, I would rather not know. The only thing I could still do for Manny was go up to the eleventh floor and talk to Linda, the social worker, about him again. I had been trying to get Manny to talk to her for months, but like many kids at West Side he was vehemently opposed to any kind of formal adult intervention in his life. One of the conditions of the probation he'd been sentenced to for his first drug charge had been that he take part in a semistructured counseling program, and he'd hated it. Hated the way adults sat down "all somber" and talked to him about his problems for five minutes every day—"Without bothering to put any energy in their mouths." So every time I'd suggested we get together with Linda he had refused.

But if Manny wouldn't talk to her, at least I could try to deliver some of her more pertinent thoughts by proxy. Though she had never met him, I had always been struck by how well Linda already seemed to know Manny. Once when I told her about a visit I'd made to his house, during which he had stayed resolutely silent, she pulled out a little yellow Post-it note and wrote, "Don't feel. Don't trust," which had been just what I had scrawled in my notebook on the way back to my apartment. She claimed that she knew so much about him because his responses were typical of a child who'd grown up with a drug-addicted parent. There was something about the steady and clinical predictability of his actions that I'd always found vaguely reassuring. This time, though, when I told her about Rich's death, she shocked me by saying that Manny was beginning to sound like the kind of kid who might seriously hurt himself. "How long will he be able to take the pressure—the weight of his life," she asked, "before he tries to take his own life?" Exasperated, I slapped my lap hard with both hands and asked her what I could do. "Nothing. Nothing until he wants to be helped," she said.

This wasn't necessarily what I wanted to hear. I had been confused for months about how far I should go for Manny, or rather how far I could go and how effective I would be able to be. I knew I was already far too involved with him. I felt guilty when I did anything at all without thinking of him, and he seemed so alone that even enjoying myself began to feel like a personal betrayal. But so far the things I had managed to actually do for Manny didn't seem to add up to much. I knew what Linda would say, that in building a relationship I had at least provided him with an alternative line of defense to the easy effectiveness of withdrawal; that at this point it was up to him, not me. I also knew that her twenty years of work with troubled teenagers meant that in some way she was probably right. Her office was certainly proof that what she offered held appeal.

Citywide, school social workers are notorious for being sloppy and second-rate, but Linda was different. Like Ed, she made no differentiation between her private and her public self and as a result her office was always packed with kids playing board games or cards, using her phone, and just hanging out. She filled most of her day with traditional clinical-therapy sessions, but she also spent a lot of time doing the kinds of things I did—sitting around, chatting and listening. Like me too, she tended to be drawn to the hardest-luck cases; the difference was that she had long ago given up trying to provide anything as egotistically heartening as redemption. Instead, she led her clients from the possible to the plausible to the achievable, step by careful step. While each of these stages required the blind faith of a leap, each was also contained and defined and only just the other side of the limits the kids had already set up for themselves.

Limits were something I had trouble seeing; that was the problem. Most of my life had been spent in defiance of those placed on me, and, for better or worse, I had burst through them blindly, leaping from one unlikely situation to another with a foolhardy readiness that appalled most of the people I grew up with. But now Manny was forcing me to confront the very real existence not only of his limits but of my own and of West Side's as well. There were certainly plenty to go round. I was an untrained amateur with only my instincts and my own chaotic past to fall back on; Manny was an average, unimaginative guy who was stuck in a rut that would lead to his downfall. The West Side staff was so overextended that despite their best efforts they could never even attempt to fill in all the gaps; besides a recent study showed that even with a perfect attendance record a teenager only spends 8 percent of his or her adolescence at school. The financial limits placed on West Side made it impossible to provide the kind of intensive programs that might have helped Manny during that time. The school couldn't even keep track of chronic absentees because they had to share the energy of just one elderly attendance counselor with five other schools, which meant that kids like Manny could fall through the cracks, despite the help he was getting from his adviser, and from Rochelle, and from me.

Still, I saw him whenever I could and asked after him and tried to engage as many teachers as I could in his plight. But whenever I mentioned his name almost all of them shook their heads heavily and then arranged their faces into appropriate expressions of benign indulgence: sad and certain that pursuit was pointless. As I wandered around the corridors though, and sat in on classes (only barely aware of what was going on because really I was thinking of Manny), I started to notice that despite their advice, almost all every teacher went out of their way to create some kind of reliable, alternate reality for the kids they had come over time to think of as "theirs." Even now, in the second half of the year, many were still struggling, apparently irrationally, to haul a variety of lost causes out of their own pockets of isolation.

Some of these approaches were more structured than others. On one end there was the trip to the Middle East, the most exalted of all of West Side's programs, which had an elaborate system in place to break down the barriers between instructor and student. Since basic introductions in December, Stewart and Ayala had led the group through a series of trust-building exercises that had prompted each of the fourteen kids to question assumptions which only a few months ago would have been sacrosanct. They had been so successful in establishing this complex and interdependent process that even Monica, the most reluctant in the group, had begun to sit up straighter in class and swing her hips in the corridor instead of hunching over herself, ashamed and apologetic about just being around.

But there were other, less glamorous examples, too, where individual teachers personalized their attention and bent all the rules in order to help out a student. Emilio was one of these kids. At twenty, he had three former arrests on his record: one for a stolen car, one for possession of a gun, and one for assault. More recently he had become what he called "the manager" of a corner of Wadsworth Avenue. It was a position in the drug trade almost parallel to Rich's, and he had risen to it quickly, efficiently skimming past the underling post of "look out" and then of "pitcher," which was where Manny had been stuck all these years. Clean, by which he meant after expenses like rent, food, gas for his car, and entertainment, he could make one thousand dollars a week. He drove his own car and had a fancy and seemingly infinite assortment of elegantly low-key gold jewelry. Women flocked to him. But he had told me that standing around all day on the street made him feel ignorant, and he was proud to be the only kid on his block who got up every morning to come to school. He had never in his life read a book. ("Oh no. I've never done that. Never. Never in my life," he told me sincerely, as though I'd asked him if he'd ever beaten up an eighty-year-old blind paraplegic.) But ever since Ed had given him a second chance he'd started to go to school solidly enough to be classed as a possible graduating senior.

Ed was in a large part responsible for this turnaround; he had stuck his neck out for Emilio when no one else had. But it was the job that David, the rapping math teacher, gave him that made Emilio really start to take his role in the school seriously.

David and Emilio had always got on; they shared a relaxed, humorous approach to life and a facility with numbers, and in an attempt to convince Emilio of his potential for success in the legitimate world of work, David asked him to be his teaching assistant for his 3rd and 4th period classes. Even David was surprised, however, by what an excellent teacher Emilio turned out to be. Hour after hour he would walk around the room, twirling a pencil with the tips of his fingers until a student asked for assistance. Then he would lean over, straight-legged in the freshly ironed linen trousers he had taken to wearing, and lead the student through the problem from the beginning. Sometimes he would walk up to the board and yell for everyone's attention and then say something like, "I got this theory, right—I got this theory, and I don't know why but it always work out." Then he would turn to the board and write it all down, slap his hands together to rid them of chalk dust, and tell them all they had to do was "do it like that" and they'd never have any problems with whatever it was—trigonometry, pi, or quadratic equations—again.

David paid Emilio for this help. Forty or fifty kids worked at West Side, and however tight the funds became Ed always managed to manipulate the budget so there was at least some money to pay them. The hourly rate was $4.25—minimum wage, but it came with a tax stub and with the student's name printed out on an official West Side High School check. In Emilio's case the checks added up to about $42 every two weeks, and if he never cashed them it wasn't because of their paltriness but because he took such pride in being able to pull from his pocket a check made out to him—legit.

Even Ann and Rochelle, both teachers who prided themselves on their crisp, no-nonsense approach to education, devised ways of balancing out their students' lives when something about a particular kid struck them. Rochelle had been receiving phone calls in the middle of the night from Jeneena for years and had even offered to put her up when she'd needed a place to stay. Ann, for her part, had set out to rescue one of her favorite students by insisting that she enroll in her new Holocaust class—and then by bringing in a Holocaust survivor to convince her of the errors of the vituperative anti-Semitic ideas she had recently adopted. To begin with the student, Reeham, refused to believe that Judaism existed before Christianity. She harumphed loudly, crossed her arms up under her breasts, and pursed her lips in a look of defiant disbelief when Ann insisted that Jesus had been a Jew. But a few weeks later, after historical texts had been presented and documentary photographs shown, Reeham collapsed. "It's disrupting everything I've been taught. I'm a Nazi," she said. The day Ann arranged for the Holocaust survivor to come into the class, it was Reeham with whom the woman sat down to chat afterward, and Reeham with whom she left too, out to have lunch, arm in arm.

Similarly, the presence of an emotional, never quite successful actress on the staff had become a life raft for an overweight boy with an effeminate manner and a high-pitched, lisping voice who had transferred to West Side after being beaten almost daily by other students at his former school. Even the bossy and neurotic computer teacher had a group of eight or nine students so dedicated to her that they stayed late, twice a week, to take extracurricular computer-repair classes with her. These were not dramatic rescues, perhaps, maybe not even extraordinary ones, and if money had been no object, many teachers might have spent their spare time dreaming up perfect, all-embracing programs for their kids instead. But money was always an issue at West Side, and these kinds of interventions cost nothing and were just what Ed had in mind when he insisted on keeping such a wide array of characters at school, both on the staff and in the student body. Because who knew what might happen when two apparently eccentric people got together. As far as Ed was concerned, computer classes worked as well as anything to encourage risk-taking and confidence-building. All that really mattered was that there be a realistic balance between what was being offered and what would be expected in return.

That had been what was missing between myself and Manny, I began to see—a series of clearly defined and attainable expectations which would lead him, not to life-challenging questions, but to minute shifts in perception that ultimately might add up. Because while it was clearly more dramatic to be involved in something as structured and well-funded as the Youthworks program, not every kid was ready for such a limitless challenge and most responded better to the gradual and almost imperceptible proddings that led them from one place to another as if by default. Emilio was only now ready to start coming to school, and though Cristy had again started to come in regularly, she still had a long way to go before she summoned the kind of confidence it took to stand in front of a class and demand their attention. Neither of them were any more ready to head off to the Middle East than Manny was, but this didn't mean that the steps they were making weren't significant. It meant only that by acknowledging their individual needs, West Side was allowing each student to stretch beyond their own expectations one small step at a time.

After all, if the Middle East program was "better" than the others at West Side, and the escape it offered just a little more complete, then the will to resist the challenge, and the tensions and fears that went along with it, were also more defined. Only the most curious and resilient would be able to cope. For almost two months Stewart and Ayala had been working hard to prepare their group for the challenges that would confront them on the kibbutz, and by now most could recite Israel's neighboring countries in their sleep, along with the dates and one-line explanations of the causes and results of the 1948, 1967, and 1973 wars too. Still, having reality shift beneath your feet is a disconcerting sensation even for the most world-weary, and with two weeks left to go some kids in the group were still balking at the idea that they were going to a distant, dusty, and war-torn country thousands of miles away, not because anyone was making them, or because they were being punished, but because they had asked to go and had fought for the privilege.

"Sitting in this meeting I look and wonder who these people are I am going to live with," Reggie wrote in his journal. "These are strangers to me, except Kevin. I think I will be very quiet on the trip. Mainly because I will be mega scared. I don't like airplanes. Every time I am in a airplane I get close to death feelings." Later he wrote: "As this trip gets closer my fear level gets higher and higher. I try not to show my fear for my mother's sake. She is scared enough for both of us." Raul began to retreat a little too. He had always been the quiet, learned one of the group, the one Stewart could turn to whenever he needed a quote from the Bible. Recently, however, he started to come to meetings distracted and angry, and to sit facing away from the others.

But after months of careful, sometimes pedantic, and often repetitive preparation, an inevitability had evolved about the trip too, so that none of the kids seriously considered dropping out for very long. By then going to Israel had become an act of saving face, of "keeping it real" and "representing," like Emilio and Sandra and Manny—like everyone who had a reality with hefty demands. And even if some in the Youthworks group kept resisting the trip, it was only because they understood the reality was strong enough to withstand it.

They finally left on a Sunday. Following what had become a tradition, Stewart and Ed arranged for a farewell party in the lunchroom on the tenth floor of the school. Not many friends showed up. As a rule, those left behind didn't mingle well with those who were leaving, and though there was pizza and soda and even a couple of balloons floating around, the mood was subdued. Besides, most of the kids arrived exhausted from having been up all night, stuffing as much of their lives as would fit into the maximum of two suitcases and one piece of carry-on luggage that the airline allowed. One after another they arrived, hauling great imitation leather cases, dragging them because they were too heavy to lift. Giant boxes of Apple Jacks, sacks of barbecue-flavored sunflower seeds, Doritos and Slim Jims were crammed next to cartons of American cigarettes. Photo albums competed for space with boom boxes and tapes and stuffed cuddly toys. And perhaps as a result of their still-lingering conviction that they were headed for the desert, the boys had brought water guns too, the fluorescent pink and yellow, semi-automatic kind that can squirt twenty yards away with surprising accuracy. With these attached to their carry-on luggage, the group looked like a too brightly colored, chaotic group of soldiers heading off to war.

After just a few minutes' wait the kids carefully loaded these bulging and oversized cases into the hold of a bus that had a green stripe down the side. Stepping back into the alcove of a camera store on the corner of Thirty-fifth Street and Eighth Avenue, I watched as in a last-minute flurry of activity mothers and fathers and grandmothers tucked five-and ten-dollar bills into their kids' pockets and gave them advice and carefully prepared emergency pouches and good luck charms and hugs. Many of these families had been through hell before this, but leaving to spend ten weeks in the Middle East was not something to be stoic about. By the time the bus doors finally opened, almost everyone was crying. Reggie was the first to turn away from his family. He was followed by his friend Kevin and their tagalong companion, the Philippine, Kenny. Enrique, the oldest in the group, kissed his quietly sobbing mother good-bye a few minutes later. Naomi and Monica and Carina followed, and then Kamilah, Fred, Ylaria, Simon, Melissa, and Raul, until it was just Michelle, her mother, and her nine-year-old sister Shawnequa left out on the corner, clinging to one another in tears. None of the kids inside the bus looked at them. Each was too intently struggling to repress the urge to run away themselves to pay any attention to someone who had given way entirely to the desire to stay. Suddenly I remembered just how that felt; remembered for the first time since it had happened, I think, climbing up the steps of a similarly painted bus to go back to boarding school after the long summer break when I was fourteen. Sitting on the rough, plush-covered seats and feeling their edges prickle my legs, I hadn't dared to look around or back to the sidewalk, where I knew my mother would be standing, looking worried and guilty and sick. It was just the same now. Mothers had approached the bus windows and were placing their palms up to the glass the way lovers do in high-security-prison visiting rooms. Stewart tapped Michelle on the shoulder. As if it were the most natural thing in the world, a joke, a day out at an amusement park, he laughed and said that they would miss the plane if they didn't leave now. Michelle's mother nodded her head, extended her arms, and held Michelle's shoulders for a couple of seconds. Over the now hysterical screams of Shawnequa ("No, no! Don't go Michelle, don't go!") she sent her daughter to board the bus, and without saying a word Michelle walked up the stairs, sat down in the front seat across the aisle from the driver, and stared straight head until the bus was out of sight.

24

IN NOVEMBER 1994 George Pataki had managed to unseat longtime Democratic Governor Mario Cuomo in the elections that realigned America's political landscape and gave impetus to the much vaunted Contract with America. For the first time in memory Republicans controlled both houses of the Congress, the state governorship, and the city's mayoralty. In a major public statement after he assumed office, the new governor proudly announced that he would be the first since 1943 to reduce real spending in New York State from one fiscal year to the next. Acknowledging that the decreased tax burden for many might bring more hardship for some than he'd initially supposed, especially for those in the city, he resolutely braced himself for the kind of vituperative opposition Mayor Giuliani was becoming famous for.

Giuliani had crossed party lines to support Cuomo in the elections. Saying that the city would be best served under Cuomo's continued stewardship, he announced that "Mario Cuomo will simply be a better governor than George Pataki," and had even done some campaigning on the veteran liberal's behalf. But as if giddy with the monumentalism of the Republicans' sweeping victory, Giuliani suddenly seemed as intent on making history as the governor. Instead of responding to the massive proposed cuts from Albany by begging, pleading and stonewalling as was customary (and expected) from a New York City mayor, he announced that the new political climate had provided "the city with opportunities to scale back poverty programs" like never before. Explaining to the electorate that state aid must be matched by city funds and that the funds simply weren't available, he not only applauded the governor's budget but requested additional, deeper cuts in mandatory programs like Medicaid and welfare. "I see this as an historic opportunity," the mayor said in a speech up in Albany, during which he repeatedly praised the governor's initiative. "It is a chance to do what was politically unthinkable just a few years ago."

When the mayor unveiled his four-year financial plan later that month, it became clear just how far he wanted to go. Reducing actual spending for only the ninth time since the city was incorporated in 1898, his plan proposed the deepest cuts in city spending since the Great Depression. Insisting that the city had been "too generous for too long," he cut back almost every city agency. The police force was the one notable exception.

These "revolutionary" reforms did nothing to improve relations between City Hall and the city's school administration. In what had amounted to the biggest cut in personnel since the Board of Education had become an independent body twenty-four years before, Cortines had already eliminated 1,400 of the board's 6,300 employees. But Giuliani still insisted it was not enough, and he now demanded that Cortines cut a further $290 million, or nearly 9 percent of the city's contribution to his budget. Given that every available extracurricular expenditure had already been cut back, Cortines insisted this would lead to an unbridgeable gap in the board's budget. While the two men argued back and forth, schools in the city started looking around for ways to cut corners.

West Side would feel the impact in a variety of ways. Teachers bumped from other schools would now almost certainly displace some of their own younger teachers, and costs would have to be clipped in everything from basic supplies to overtime. Most disheartening, however, was what the cuts would end up meaning for the school's still unresolved real estate problem. It had been three years since West Side had moved to Thirty-fifth Street and nearly two since they had first heard that they were not going to get a new building. Until very recently, the possibility of renovating the old Château on 102nd and Amsterdam had been dangled tantalizingly before Ed and his staff. But now it began to seem that the board's previous hints about the cost-efficiency of razing the old place were to be taken seriously. With the roof useless and the outer walls bulging with water saturation, they began to hear that repairs would cost more than starting from scratch. The building might once have been grand, and it was clearly of some architectural interest, but Ed knew that the board was more concerned with short-term efficiency than historical preservation. Sallejane Seif, the woman in charge of leases and buildings for the alternative superintendancy, had stepped in to try to turn the tide. But whatever she tried, however many surveys and architects and engineers she brought in to testify to the building's fundamental soundness, the board seemed to have already made up its mind that the building was unsafe. In fact, not long after she found an independent buyer for the building she learned that they had already signed a multimillion-dollar demolition contract.

Ed was not surprised. The board had been toying with West Side since well before he had taken over the school, and while he went along with every last-ditch effort to revive the renovation plan—scheduling a series of meetings, drafting several versions of protest letters and even calling in favors where he could find them—he didn't expect anything to come of it. The board's capital budget had been cut from $7.5 billion to just $3.4 billion, which left sufficient funds to build only eight of the proposed thirty-three new schools. School district 3, which included his old school's neighborhood, was to get one of these new buildings, and though the district would still be grotesquely overcrowded, it would be hard for anyone to justify the added expenditure of a major renovation project in the same area. Besides, having left the area, and having been forced to accept kids from across the city's five boroughs, Ed had lost the mandate he once had to rile up local activists, like the still very involved Doris Rosenblum. West Side was no longer a District 3 school. It was a school for the city, and because the city didn't have a unified constituency, he was out of luck. The day after the deadline, when someone in Family Group asked him how it had all turned out, Ed fished around in his pocket for four subway tokens and placed them on the table in front of six kids.

"Total financial recourses," he said. "How do you split them?"

Emilio answered first. "I take one. Anyone who wants my token will have to deal with me."

"I'd give them to the ones that don't got no train passes," a pretty girl who wanted to impress Emilio with her kindness said, smiling shyly.

"I'd take one and go someplace where I can get more and bring 'em back," Cristy said.

"The first one that finds them, gets them. I'd take them all," a third girl ventured.

"And what would you do, Emilio, if she just took all the tokens right now and announced that they were hers?" Ed asked. Emilio didn't have to answer. As one of the most successful and debonair of the school's drug dealers, he had a well-known reputation. He simply raised his eyes to the girl's and after a moment added, "And I'd bring my peoples."

"I'd bring my peoples too, then. More peoples than you," the girl protested, not quite managing to hide how rattled she had become. And so, in three or four minutes and with a pocket of change, Ed managed to illustrate the pattern of divide and conquest that, as far as he was concerned, pretty much defined the last thirty years of New York City politics. The kind of politics, he added in the teachers' room a day or two later, that had led to the demise of a once grand and formidable building like the Château when forty years ago all it would have taken was an annual visit by a drain cleaner, twenty years ago a modest revamping of the drainage system, ten years ago larger but still feasible adjustments to the roof, and even five years ago a viable renovation project, to have kept the building standing. At a time when both funds and space were scarce, such shortsightedness seemed almost wanton.

A couple of weeks after the demolition, Jim, the former dean, came to school carrying a big black garbage bag filled with bits of brick and stone from the rubble of the old Château, and a ripple of anger spread through the classrooms and offices of West Side. It was hard, usually, to get most kids at the school actively involved in anything that might be considered political but, feeling genuinely threatened now, the students responded. Many wrote letters to the chancellor announcing their loyalty to the West Side and asking him to at least guarantee that the lease on Thirty-fifth Street would be renewed. Sandra started coming into school wearing a black band across her arm; "Pataki's death," she would say whenever anybody asked her what it was for. And a student in Rochelle's class, a shy boy named Frederick who otherwise kept to himself, even wrote a story one afternoon titled "The Police Opened the Door . . ."

> The police opened the door and discovered mutilated bodies all over the house. One police officer threw up on the spot. Another officer's face turned white like paper. Then the phone rings (ring ring ring) the officer picks up. "Hello . . . Hello?" As the officer is about to hang up someone on the other line speaks "How do you like my work?" said the man on the other end (the killer). The police officer asked "Who is this?" and the killer stayed quiet for about 8 seconds. Then he spoke "I'm just a good citizen doing the community a big fava." "What do you mean?" asked the officer. "Go look in the oven, the best parts are in there, " the killer says. The officer on the phone tells the other officer to go look in the oven. The officer's heart is beating as if he just ran 100 miles. He opened the oven, looked inside and passed out. He had seen two heads. But they weren't just any heads, they were the heads of the mayor of New York and the Governor of New York (Giuliani and Pataki). On the phone the killer told the officer "They wanted budget cuts, so instead I gave them body cuts!"

Rochelle had given him a B plus for his story, had written, "Frederick you are *really* clever" across the top in red, and had then pinned it up on a board down the hall from some of the headlines announcing the latest in a round of cuts from City Hall and Albany. One of these quoted Giuliani as saying that the city's high schools should be able to replace the after-school, sports, and enrichment programs he had cut by raising the required funds privately. And perhaps because it had just been announced that $20 million in cuts in youth employment, educational, and training programs would also be implemented, months of quiet acquiescence were giving way to protest elsewhere in the city too. While student leaders in both the state university and the city university systems had long been speaking out against what seemed to have become the mayor's pro-business, anti-youth stances, they now stopped writing editorials in school and community papers and began to plan a citywide demonstration instead.

During the weeks leading up to the protest the chancellor repeatedly insisted that the city's public school students remain in their classes and avoid the downtown area on the day of the rally. But at West Side, Ed stayed resolutely mute on the subject. Mysteriously, one or two smallish posters advertising the march appeared on the notice board downstairs. It was common knowledge, too, that Jim had begun to organize a group of kids from the eleventh floor to take to the protest. Ed did nothing to encourage this, but nothing to discourage it either. And while he privately doubted the effectiveness of a massive public rally right then, he did start to evoke the image of peaceful protesters from the past in some of his Family Group meetings. Spinning yarns that linked the trials of Montezuma to Rosa Parks and Parnell's blighted struggle for democracy and self-rule in Ireland, he pulled down the world map above his classroom's blackboard and skipped from continent to continent, century to century, sketching stories of Gandhi, Solzhenitsyn, and the White Rose anti-Nazi German resistance group with such enthusiasm one morning that he started to sweat. "And it's cold today!" Cristy whispered to Sandra. "Imagine him in the summer!"

At most other high schools in the city, the chancellor's order to avoid the upcoming demonstration was taken more seriously. But student leaders still continued to organize. They sent messages to one another by fax, phone and e-mail and printed up pamphlets, which they then distributed on the sly outside their schools in the afternoons. Students at Bronx Science and Stuyvesant referred to the rally as "the thing" to keep their teachers from knowing what they were up to. And on the day of the protest the Board of Education reported that fourteen thousand students ignored the public-address-system message from their principals and walked out of sixty-two high schools early that day. Some students marched around their own blocks in solidarity and then returned to school. Others, of course, used the event as an excuse to cut classes for the afternoon, but most made it down to City Hall. By the time I arrived, shortly before noon, there were maybe five thousand high school and college students gathered in the small park outside the mayor's office. Jim had brought a group of ten or fifteen kids down from West Side at eleven, but I had had to come to the rally straight from yet another court appearance with Manny, and after twenty minutes or so of scanning the waves of students marching down Broadway I had yet to see a familiar face.

By midday close to ten thousand people had gathered in the tiny triangle of grass and trees. For what seemed like hours, kids shouted slogans like "Education is a right! Fight! Fight! Fight!" and "He's mean.

He's wacky. His name is Pataki!" with a righteous look of certainty that the protest would roll back the budget cuts and change everything. Huge banners billowed out like parachutes over the heads of students who linked arms as they marched down Broadway, high on the energy of seeing thousands of others ahead of them. Handwritten signs on sheets of construction paper and computer-generated pamphlets were being stapled to trees or shaken in hands stretched high over their heads. The communal sense of focused optimism was so infectious that within an hour I had allowed myself to succumb to it almost entirely. Perhaps, I even thought, standing on top of a shiny black park bench on one of the first sunny and warm days of spring, the protesters would even be able to extend their optimism to kids like Manny, trapped in his corner of Knickerbocker Avenue out there in Bushwick right then, I assumed, selling heroin for two dollars a bag. And as I watched a ten-foot-long coffin draped in a flag reading "Our futures are smashed because of no cash" being carried down Broadway to the edge of the park, I thought that maybe, at last, people would have to sit up and take notice of the thousands of peaceful teenagers that were gathering outside City Hall that afternoon.

More were still pouring in from every direction, and in an attempt to see the stage some were climbing up trees and falling off again as branches broke. At one point, I thought I recognized a girl named Stacia from West Side trying to climb onto the shoulders of a barely willing schoolmate. It wasn't her though; this girl's voice was too screechy, and a few minutes later I decided to give up trying to find the West Side contingent and focused instead on the stage. Speakers had been up there since I'd arrived, but the sound system wasn't carrying well, and as I hustled across the park, squeezing through the crowds to try to get close enough to hear, I remembered a story Ed had told me a few days before. He had been at an alternative-school conference that had gathered to talk about the possible impact of the city's new budget crunch and had overheard a vibrant teenage girl trying desperately to explain to a man in a suit the financial straits her school already found itself in: "And furniture! Forget it! We haven't had new furniture since the school opened!" he had heard her say. "You can't walk by a chair without getting a run in your stockings! Our assistant principal? She went from three-ninety-nine panty hose to ninety-nine-cent panty hose. It's pathetic!"

Ed had been delighted by that. It summed up all the energy and humorous, down-to-earth outrage that so many students had developed in response to their lives and to their educational futures as well. He had even spoken about the girl's outburst in Family Group. Sucking in air through gaps in their teeth, his advisees compared their school to others they had attended in the past. West Side had it worse, they agreed. While most schools were appalled that they might have to reduce time in science labs and end music classes, West Side had never had them in the first place, and the students discussed everything from the basketball team's secondhand, softball T-shirts with strips of white sheets sewn over the invalid numbers, to the lack of a gym, of functioning cooking facilities, and even of books that they could take home with them instead of having to turn in at the end of each class period. Ed encouraged them to ask themselves why and to consider what they could do about it, and that day a handful of them had left Family Group with the telephone number and the address of the governor in Albany, determined to write him a letter.

Making my way to the front of the park I passed tightly packed groups of high school kids holding placards representing schools from all over the city: Central Park East, Whitestone, Edward R. Murrow, James Monroe. Closer to the stage, a group of cheerleaders danced in complete synchronization, simultaneously shaking clenched hands as though holding pompoms, in rhythm to some protest-oriented, freestyle rap lyrics. Earlier I had watched as a group of kids had taken turns with the microphone onstage, announcing the name of the school or college they represented in imitation of the way states declare themselves during roll calls at national Democratic and Republican conventions. I'd been looking forward to hearing these same kids make their political debuts, but as I approached the stage I saw that they had been deposed by a group of much older speakers.

"This rally is not about budget cuts or tuition increases. It is about a defunct system of government which promotes the rich and cares little for the poor," an angry, gray-haired woman in a long skirt shouted as I drew near. Like the other adults onstage, this woman held notes in her hands, and as she read from them it became clear that she cared more for the glamor of worldwide revolution than the more mundane matter of improving secondary and higher education in New York City. Long stretches passed during which she seemed barely aware of the audience at all; occasionally, she even turned away from the crowd to address herself directly to the men at her back. They registered their appreciation with a variety of solemn nods and self-conscious sidestepping jigs. And though they seemed sincere in their commitment to end cultural imperialism the world over, their message didn't seem to be galvanizing anyone in the park right then and certainly didn't seem helpful to students trying to get a simple point across to a city that seemed eager to write them off as lost.

Looking around I started to notice a growing contingent of middle-aged, middle-class white people giving away socialist newsletters that were eagerly taken up by the kids, only to be glanced at and then discarded two steps later. Small groups of ex-hippies had also gathered in front of the stage, seemingly oblivious to the sidelong glances they elicited when they linked arms and chanted songs that made no sense anymore. They weren't the only ones to have arrived, either. Around the edges of the park, militant Afrocentrists had set up stalls, calling for a return to Africa; union representatives demanding better working conditions circled a statue holding mass-produced, two-color signs stapled onto splintery wooden poles; gay and lesbian groups had come too, as had the antipornography zealots with their grimly decorated stands. Even a handful of petitioners demanding the release of Mumia Abu-Jamal had gathered at a park bench. So when, about half an hour later, two of the ex-hippies helped each other up onto the bench I'd found, and then unfurled and quietly waved their "mourning black" banner in front of me, I complained just loud enough for them to hear, and then gave up and started to leave. After all the students' effort, all the work and energy and idealism, and even after a rare moment of actual belief in the possibilities of working within the system, I couldn't help but feel exasperated that the students were being shunted aside again—not only by the governor, who would later call the rally "an outrage," or by the mayor, who seemed more impressed by the misspelling of his name on some of the placards than the fact that he was being faced down by the largest student protest in years, but by purported members of the rally themselves.

Apart from an occasional chant that still rose from one corner of the park, the crowd's once ebullient focus had largely dissipated by then. No one under the age of forty had been up on the stage for at least an hour. I no longer knew what they were talking about, and to tell the truth I didn't much care. Like most of the kids, I was paying more attention to the police officers who had begun to surround the little park. In full riot gear, on horseback, and in fleets of motorbikes decorated with ominous posies of milky white plastic handcuffs, they soon completed their cordon and the mood in the park turned from frustration to panic.

The crowd swelled and surged; people in the center started to get crushed, or started to think they might get crushed, and in ten, single-minded minutes I had picked my way around to the edge, where I skirted along the splintered blue wooden planks that read POLICE DO NOT CROSS until I found a cop who acknowledged my press pass and allowed me to leave.

According to news reports it wasn't until half an hour later, when a group of students tried to lead an unauthorized march out of the park, down Broadway, to the spaciousness of Wall Street, that the police finally moved in. Spraying Mace and thrusting batons into the almost entirely peaceful crowd, they forced kids back into the park. The West Side contingent had already left by then, but most other students were still there. The ensuing commotion lasted more than an hour, led to a sit-down protest, and ended in the arrest, mostly for disorderly conduct, of sixty students. Sixteen police officers suffered minor injuries, and two well-identified press photographers were sprayed in the face with Mace. And though I watched footage of what was now being called "a riot" on several television stations on the six o'clock, ten o'clock, and eleven o'clock news, I never saw even one of the professional protesters who had taken over the rally—the union representatives, antiporn protesters, and return-to-Africa sponsors. Like me, I realized, they had seen what would happen and had left before the trouble started. As for the mayor? He was reported as having this to say about the afternoon:

"They're supposed to be in class today, and they're not. And they're not paying for their own education. Somebody else is paying for it. So I think that's an issue that should be raised. . . . To ask students to pay a few hundred dollars more, to work a couple of extra hours, maybe, instead of protesting, to go find a job for the day so you make a little extra money so you could pay for your education, you might actually be preparing them for the rest of their lives better than what is happening right now. Maybe they should study harder," he said.

25

"THE ISSUE OF organized kids working together—and we can call them gangs; we can call them anything we want—is a very powerful force in this city. It is here. And it can destroy us," Lawrence Edwards, the assistant administrative superintendant for high schools had said by way of introduction to the Board of Education's citywide conference on gangs, Gang Affiliation 101: Perspective for Educators. "It can do what in my mind nothing else can. It can erode the very fabric of what we are trying to do."

As if to prove a point Mr. Edwards directed the audience's attention to the dusty white posterboard that made up the NYPD Gang Intelligence's "Gang Bead Presentation." Scuffed around the edges and covered with fingerprints, the display was hung with several strings of variously colored beads—the actual, if slightly damaged, captured proof of the gangs' structured and highly dangerous existence. The Latin Kings, the Netas, the Zulu Nation, and La Familia were represented, as well as smaller organizations I had never heard of before: MUP (Mash Up Posse), SOK (Souls of Krylon), and the spectacular-sounding Ghost Shadows Gun. Some famous necklaces were missing, and some had the names scrawled in underneath them crossed out—a sign, we were told, that the organization no longer existed. One or two *collares* had even been broken, leaving empty strands of nylon stuck with tape to the board. It wasn't a very impressive display, and the detectives were the first to point out that it was neither exhaustive nor entirely up to date. But like a collection from an historic local battle displayed in a small museum somewhere, its very concreteness made it magnetic. Here you could reach over and touch these usually untouchable plastic beads, and though I didn't catch anyone doing so, I did see, later in the day, a middle-aged man and an older woman arguing over the right "gang" way to greet each other—clumsily struggling to twist their fingers into the appropriate shapes and combinations for the Kings' "crown," which seemed to me to be pretty much the same thing.

Over the past year the New York City school system had become increasingly worried about youth gangs. The revolutionary politics that many groups espoused, combined with the ready-made sense of community they offered, had been a potent call to teens all over the city, and many schools administrators had become alarmed as more and more of their troubled students began to turn up at school in multicolored *collares*.

Seventy deans from all five boroughs were in attendance on the day of the conference. Charl hadn't wanted to go, and Ed, who was to be busy most of the morning collecting supplies donated to the school, had sent me along in his stead. He had been on the planning committee but had been a "member in absentia," he confessed: he didn't give much credence to many of the Board of Education's theories and frankly had better ways to spend his time. Several students at West Side were involved in gangs, he knew. But he could rattle off a list of similar groups stretching back to the early 70s, and while it was true that girls like Sandra had continued to attend school only sporadically since joining the Netas, Ed knew them well enough to understand that his best chance of getting them back again was to sit back and wait for them to get bored.

Whenever I saw her up at PS 143, I had to admit that Sandra was as well as I'd ever seen her. In fact, it soon became clear that though she had pretty much given up on school entirely by then, she wasn't the type to lead the lazy life typical of a seventeen-year-old dropout with only 17 credits, no job, and no prospect of getting one. On the contrary, for the first time in her life Sandra's leadership skills were being recognized, and she was blooming as a result. Recently she had even been promoted to the upper echelons of the citywide junta, over the treasurer and disciplinarian and assessor and ahead of all the chapter heads too, so that suddenly she was more powerful even than Ramón.

Such a rapid promotion in the Netas was almost unheard of. As in the army, or any discipline-conscious organization, promotions tended to run along preordained paths and could be bestowed only when approved by the central governing board. But Sandra had been a full-fledged *hermanita* for a mere two months when she had been catapulted into the ranks of the junta. It had happened almost by chance at her first universal meeting when the most powerful female Neta in New York, a woman known as the "Godmother," had singled out Manhattan for its particularly poor attendance. Six hundred Netas had assembled that afternoon and had been corralled into a traditional unifying circle by selected enforcers who patrolled the outer rim to ensure that everyone maintained their "proper respect." Still, Sandra couldn't help but speak out. Brushing aside the rigid hierarchy the Netas held so dear, she had stepped into the circle and explained how Manhattan was so unorganized that a lot of chapters didn't even know there was a universal that evening, let alone where it was. There were at least five chapters she knew of, without even really trying to think about it, she said, who weren't even registered or certified by the *junta central.*

The Godmother stood silently for a minute and then asked what she would do to change the situation. Sandra replied that there were such things as telephones and beepers and mailboxes; that letters could be written and phone calls made, and that though she understood these methods weren't foolproof, they should at least be tried.

"I like the way you think," Sandra remembered the Godmother saying then, right there in front of everybody. "You wanna be coordinator of Manhattan?"

Sandra, of course, had been exultant. She had stayed late in Brooklyn that evening and had conversations with both the Godmother and the green-eyed Primero-of-all-Manhattan, about what she could do to improve communication and cohesion in the borough and had then returned triumphant to PS 143, where she was greeted like a hero. But it was hard work being a Neta coordinator. Despite their purported desire to get organized, it wasn't easy to convince individual chapter heads to pay attention to paperwork, she told me. Most simply weren't interested in keeping up-to-date records on their *hermanitos*—especially as many had criminal records and were sensitive to official documentation of any kind. But Sandra believed it was essential if the Netas were ever going to become a cohesive cultural force. She exhorted them to at least try to keep track of things as basic as the payment or nonpayment of membership dues and dates of individual promotions and demotions within each chapter. She also left each head with a list of beeper numbers and codes so they could keep in touch with either herself or a member of the *junta central* and stay abreast of upcoming universals and changes of citywide policy.

Her travels took her all over the city—even to the East Side, she told me, as if it were the moon. ("The *East* side!") And though her schedule was so busy that she sometimes missed an evening at PS 143, she tried to spend as much time there as she could between the hours of six and nine, helping to make sure that every one of the over four hundred people who used the building in the evenings signed into the book and took off their hats and didn't run in the corridor or disrespect one another.

Over the past few months, I had been visiting the school with at least as much regularity as most junior *hermanitos,* and the truth was that the more time I spent with the Netas of Capítulo Seis, the more confused I became. There was something ominous about the blank-eyed way kids jumped to respond to an order from Ramón, I couldn't help thinking. And something too about Ramón's own ease with violence gave me the feeling that if he wasn't trying to pull the wool over my eyes, he was certainly trying to blinker his own. The scuffles outside of the building were becoming more frequent; almost each time I went up there I would hear of one or two fights in the area. And while Ramón officially frowned on these displays, he was rarely above joining in the macho contests as to whose slash wound or bruises were deeper.

On the other hand, I had listened to so many heartfelt exhortations to ignore the temptations of the street and to concentrate instead on the infinite possibilities of the future, that I felt sure the chapter was at least trying to bring about positive change. Even if they sometimes failed, their efforts still seemed preferable to the inevitable drifting to crime and incarceration that most of their members would be following without them. And by that point I had witnessed so many pleas for safe sex and antiracism drives and lectures with names like "Squashing It" and "Keep the Peace" that I wasn't the slightest bit taken aback to hear Mickey, the *capitulo*'s second in command, suggest one evening that they start cooperating with the police in the neighborhood.

Still struggling to improve their image with the community, Mickey had dropped by the local precinct house one afternoon and, to his surprise, had found the detective there amicable and eager to get involved.

The detective had suggested a joint help-the-aged program, which, he'd implied, might later be extended to educating elementary-aged schoolchildren. In the end, this kind of collaboration had been a step too far even for Chapter 6, and the plan suffered its final blow when Sandra commented that she could no more think of joining forces with the police than with the lurking members of DP outside the school gates. But up until then, the gathered *hermanitos* had entertained Mickey's proposal as seriously as they had all the other "works of positivity" that made it onto their weekly agenda. In fact, there was something about their doggedly shared belief in their power to change society that lent them, often, the same pedantic, driven tone as a politician running for office against a long-standing incumbent. And the group's collective and earnest obsession with detail frequently ended up boring me at least as much as the most uninspired class at West Side.

Once I had even tried to sneak out of a meeting during a long, incredibly arcane debate about whether Carlito was killed on the morning of the twenty-seventh of March and buried on the thirtieth or was in fact killed and buried on the same day. One of the *hermanitos* sitting onstage that night was an acknowledged expert on such matters because he had read five books on the subject ("that's five books, *manos*"), and there seemed to be no stopping him. There was so much literature in circulation though, that despite his expertise no one was sure whom to believe, especially after a young *hermanita* pulled an official-looking Neta pamphlet from her bag that explained clearly and concisely how Carlito had rested in state for three days before being buried. I was edging out of my seat when the talk was brought to an abrupt end by the burly head of security, who had been working off some of his own boredom by pacing the aisles and radioing his men upstairs, and who now stopped suddenly and pointed to an *hermanito* sitting in the middle of the fifth or sixth row.

"You—open your mouth," he shouted. There was a brief moment of confusion as the boy realized it was him that was being singled out. "Who, me?" he asked.

The head of security nodded. No one moved. "Gum," he said after a pause.

"Oh!" the young *hermanito* practically shouted in relief. "My bad. My bad." And then, standing up and walking across the auditorium, he dropped the piece of gum into his hand and deposited it in a regulation Board of Education garbage can.

"Corazón!" the head of security said.

"Corazón!" the young *hermanito* replied as he made his way back to his seat.

This was hardly what the deans who had gathered for the board-sponsored conference would have imagined to be going on in these infamous "gang" meetings. And yet over a buffet breakfast of bagels, croissants, coffee, and orange juice, I glanced at the shiny yellow folders marked "Gangs 101" that we had been handed when we registered, and was surprised to see that most of the articles included were entirely rational and right-minded. Ranging from the practical to the philosophic, there were step-by-step guides for performing intergang mediations, gang-affinity indicators, and lists of reasons most kids join gangs in the first place (friendship, a sense of belonging, pride). A good half of the package was even dedicated to previously tested and successful gang-intervention suggestions: "We cannot create some national curriculum that will magically solve the need for safety, for membership in the community," one such paper began.

> Nor can we, in most cases, involve the family in such a way as would improve the "curriculum" of the home. We can, however, develop a curriculum that incorporates the school into the community and gets the community into the schools. We can make positive rites of passage available to students through various programs at school that, we hope, will draw them away from the hazardous rites of passage they now seek out. These connections would provide students with a sense of belonging to society; they would also, significantly, impress upon the community the realization that these kids are not villains, but their kids, *our* kids.

This was exactly what people like Oscar Ramos at PS 143 had been trying to do and why he'd invited Chapter 6 into the school. But perhaps because of the bleakness of the future economic horizon in New York City, a landscape where increasingly even the most perfunctory of extracurricular programs were now all but defunct, most of the deans gathered at John Jay College seemed reluctant to consider the more practical suggestions offered: the creation of after-school programs, self-esteem workshops, and school-based group activities. Instead, a consensus seemed to be building around the much simpler notion of eradication by force. According to our packages, even people in Ohio knew that "overreacting and resorting to extreme measures will do little to alleviate gang violence"; and out in Los Angeles, where citizens really were beset by gun-crazed, car-screeching gang battles, they at least knew that "the need for safety and protection, the need for respect and identity among gang-involved youth do not go away when several gang members are expelled from a school." But in New York that day, the deans didn't seem much interested in what the experts had to say. Refusing to even consider anything that might muddle their clear-cut scenario of threat and counterthreat, they spent most of the rest of the conference listening to local principals talk about their encounters with a group of particularly ferocious-sounding gang members.

One such principal, a woman with a jowly and chalk-white face, told of her ordeal with the exaggerated gestures of pantomime. Two kids in her school had beaten up a member of the Zulu Nation, she said, and their members immediately called for retribution. Gang Intelligence suggested she speak with one of the gang's representatives in the school. But she had heard about "these Zulus" before, she told us conspiratorially, and she in no way wanted to validate them by talking to their representative one-on-one, as if they were equals, as if he were a dignified human being—"even if his name was *Brother Righteousness*," she said.

A principal from Staten Island was so awestruck by his own experiences with gangs that he outlined every moment of even the minutest encounters he'd had at his school. His talk went on for forty minutes, and included detailed descriptions of how a certain gang leader had been sliced across the cheek and what this did to the rest of his face, both before and after surgery. He talked about his run-in with one of the "leaders" alone by a pay phone opposite the school, and with another, seen counting great wads of money, and on and on, until it struck me, sitting there among all those deans, all those people that dealt with the self-indulgence and vagaries of teenagers all day, that gang activity, or talking about it, at least, was a break for them in some funny way, an occurrence, an episode, a thrill. Then I thought that perhaps that thrill, that titillation, was what made gangs "gangs" in the first place. Because if you are a teacher or a policeman or a journalist even, isn't it better to be tackling a superdemon than a more or less random gathering of confused and incorrigible kids?

The administration at High School for Humanities was certainly trying its hardest to stick to the parameters of complete negation. Just ten years before, it had been the school of choice for private-school students who'd been thrown out for discipline problems. Back then its population was 65 percent white, but now it was 97 percent minority, and as one of the city's largest comprehensive schools it had the problems common to all overcrowded and understaffed schools. Sandra had been told about the gang situation there by her cousin Nikole, who was a fellow *hermanita* and a student at the school. Angrily checking the atrocities off on her fingers, she had told Sandra how she had even heard the deans vow that they wouldn't rest until every member of every gang ("that's the word they use—'gang'!") had been thrown out.

Gang members were often treated this way. What made this situation different, Sandra told her *hermanitos* the following week, was that these students were actually trying to do something about it. With the help of a couple of counselors from Spark—a drug-and-alcohol-prevention program in the school—the Humanities "gang girls" had been meeting during their lunch hours, in free periods, and after school and had come up with a plan to stop what they referred to as "the Intimidation." To this end, they decided to start a schoolwide newsletter and initiate clean-up crews for removing graffiti in the bathrooms. One of the Spark counselors, Miriam, was an engaging and convincing ally, and under her auspices the principal had agreed to let them try it. This was an impressive enough example of the positivity that came about through organization, Sandra said. But now, these same *hermanitas* and *primas* and friends at Humanities were trying to put together a multination feed-the-homeless drive and Sandra wanted to get in on the act.

Identifying herself as Nikole's cousin and as coordinator of Manhattan's Netas, Sandra began calling Miriam at her Spark office at the school. Because she was nothing if not convincing, she had soon persuaded Miriam to call an open meeting for all "youth organization" members interested in changing their image. The meeting would take place after school at Humanities. There would be no arms or drugs or liquor allowed, and they agreed that no one should go who wasn't genuinely interested in turning the situation around.

As was usual the turnout was a little disappointing. Sandra had hoped that at least half of her chapter would show, but less than forty kids made it down to Humanities that day. It was freezing out, one of the last really cold days of spring, but Sandra had wanted to "look nice for the meeting," she told me, and so had dressed in a summery white cotton Polo shirt, a short tartan skirt, and thick white nylon tights. It wasn't the most appropriate outfit for the occasion but it was the only "pretty" thing she had to wear, and she had no trouble overcoming the hesitation the other gang members greeted her with when they first saw her. Drifting into the once grand auditorium with water-ruined murals and a crumbling ceiling, where we had been sent to wait by the school's security guards, each new arrival was greeted with a round of variously intricate handshakes and *Primo!*s and *Corazón!*s and back-slapping hugs.

At 7:30, one hour exactly after the appointed time, we were finally ushered up to a small but cozy advanced-placement English classroom on the second floor. There, the head of Humanities' Zulus, a tall, beautiful girl named Chante, opened the meeting by standing up from her chair, gathering the two hundred or so braids in her hair—each one tipped with the Zulu Nation's royal-blue beads, and letting them drop back in a cascade of tiny clicks round the back of her neck.

"This meeting has come about partly because of the abuse that our Nation and other association members have been taking at Humanities and partly because we want to change our image," Chante said. "If we don't take steps to make it happen, our names are not going to change, no matter what we say or how we feel. For me, I am proud of my beads. I am a black woman Zulu and want to represent being black, being a woman, and being a Zulu—they all equally important to me.

We must let the school administration know that we were never what they thought we were from the get-go."

Sandra listened intently. When she had to she could summon the concentration of a world-class chess player, and she needed to now because this was her first official mission as coordinator and she wanted everything to go smoothly. As the only one in the room with a citywide title, she was treated with a deference that had an aggrandizing effect. When the other kids became overexcited, and when Willie, the nominal head of the Netas from Humanities, tried to calm them with cries of "Keep the order! Keep the order!" Sandra only needed to yell "Shut up!" once for the room to collapse immediately into a pit of silence. This, however, didn't happen very often. Like young community activists everywhere, the gathered gang members were eager to work, and to do good, but they were unruly and easily distracted too. They spent the first few minutes calmly discussing a school clean-up campaign but quickly segued onto the potentially more explosive issue of dealing with a particularly heinous dean. Sandra was as entertained as anyone by the disparagement heaped on the woman, and it was only after half an hour that she remembered they were there to discuss citywide initiatives, and guided the subject back onto the possible creation of a feed-the-homeless campaign.

Here, noble intentions soon led to grandiose schemes and blindly unrealistic discussions of citywide van-delivery networks for the needy, twenty-four-hour community kitchens, and hot-food courier systems featuring uniformed messengers with aluminum-foil-coated backpacks. When Chante finally refocused the discussion on the best way of attaining positive media coverage, some suggested they should feed "the kind of homeless men with no legs who travel round on skateboards on the subway." Many *hermanitos* and *primas* and Zulus thought this was going too far. There were squeals of disgust and flat-out refusals until Mickey called out: "But we don't gotta feed them—feed them like with a spoon and shit—we just gotta give them the food!" The room didn't calm down again until a young member of La Familia who couldn't have been more than fourteen stood up. At a nod from her "head," she told the room that every day she walked past a soup kitchen on Ninth Avenue that she was pretty sure would be happy to take volunteers. It wasn't much, she said, but maybe it would be a good start.

"It's run by"—she unfolded a little scrap of worn, lined paper and read—"by *the Reverend William Greenlaw.*" Then, relieved to be out of the spotlight, she sat down.

"Sound like a government thing," said a boy who had until then had sat slumped in the middle of the circle. "I don't want to work with no government organization."

"Yeah, if you going to do a half-assed job it ain't going to work," another responded, setting off a lively debate about whether they really wanted to help people who were fit enough to get to a soup kitchen in the first place. Wouldn't it be better, many of them asked, if they went round the streets themselves in small groups with hot meals for the people who really needed help?

"We all got—what do you call it—those, what do you call it—we all got coolers, don't we?" one girl asked.

"No," a couple of boys groaned.

"Well, I got a cooler and we could kind of set something up with that. Or maybe you got a mad cool mom who would let you heat up twenty boxes of Rice-A-Roni—we all got kitchens."

But in the end Oscar managed to convince the kids still in the room that it would be better to do something specific and visible right now rather than work to create an elaborate scheme that no one would know about for months. Sandra agreed, and after another twenty-five minutes of increasingly sarcastic debate she finally brought the issue to a vote. The soup kitchen won out 14 to 11.

"Break it. Buss it down, kick it with them, the whole nine," Sandra then instructed John, who nodded his head, turned to the young Familia member for the priest's name and telephone number, and headed downstairs to a telephone as if he himself were one of her obedient *hermanitos.* Both Sandra and Chante were pleased. Feeling sure they had come up with at least the first step toward public recognition, they announced that each *hermanito* or *primo* or Zulu should volunteer three times a week. Anyone could volunteer more, Sandra added, but three afternoons would be the minimum. Thrilled with having seen the process through, Chante started to draw a weekly schedule chart on the blackboard.

Five minutes later, though, Oscar returned looking rueful and abashed. The soup kitchen needed help only in the mornings, he told them—from 9:00 to 11:45, in preparation for lunch—and though the priest had been more than enthusiastic about their offer, he had been worried that the hours might interfere with their class time.

"What about dinner? They don't serve dinner?" someone asked.

"Lunch is the only meal that they serve," Oscar replied apologetically.

"But everyone knows it's late in the evening that people need something warm inside of them!"

"Dang!" a girl sitting next to me said.

"Like I said—dumb-ass government thing," the boy in the middle concurred, and Chante reluctantly started to erase the intricate schedules she had been filling out on the board. Slumping down into her seat, she spent a good twenty seconds methodically brushing the chalk dust from her sleeves. "OK, who wants to volunteer during the vacation next week?" she asked without looking up, and across the room everyone's hands shot up into the air. Chante nodded to a younger girl and handed her the chalk.

"OK, what day?" the girl asked Sandra.

"Every day!" Sandra replied, offended.

26

IT WAS IMPOSSIBLE to say exactly what it was that brought about the kind of change in an individual that Rasheem was experiencing then. It was far more complicated than switching allegiances from Maurice to Roland, or finding a job, though both these things were symptoms of a transformation that clearly got going with the move to his new apartment. The same thing happened periodically with many kids at West Side, and the staff had learned long ago to be encouraging but not overbearing when a once reluctant student suddenly started to work harder than even the most studious child. With Rasheem, I think, the impulse stemmed more from a deep-seated desire to re-create himself than from any more mundane wish to graduate. Like many kids before him, he had started to work not only hard but with a hint of desperation too, as if through an act of monumental will he could wipe out his past and replace it with a more controlled and orderly set of circumstances.

Over the past few weeks Rasheem had been maintaining the insane schedule he had laid out for himself in mid-February. The art store had been doing inventory, and he'd been working there most nights until ten; he was spending a fair amount of time in New Jersey, doing "something with my uncle—family matters"; he came to school every day; and he spent hours every night on his homework. And he still managed to make time for Roland. The two had become almost inseparable, and ever since Rasheem had had his hair twisted into the same palm-frond plume as Roland, strangers had been asking them if they were brothers, at which point one or the other of them would smile and then pull out the shoe box they still almost invariably carried around. Opening the lid, they would thrust the exposed snake forward and say, "This is our brother, man."

Ed had been hearing reports from teachers about Rasheem's turnaround for some time. And though he didn't want to increase the pressure by mentioning it too often, he did make every attempt at encouragement. Rasheem's was the kind of progress that made you hold your breath, Ed said, over and over again, and he told Rasheem that if he ever needed any help, if he wanted to cut himself a little slack now and then, all he had to do was come talk to him. Certainly the fact that Maurice had been pulled back by Williamson's in early March made it easier for him to steer a straight course, they both knew. Maurice had set himself against Rasheem's attempts at reform from the start, and Rasheem had been subjected to increasingly vicious put-downs as his efforts started yielding results. Then, suddenly, just as the situation was becoming unbearable, Maurice wasn't there anymore. Nobody knew why, Williamson's hadn't given Ed a reason, and though Ed correctly surmised that they didn't pull kids back unless something serious had happened, it seemed unlikely he had been involved in a plot to kidnap Lucille, the way Maurice had told me over the phone.

Whatever the case (Cristy heard he was caught dealing drugs outside the center by the park, Georgia that he had been busted shoplifting porno magazines from Shadi's father's store), Rasheem and Roland had too much going on to pay his absence much mind. On top of everything else, Roland had recently bought himself a Rottweiler named Lucy, and they'd been spending hours in the park training her to sit, lie down, retrieve, and play dead. She was all they talked about in Family Group those days, and it was fun to listen to them chatter about how she just sat quietly and watched the snakes without bothering them, or how she chased after bugs in the park, and snored when she slept. In a more blustery moods, or when a pretty girl was around, they puffed up their surprisingly narrow chests and bragged about how Lucy would make a wonderful fighting dog too, when she was older, because she was strong and brave and they had trained her just so. They would generally turn to each other and grin at this point though, so I never believed them. Lucy was simply too docile to make a good fighter. So docile, in fact, that when she started to act the way most members of her breed did—barking at the door when anyone walked past it, for instance, or snarling at a stranger—Roland became convinced she was getting her period.

When nothing had changed a week later, he dragged Rasheem to the local Barnes & Noble, where they searched for a better explanation. Between them they paged through seven or eight reference guides but didn't learn anything new. Then, three weeks later, when Roland got home one afternoon, his foster mother told him to go look in his room.

"Why? One of my snakes die?" he asked.

"No. Worse."

"What? The dog ate one?"

"Nope. You'll see," she told him and pushed the door open to reveal seven puppies sprawled in a heap, blindly nuzzling the side of their exhausted mother. Roland was beside himself. If he'd been enthusiastic before, he became downright obsessive now, and like a proud godfather so did Rasheem. For days they kept Family Group entranced with stories of these soft, blind balls of miniature Rottweiler fluff battling for the mother's attention. One morning Roland even performed it out for us. Closing his eyes and scrunching up his nose and chin he brushed the air in front of him with his cheeks as if he were blind. Then he took questions. How many boy pups were there? How many girl pups? Would they all live? It had been a long time since I had seen Family Group so lightheartedly engaged, and with typical good humor Roland slumped back in his chair, his lanky body completely relaxed as he explained his latest predicament: while humans weren't usually supposed to touch newborn puppies, Lucy had rejected three of them, and now he was trying to feed them with milk from a baby's bottle.

Rasheem was helping out too, and he'd been so attentive that Roland's foster mother offered him his pick of the litter. Animals weren't allowed in his mother's new building, though, so he had to content himself with a Rottweiler cartoon character he designed, who was constantly accompanied by a litter of puppies that transformed themselves into flying superheroes with wings like a bumblebee's whenever an innocent bystander was threatened. Sometimes Rasheem even spent the night with Roland and the puppies uptown, and once they were old enough, Roland would sometimes let him bring one into school with him. Tucked into their jackets the way Roland used to carry his lizards, the puppies looked irresistible, especially to girls. Not long after that Rasheem started to spend time with a new friend from the High

School of Art and Design. She was not actually a girlfriend, he admitted; she was shy and awkward and no one would call her beautiful. Besides, "she don't know how to show affection," he told me. "Like usually when you see your boyfriend you say 'Hi,' don't you? She don't even acknowledge me." But for the meantime anyway, he felt proud walking along Seventh Avenue with her beside him, a skimpy and pale shadow of Roland's girl, who was bigger than Cristy and dark and voluptuous, but a girl nonetheless. His girl. And when he took her to the food court in A&S Plaza and asked her if she wanted a soda or something to eat, she would always reply that she would like one of whatever he was having, which made him feel kinder, more generous, and more of a man than ever before.

Then one Saturday at around ten in the morning, three men in suits arrived at Roland's door and demanded the removal of all animals and reptiles from the house. Pretending to think they were Jehovah's Witnesses, Roland refused to let them in. But when they returned with a uniformed policeman he had little choice but to submit to the warrant they had and to stand by and watch as, one by one, they transferred the snakes into boxes and the puppies into cages. Fixing a muzzle to Lucy's mouth, they loaded her into the van without saying a word. The men didn't tell him where they were taking the animals, or why, though Roland repeatedly asked. Something was mentioned once about having received a complaint, but no one ever said from whom, and as they left they handed Roland a fine of twelve hundred dollars and told him that as long as he paid it he wouldn't be prosecuted any further.

Rasheem and Roland spent the following Monday calling every animal center in the city. For some reason Roland had a hunch they were being held at the ASPCA on Ninety-sixth Street, and he spent most of the morning trying to get through to them. But the few times he managed to get past the mechanized answering machines, he was told that they couldn't give out that type of information, that it was confidential. He and Rasheem went down to the center in person the following afternoon, and after having their questions deflected and ignored for hours they were finally informed that the animals had been moved to a site on 103rd Street. A worker there told them that the dogs were in transit somewhere else. And though one vet gave a terse little nod when Roland asked if his dogs seemed well looked after, the majority of workers assumed the worst and glared at the boys as though they were criminals. The situation was becoming impossible. But Rasheem, at least, refused to give up. He goaded his friend out the door to follow more leads the following day, and the search would have gone on for weeks, I think, if Roland hadn't heard the following Monday that Lucy had been put down.

She had shown aggressive tendencies when a vet had tried to place her on the examination table, he was told, and was "put to sleep" by injection. Roland didn't come to school the following day, or the next, and when he finally did show up he had already bought himself a child's stuffed cuddly chow dog. It was brown and white and had silly-looking bulging white chops, and without the slightest self-consciousness he had carried it all the way to West Side on the subway. All day he walked around school with it, holding it under his arm, wagging its head and making it look real. He had found out by then that his puppies had passed their health tests and that they had all been put up for adoption at North Shore Animal League. When I asked him why he didn't go there and re-adopt one of puppies, he nodded the dog's head up and down and, pretending to be a ventriloquist, he giggled nervously. Trying not to move his lips at all he had the dog say: "I'm not quite ready for that yet."

For days after that Rasheem tried to persuade Roland to restart his pet collection. They went down to Canal Street and to Houston Street and to midtown on the east side, where all the biggest and best pet stores were. When Roland managed to convince Rasheem that he wasn't ready to look at dogs, Rasheem steered him to snakes, and then, finally, to a tank full of piranhas, which did seem to interest Roland for a time. They saw a baby rattlesnake and a spitting Asian cobra up at Roland's favorite pet store in the Bronx. They saw a pair of spider monkeys too, and a baby gray shark, both apparently illegally imported, which explained their huge cost. But they were still too drained by the recent confiscations to even think about buying anything, and they always left the stores emptyhanded, wondering why it was they kept seeking animals out in the first place. After a week of crisscrossing town, their other responsibilities began to slip by the wayside, and the second day in a row Rasheem sauntered in to his Holocaust class fifteen minutes late, Ann decided to prod him about it. "Sir Rasheem has decided to join us, I see," she said. "What an honor." Rasheem's already edgy humor fell away instantly. "You want a note, Ann? You want a note explaining why?" he spat out. "I'm too tired, man! I'm so tired I fell asleep trying to do your homework yesterday—for real—you wanna see it?" There was something in his tone that stopped Ann from going any further.

Maurice was back in school by then, which didn't help. There was still no explanation of what had happened up at Williamson's, but a few days after Roland's run-in with the animals-rights workers Maurice's mother had brought him to West Side and told Ed that her son would be living with her from now on, in the two-bedroom apartment she shared with her daughter. Neither Rasheem or Roland wanted anything to do with Maurice, and at first they managed to maintain their distance by sitting together out in the lobby opposite the seventh-floor elevators, taking turns playing ventriloquist with Roland's by now sagging toy dog. But it was difficult to resist Maurice's pull when the momentum had gone out of their own lives. His very first morning back Maurice had registered for all of Rasheem's classes and had come into Family Group waving his new schedule in the air as if it were the winning lottery ticket. He brought in new Nintendo games too, and took them to lunch at McDonald's, and in just over a week the two of them were beginning to accompany him to the steps of the main post office, where they'd watch him pick up girls and then maybe sing a tune or two. With his mom away at work, they were free to go to Maurice's house in Brooklyn, as well. And though Rasheem snarled, "So does mine," when Maurice boasted that "my mother lives in a white person's building," it wasn't long before all three of them were spending their early afternoons together out there, hanging out in the basement, listening to music as Rasheem constructed ceremonial fires and the other two got high.

So it seemed almost superfluous to hear, a few days later, that Roland had been shot. He wasn't seriously hurt: the bullet had grazed his chin in a straight line an inch and a half long, from one side of his face to the other. One millimeter closer, though, and he might have been dead. He'd been on his way to see a newborn Rottweiler when it had happened, and he never even saw who shot him. The last thing he'd seen had been a small group of people arguing on the corner. To avoid them he'd tried to cross the street, and the next thing he knew he was ducked into a crouch, staring down at his blood-drenched T-shirt. By the time he got to the hospital he had no idea what was going on. His foster mother told him they were there for just forty-five minutes, during which a doctor took him away and sewed nine stitches into his chin. There was very little talking and no counseling or treatment for shock. Nor were there any questions from the police, and he was back in Family Group the very next day with a white bandage across his chin, the bottom of it heavy with blood seepage from the wound.

Ed tried to convince him to spend the day on the bed in the nurse's room and to talk to Linda about the incident. But when Roland insisted that everything proceed as normally as possible, Ed spent Family Group carefully maneuvering the conversation onto any topic that was unrelated to the incident: lunch forms to be filled out again, a movie he had seen called *Speed,* which he'd enjoyed because it was so true to life, he felt—didn't homicidal maniacs like the character played by Dennis Hopper really behave like well-brought-up bourgeois men most of the time?—and a discussion about a girl named Alana's upcoming divorce, for which she still needed to be convinced to reveal the fact that she was raped repeatedly from the age of eleven by her "husband." One way or another, Ed kept his family group so entertained that though the other kids in the room sometimes stared at Roland, no one said anything and he was pretty much left alone to rest.

But a shooting was always news; its victim always an object of fascination and pride, and after Family Group the cozy closeting Roland had experienced couldn't be maintained. Maurice was probably most responsible for making sure the story got around—"Did you hear my boy got caught in the chin, B?" I heard him saying to a fresh-faced young girl outside Rochelle's English class—and by third period kids were gathering round Roland like he was a good-luck talisman. Mostly they joked about bullets. Sometimes someone would ask what kind of gun it had been. Several people chided him for being a dumb fool for running toward a bullet instead of away from it, and a couple expressed themselves by simply saying, "Damn!" admiringly as they passed. No one spoke about pain or fear or death. And apart from seeming slightly more wide-eyed than usual, and for protecting his back by clinging close to the sides of the corridors as he walked along, Roland seemed to be taking things more or less in his stride. His chin hurt, it was true, and he couldn't help but feel rattled and edgy, but Rasheem was there for him and he was coping.

In fact, the combined traumas of the past few weeks seemed to effect Rasheem almost as much as they did Roland. Even before the shooting Rasheem had seemed unable to rein in the anger he felt over the confiscated animals. He saw it in the most cataclysmic of terms. ("Roland was heartbroken by them taking his animals away. Heartbroken," he told me once. "It's the equivalent, I guess, of if a fire were to sweep through my house and burn up all of my sketchbooks along with it.") While Roland responded by shutting down and retreating inward, so that for the first time he was happy to dumbly follow Maurice wherever he led, Rasheem became increasingly frantic after the shooting. It was as if he had stepped over a precipice and had realized, too late, the value of all he was leaving behind. And there was something so frantically willed about him now, a vertiginous panic at all he had lost, that made me worry almost more about him than about Roland. He kept losing his travel pass, for one thing. A few days after the shooting, when Julia, the secretary, refused to give him another one, he exploded into a tantrum, screamed at her, and then stormed out of the building in a hail of threats so serious that Ed had to be contacted. From then on it was as if his driven determination to succeed had just snapped.

His math class was the first to go. It was the period just before lunch, and none of them had attended with anything like regularity since Roland's animals had been taken. Art was the next, and then science. And when Rasheem agreed to go uptown with Maurice on the morning Ann had scheduled to screen *Schindler's List,* I knew the double-period Holocaust class would soon follow. Ann had been emphasizing the importance of the movie for close to a month by then and had made it clear she would accept no excuses for nonattendance. Anyone who didn't come to her classroom by 2:00 that afternoon would automatically fail the class. But at 1:00 Maurice and Rasheem were still hanging around the video machines in the foyer of a movie house uptown. I reminded him about the class every five minutes or so. By 1:30 I was frantic. Watching him resolutely ignoring me and frantically tap-tap-tapping away on the round red disk of the Dragon Slayer attack button, I knew that in one move he was evicting himself from his desperate journey to success. And when he looked at me, shrugged and said, "So?" when I told him he had twenty-five minutes to get back to West Side, I knew something elemental had shifted.

Three weeks later he had been kicked out of every one of his classes except Family Group. He still came in every morning, but for the most part it was only to hook up with Maurice and Roland, and they all usually ended up leaving at 10:00. One morning I saw them get caught by a teacher named Tim.

"Where are you all going?" he shouted down the stairwell, having trapped only Rasheem on the seventh-floor landing.

"Mind your business," Maurice shot back from a couple of floors below.

"You'll be doing that in another school, young man," Tim replied and then turned to Rasheem, who insisted, truthfully, that he had no more classes to attend. He had been thrown out of his Holocaust class for missing a movie, he said, and in a rage now, he jerked his thumb in my direction and added, "You can ask her. You can ask her to tell you how I got kicked out of my other classes."

Tim was still incredulous. "You have nothing after Family Group? Then at this rate you'll graduate around the time when you are forty, with a specialty in electives," he said with a chuckle. It was more than Rasheem could take. For a moment it looked like he was going to hit the bespectacled, grinning teacher in front of him, but he brushed past him instead and stormed down the stairs shouting, "I can't learn here, they don't teach me nothing here. I am going to Art and Design. I could learn there, man. Damn! I used to be an A and B student. I'm out, man. I'm out, tha's it. I can't learn here no more."

27

I HAD BEEN in intermittent contact with the Israel group since they had left in March and had heard nothing from them that made me want to join them. They had access to a fax machine on the kibbutz, and every now and then, when I remembered, or when I just wanted a little respite from the craziness of the seventh floor, I wandered up to the Youthworks office—the tiny cubicle that Stewart, in a fit of frustration at his lack of privacy, had decided to build for himself one year—and rifled through the pile of recently arrived faxes to see if there were any for me. Few were. But the kids had also agreed to take along a couple of tape recorders and had promised to record their first impressions for me, the idea being to fill in the blanks until I went out to join them for a couple of weeks in the middle of their stay.

These I received piecemeal. Filled with requests for fast food and complaints about their health, they were grating examples of how difficult it was to adapt from the known to the bizarrely exotic. The kids had arrived at night, and the days that followed were filled with the chaotic clashing of resistance and adjustment. "Michelle, Naomi and Kamilah got on my fucking nerves—I'm not sure why exactly, all I know is I was ready to fuck all three of them up. Badly. Especially that little bitch Kamilah," Monica recorded one evening. The next day she continued: "Stewart got me crazy heated today. Must you be spitting up blood in order for him to consider you being sick? Just because you sick doesn't mean it have to be written all over your face cause if you have what I have it won't show unless you talk and I ain't gonna talk! Not to get out of no lousy job anyhow." Naomi, for her part, had this to say: "I feel that I'm lost. I feel that I'm on my own. Shit is real." Kevin wrote that "My first day at work weren't exactly what I thought it was going to be. We weren't gardening. We were doing what's called landscaping. I had to cut down a thorn bush and uproot weeds. You wouldn't believe how many times I got stuck in my hands. My first day sucked." This sentiment was echoed by Reggie a little more directly: "Today fucking horrible. My boss is an asshole. I had to wash pots the size of car tires, no-no-no, truck tires and by myself I might say. Dumb ass Bullshit."

I was going through my own personal dislocation right then too. Having recently left my home of six years, I was trying to adjust to a one-bedroom apartment that I was sharing with an old college friend, our spaces divided by sheets hung from string pinned to opposite walls. And as my own departure date drew near the idea of leaving for Israel filled me more with fatigue than with any kind of excitement. As it had for the kids, routine, no matter how deadening, was becoming more and more attractive.

Then I heard the following from Monica and everything changed.

> Egypt: Today we went to the market—I had a couple of men ask for my hair, talking about "I give you 100 camels, 100 camels 100 sheeps!" We went to the pyramids. They was real hard to get into. We had to slouch all the way down. It would have been better just to roll in but you couldn't. I tried. Once you get to the pyramids it's so hot and humid you start sweating—it's all funky and stinky, just disgusting. We went to the step pyramid though and that was nice. My favorite part was going to the Mohammed Ali Mosque. Carina is Muslim so she took it upon herself to pray. I took it upon myself to pray also. But we didn't know which way was East, so one of the men that was working there came and showed us what to do. We had to cover our hair with the robes they gave us and cover our skin with the robes they gave and he pointed us East toward Mecca and he was saying something like "Ra-Ha, Ba-Ha, Le-Ha, La-Mohammed," something like that. And he would go "Allah" and bend down and bow and we would do it behind him. And at the end he told us what he said and he made us repeat after him and he said, "Now you're Muslim." They greeted us with tea. That was nice. I mean it was the first time that someone actually gave us something that wasn't like money, that wasn't asking for money. It was nice. I felt good. I felt wanted. I mean Muslim—I could be a Muslim. The only part of it is

> Muslim females can't date out of their religion and I can't hang with that. I mean, if I could date whoever I wanted to and be a Muslim I would do it. I guess going into any religion you have to make some kind of sacrifice. Maybe if I could cheat a little bit? But the mosque was nice though. I felt good in the robe. It was just so pretty. After it was over I felt like if my soul been touched. If I been lifted. And I just felt so good. I swear it. I just felt so good. I mean the whole day—going to the market, buying a whole lot of stuff, stealing a lot; I ain't going to lie, stole a little bottle at the store. Jewelry. We almost got caught this time but we got away with it. The whole day. Ah well, it's weird.

The kibbutz was nothing like I'd thought it would be. Established in 1940 by two groups of immigrants from Germany and Eastern Europe, Lehavot Habashan was one of the oldest kibbutzim in the country. Lying just half a mile from the Syrian border, it had seen its fair share of danger until the 1973 war pushed the borders back over the Golan. Since then it had expanded and prospered to the point where it now resembled a not very established company town, or a refugee camp left for so long that it has become semipermanent looking. There were only the barest traces of luxury. The residential areas were arranged in suburban-style tracts with paths running between concrete, boxlike bunkers all painted the same off-white. The communal dining room was large, but functionally so rather than grand, and the less important buildings, like the library and the even older children's dormitory, were overgrown with stringy vines and largely ignored.

But it was a beautiful place too. There were still plenty of wild scrub areas and most of the remaining open space was covered with ankle-high grass. With only one or two streets wide enough for vehicles to pass each other, it was like a huge working farm. In the early morning just before breakfast, you could sometimes see an old gnomelike man in a blue-and-white woolen hat, walking up the hills with his English Wellington boots and his stick, *jahing* the cows to pasture. Otherwise it was still. Tucked up next to the base of the Golan Heights, which rose to soft, worn curves on the horizon, the bottomland surrounding the kibbutz was covered with orange trees. One dusty road skirted the edge of a fish farm and led to the Jordan River, little more than a stream up there, lined on each bank with thousands of yellow flowers. Because no one had much business in the mountains or the willow-shaded valley, the kibbutz seemed to exist in the middle of an ancient, worn-smooth nowhere.

Stewart had deliberately chosen Lehavot Habashan because of this. Many of the more successful kibbutzim had become industrial over the years, running mostly on profits from factories. Lehavot Habashan, however, was still predominantly agricultural. The sense of sedate, bare-bones simplicity that this brought to the community was essential for kids used to the brash squawks and turbulent chaos of life in inner-city New York. Neither Stewart nor his co-leader, a Californian-based teacher named Lucy, believed in force-feeding the kids, but they knew that the shock of so much empty openness was as disturbing to them as a flash visit to New York City would be to someone who grew up in the countryside. Like gawping tourists from the farm belt, the kids had to be continually reassured that it was all right to leave their clothes out on the railing in front of their dormitories, that nothing would happen to them, and that it was fine to start up conversations with strangers, and to smile and look them in the eye, and even all right if they wanted to go for solitary walks in the middle of the night. After years of living in the concrete canyons of the city, it was as if they had developed a kind of agoraphobia. Even the birds chirping and the crickets and the rustling of trees was hard to get used to.

But then everything was different in Israel. Everything. Visiting soldiers walked around with M16s slung carelessly over their shoulders and no one seemed to feel the slightest bit threatened. No one cared about what clothes they wore either, or how their hair looked, and many of the children wandered around naked. People spoke to each other in what the kids called a "disrespectful way" before barging ahead in line. And though most of the kibbutzniks had grown used to the annual pilgrimages from New York, when a new group walked into the dining room, it still silenced all conversation. The older people—those who'd moved to the kibbutz after being released from Auschwitz or Dachau or Belsen—couldn't help but stop eating their salad and look up over their glasses of water and stare for just long enough to make someone like Monica long for the anonymity of being one of Grandma Doreen's kids back on 213th Street in the Bronx.

To orient themselves and at least partially balance out all this newness, most of the kids had made little uptown shrines in their dorms. They all lived together in a one-story concrete structure with a porch and four rooms, two for the boys and two for the girls. Monica shared a room with Michelle and Kamilah, and like all girls forced to share living spaces, each had defined her own area by decorating the walls. Monica's were covered with the school certificates she had earned in her past year at West Side. Carefully smoothed out and stacked and packed for the journey, they were tacked to her wall now, in perfectly straight lines. Above Michelle's bed was a poem by her little sister Shawneequa: "I know you are sad, and me too/ I wish I can come with you/ because I do have no one to play with/ you always said I always be next to you/ I always love you." And though a single picture of a lizard decorated Kamilah's wall, the mounds of chaotic mess at the base of her bed delineated clearly what part of the room she felt was hers. Next door some of the boys had done the same kind of thing. Fred had brought along his collection of toy cars, and though he had kept them in his suitcase for the first few days, he'd soon brought them out and braved whatever mockery they caused. Reggie had filled his area with junk food and tapes from home, and everyone displayed their alarm clocks in the most elaborate ways, apparently attempting to establish once and for all whose was more effective, louder, uglier, better, "flyer," or just plain more sensible.

By the time I arrived, waking up on time for work was still something the kids hadn't adjusted to, and though they set their clocks to go off in unison, almost every morning either Stewart or Lucy would have to storm over to the dorm and haul one kid or another out of bed. Work was obviously an important part of the experience. I'd been hearing their complaints since their very first day. But three weeks into their stay, they had settled into a softer kind of noninflammatory grumbling. Their work days were long, stretching from seven in the morning until two, but even the youngest kids in the kibbutz took part in the routine and there was a fair amount of variety. Aside from the agricultural labor, working with the cows, chickens, and turkeys or out on the kibbutz land itself, there was work in the kitchen and the dining room, as well as in the laundry, the small fire-extinguisher factory, and the machinery shop, where Kenny spent weeks spray-painting steel girders.

In the beginning the kids had been shuffled from one job to another until appropriate fits had been found. Most started out raking leaves and waiting for the head gardener, Kobi, to come by with his tractor and pick up the four or five piles they had gathered into neat little volcano shapes. He was infamous among the group for being a demanding and unpleasant boss, and a few of the kids, including Reggie and Monica, had refused to work with him. Michelle, however, didn't seem to mind; the work was hard, but she was left alone most of the time, and as long as the weather stayed cool and the snakes kept sleeping she was quite happy. Besides, Stewart had promised that when an opening came up he would get her a job in the fish farm, where she'd wanted to work ever since seeing a photo of a former participant wearing the required waist-high gray rubber boots with suspenders that strapped over the shoulder and the matching, steel-clasped jacket.

Tucked away in the kitchen, Melissa and Naomi may have had the best jobs. Their hours were regular and relatively relaxed, and because they were handling food they could at least be assured of clean working conditions. While there was much debate about who had the worst, it was obvious to me that Carina did. She was stationed in the egg house, where 11,500 chickens sat, three to a minuscule cage. The only light in the building came from a four-inch gap between the ceiling and the wall and from under the slatted metal walkways suspended in the air twenty feet from the ground. The first time I walked in, the air, thick with guano dust and feathers, almost made me gag, and the scale of the place—two hundred feet of caged and stacked chickens stretching to a vanishing point like a child's neatly plotted rendering of perspective—made me feel so small that I had to sit down. Carina recognized my reaction. "I know," she said kindly, almost indulgently. "It makes me think that I should go out and do something with my life. I mean we have choices and they don't, and it's time to stop being lazy and hanging around because before we know it we'll be old and it'll be finished and over. When I look at these chickens I think it's, you know, kinda like the way people think of women—make kids, make sure everything goes OK with them, with everyone else, and then die."

However much kids grumbled about work, though, the food had presented the most concrete cultural hurdle at first. Fare was plentiful but simple, as the community survived mostly on their own fruits and vegetables that were too small or too blemished to be sold. Most days there was salad for breakfast and sometimes eggs or cereal; a hot dish and salad, for lunch; and then more salad for dinner. Stewart had warned the kids about this for months, but their reactions continued to be emphatic: they hated the food, hated the way it was always cold and "straight from the ground," and especially hated the way it was "greaseless." After a few days with them there in the kibbutz, however, I began to realize that their horror of the food stemmed more from a need for commonality than from a genuine feeling of disgust. Among all this strangeness it was important to have certain bedrock customs to fall back on. And whether you were Latin or African American, male or female, sixteen or nineteen, whether you lived in Brooklyn, Harlem or the Bronx, cold salad—and not even salad like in the salad bars at home, but entire leaves of lettuce and whole tomatoes and cucumbers that you had to cut up yourself—was just not an appetizing way to start the day. Ironically, their constant griping had led to the group's first real breakthrough: Kamilah's discovery that when she flipped her room's bar heater onto its side it made an almost perfect cooking ring.

She found a pan that had been holding grain in an incubator room, and every afternoon she used it to boil eggs that had been "borrowed" from the kitchen. On special occasions, after their once-weekly visit to the kibbutz's only store, she would prepare hamburgers too. The pan was big enough for only one burger at a time, so she'd carefully place each patty in the middle, flipping and flipping it until it was brown and shiny with the grease they so missed. Then she'd drape cheese over the top and wait for it to melt. Kamilah had always been inventive. Most of the time she lived in her grandmother's two-bedroom apartment with eleven other people. The cramped quarters of their new living situation on the kibbutz was something she was already used to, and she was more relaxed about boundaries and sharing than the other kids. So while at sixteen she was the youngest of the group, her generally easygoing nature and her control of the "kitchen" gave her an unquestionable position of leadership within the group.

It was all very subtle, of course, this slow construction of a legitimate hierarchy separate from the one they had already established in New York—particularly as it was female led. Unsurprisingly, perhaps, the largest factor in its evolution were the romances that had sprouted like mushrooms after rain. The kids had started to pair off almost as soon as they got to the airport. Within three nights, Reggie had kissed a girl in the group who he had been secretly adoring since the first meetings at school. "I kissed a lovely young lady for a while. She has very soft lips," he told me one evening. After days of Zen-like contemplation in the chicken house, Carina was coming out of her shell too, and even as she was having what she called "a nervous condition" she began to flirt quietly with Simon. Monica hooked up with Kevin in just about as uncomplicated a fashion as was possible under the circumstances. Naomi and Raul had been spending so much time together since they'd arrived that they were beginning to get on everyone else's nerves. Even Michelle, until then a shrewd, eyebrow-raising boy mistruster, had fallen for a burly white boy from the suburbs who had been in so much trouble that his mother had begged Stewart to take him to Israel after reading about Youthworks in a magazine.

Tall, blond, and chunky, every high school's dream of a linebacker, Kirk had instantly fascinated the girls when they'd first met him at the airport. Monica sashayed around him as Naomi and Carina entertained him with cards and Gameboys that they'd pulled from their carry-on bags. For her part, Michelle insisted she didn't pay him much mind and was surprised and only quietly pleased when he ended up sitting down next to her on the plane. Michelle had been in planes before. She knew all about the food service and the headphones and she knew about taking off and landing too, how you had to sit back in your seat and grab onto the armrests and suck and suck and suck on a piece of hard candy to stop your ears from "bursting." The eighteen-year-old Kirk was clearly impressed. He had never been out of the tri-state area before and was as nervous as Reggie about flying. But according to Michelle he had another kind of worldliness. "He kisses surprisingly well for a white boy," she said. Every afternoon they met in the dining room and went for strolls round the kibbutz, where they once discovered a pond hidden behind a locked set of gates. Kirk didn't sleep with the other Youthworks participants. He had his own room with the kibbutz's "regular" volunteers, but it wasn't long before he started spending most of his time with Michelle in the Youthworks dorm. He preferred the company, he said.

How much Stewart was aware of all this I really don't know. Both he and Lucy had backed off after the first two or three weeks, and aside from the hour-long Family Group meetings they held in the afternoons, and the more casual chats over meals in the dining hall, they seemed to pretty much let their kids be. There was no real danger on the kibbutz after all, and each of the participants had signed a contract stating that they understood the rules and would abide by them. Besides, Stewart believed that as young adults they were capable of resolving most of their difficulties on their own. There was plenty of grumbling about their work duties, and the food and their living conditions, but nothing they didn't seem able to cope with, and he was more interested in watching how they dealt with the intangible challenge of filling the time they now had on their hands than in interfering with the details of their everyday life.

I'm not sure what I expected to see when I arrived at the kibbutz. For months I'd listened to past participants of the trip speak about how the trip had changed them, how it had matured them and made them see the error of their ways. Perhaps I had learned nothing over the past few months, and continued to expect some great earth-shattering transformations to be under way, or at least to find some meaningful cultural exploration. But the kids couldn't have cared less about being in Israel. They ate every day with survivors of the Holocaust, picked up the occasional strange-sounding Hebrew word, and were vaguely impressed by the warlike elements of the country. ("Just in case," they would say as they lounged on the poppy-covered roof of the bomb shelter close to their dormitory.) But for the most part they remained strangely unaware of both the history and the culture that surrounded them. Instead they tended to drift through their days locked in their own personal identities—exploring a pond or staring at the way a tree bent almost to the ground when the wind got up. Sometimes they even slipped into the belief that they were back in the States somewhere.

"Sometimes I feel like this is upstate, 'cause they are similar, I think," Kevin told me one afternoon as we sat by a pond filled with goldfish. "Like the animals all over the place roaming free and the way the clean air is and the trees and all that stuff, the way the environment feels."

Gradually I began to realize that it was this very sense of normalcy that allowed even the potential for any behavioral adjustments to be made at all. The kibbutz reminded the kids of upstate, they said, but many of them had never been upstate in their lives and had never experienced the languorous freedom of an empty summer outside of the city's edgy bustle. Now, for once, they had time on their hands. With no chaos to fill their days, the open space and heavy abundance of slow passing emptiness was what the kids railed against and what they also praised to the skies, depending on their moods. Lying on their backs in the grass they would sometimes swear, vow, and pray that they would be able to grow up and come back to the kibbutz to live; more often, however, and especially in the beginning, they would lie in the same grass and dream of crowded subways and grime and all the action they were missing back home.

There just wasn't that much to do. Sometimes a few of the kids would be invited to the house of their assigned kibbutz family, where they would be fed more or less the same food as was served in the dining room and where there might be a TV and a few American shows, dubbed into Hebrew, to watch, and perhaps even a younger child or two to play with quietly in the living room. But a lot of the time, the hovering quiet, empty spaces and dark nights closed in on them like the busiest city never could. For the first few weeks the boys tried filling the time by playing basketball on the old but still functioning court opposite the zoo. But although they could handily beat the kibbutz kids and the South African and Danish volunteers, none of them were particularly athletic, and the novelty of being good at something wore off when Reggie almost got into a fight with a South African volunteer who kept pushing and bumping into him as if the game meant anything. Most of the time they just hung around and stared at the worn silhouettes of the Golan Heights against the dark night skies and reminisced about impossibly romanticized versions of their lives "back home in the city."

"I'm about ready to break out and to hell with the consequences," Reggie said one night, driven mad by the boredom as much as by the fact that the pet dog he had adopted as a mascot had just lost a fight to the dog sported by a group of Russian volunteers. "It's so boring here. So boring. I'm just so bored. I would die if I had to live here—the people they cool, but I guess I'm really a big-city boy at heart. I just can't take this."

It was 10:30 at night when he said this, and he'd been sitting by himself out on the porch of their dorm building with his brown hoody pulled up tight around his face, his shoulders hunched, music from a tape he'd brought from home playing softly next to him. I knew what he meant. The days started early with a 6:30 breakfast and skidded along with work until lunch. But with only a one-hour Family Group meeting to distract them, the afternoons stretched endlessly, and after supper in the evenings, there really was nothing whatsoever to do. Nothing. After just five days there, even I was going stir-crazy. There was a kibbutz bar—the Pub, they called it—but it was only open twice a week. The three bottles of Johnny Walker Red Label on the shelf perked me up when I first walked in, but it didn't take long to notice the layers of dust and the old candle-wax drippings down their sides—decoration rather than solace—and I had to settle for a beer, which I ended up sharing first with Reggie then with Kevin and then with so many of the kids that I felt sure Stewart would hear about it and send me home, and I decided it was best to leave and drink the last drops of my airplane-bought mini-scotch, which I had been saving in my room, by myself. When I asked Reggie that night if he felt that he was in Israel rather than say, New Jersey or Iowa or New York State, for once he said "I'm in Israel all right." Then he jutted his chin out toward the pub, somehow encompassing with that gesture the sack-cloth walls, the neon orange and pink dart board, the hard-rock music, and the elderly Danish visitors dancing "rock and roll style," and said, "You could never get away with this in the States."

So although the one rule Stewart did seriously emphasize was that no one ever leave the kibbutz unattended, even Michelle pointed out that, "the guards are practically never at the entrance and Stewart doesn't really have any way of knowing where we are." To begin with, once the most immediate hurdles had been overcome at least, the boys frequently left the kibbutz to hitchhike into the mountains, where a nearby kibbutz had a late-night disco. They didn't take the girls with them, and this caused some friction. The way they saw it, they'd have to be "crazy irresponsible" to take a group of beautiful "New York females" out into the countryside to hitchhike with strangers in unlit cars. None of the girls would have dreamed of going by themselves. Instead they sat in their dorms listening to music, doing their hair, chatting, and writing their journals for Family Group the following day.

Sometimes the boys even hitchhiked into Qiryat Shemona, the local town where Katyusha rockets sometimes had a habit of falling. But they were strangely shy of the small town's bluster, and though Fred and Enrique had their ears pierced in a little beautician's store in a mall there once and Kirk had his name tattooed in Chinese round his bulging biceps, mostly they loafed around the shopping district, where they soon learned to order pita bread stuffed with french fries and meat from a gyro stand before hitchhiking back with a couple of take-out orders for the girls.

Not such a very dangerous pastime. They were always back in time for Family Group, and though the occasional work morning saw some of the boys really struggle to get out of bed, the kids, for the most part, kept out of trouble. In fact, the kibbutzniks had noticed an increasing docility as Stewart's groups progressed over the years. "These ones are a bunch of poodles," a disappointed middle-aged man told me one day at lunch. Only Reggie had been causing any real trouble. Of all the kids in the group his background was the most stable. "He has two parents in his home and both of them work and there is no real reason why he should be a mess," Ayala had told me, which had made me think of myself. He had worked at and been fired from landscaping, the kitchen, the dining room, and the factory since arriving in the kibbutz. And it wasn't until an eccentric character named Alon took him on that Stewart no longer had to storm over to Reggie's dorm and shake him and shout at him to wake up and get out of bed.

Alon was head of the poultry division, a large profit-making industry for the kibbutz. Because of its centrality, he had never allowed anyone from New York to work with him before. But something about Reggie struck him as amusing one day in the dining hall, and he agreed to try him out. Alon himself had been a problem kid when he was growing up and was still viewed with suspicion by some of the older members of the community, who demanded his expulsion whenever they caught him growing marijuana on the Golan Heights. Reggie didn't know this, of course. Nor would he find out. Instead, he found himself working for an intelligent, hardworking, and eccentric middle-aged man who looked like a pirate—long hair pulled back into a dashing ponytail, a scar across half of a cheek—who loved what he did and who expected the same level of dedication from all those he worked with. Almost from the minute Reggie started working for him things started to change. He woke up early and without much complaining every morning and worked hard until lunch, when he would stroll into the dining room with his mask still covering his face or pushed up to the top of his forehead like a warrior's helmet. When he first began to work there he had mistakenly left the door to the chick house open, but Alon had decided to give him a second chance and Reggie had been so careful since that I could see he was nervous just showing Kevin and me around.

"I just want you to keep quiet once you're inside, and to watch where you walk," he said before unlocking the door. He raised his hand for us to wait just the other side while he turned and relocked the door behind him and then flicked on the light. Like Carina's egg house, this building was also about two hundred feet long. There were no cages though; instead the floor was covered with thousands and thousands of tiny yellow Easter-card chicks. "My workplace," Reggie said regally. Carefully picking his way through the carpet of yellow, he showed us the heaters that hung from the ceiling and the automatic water feeds and the computer in the office that kept the whole thing going. Afterward he picked up a chick, which he handed to me; picked up another, which he handed to Kevin; and then picked up a third and tried to show us how to feel for the remainder of the yolk in the inside of the throat. He'd been trying to find this for days but hadn't managed to. He told us that it's a sign that a chick is sickly, and perhaps because it was part of his job to pick up and throw out all the dead chicks in the morning, he had a morbid fixation with diagnosing one in time to save it by placing it in a special incubator. "These little suckers, these shorties, you might think they look cute, but they kill each other. Like, this one is fine," he said, picking up a perfectly yellow and fluffy dead chick. "But some of them, their heads are all picked away at."

Kevin nodded knowingly. Since shortly after arriving at the kibbutz he had been working in the petting zoo—a leftover from the time when there had been enough kids on the kibbutz to warrant such an extravagance. He worked with Kamilah, who had always loved animals and who had wanted to become a vet all her life. She had instantly taken control and made it one of Kevin's regular duties to gather the birds mauled by the stray dogs that snuck in through the zoo's old wire fences at night. Almost every morning he found one; sometimes he found three or four; and he soon chose a spot to dump them out by the basketball court where great heaps of scraps and leaves and straw were piled into "smoking wigwams," he said.

Born and bred in Bronx, Kevin had never been out of the city before. He was raised in the shadow of Yankee Stadium, but he had never been to a Yankee game either, because "kids like me isn't wanted there." It wasn't until he came to Israel, in fact, that he confessed he had never learned how to catch a baseball or to ride a bike. He wouldn't have said anything about either deficiency if Reggie hadn't magically arrived outside their run-down old dormitory one day, riding a red bike and hauling along a tiny silver one by his side, frantically shouting for Kevin to join him. He'd swapped the use of them for some American junk food and a few hip-hop tapes fresh from uptown—that was what clinched the deal, he said, the freshness of the tunes and the promise to teach the kids how to dance to them too—and Kevin had only stood there, sleepy from the nap he had been taking, shrugged, and said, "Don't know how to ride, Reggie."

Two weeks later he was still wobbly but confident enough to ride down to the Jordan River most afternoons, and to spend most of his days circling the ringed outer perimeter of the kibbutz, right next to the ten-foot wire fences topped with razor wire. This annoyed Kamilah. She blamed his obsession with biking for the terrible condition of the zoo and the animals it housed. She warned that unless he started devoting more time to the animals, she would have to report him to Stewart.

The Zoo wasn't much, it must be said. After years of only the most perfunctory care it was the kind of operation that had a few sheep who never got sheared, some skinny, bleating goats, plenty of rabbits, a wheezing old horse, and a handful of birds in feather-stuck cages coated with guano. But to Kamilah it was paradise. By the time I arrived she had painted most of the animal cages, scraped and cleared the paths (which she called sidewalks), and even housed the old horse, Smooley, in a hastily constructed but reasonably sturdy stable. Recently, she had also begun asking the kibbutz to pour cement over the now cleaned pathways. Her real concern, though, was that they mend the gates and patch up the fences to stop her animals from being eaten by the scrawny, long-legged dogs that roamed the kibbutz. Animals were being killed every day, she told anyone who would listen, and she had become famous around the kibbutz for storming across to the dining hall with a wounded or dead animal in her arms, demanding that someone somewhere pay attention to her. "The Zoo Girl," the older kibbutzniks called her, and though all she had been able to do about it was to insist that Kevin clear the carcasses away in the morning, she continued to make what headway she could in other areas of her domain. She had even persuaded Naomi and Melissa to replace the rotting scraps they were sending her animals with fresh, tasty leftovers—"You know who's getting this," she told them. "So throw some good stuff in there." The girls were continually caught throwing big juicy tomatoes into the "zoo waste pot," but the system had inexorably established itself by the time I got there and every morning Kamilah served her rabbits still crisp lettuce and her horse whole, earth-encrusted carrots.

It wasn't until she reported Kevin to Stewart that the orderly progression she had established began to disturb, rather than advance the group's sense of unity. It was part of Kevin's nature to be lazy, Reggie maintained, and, insisting that Kevin worked as hard as any normal person would (Kamilah being not normal but obsessed), Reggie and Kevin tried their best to cause a scandal. They scheduled private meetings with Stewart and Lucy, and brought it up in Family Group and whenever they could in the dining hall, at breakfast and lunch and dinner. But Stewart stuck to his plan to move Kevin over to Kobi's landscaping team and when it became clear that the decision was final, Kevin slipped into a sulk. He still insisted he liked elements of the kibbutz—"It's like a huge family growing up with just one big parent, ain't it? Like a bunch of brothers and sisters and this one big parent who has a really good job and supplies for everybody,"—but after being evicted from the zoo he started to mope around more, sulkily longing to go home.

Over and above the feud between Kamilah and Kevin, the tension brewing in the girl's number-two room had become the focus of group gossip, however. Since arriving in Israel Naomi had been paired up with

Raul, the quiet, scholarly Cuban boy, who spent most of his time standing proudly behind Naomi with his arms wrapped around her middle while she chatted with whoever would listen. Kamilah, in contrast, was spending a lot of time with Fred, an ardent malingerer and the best thief, "the quickest fingers," of the group. The two couples did not get on and whenever Kamilah got mad, she picked up the closest thing to hand and threw it at Raul, shouting at him to get back into his own room. At this point Naomi would unleash a stream of high-pitched invective against Kamilah and the filth of the zoo she brought into the room with her, not to mention the cooking, and the constant noise from the music she and Fred liked to listen to late at night. When Kamilah walked into the dorm one afternoon with two abandoned kittens the tensions between them exploded. None of the girls wanted the cats in their room. They sometimes used the litter tray Kamilah had made for them out of an empty cereal box filled with torn up newspaper, but for the most part they didn't and soon the room began to reek with the acrid ammonia smell of stale urine—a situation particularly unbearable to Naomi, who prided herself on her cleanliness and fastidious sense of order.

"I am learning a lot about human nature here—Michelle, Kamilah, and Monica are the most unbelievable females I have ever lived with! God help me to be able to find a way to never end up in a situation such as this. Willpower is the weirdest thing. I wouldn't wish this on my worst enemy!" she recorded into the tape. Minutes later Kamilah's voice came on:

"She pissed me the fuck off. She is always taking the bullshit about she's the peacemaker when really she is the instigator. Always reporting back and forth and giving the wrong info. I also hate it when she tries to talk like she's educated. She is really a dumb bitch. That's why her ass is nineteen and still in high school. Her and Raul belong together. Two stupid motherfuckers."

Within days the girls were refusing to room together, beds were moved, joint chores avoided, dining tables abruptly left when members of one camp came too close to members of another camp. Soon Family Group meetings became almost unbearably clogged with whining and bitching and blaming.

It began to seem like the group would not hold. The cramped living situations, dearth of private space, and impossibility of escape were beginning to take their toll. But Stewart was unfazed. Telling the kids that they'd known all along it was going to be hard, and that there was nothing he could do about the living arrangements, he clung to the belief that nothing he could do or say would change them as much as working through the problem themselves. "The key is giving them the space and a loving environment," he insisted. "It's painful watching the process unfold, but it's very rare that we need to rush in. If we get involved, then it never really resolves itself. What we are trying to do as educators is modify their behavior so they will become successful, empowered young people, and what we provide for that to happen is a very challenging situation in terms of social dynamics that are created by them living with each other."

In theory at least, this made sense. And Stewart was right that, on the surface of things anyway, the program continued in much the same way as it had before. Despite the social difficulties the kids were having, their punctuality and attendance rates improved every week. Naomi and Melissa had been called two of the best bakery workers the kibbutz had ever had. Reggie had been promoted to the turkey house. Even skulking Fred had become the head dining-room worker, though he had always been on good terms with his boss because they had Spanish as a first language in common and it made them feel special and superior to talk to each other about Hispanic culture in the middle of Israel. Kamilah had even prepared a kibbutzwide Easter egg hunt and had brought all the kids from the kibbutz together to teach them how to paint eggs, a scene so intimately picturesque that Stewart must have spent four rolls photographing it.

But back at the dorms the situation continued to deteriorate. Briefly summarized, the dynamics of the group now ran something like this: Kevin had been fired from the zoo, for which he blamed Kamila, who found solace from Fred, who hated the way Raul would tell him to turn his music down all the time. Raul in turn was snide about Reggie, who was feeling deserted by Kevin and shunned by Carina, who hated her job, especially when she had to work with Naomi, who bossed her around. Everyone was mad at Michelle and Kirk for keeping to themselves too much. And everyone loathed Kenny, who had lost the meager kudos he had managed to earn since arriving at the Kibbutz, by getting completely drunk one night, giving a Russian girl a hickey on her neck, and then confessing to Stewart that it had been Kirk who had been buying them liquor. Enrique, of the green contact lenses, ignored everyone in the group in favor of the pretty young volunteers from South Africa.

Passover was also coming up, and the tradition that the Americans perform during the evening's festivities only added more fuel to the fire. Stewart made it clear that they had to perform something but he stuck with his policy of nonintervention. As far as he was concerned, the kids had to perform on Pesach whether they were organized or not. If working as a unit was impossible, he told them one Family Group when they continued to insist that it was, well, they would all just end up looking like fools.

As the days went by, he did nothing but mention it casually at the beginning or the end of meals: "How's the rehearsing coming, by the way?" or, "So, have you started anything yet?" which invariably led to a stunned, embarrassed, anxious silence until, finally, two days before Passover, the kids called a preliminary meeting on the porch in front of their dorms. At first the boys remained sullen and reluctant. Kevin insisted that he couldn't perform because his feet hurt from landscaping all day (a piercing glance over to Kamilah). Others avoided the girl-led debates about what they could do for the ceremony by playing the fool or just goofing around. "Animal go bye-bye," Kenny kept saying, while Simon made up a rap song in baby-talk Hebrew.

Among the girls, Naomi was trying desperately hard to take charge. She complained about cramps more often than she made suggestions, though, and Kamilah burst out laughing at any idea Naomi came up with and then scrunched her lips and exhaled sharply. But after almost an hour, Michelle, Ylaria, Melissa, and Monica seemed suddenly to have had enough of other people's feuding. Driven by fear at what might happen if they didn't plan anything right then, they insisted that at least they divide into two groups. The boys would sing "Swing Low, Sweet Chariot," Ylaria announced; the girls, "Amazing Grace." None of them could hold a tune and no one seemed to know the words for either song, but after forty-five minutes or so the girls had sketched the outlines of a dance for their number and the boys had invented their own, vaguely manly, stomping V-shaped arrangement. By ten that night, missed steps had became hilarious instead of irritating, forgotten lines absurd instead of typical, and even when they needed to borrow one another's clothes for costumes, they all ended up getting along fine. By the dress rehearsal the following afternoon they were as good as they were going to get: almost friends again, they were clumsy, out of tune but eager and proud.

Most spent the next day away from their regular jobs, helping camouflage the usually industrial, linoleum tone of the dining room for Passover dinner. Great historic murals were hauled from a dusty back room in the library and then displayed against the walls. Tables were draped with purple cloths and deep-blue napkins. There were bottles of wine and special plates and serving dishes; and through the doors of the kitchen, bowls and bowls of food and breads and fancy tidbits were being prepared.

That night the boys walked into the dining room right on time, dressed up in their city best: crew-necked sweaters and shirts with collars, baggy pleated dress pants and leather shoes. Kenny even wore the suit that his mother had sent him without explanation one afternoon, all folded up in a brown paper parcel. The kibbutzniks were dressed up for the occasion too, the young men in smart trousers and sweaters much like those of the boys from New York, the older ones in thickly woven three-piece suits. Their wives wore ankle-length dresses and elaborate and beautiful shawls, and some of the younger women were in tight, sparkling evening dresses, dangling gold and bead earrings, and high heels.

Looking for and finding the table set aside for them, the boys took their places and had more than enough time to sneak samples of wine before the girls arrived. Simon insisted that the red wine was alcohol free—"My mother used to send me this all the time, it's grape juice"—but most agreed that the white had alcohol, and they had finished a bottle of it when the girls made their entrance half an hour later. Monica had used the hair extensions she had been saving for a special occasion, and now long braids were piled up high on her head so that she looked like an Egyptian empress. Naomi was wearing a short, tight skirt, sheer stockings, and a pair of patent leather, high-heeled stilettos; Ylaria was in a tight-fitting satin evening gown with a plunge back; even Kamilah had taken off her work clothes and changed into a bright red, knee-length skirt. They looked magnificent. As they walked in, a hushed gasp of admiration filled the room. The younger kibbutzniks all stopped what they were doing to watch the girls as they moved in a wobbly single-file line across the back of the room to their table. But the older kibbutzniks' former inquisitiveness had by now turned to blind disregard and they resolutely concentrated on their food until the boys, following Raul and Simon's lead, leapt up to pull back empty chairs, and the girls sat down.

For the next forty-five minutes excerpts from the Torah were read, and a succession of dances, one-act plays, and Hebrew songs were performed onstage. Sitting a little removed from it all, the New York kids tried to relax before they had to perform. The boys went first, the program said. They were performance number 26, and as soon as they stood up the entire dining room fell silent. Even the children stopped talking when Enrique stepped onto the stage. For a moment there was a terrible pregnant silence, during which the boys just stood there staring at the audience, their hands hanging heavily at their sides. Then Reggie lunged forward onto his right foot, spread out a palm, and sang, "Swing—" The others were with him for the "low," and two and a half or maybe three minutes later they were done and the room was cheering, and they danced off the stage chanting, *"Lehavot Habashan, Lehavot Habashan,"* to the loudest applause of the evening.

The girls had watched in utter silence as "their boys" had struggled through the number, and they yelped and cheered and greeted the returning heroes with cries of "You didn't make one mistake!" and "Fly, nigger, fly!"

When the girls filed out onto the stage ten minutes later, the boys returned the favor by rushing up to the end of the aisle to get a good view. For the next three minutes, the girls cracked and spluttered their way through "Amazing Grace." They sang the first verse second and the second verse first and even though Michelle never did manage to fit her lip-synching to the words that were actually being sung and at one point tripped and nearly fell off the stage, the kibbutz gave them a rousing cheer, and the boys applauded and whistled and grinned at one another, secure in the knowledge that if they weren't the most talented kids ever to have come over from New York, then at least they hadn't failed altogether. "I told you we'd be able to do it!" Naomi screeched as she wobbled her way back to the table, her high shoes slipping off the back of her heels every time she took a step. "I told you, I told you!"

They were too pumped up to stay at the dinner long after that. Kamilah, Monica, Reggie, and Enrique each grabbed the bottles of wine nearest them, tucked them under jackets and down trouser legs, and headed back to their dormitory building, leaving me to look as surprised as I could when Stewart came over afterward and told the story of how the first group he had ever brought over had stolen the Passover wine and stashed it in their rooms. But he was as exultant as the kids and wouldn't have noticed if there wasn't a bottle left on the table. "The kids were great. They were great and they did it all on their own," he kept saying.

I had been at the kibbutz for almost two weeks by then, and New York had never seemed so far away and irrelevant. The kids were the kings and queens of the walk that night. And they knew it. Everyone they passed smiled and thanked them for their participation in the celebrations. The bartender even stopped playing seventies rock music in the pub and started to play hip-hop from the kids' tapes instead. This open and acknowledged acceptance helped to ease them over any lingering feelings of estrangement, both from one another and from the kibbutz. From then on they slipped into a prolonged period of calm, rational quiet. Doors were left unlocked, clothing and tapes and even occasionally Walkmans and Gameboys were left unattended as they ambled over to the dining hall for meals, and sometimes a group of kibbutz kids could be seen hanging out on the New Yorkers' beds, listening to the latest hip-hop tunes through fancy American headphones with oversized earpieces. There was still the occasional problem, of course. Kamilah found a small snake in front of her dormitory door and put it in a jar only to be told the next day that it was poisonous, work still started too early for some kids, the laundry still lost clothes, and food kept disappearing from their communal refrigerator. But overall it was amazing to sit back and watch how relaxed the kids had become.

On a Sunday afternoon Reggie was sitting on the porch reading car ads in the local English-language paper, Kamilah and Monica were braiding two South Africans' hair for thirty shekels each, Naomi was lounging in the sun with a book, Carina was wandering around in her dressing gown and slippers, Michelle and Kirk were fiddling with each other's clothing and smiling at each other, sitting astride a tree trunk, and just inside Kevin was asleep in bed. It could have been an old folks' home. Watching them, I understood for the first time everything Stewart had been trying to tell me about the calm, empty, weightless exterior of the kibbutz becoming internalized.

Perhaps I recognized it because I was feeling it too. It was funny how time stretched out there, how, for me anyway, leisure and work actually seemed to have become one, and how long and wonderful an evening could be with no liquor, no music, and no one in particular to talk to. Boredom had become like a pillow to stretch out on. Like the kids, I'd freaked out in the beginning, but like them I was now starting to get used to it. Leaning up against a tree I could pass hours, it seemed, doing nothing at all. Looking around me one day, after lunch but before the daily Family Group meeting, I realized that this was the transformation the past participants had been talking about and that it was the boredom that had allowed it to happen—the boredom and the routine and Stewart's determined insistence on letting them be.

Work still went on, but routines as comforting and confining as any I'd had in New York made the days pass in the same random and humdrum way as they might in any real-life existence. Reggie had finally found chicks with their yolks still undigested—five of them—and saved them. Kevin, landscaping permanently now in place of Michelle, who had finally been moved into the bakery, had developed what he called the Five Rules for Survival. (Rule number 1: Whether you need to go around the other side of the truck to load branches or not, you do so every time and there spend as much time as you dare doing nothing. Rule number 2: Pick up as little as possible at a time. Rule number 3: Always walk to the farthest branch to pick up. Rule number 4: Only applicable if you are working with someone like Stewart: you stand back and watch them work because they're so busy they don't even notice. Rule number 5: Stretch out as often as you think you can get away with it.) Even Kenny was excelling in the machine shop, spray-painting a mural and designing the T-shirt for the group and Kamilah, left alone to look after the zoo, had revived the old horse to the point where he was now strong enough to take children on short rides around the kibbutz. She was ecstatic about this. "Here they know me as Zoo Lady. In New York they know me as bitch—see the difference?" she told me one morning. "I tell you, I'm going to go back home and grill my family and find out if there's any Jews in it—any Jewish blood at all, because I'm sure there must be and I want to come back here and stay here longer than nine months, which is the longest a non-Jew can stay without getting their visa renewed."

Michelle was happier than I'd ever seen her. She still couldn't be certain that she was in love, though when I asked her she became girlish, the way I had only seen her act with her mother before, and occasionally with Ed, so that all her weight settled on one foot as she twisted her body into a balanced position above it like a child ballerina. Kirk wasn't an official member of Youthworks and so hadn't taken part in the Passover show, but he had adoringly watched Michelle's terrific and lovably awkward performance. Afterward he'd hugged her and whispered in her ear that he had something to ask her, at which point she became so nervous that she'd torn herself away from him to come and ask if she could borrow my good-luck beads because she felt sure she needed them. Something about the hyperactive way she jiggled around as I looked for the wooden beads my younger brother had given me years before made me think that she thought he was going to ask her to marry him. But the next day when she came to my room to give me the beads back, she looked ashen and quiet and never mentioned anything about marriage. Instead she showed me a silver chain with a heart-shaped pendant that he had given her the previous night. Michelle had only ever worn gold before, delicate strands of interwoven threads. It looked better with her skin, she said. But now Kirk's chain was hanging proudly around her neck. "It's so beautiful—not necessarily the chain itself, but more because it came from him. I've never received a gift from someone that I felt was given to me with such meaning. I really care about him. If our relationship was to ever come to an end (I hope not), we will always be friends, good friends. There's probably nothing in the world I wouldn't do for him. He's quite special to me," she said.

Even Naomi had given up her compulsive desire to straighten every rumpled corner around her and was at least trying to let others be. Most nights she'd take long, solitary walks out to the children's playground and swing there gently for a while. One night she recorded the following: "Alone at last. There's so much I would love to do in my loneliness. So little time. Before I know it I'll be surrounded by people. What to do? How to act? I wish I could videotape myself in my loneliness to always cherish it when it's gone. To act silly, funny, cry, depressed, angry—all these feelings I cannot or choose not to express in company. I'll tell my grandchildren and their children the wonders of my loneliness. I love alone, I love company, I love to love!"

By the end of my stay the kids had established themselves into such mellow order that it almost seemed a shame to tear it all up and pile on a bus and head off for a four-day trip to Jerusalem. But the trip had been planned for months: a day's sight-seeing around Galilee, just a few miles north of the kibbutz, and then two days in a hostel in Jerusalem, followed by a day at an archeological dig south of the city. A lot of the kids had grown up in religious households and had promised their relatives whole troves of sacred memorabilia. One or two of them had even been given special outfits by their mothers and grandmothers to wear while in the Holy City—pilgrim's white shirts and skirts with touches of yellow and gold. But for the most part the kids themselves had only the vaguest interest in the historical or religious backgrounds of the places they were seeing. We saw the Church of the Beatitudes, the church at the site of the feeding of the five thousand, and the town of Cepernium, where our American guide, Kate, dwelled so long on an infinitesimally accurate account of an Old Testament tale that there was neither time nor interest for anything else. "Oh my goodness, she so boring!" Ylaria whispered at one point. "I mean, we're just young, we're not really so religious, she doesn't have to go into so much detail, you know?"

Bored and bus weary even halfway through the day, the kids tended to focus mostly on shoplifting opportunities in the afternoon. "Sticky fingers" and "five-finger discount" had become the key words of the trip, and as we passed through one religious shrine after another, Fred continued to build his collection of key chains; Kevin focused on rings, Reggie on onyx crosses; and even Kenny managed to steal a lovely carved silver pillbox for his mother. They did the same thing in Jerusalem too, though after Enrique narrowly escaped being beaten up by an irate stall owner who caught him trying to steal a large leather book bag, things calmed down a little. Besides, even the most reluctant of the group couldn't help but be impressed by the array of Christian priests, Muslim clerics, and Jewish rabbis that were packed into the already overfull Old City. They started reaching into their wallets to pay for the trinkets instead.

Laden down and hot and exhausted ("And then which king came after David?" Kate was still asking as the bus pulled up outside of the youth hostel. "What significance has Jericho got in the present political situation?"), the kids trooped into small dorm rooms to wash and change before going out. They had been looking forward to their upcoming "night on the town" for weeks. Past participants in the program had given them the name of a club in the center of town which played reasonable music and served drinks to minors. But by the time they arrived the small space was filled with a group of drunken and vacationing Germans, and the music was hard neo–punk rock. Tired anyway after their long bus ride and sight-seeing tours, they stayed only about five minutes. Six weeks in the kibbutz had softened them, and their pace was all wrong for a big city like this.

All wrong too for the planned trip to the Holocaust museum the following day, and they were clear about the fact that they didn't want to go.

"It's a history which we know about already, Stew," Monica said. "We know about the six million Jews killed." But as was always the case when Stewart made up his mind about something, they went nonetheless, and after looking for and finding Schindler's grave, Stewart shooed them reluctantly into the museum, where they quickly dispersed. Raul and Naomi walked through the exhibits looking interested and serious, like scholars having their opinions on life verified. Fred and Enrique and Carina followed suit. Clustering silently around an exhibit of prisoner ID cards, touching one another's shoulders, even holding hands for reassurance, they made their way quietly and respectfully through the rooms of large black-and-white photographs and locks of victims' hair and their eyeglasses. But Kamilah became enraged when she saw a life-sized photograph of a Nazi soldier aiming his rifle at a woman holding a child in her arms. When she saw another, smaller image of a frightened old man looking shakily up at a smirking German soldier, apparently pleading for his life, she spun around on her heels, clasped her hands to her face and, swearing only just under her breath, stormed out of the museum.

By the time I exited the building Ylaria and Monica were struggling not to show they'd been crying; Melissa was sobbing openly, and, sitting in front of her, Michelle stared down at a remembrance pin she had bought from the store. Every now and then she raised her little finger to wipe away tears from behind her dark glasses. Kamilah, dazed, walked slowly through the orchard. And long after most of the others had exited, Reggie strolled out alone, muted and harrowed and shocked to the point of such sullenness that he spent the rest of the day sitting in the back of the bus with his Walkman turned up loud. "They just people," Naomi said, as the bus pulled away. "Regular people," Raul agreed. "With a hard, hard history."

Twenty-five minutes later the bus pulled to a halt at the top of the Mount of Olives, where Stewart always took a group portrait. I was going to be leaving on a flight from Jerusalem later that day and, perhaps because this was going to be the last time I'd see them, I found myself watching the kids arrange themselves in front of the camera with more than my usual attention. With Jerusalem stretched out behind, and the Dome of the Rock glinting gold in the sun, the setting was fine and elaborate and exotic—proof of a once-in-a-lifetime dream fulfilled. Sitting in front of it, wearing shades and Egyptian necklaces, most of the kids looked happy. But as they smiled and posed and shifted their weight I could also see the telltale signs of sadness—a smile gone flabby at the ends, a too straight back or a mouth covered by fists—and I realized they were all shocked right then too, with the growing realization that life was both more complex and more open than they had ever dared imagine. Off to one side, Monica was growling as Stewart struggled to reload the camera, and Reggie, who'd been ordered to join the group as soon as Stewart noticed his absence, was sitting glumly on a short stone wall doing his best to ignore everyone. Naomi looked well and strangely complete leaning against Enrique's back, but even Michelle looked worn, I noticed, her eyes just visibly swollen and her necklace, hung now with the remembrance pin she'd just bought, blending whiteness, blackness, and Jewishness together around her neck.

28

IT WAS A strain to come back to West Side after two weeks of stretching out in Israel. Before I left I hadn't realized how the routine of school five days a week had been changing me. The day-to-day crises and horrors had grated on me so constantly that my once-sharp sensitivity had become scabby and numb from the irritation, and without realizing it I had become as oblivious to standards of what was normally acceptable as many of the kids. Ed had told me about this when I had first met him, how he sometimes felt he had lost touch with standard behavioral mores and that he often found himself shocking journalists or other visitors by being overly blasé about the horrors of life in the inner city.

But now, returning from the arid but welcoming space of Israel, I was again firmly rooted on the side of the positive. I knew who I was and where I was and, having rediscovered my own sense of proportion, I didn't want to go back to the school, where, only three weeks before, a shooting around the corner from Sandra's house had merited a glancing, four-word note in the corner of my notebook and where Roland's own brush with death had only made me exhausted and wary. So I played hooky for a couple of days, not letting anyone know I was back except my roommate and a visiting friend of his, who escorted me for hours around farmers' markets and introduced me to martinis. I listened to music, watched the news, and read the paper. Occasionally I thought about some of the kids here in the city and some of them still in the kibbutz. How would they feel when they came back if just over two weeks had had this kind of refocusing effect on me? What would ten weeks do to them?

Trying to sound cheerful, I wrote them a fax extolling the benefits of being back in the city and then switched off again, listened to more music, and went for even longer walks in Central Park and along the edge of the Hudson, on the New Jersey side, where picnic tables sometimes washed up on the beach. I would probably have given myself a few additional days if I hadn't walked past the site of the old West Side building one afternoon while baby-sitting my niece on the Upper West Side. I already had a chunk of mottled red brick that Jim had given me from the ruins of the demolished old building. But this was the first time I'd seen the empty, flattened, still rubble-strewn lot, and the sight saddened and angered me and made me think of Ed.

Before I'd left, and in what I now understood to be a dazzling display of blind defiance, he had invited a group of volunteer designers and architects to West Thirty-fifth Street and had encouraged them to lead a group of students in a renovation project. There was no money for the project and they would have only donated materials to work with. But after just one brainstorming session, the group of students and professionals had come up with the following wish list: build a new weight room, make a candy store, repaint the stairs all the way from the first floor to the eleventh, vary the colors of the floors, do anything to stop the building from looking like a factory, decorate the girls bathroom, add curtains to the classrooms, install carpeting and pay phones and ashtrays and escalators and a trophy wall, build a student lounge, a child-care center, a permanent honor roll, and lockers of some kind so that students could leave their stuff safely unattended. By the second week they had put the matter to the vote, and because it was both conspicuous and affordable, they had decided to focus on the lobby, inside and out.

It was a plan on a typical scale for Ed. It would need the participation of at least forty students over a period of six weeks, and at times even he had had serious doubts about its feasibility. "I don't know," he'd told me one afternoon after a representative of the Board of Education had again refused to guarantee that the lease on the space would be renewed. "Maybe we are trying to do too much. It's just that I think my job is to continue to generate life at all times and to keep things going, so when people are tempted to give up they don't, they keep driving and driving instead. Sometime's its hard. But, OK—my vacation's in June—I'll just basically collapse then."

Back before Roland had been shot, Rasheem had been one of the first students to sign up for what came to be known as the redesign-your-school project. Because he was the most talented draftsman of the group, he had been slated to head up a mural on the wall to the left of the entranceway. There had been a mosaic planned too, and some painting and furniture construction. But those things had still been in the planning phase when I'd left, and I couldn't believe the amount students had achieved when I finally went back. The flat, gray dullness of the old entranceway had been completely repainted. The door was now coated in a deep, full-gloss midnight blue and over it, in sunshine yellow, were the words "West Side High School." There was a neatly stenciled "West Side" down the edge of the once urine-stained garage entrance next to the front doorway, and at the bottom was a handwritten list in yellow of the kids who were responsible for the work.

Inside, the lobby was equally transformed. The walls were a fresh shade of light sky blue. The elevator doors were indigo, and even the notice boards had been reworked into irregular curves, so that they echoed the new kidney-shaped guard's desk. I couldn't see Rasheem's mural anywhere, but the mosaic was there, leaning up against the wall, still waiting to be hung. About three feet by five, it showed a raised fist clutching a diploma in front of a blue-and-green globe; the phrase "Knowledge Is Power" was bravely emblazoned in blood-red halfway up the arm. It had taken two full days to chip the pottery and cement the pieces together, and it looked so impressive, even propped against the wall, that for a few minutes I was lulled into the hope that the freshness and the vigor downstairs might presage a shift in the mood at West Side.

But nothing seemed to have changed up in Ed's Family Group. Over in one corner Dayna was eating her Egg McMuffin and chatting with Anna, who was still in the process of battling for custody of her kids in the courts; to the left sat Cristy, sprawled, as usual, over two seats at a time, leaning down over her desktop, staring out of the window. Maurice wasn't there when I arrived, but his jacket and book bag were slung across the cabinet at the side of the room the way they always were, and when he came back Ed screamed at him the way he always had, threatening to steal the clothes himself if it happened again.

"You touch my clothes and I'll break both your kneecaps," Maurice said, with enough of a smile for it not to be a threat.

"You can do whatever you like, Maurice, as long as I don't see that lump of stuff all alone in here again. You may as well hang a sign from that jacket saying 'merchandise to be stolen'. And where was Rasheem last weekend?" Ed asked then. "He was supposed to paint the mural downstairs. There were thirty-seven people waiting on him with nothing to do for three hours. Doesn't anything ever mean anything to you guys?" Looking around the room he slumped a little farther down into his chair as he realized that Rasheem wasn't in.

"I know where he was, Ed," Maurice said pseudomournfully. "He was up on One twenty-fifth Street pit-bull fightin'. I tried to tell him to come down to school, I tried, but he wouldn't do it Ed—"

Roland was sitting in the back of the room, in the corner where he always sat, nodding in agreement. I couldn't help peering at his chin, which had been swabbed and swollen the last time I'd seen it and which looked completely normal now, the scar neatly tucked up under the bottommost curve of his face. But he ignored me when I offered him a smile and a gentle hello, and the rest of the group treated me as if I'd just returned from a ten-minute trip to the coffee shop. There was a fair deal of talk on my color: two weeks in the sun had browned me up well enough, most of the kids thought, and they were relatively interested in trying the Israeli candy I'd brought back with me, though not many of them liked it. The most enthusiastic response I got was a shrugged "It's OK—a bit stale tasting," although Cristy loyally stuck by both me and my candy and had even brought in the postcard I'd sent her, saying that neither she nor Ray had been able to read a word of it and what was I trying to prove by writing like that?

Ed was pleased to see me, but he was tired. If the redesign project had enlivened his usual school routine, it had also extended it, and he'd hardly had a day away from West Side since I'd left. Aside from the regular school week and the extended Tuesday-night school hours, he'd also been in every Thursday evening until nine and on the weekends too with the architects. It was worth it, of course. Just walking into the school felt different now, more permanent and promising than it had before. Ed had even sent a series of before-and-after photographs to the chancellor. But what he'd most enjoyed were the reactions of the students. Almost all of them had commented on it, and those who had actually done the work were still strutting around the school wearing the bright pink T-shirts that had been given to every participant.

It was the kind of reaction that most gratified Ed. But other less inspiring events had taken place while I'd been away as well. Over lunch at a fancy Chinese restaurant with pink tablecloths on Eighth Avenue, Ed told me that Carlos, the mild-mannered Neta who joined our Family Group in January, had been busted for carrying an illegal weapon and was now waiting for his trial at Rikers; that James's mother had been seriously ill; that Sandra hadn't turned up once while I'd been away, and that Maurice, Rasheem, and Roland had now fully reverted to the worst of their past behavior patterns. More seriously, they had also started stealing supplies from teachers' rooms on the other floors and taking the bus to New Jersey, where they indulged in massive shoplifting sprees. They weren't foolish enough to do the stealing themselves, of course, Ed sighed. They used young Maurice-wanna-bes as "carriers" instead—something he knew about because the mother of one had complained. They had all denied it, though, and because Ed had no tangible proof he'd had no choice but to let them go with a warning. He couldn't even split them up because no other Family Group adviser would take them, and in desperation he had been forced to make them sit on opposite sides of the room in Family Group, he told me, which made everyone feel like they were in elementary school again.

Determined to hold onto the balance I'd gained in Israel as long as I could, I tried to leave school early those first few days. But within a week I'd stopped going for long walks by the river in favor of passing the afternoons in the stale Formica booths of McDonald's, where I listened to kids like Danny Figuera explain how he'd come to live in the subways for a fortnight. He hadn't eaten at all the day before, and when I'd told him to order whatever he wanted he very politely asked for two cheeseburgers, a six-piece Chicken McNuggets with two extra sweet-and-sour sauces, a supersized fries, orange soda, and a frozen yogurt with caramel topping, no nuts. When we sat down he looked at his tray of neatly wrapped food for a moment and then decided to go wash his hands. Trying to deny he was hungry at all, he even insisted on making small talk before finally unwrapping his meal. And if I'd ever had any doubts about just how shifting and elastic reality could be, he said, "I bin sleeping in the train so long now I'm even starting to like it. At the beginning, when I woke up and there was a lot of people on the train, students and stuff, I didn't want to lift my head, so I just stayed there like that until it got empty again, but now it's like I'm home. I mean, I just lay down relaxed like I'm at home—no worries about no one beating me or robbing me or nothing."

It was as if I was having to absorb the force of all I'd discovered during my first few months at West Side in a matter of days. At least the previous fall had provided a period of gradual acclimatization: I'd been protected first by my fear, then by my ignorance, and finally by the slow process of building trust between the kids and myself. I had shed my fear of the kids after a few days at the school, but my fear of the realities that lurked in their private lives had only grown more acute during my time away. And now that the kids felt comfortable with me they were unloading it all at once, often just after saying "hello."

In the days that followed, I discovered that Manny's mother was pregnant again with her bus-driver boyfriend; Cristy had stopped working in the movie theater because Ray didn't want her to be alone with the male manager all those hours every night; and James's mother had narrowly avoided dying of an asthma attack. He'd been the one to find her, gasping frantically for breath in bed, and he'd been overwhelmed ever since by the notion that she would have died if he'd simply missed a train or hung out a few minutes more with his friends. Nicole's biological mother was dying in the hospital; another girl's uncle had been shot in the doorway of his own house; and the mildly retarded brother of a student had been arrested for dropping a baby out of a window.

The stories never ended, and listening to them made me appreciate—even more than I had before I'd left—what West Side offered to so many of its students. If the light-blue classrooms of the tenth floor seemed a bit faded after the open fields of northern Israel, then they were still a big step above the harsh loneliness of so many of the kids' lives. As graduation approached I even began to realize that the air of quiet desperation in the school came not from a desire to escape but from anxiety about having to leave. Eighty-five students were to graduate that summer. In theory, at least, they were incredibly and incessantly proud about this. It was just that most of them had never believed they would reach this point. Realizing that they were now actually on the verge of achieving the impossible, they were beginning to panic.

Even Cristy, who seemed fine on the surface of things, admitted that the thought of leaving West Side filled her with dread. Ray had become so jealous by then that she had to call him every half hour after school. Even when she was out with me for coffee or a walk or a quick bite to eat, she sometimes had to drag me to the phone to reassure him that it was not some lustful classmate who she was spending her time with. This embarrassed her. It made her feel like a child, like someone's pet cannery, she said (meaning canary). And though I could see that her foot-stamping outrage held something of the grandiose bluster of a pampered child only too happy to please her proud but demanding father figure, it was also clear that his tightfisted control meant that, at eighteen, her world had been reduced to the narrow strip of stores where she went to shop in the afternoons and her apartment, with its color TV and afternoon game shows. Once she graduated she would have no reason to ever leave the neighborhood. Without West Side to come to every morning, she was worried that she'd end up like the hundreds of other girls "on lockdown" who stopped even bothering to get dressed in the mornings and walked to the store in their house shoes, with their hair up in curlers.

Few people were courageous enough to discuss any of this openly. But when Emilio brought it up in Family Group one morning, I saw that others besides Cristy felt this way too. Sitting askew in his chair, pretending to be asleep, James was listening hard. So was Dayna. And though Roland and Maurice were flicking through the reflective silver covers of the "Death of Superman" issue that Rasheem had bought five of in the hope that one day they would become collector's items and make him rich, I could see by the way Roland was nodding his head and scrunching up his mouth in agreement that he was paying more attention to Emilio than to Rasheem's investment.

Emilio, of course, was already rich—that wasn't the problem. He didn't have a bank account because he was uncertain about how to go about getting one and just what to say about how and where he got his money. Instead, he gave it to his brother, a college student, to look after. So far he had saved nineteen thousand dollars toward what he called his "college fund," but it was easy to see that he'd never really believed he was on his way to college and that the thought of living the rest of his life on 177th Street destroyed him. Not that he disrespected his coworkers, he told us. They were keeping it real, he said, and they all belonged to an organization named FBI—Far Beyond the Imagination—which showed that they thought a lot. It was just that "in the 'hood, all they talk about is rap and guns and what happened yesterday when the police came and this and that. You know tha's stressful to think of, that being your life, you know? And it ain't only me either," he concluded, leaning back in his chair and scanning the room for some acknowledgment. "All my friends round West Side feel this way too, Ed. Scared. Scared, you know, because they feel the summer coming up and now finally they going to graduate—finally! Only they don't know what to do next—they don't have jobs and they don't know nothing about college. It's not that we don't want to advance, Ed, it's just we don't even know how to."

Ed would never have denied this trepidation, or the rationale behind it. He understood there was a gaping ravine between their current present and the unknown of their future, he told them. He knew, too, that graduating from high school was only the first step of hundreds they would have to keep making for the rest of their lives if they wanted the best the country had to offer for themselves. What they didn't realize, he kept telling them, was that they were already doing it; that by graduating from high school they were already beating the odds and had shifted into a new world with a new set of possibilities and opportunities. All they had to do now was relax enough to be able to accept it.

Just as he had responded to the destruction of their old building uptown by taking what he had and improving upon it, he then went a step further by reminding them of the upcoming prom. It was not the first time he'd mentioned it, but today he had some brochures of the fancy luxury yacht that Esther had rented for what was sure to be West Side's best prom yet. The brochures showed a three-story luxury liner, layered like a wedding cake and lit from the outside with spotlights so that it glowed, ghostly and ethereal, as it glided on ink-black waters like a swan. The kids were impressed. If they'd expected anything at all, it would have been more along the lines of a classroom decorated with blue and white balloons, a few jumbo bottles of soda, and a tinny tape recorder in the corner. But this was the real thing. Even those who were not graduating asked for a pamphlet, and though everyone in the room sighed and oohhed and aaaahhhed, it was pretty clear too that most of the graduates were having a difficult time imagining that they would actually ever walk along the deck of the fairy-lit boat with a cocktail in their hand, the way the blond woman in the photograph was. The evening would be expensive, but it was more the idea of celebrating their eviction from West Side that got in the way of any real anticipated pleasure. Kids like James were reluctant to even sit up and look at the photo. Though the temperature must have been 70 degrees, he was still wearing winter clothes, thick heavy jeans and a sweater and a jacket in dark blacks and browns, as if by refusing to acknowledge the changing of seasons he could stop time from passing. Ed had told me to look out for him, that he'd been having a hectic time at home with his mother's near-fatal attack and with his girlfriend too, and a baby that may or may not have been his, but it wasn't until he burst out with "Yo, bussin'—they attacked my sister this weekend" that I understood how surreal a prom night on a fairy-lit cruiser must have seemed to him then: simply too distant for him to even consider.

In all my months at West Side I had never really thought of what happened to students once they graduated. Many went to college and then on to successful lives in the city or elsewhere. Occasionally, some would drop by the school just to say hi, or to talk to the kids and offer encouragement, and though I knew that some in that room would do the same, watching the effort Ed was having to expend even to convince some of his advisees that they deserved a night of glamour at their prom, I too began to worry about what might become of them once they graduated. Without the bulwark of West Side to protect and bolster them, would they disappear back into the quiet, limited confines of their lives the way Cristy might? Or, like Roland, would they roam listlessly and unchecked and simply slip away without a party, or even a graduation for that matter, into private lives that they'd busily set about just making worse?

It seemed inevitable that my reintroduction to the world of West Side be completed with Emanuel Martinez, a kid who had never been a full member of the school in the first place and whose position had grown only more tenuous since I'd been away. My relationship with Manny had never been simple, and perhaps because I felt that I was his only remaining link to a world outside of the Ave, I had always been reluctant to push him so far that he would sever his ties with me too. Sometimes I had grown impatient and had made suggestions that he hadn't been able to hear, let alone comprehend. But I'd never risked total disapproval, and had spent hours listening to stories of life on the Ave which I would have rather not heard.

He could still win me over. Hanging around the seventh-floor lobby, anxiously adjusting his hat and glancing around and smoothing the edge of his trouser creases by running pinched fingers along their spines, he smiled when he saw me, and I felt just as I had when I'd first met him out in the corridor, where I was to tutor him for Rochelle. Now, though, he told me with a frown that he had a favor to ask. His cousin Lazarus had been arrested, he said. Little Lazo. He wanted me to accompany him up to the Spofford Juvenile Center, where he was being held. Af fifteen Manny was too young to be admitted as a visitor on his own, and he wanted to deliver a fresh set of clothes to his cousin so he'd be able to "represent himself right in the courts," he explained, smiling sadly and patting a bulging and torn white plastic bag down by his feet.

Lazarus was only thirteen, and he'd been living with Manny and his father ever since he'd run away from a juvenile-detention center upstate. He was as close a friend as it was possible to have out on the Ave, and Manny had often told me proudly that as Paco was to Manny, so he was to Lazo, so of course I agreed to accompany him up to the South Bronx where Spofford was located. At first Manny was grateful and pleased. Even when his mood became darker, I assumed he was just trying to cover the loneliness he must have been feeling, and I tried not to listen too hard as he insisted that Lazarus was a failure and a liar and a cheat and a phony as we headed uptown on the train. Sprawled on a seat across the aisle from me, working himself into a mad froth of self-pity–induced anger, it seemed he wanted the whole car to know that not only had Lazarus sold to an undercover when Manny had expressly told him to stop working but that he had broken down in the precinct and sobbed, too—sobbed like a little boy who didn't know a thing. Sobbed like the frightened child he used to be when Manny had first met him, the apartment nerd who was afraid of the street and who used to stay in and watch television and who could never think of anything to say. Imagining his cousin's breakdown a thousand different ways, he told the crowd over and over how he had snitched too—how he had cooperated with his arresting officers and told them whatever it was that they wanted to know.

"I tell you. I'd be feeling upset if it were any other nigger, but that nigger don't listen, man," he said. "He ain't no good 'cause he ain't true to the game. I ain't going to even hang wid him when he gets out, man. He a fake motherfucker." His rage was even making him speak differently.

"Why are we taking him fresh clothes then?" I asked, finally trying to at least calm him down.

"The clothes he was wearing are worth five hundred dollars," Manny replied, his face a mask. "Five hundred dollars, Tina! A blue Polo hat, a Polo hoody with patches, a Polo jacket with the flag, Guess jeans, and a brand-new pair of Nike Uptowns. He don't need them where he is. They give him rejects and a uniform. That's what they all wear. Reject sneakers and uniforms. Green or blue. His clothes'll just get all doggy if we leave them in there."

That was when I realized we were going up to Spofford not to help Lazarus but to steal from him. Manny had stumbled onto the perfect crime, and inadvertently I had become his accomplice, because what could his cousin do? Trapped in a cell in Spofford, he was powerless to stop Manny from waltzing out with his best Polo gear. I looked at Manny again. He was staring up at the ads above my head, absent-mindedly polishing the new removable gold tooth caps he had bought against the pocket of his jeans. When he noticed me looking at him, he glared, his eyes flat and dark and challenging. It was not the first time that I'd run into the brick wall that seemed to be becoming Manny's future, but it seemed more complete suddenly, a finished project between him and me.

It was one of the longest train rides I'd ever taken, half an hour in which my conflicting roles of writer and friend can into painful opposition. I had come to the school as a reporter and had crossed over to try to help and be a friend. But it wasn't until that moment that I realized that rather than help Manny out of his hole, I had leaned so far over into his world that I had fallen in myself. Stuck there at the bottom with him, there was nothing left that I could say or do but witness the death of my hope that I could make a difference. What Manny really needed wasn't rehabilitation, but habilitation, I thought. "To make suitable or qualify," as Webster's defines it. Feeling the finality of the situation as we ricocheted our way up to the South Bronx, I felt sick and used and hopeless.

Only the bland nastiness of the Spofford Juvenile Center itself seemed to calm Manny down a bit. It was a monstrous construction—half Victorian brick, half gray concrete, surrounded by a thick dark metal gate topped with rolls of barbed wire—but as though reassured by the fact that it was an actual building instead of the mad wizard's castle he had feared for so long, he relaxed into one of the orange plastic bucket seats in the waiting room and made his sneakers squeak against the large checks of the linoleum floor. "Guess this is what the rooms look like?" he said, settling in now. "Beige walls, huh? Not bad."

Still stunned, I sat there and did nothing while the guard searched for Lazarus's old set of clothes. Ten minutes later he handed them over to Manny, who thanked him politely and then asked him please to tell Lazo he said hi, that he'd try to get back to see him some other time. But as soon as we stepped out onto the street again, his poise evaporated. Frenzied and jubilant and horrified at the same time too, he ran halfway across the highway, and then turned to grin at me. The image froze in my brain: Manny under a raised highway in the South Bronx, with his earphones on (white and stiff so that they looked like some kind of collapsed halo) and his gold fronts glinting and his arms full of his cousin's Polo clothes half-stuffed into the white plastic bag, a brand-new pair of Nikes still done up, the laces flat and broad, hanging down from his left hand and the happiest, most manic-looking expression I had ever seen on his face. Click. It was like that. Just like the shutter of a camera. Frozen. Captured. Happy, deranged youth. Deprived, but not this second, because right then he was fulfilled. Five hundred dollars' worth of clothes from his betrayer cousin. Betrayer of his betrayer cousin—revenge achieved. Click. Kept. For keeps. Tha's the way it is, man—he won't be needing them in there (poor kid).

29

EVEN BEFORE I left for Israel I had known that life was becoming increasingly tense for the Chapter 6 Netas. Oscar had told me, "Word of our positivity and stuff is starting to get out, and there is a lot of people who want to get a piece of it. Now, I don't mind people coming from other chapters and other groups and organizations to encourage. What I don't like is when they come in to discourage." When I'd asked him what he meant, Oscar had only shrugged, but I knew they had been encountering resistance not only from other groups but from within their own *capítulo* itself. I couldn't help remembering Sandra's outrage when Mickey had suggested they team up with the local police, and while I still believed that most outsiders had it backward, that groups like the Netas didn't take honest kids and turn them into hooligans but the other way around, I was also beginning to realize how hard that turning around could be.

The main problem was the ever growing crew of kids that had taken to hanging out on the sidewalk just outside of PS 143. They called themselves the DPs, but they weren't really a cohesive group at all. Even though they all wore the same intricately beaded, flag-shaped *collares,* the organization was more of a catchall for any Dominican who felt the need of a little power, a little camaraderie, a little macho swagger but who was too lazy or bashful to join one of the more bona fide groups in the neighborhood. Because they were a group without official membership, they were also a group without even the most rudimentary of rules or aims. There could be twenty of them outside PS 143 one evening vowing eternal enmity to the Netas, and the next night those same kids could be inside the building, their beads no longer around their necks, playing basketball or hanging out with the Netas working security because they just happened to be old neighborhood buddies.

What was particularly offensive to the Netas was that the DPs committed crimes wearing their *collares*. If a Neta was ever caught dealing drugs with his beads clearly visible he would receive an instant "ten knuckles," and the DPs' practice of flagrantly breaking the law with their beads around their necks gave all youth gangs in the area a bad name. It led to a lot of extra work for Capítulo Seis's junta: door-to-door campaigns to make sure local merchants knew the difference between the Netas and the DPs and more sweep-the-street programs. The Netas' efforts nonetheless failed to prevent their image from slipping because no one could stop scuffles between the two groups from breaking out occasionally, and the image of five or six kids beating one another up did more to convince the neighborhood of their character than any public relations campaign ever could.

But the pressure facing the junta of Capítulo Seis wasn't only external. An encroaching sense of boredom had begun to take hold within their own ranks as well. The initial fun of playing teacher, of hanging out in an elementary school all evening, giving directions to newcomers and telling little kids not to run in the corridors, had begun to wear off. A dramatic thinning of the ranks was the result. Ramón had always said there were close to eighty full-fledged *hermanitos* in the chapter, and though I had never seen that many gathered there, it was rare for less than thirty to show up for a Friday-night meeting. Now, though, the junta was finding it increasingly hard to come up with even a full complement of guards every night—a situation that hadn't been helped by their handling of an accusation of robbery from a DP.

In an attempt to keep the peace, Ramón had called a meeting with the DP who had alleged that two Chapter 6 *hermanitos* had jumped him. Oscar had agreed to be mediator, and he'd managed to keep things relatively orderly during the long, highly charged meeting. When the DPs produced a string of eyewitnesses to the crime, Ramón felt he had no choice but to agree to pay restitution, though only on the condition that doing so was not an acknowledgment of guilt. In the equivalent of an out-of-court settlement, the representatives of the two sides had shaken hands warily and stated they were determined to "keep the peace." But the accused *hermanitos* had been furious. They had insisted all along that they were innocent, that they'd been nowhere near the DP when he was robbed. *Guerreros humilde* was one thing, they said, but being a sucker was another, and they had stormed out of the conference room, stridden across the hallway, flung back the bolt from the door, and left, barging their way through a nest of DPs out on the street. "DP, what that stand for again? Dominican Pussy?" one of them asked under his breath.

Trying to prevent further escalation, Ramón ultimately decided that some of their younger *hermanitos* were not "comfortable with themselves enough yet" to be "Netas from the heart," and he'd asked all male members under the age of seventeen to leave. It had seemed a desperate measure to regain some kind of cohesion. In the end, in fact, it had ended up making things worse, because the expulsion spawned a rumor in Washington Heights that the local Neta *capítulo* was expelling everyone but Puerto Ricans in an attempt to keep their association pure.

By the time I got back from Israel the scandal had become so widespread that people from other chapters—Neta bigshots from Staten Island and the Bronx—had started to show up at Chapter 6's Friday-night meetings. They always fabricated a valid reason for being there, Sandra snarled: one *segundo* from the Bronx had come down to warn them that Jimmy Pio, a.k.a. Al Capone, was not who he said he was. The *segundo* explained that Pio was not in fact leader of the Bronx chapter and that he was dangerous and deranged and if any of the *hermanitas* or *hermanitos* were ever to run into him they should know this. But Sandra was certain that no one by either name had ever been in charge of any chapter and that the story was just a ruse for other Netas to come and check up on their meetings.

Her suspicions were verified my first Friday back when an *hermanito* from lower Manhattan, a young man who didn't have a title but who Sandra recognized as a facilitator in waiting, came to visit. Halfway through the meeting he brought up a story about an *hermanita* who had been threatened by a group of girls at a baby shower. She had called the Netas of Capítulo Seis for help, he said, and had been refused any assistance. Clearing his throat, he asked if the members could assure him now that they would come to the aid of an *hermanito* like himself should the need arise.

"We would certainly be there to discuss it," Ramón said.

"Would you come, or would you just sit there asking questions?"

"It's just not always the best thing to go charging into situations like that, you know? I am speaking from experience. It can lead to stuff."

"But don't you think it's embarrassing to know that even the Zulu Nation will drop everything at any time and come and help out one of their own and we do nothing?"

Here Ramón hesitated. He glanced at the young Neta from downtown and then around the room. He flashed a quick glance at Sandra, and something about her intense look back made him acquiesce.

"Look. You gotta do what you gotta do," Ramón said flatly. "All I can say is that there are some people out there who can't listen to anything else and in those cases we will be there." This answer at least partway mollified the visitor, but the exchange left everyone else in the room feeling muddled and vaguely ashamed.

By the following week things had come to a breaking point. I had long grown used to the journey up to PS 143, but the recent increase in DP activity made me nervous as I walked down the two long, empty blocks to the school. Sandra and Oscar had warned me to expect a larger group of DPs than usual that week, but I was still surprised by how many I had to make my way past to get into the school. One of them, a skinny, pale-looking boy with green eyes, reached out his hand and tapped my shoulder as I reached the front door. "Hi," he said. It was Rankin, Sandra's ex-husband, the son of a Neta and so a Neta from birth. Around his neck hung the intricately beaded Dominican flag of the DPs. He grinned. I hurried inside.

There was a nervous, edgy feel to the Netas already gathered in the lobby. Gone, certainly, was the cozy, slightly sullen, but friendly air I had become used to; and instead of the anticipated boredom that usually preceded a Friday meeting, the *hermanitos* looked riled and tense. For some reason they had decided to have their meeting in the dining room upstairs instead of the auditorium that evening and, variously milling around in tight little knots, charging across the lobby, and bursting through the door, they shared the kind of intense hostility of a group under siege. Behind the security desk, even Sandra and Ramón were arguing. Spreading as relaxed a smile as I could muster, I walked across the main hallway toward them. "*Y ella! Ella es otra cosa.*"—"And she! She is another thing!"—Ramón said as I approached. Then

Sandra spun around on her heel and stormed down the linoleum corridor, through the swinging doors, and out into the street without even saying hello.

"Ramón, we got company" someone whispered. Ramón raised his hand to quiet him and nodded to the head of security, who ducked out the door and then came back in. As inconspicuously as possible, he pointed at specific *hermanitos,* beckoning them to his side, and then left with them again through the clanking door.

I had no idea at that time that the neatly dressed, lanky man standing at the entrance to the dining room with the perfectly curved baseball hat beak pulled low over his green eyes was the *primero* of all of Manhattan. I did notice him, though; it was hard not to, even through the chaos of people charging around, because for the past five minutes he had been leaning completely immobile against the doorjamb. I thought it might just have been his pockmarked complexion and his teeth, which sloped inward from his lips, that made him look so angry, but Felipe soon set me straight. The *primero*'s appearance had been so surprising to the Netas of Capítulo Seis, he explained skittishly, that earlier, in an overzealousness brought on by nerves, two young *hermanitos* from security had spread-eagled, patted down, and then pocket-searched him in front of everyone. "He very steamed up," Felipe told me in a half whisper. "He's the *primero* of all of Manhattan, and he didn't like that at all. He is very, very steamed up."

The *primero* of all of Manhattan. That was what they called him. Never *primero* of Manhattan, or *primero*, and though I supposed it was a sign of respect, the words were always run together as if spoken in fear, so that at first it was hard to make out: the-*primero*-of-all-of-Manhattan. But despite his presence, Ramón's authority seemed to be holding. As part of the ongoing hunt for DPs, he had supervised the search downstairs and had cleared the auditorium, the art room, and the citizenship classroom. Now his team was focusing on the gym, and though he was clearly more harried than usual, he was still distributing orders with the calm certainty that they would be obeyed. At one point he noticed a group of Netas standing around in the corridor outside of the dining room and, with a glance at the *primero* of all of Manhattan, he ordered them inside and told them to take their seats. Soon afterward, I was ushered into the unfamiliar room by Oscar, who sat down next to me, as seemingly immune to the high-pitched stench of the eight industrial-sized garbage bags lined up against the front wall as everyone else in there. Dropping his head, he rubbed his hands through his hair as if massaging his brain and didn't say a word until, two or three minutes later, Ramón started the meeting with a booming *"Corazón!"*

For the moment things seemed to be back in control. But just seconds after Mickey and Felipe joined Ramón up at the front of the room the *primero*-of-all-of-Manhattan came in, accompanied by five other Netas who looked older and more seasoned than any Neta I'd seen. Walking single file between tables, these men all wore the same trousers, the same crisp, minutely checkered, black-and-white shirts, the same baseball caps with the same perfectly curved bills, and the same ostentatious Neta *collares,* each bead the size of a grape, which hung down to the same point in their torsos, just slightly above the belly button. Silently they filed into the back row, the row right behind me. In unison they removed their baseball hats and then placed them, beaks facing forward, on the table.

For the first time since I had persuaded Ramón to let me into the meetings I was scared. Quietly, I leaned over and asked Oscar if everything was all right. He didn't even try to pretend. "No," he said, looking down at the table in front of him. "It's not," he said. "Not at all."

Meanwhile Ramón, Mickey, and Felipe were trying to run as reasonable a meeting as possible. They were talking now about the statistically increased risk of a violent death if you carried a weapon. "And I'm not just talking guns," Ramón said. "I mean any weapon—a knife, a box cutter, whatever." For a few minutes the room was quiet as the gathered *hermanitos* at least pretended to listen to whatever it was that Ramón was saying. But the stiffness of their backs showed that most of them were paying far more attention to what might be happening behind them than in front.

"You know there's someone out there—an ex-Neta boosting somebody else's colors? There's DP out there," the *primero* of all of Manhattan said finally.

"No, I hadn't noticed that," Mickey replied.

"It's Rankin."

"Oh. Rankin," he said. "I haven't seen him for a while. I didn't notice him, but I know where he lives, and I'll deal with him later—

OK?" Silence. Nervous and shuffling in front of me, solid and piercing behind.

"You guys got beef with DP?" Felipe asked then, swinging his legs like a little child from the table on which he sat.

"Everybody does. Everybody who's a Neta," the *primero* challenged.

"Yeah. Yeah. But the way I see it? Mostly we can talk it out."

"Then you ain't got no beef," one of the *primero*'s aides said not quite under his breath, which made them all laugh.

That was when the *primero*-of-all-of-Manhattan decided I should leave. He didn't say anything, but in response to some sign from him Felipe was up on his feet suddenly and walking toward me, and as the conversation between the junta and the *primero* continued, he very politely asked for a quick word outside.

"See. Like. See. I seen DP. I seen them, but not around here," Mickey was saying, desperately trying to remain philosophical. "And I'm, like, they don't bother me, why should I bother them?" Then the doors swung closed behind us and I couldn't hear the rest.

Felipe apologized as he explained that the *primero*-of-all-of-Manhattan wanted me out of the room only for certain parts of the conversation. He reassured me that I'd be allowed back in later on and, apologizing again, went back inside. With nothing else to do, I folded my coat at the base of a pillar in the now deserted school lobby and pretended to read the only book I had on me—Willa Cather's *Death Comes for the Archbishop,* a not very convincing alternative to whatever was going on just the other side of the closed doors. People kept coming in and out. Every time the door swung open it hung there for a second or two, and I could hear shouting and once even a semi-organized stamping of feet, as if in protest. But the door always swung closed again, and all I could see through the thick, wire-enforced glass windows were the backs of the heads of the security guards standing in front of each door.

For the first time since I'd gone into the meeting I realized that Sandra hadn't been at her habitual position next to Felipe. I hadn't seen her come back after storming out of the building earlier that evening, and I wondered if her absence had anything to do with Rankin. She would certainly have been outraged to see him wearing that red, white, and blue flag around his neck. Sandra had always been adamant about the trouble inherent in crossing colors, even for a fleeting sexual liaison, and though she'd often told me she thought Danny Figuera was the sexiest boy at West Side, she refused to even consider approaching him. "Can't cross colors," she'd said simply. But here was her ex-husband, a Neta from birth, and now a DP. It was one more thing to worry about, and she already had the shaky situation at Chapter 6, her coordinator duties, and her boyfriend and his family up in the Bronx to occupy her.

I hadn't seen much of Sandra since I'd been back. The week before, we had shared an appointment at the beauty school on the twelfth floor of the building that housed West Side, where she had nail extensions fixed to her own well-manicured naturals and asked for them to be painted in black, white, and red. But it had been crowded that day (by then almost all the staff at West Side knew they could get free manicures if they showed up on Friday between 11 and 2), and we ended up sitting on opposite sides of the room. Because her appearances at West Side had become increasingly sporadic, the only times I had been able to count on seeing her regularly had been at the intergang meetings down at the High School for Humanities. I had gone to several of them with Oscar, and along with Miriam, the counselor from Spark who had arranged them in the first place, we often slipped into an excited kind of optimism after they were over.

There had been good reason to be hopeful too, I still believe. The feed-the-homeless drive had been short-lived but successful: the students had stopped only when classes resumed at the end of their vacation, and they had immediately started looking around for another site with more flexible hours. Within the school, members of Zulu Nation had gotten a good start on their clean-up-the-school campaign and plans for the first issue of the intergang magazine had been well under way. After two full meetings of debate, they had finally decided to call it *The Third Eye. Combi-Nations* had been considered for a while, along with the less clever *The Truth, All Together,* and *Power Combine. United Colors* and *United Nations* had also been suggested but had been quickly dismissed for sounding too governmental. Besides, members of La Familia were bound by an obscure rule that forbade them from ever speaking the word "united," or any derivation of it (like unite or unity), in public.

Sandra had been particularly excited about the magazine, and it had been she who had finally settled on the name. The term "third eye" came from "some Egyptian something," she said, and it suggested the ability to see the invisible and understand the incomprehensible, which she thought fit well with their aim of exploding the myth that still clung to youth gangs. The *Third Eye* had never been intended to be fancy. No one in the room had any money, and they didn't want to stop anyone from reading it by charging for it. It was to be designed on the computer in Spark's office and then xeroxed. If there were enough pages to make it necessary, it would be folded down the middle and stapled.

By the end of April they had gathered fifteen complete articles and a good-sized stack of illustrations. Sandra was the editor of unsolicited submissions for a column named "Positivity." Anyone could contribute a piece as long as it focused on potentially bad situations that were resolved by young people keeping cool and thinking well. She had also turned in an advice column and a complete set of horoscopes. Chante, the head of the Zulus, had designed a health and beauty page. Felipe had submitted some poetry, and another young *hermanito* from Capítulo Seis had come up with a column named simply "The Street," in which he hoped to discuss issues that confronted young African American and Latino men every day.

In addition to the magazine, Miriam had also managed to keep "her girls" going to their classes at Humanities by insisting that if they skipped even one, they would not be allowed to participate in any of Spark's activities for a week. It had worked. For the first time ever the school's worst truants had actually begun to turn up at their classes and to proudly hand over their attendance sheets to their teachers for comments afterward. But ironically it had been just this sort of effort that had aroused the suspicions of some members of the school administration. Arguing that the kind of selective attention they were receiving encouraged others to see "gang girls" as sources of both illicit and school-sanctioned power, many demanded that all "gang-specific" activities cease. When the principal didn't immediately agree, individual members of staff had taken matters into their own hands and had begun to suspend the girls for the slightest infractions: showing up at class ten minutes late, talking during class, hanging out late in the hallways. When one dean saw a group of La Familia girls scrubbing the bathroom walls, she screamed, "They are beginning to run the school!" before confiscating their brushes and buckets and marching them down to the principal's office to complain.

Miriam had been both appalled and dismayed. Her gang meetings had been optimistic, civic-minded affairs, and while she readily admitted that some of the girls had misused their newfound authority, she argued that missteps were bound to occur, and that the staff members in question had grossly overreacted. "I mean, the level of harassment was unbelievable. It's like they forgot they were dealing with fourteen-year-old girls," she said. "They acted as though they were dealing with hardened criminals who had been in prison for thirty years. Really. I mean, yes, they have had experiences, they have leadership qualities, and they may misuse those occasionally, but they are fourteen, you know," Miriam told me. "And with just a little bit of help they could have been turned around."

Instead, after weeks of complaints about the uppity gang girls, the principal finally agreed to call off the experiment and dismantle the program. On pain of arrest for criminal trespassing no non-student from Capítulo Seis or any other organization would be allowed in the school again. The clean-up-the-school project and the newspaper were banned. The feed-the-homeless campaign stopped, and, concluding that Miriam and her co-workers at Spark were "acting as enablers" and encouraging increased gang activity in the school, all gang meetings, special programs, group counseling, and work incentives were brought to an abrupt end. Several weeks later, when the city offered an employee buyout to reduce payroll costs, Miriam took it and left. She couldn't see the point in staying if she wasn't going to be allowed to do her job, she said.

Sandra had been furious. For the first time she'd be working with representatives of legitimate authority, and it had all come to nothing. Though she knew Miriam was not to blame, I couldn't help noticing in Sandra a new kind of wariness about trusting even someone like Ed anymore.

* * *

I'd been out in the hall at PS 143 for a good half hour, and was still hoping that Sandra might show up, when the door to the dining room opened again. A plump *hermanita* in tight jeans and a tight black T-shirt came out with one of Oscar's assistants from La Alianza Dominicana. She was crying. All the chaos and shouting in there had stressed her out, she said in between wiping her tears with the part of her T-shirt that covered her shoulder. It made her nervous, and she couldn't bear too much excitement because she had a heart murmur. "It runs in the family," she sobbed.

"You want me to call an ambulance?" the PS 143 counselor asked, looking genuinely concerned. "You been to the hospital before?" The girl shook her head and said that she thought she would be OK, and after a while the two of them went back in again, though the counselor suggested that this time she sit in the back, where she would be farther from the trouble and closer to the door

"But we're not allowed to," the girl said, pitifully. "We're not allowed to sit in the back, Ramón always says so."

"It's OK. I'll explain, just sit in the back," the man said as the door closed behind them. I had no idea what was going on inside but the *primero*-of-all-of-Manhattan and his boys didn't look like the types to get excited about that day's violence-prevention theme. After a while I began to get nervous again and started to think about leaving. I might have done it too, if I hadn't have been worried about the DPs. I gathered they were still outside the school because of the way *hermanitos* with walkie-talkies kept strolling in and out of the lunchroom, desperately trying to look casual until the doors closed behind them, when they broke into a run.

After what must have been at least another hour of sitting there on the floor, my Willa Cather hopelessly open at the same page on my lap, Felipe finally came out and offered to escort me to the train station. For some reason, the *primero* had changed his mind, he said, and I would not be allowed back into the meeting. Four guards came with us to the front door and then stood at the top of the stairs as we made our way through the still languorous group of DPs and up the block. We were taking the long way around to the train because Felipe said he was in no hurry to get back to the meeting. "I need some air," he said, and he sounded so tired that I didn't want to push him right then by asking any questions. We walked awhile through the deserted streets, past the makeshift wobbly corrugated-iron-roofed car-repair stalls and liquor stores and Santeria boutiques with thousands of candles stacked in their windows, which between them made up the small business community in the neighborhood. It had been raining; there was still a misty dampness in the air, and the sidewalks were wet enough to reflect the golden street lamps and the harsh white glare from the naked bulbs that hung from the auto mechanics' workstations. It was so quiet that I could tell Felipe's boots needed resoling because of the way their hollow wooden heels clacked against the sidewalk.

"That was kind of frightening," I said at last.

"Yeah," Felipe acknowledged. He walked a little more before adding, "Sometimes it's hard to keep it together—I think it's because we're the most advanced *pueblo* of them all."

Pueblo. I had forgotten all about that. Before I left for Israel they had been planning a vote on whether to maintain their name as *capítulo*, or "chapter"—that imitation of northern, Anglo-Saxon associations like Rotary clubs and Masonry—or to reclaim their heritage and call various groups *pueblos,* "little towns," as they had done back in *La Isla*. Felipe was too obedient a Neta to forge ahead without Ramón's OK, so I guessed then that the vote must have passed. I wondered what had happened with the equally radical move to abandon *collares* altogether in favor of ID cards. "We getting stereotyped because of these colors right here," one of the ex-cons up at a Chapter 6 meeting had said, holding his beads almost disdainfully up to his chin. "Without these we wouldn't have so much trouble, because these here are a target. And we don't need them 'cause it's all in the heart, *hermanitos.* Beads break, the heart don't break. Live your life in harmony." But looking at Felipe now, lost in thought as he strolled along a familiar street in his neighborhood, hands tucked deep into his pockets, his beads swinging slightly from side to side as he walked, I realized that that must have been a step too far even for Pueblo Seis.

It's hard to say that it was as a direct result of the *primero*-of-all-of-Manhattan's visit that night, but if what happened the next day was a coincidence, it was a fairly extraordinary one. A Neta saw a DP walking along Dyckman Street and, instead of walking past as he usually would have, he turned around and stripped the DP of his beads. He didn't do it gently, either. "In fact, he almost strangled him to death with his *collare*," Oscar told me the next day. In apparent retribution for this, Sandra and a couple of *hermanitos* were jumped by a group of DPs outside George Washington High School, where they were waiting for some friends. No one was seriously hurt, though one DP was slashed lightly across the cheek. Because no one knew what would happen next, Oscar advised me to stay away for a couple of weeks, until things calmed down. But I couldn't. Like Cristy before me, I spent the whole week trying to get in touch with Sandra. I even beeped Ramón and Felipe and Mickey, but I never got a call back from any of them. And when I went up to PS 143 the following Friday, I was surprised to find not a single DP outside of the school and only Ramón and Felipe and Oscar inside. They weren't even sitting behind the central security desk at the top of the stairs, where they usually did, but were at a seemingly random spot halfway down the corridor, and without the ten or twelve minions that had always hovered around them, they looked younger and less powerful than they had before—more like college students than gang members.

A peace had been brokered between the DPs and the Netas of Pueblo Seis, they told me, after Felipe fetched me a chair from the gym. It was a shaky peace because no one could be sure of whom to negotiate with in the DP camp. But after the slashing even a shaky peace was better than nothing at all. They had to think of the safety of innocent bystanders first, they said, and for that reason they were not holding any more meetings in the school. "Tha's right, no more meetings here, ever," Sandra said then, oddly cheerful, as she walked up the corridor to join us. "Not today, not next week, not ever." From the way she spoke, it was impossible to tell who had sponsored this idea, and when I asked Ramón he looked politely to Oscar for an answer. Oscar said that of course the decision had been mutual, but he was always diplomatic and I was none the wiser.

"What about the *primero* of all Manhattan?" I pressed. "What did he have to do with all this?" Sandra answered only by waving her hand dismissively. The conversation was over. No one wanted to talk about it. We sat for almost a minute before Sandra broke the silence.

"It's just that we had too much difficulties with the other gangs to keep focused on the important things here. And anyway, it could have got dangerous, having meetings in such a public place, and there are kids in here too, remember, little kids." Then the silence descended again, gaining weight and depth all around me. "Anyway, we don't need so much space anymore cause we kicking almost everyone out of the chapter." Sandra added. "By the time we through, there will be no more than seven members: Ramón, me, my cousin Nikole, Mickey, Felipe, some others. The rest don't take things seriously enough."

"But you're still going to be Netas?" I asked.

"Mmm-hmm," Sandra replied, getting up to escort me to the door. "With me and Ramón as heads. But being a Neta isn't just what they all think it's about, see," she said and then trailed off as we reached the steps to the street. "Its funny though. I always knew I'd have my own chapter one of these days, even back with R3, but I didn't think it would be like this. I used to want to have a chapter just for girls. Only girls, the leanest and meanest girls, so that people would say, 'Don't mess with them, they are Sandra's girls.' But it's not like that at all when you've got one."

30

I CAN'T SAY I was surprised to notice Maurice wearing a string of black and blue beads around his neck one morning in Family Group. When I asked him what they were he produced an overly designed scroll proclaiming him "head" of a new citywide group called 3RM, and then smiled as he said—"but we're not a gang; we're more like a family, you could say."

Standing for "Three Real Men," "Thirty Riotous Maniacs," or "Three Thousand Raping Marauders," depending on whom you spoke to, 3RM was incredibly small time. Consisting of Maurice, Rasheem, and Roland, their main aim seemed to be to increase their own importance and to humiliate others. And though they had taken to dressing like dapper turn-of-the-century gentlemen (Roland all in white with a flat cap and two-tone golfing shoes; Maurice, more businesslike, in a dark-gray suit, just a fraction tight around the biceps; Rasheem in black imitation alligator shoes and a thick orange Calvin Klein tie) their newfound aura was never convincing enough to attract even the most desperate of Ed's advisees.

Outside of Ed's Family Group, however, there were plenty of less established boys, special-ed kids mostly, who jumped at the chance to belong to anything. Down on the street in the mornings and at lunchtime, this collection of hopefuls would cluster around Maurice and Roland, mutely appreciative of their new right to be there, and would listen, wide-eyed and eager, to whatever the founding members were saying. Sometimes they would go to the store to pick up a tea or a couple of donuts for Maurice, or they would trail behind the three boys as they slunk off into the subway, or onto a bus headed for New Jersey, where they'd been guaranteed a portion of whatever they managed to get past the department-store security systems.

Within three weeks of 3 RM's formation, one of the boys who stole for them was rewarded for his efforts with a beating in the stairwell. This I knew because I overheard Rasheem and Roland boasting about it the next morning in Family Group. The boy's name was Q. He was geeky and slow and good-natured, and he'd wanted to hang out with 3RM so much, and maybe even become a member one day, that he had just stood there and taken it while Roland and Rasheem took turns pummeling him. Maurice was very proud of the way everyone handled themselves, he told me later that afternoon. Playing with the band of black and blue beads that hung around his wrist now, he said, "If I were still younger I would have joined in the beating. But now I'm older I made the choice not to do that, see?"

A week later they picked another kid to bully. Charles was also a special-ed kid. He was a little hyper, sometimes giggled for no reason, like a preadolescent girl, and he spent a lot of time chasing students who might have borrowed his pencil, or snatched his bookbag from him, just for the fun of teasing him. One afternoon he had been lounging in the corridor up on the tenth floor as he usually did, flipping through a glossy high-priced car magazine, when one of Maurice's girlfriends took his magazine and ran with it. In response, Charles reached out and grabbed her breast. According to Maurice, who heard about the incident five minutes later, this was sexual harassment, and it called for revenge.

Unsuspectingly, Charles proudly agreed to accompany Maurice, Rasheem, and Roland to A&S Plaza later on that afternoon, and he didn't notice when, on the way out, Maurice ducked into a couple of classrooms to brag that they were "on their way to beat up a kid." Dressed in their usual snappy gear, they walked past Macy's and then around the corner to the entrance of A&S Plaza, casually talking about shopping malls and video games and getting high. It wasn't until they had turned the corner onto Thirty-fourth Street and then doubled back and headed for Madison Square Garden that Roland asked Charles why he had touched Ruby. "You like her titties?" he asked as the others pinned his arms behind his back and frog-marched him to the lot behind Madison Square Garden where trucks unload. Continuing to insist that nothing had happened, that Ruby had taken one of his car magazines and that he had simply tried to get it back, Charles started to panic. Roland spun on his heels, looked at Rasheem, looked at Maurice, and then-*bam!*—punched him smack in the face.

No one was very specific about who did what when, after that. But this wasn't the first time the three of them had attacked someone, and I knew by then that Rasheem enjoyed kicking. When I'd heard them talking about the incident out in the stairwell with Q the week before, Rasheem had been zealous in describing how he wished he had kicked the boy in the knee "Just so—I kid you not, right exactly perfectly there," at which Roland had doubled over laughing, nodding his head up and down, wordlessly agreeing.

Now, around the back of the world-famous Garden, where the New York Knicks and the Rangers play, Maurice rummaged through Charles's pockets for cash. Charles begged that he be allowed to keep a dollar twenty-five because he had lost his train pass and had no other way to get home. While they laughed about this, he managed to run to a loading-dock guard, screaming, "These kids are attacking me—they beating me!" The guard, however, didn't want to get involved. Without so much as a backward glance he reached up and pushed the automatic door-closing button. Trapped again and with Maurice, Rasheem, and Roland demanding he give them his jacket, Charles tore it off, scrambled his way under a detached truck trailer, and sprinted all the way back to school.

3RM had played Charles like this before. He was one of those kids who through his very pliability seemed almost to demand abuse. In New Jersey, he had been only too happy to stuff his bag with stolen goods and had done it repeatedly until he had been caught. In fact, it had been Charles's mother who had first warned Ed about the formation of 3RM and who had given him a list of rules and typescripts of group oaths that she had found in his backpack. Nonetheless, the three boys were strangely secure of their immunity as they walked back to school the following morning and were as surprised as anyone to see policemen strategically placed throughout the seventh floor.

Policemen hadn't been inside the school since the would-be gang fight the previous fall. Ed hated to have control wrested from him, and he did everything in his power to keep all elements of street life where they belonged. In an attempt to diminish the mistrust between most kids and cops, Esther ran a program where once a week a team of officers came in to talk to her kids. But in general people in uniform made the kids jittery, and Ed had even discouraged a marine from coming to recruit in the school. The morning after the attack, however, even the most naive student could guess that the men standing around the seventh floor were policemen from the way they stood, their hands lightly clasped in front of their groins, and from their hairstyles and the cut of their suits. They were everywhere, one by the elevator, one in front of the special-education office, two by the receptionist's desk, one by the stairs, and one roaming, casually circling the corridor as though he'd lost something.

They found Maurice first. Advising him of his rights, they escorted him out of the building and then handcuffed him. A few minutes later they did the same with Roland. Rasheem wasn't in the building at the time. He often missed Family Group these days, but when Charyl saw him later in the day she hauled him into her office and told him what the police had told her—that he was under no suspicion himself but that they simply wanted to ask him some questions. Skirting over anything that might have been detrimental to himself, Rasheem painted a confused half-picture of a robbery featuring a strange kid he'd never seen before who had demanded Charles's jacket and then left with it. When questioned, Rasheem agreed that he should probably have done something to stop the boy, but at the time he hadn't dared, he said. Twenty minutes later, with Charyl's approval, the police escorted him out of the school for the day. As soon as he stepped onto the street, one of them grabbed Rasheem's left hand, wrenched it behind his back, and handcuffed him. "What's going on? I didn't do nothing!" Rasheem protested.

"That's not what the law says."

"Hello! That's what I say and I was there."

"Yeah? Well, from what you told us, you were acting in concert, and that's enough to put you away."

Ed had always said that it was a crap shoot, that you could look at a group of kids in the fall and think you knew which way each of them would go—that one would end up in jail, the other would graduate with honors—but it never worked out that way; there was simply too much environmental chaos out there to make any of their lives predictable. I knew he was right, but halfway through the year I'd also thought I knew at least some of the kids well enough to make a calculated guess against the odds. When Rasheem had moved into his new apartment I'd felt sure that with a little encouragement he would finally claim his own talent and start to make use of it. It seemed like such a perfect piece of luck that he'd moved in right opposite an art store, and that he'd then found himself a job there. But since the shooting it was as if he were angry with the world, and in taking it out on every representative of that world, he didn't realize that he was really taking it out on himself. I was still reeling from trying to absorb how far he had fallen and how fast. Roland, of course, had tumbled just as far. For a time he had clammed up entirely, jutting out the scar on his chin to answer most questions. But at least he now seemed to be holding his rage in check. It was as if he were finally coming out of the shock induced by the shooting and for the first time was able to look around himself and see the evidence of his decline staring him full in the face. The sudden self-recognition was making him dumb with horror and shame and awe. Rasheem, on the other hand, showed a surprising lack of introspection. To him it seemed as if the world had inexplicably turned against him and was sectioning him off for special, unremittingly unfair treatment.

When Rasheem had been thrown out of his Holocaust class, Ed had said, "It's a shame. It's a shame because he is a smart kid, that Rasheem, but as it is he hasn't got a chance. Not a chance." It was one of the bleakest things I had ever heard Ed say, and the most final. At the time I hadn't been able to see why he had picked Rasheem for such a dire appraisal. But I understood now. Despite his penchant for orange, Rasheem was a follower, not a leader, and though that's not always a life-or-death problem, I was beginning to understand that when you chose Maurice to follow it can ultimately have serious consequences.

Officially, of course, Ed had no choice but to ask them all to leave. The rule "No physical or verbal abuse of any kind by anyone to anyone" was fundamental. No matter how much hope he still held out for someone like Roland, Ed simply had to let them go. It wasn't a simple process. West Side didn't throw students out without making sure they were appropriately placed elsewhere. And though all three had been arrested, charged and detained in a holding pen in downtown Manhattan for close to thirty-six hours before being arraigned, their first hearing wasn't scheduled until the middle of June. Until then, in the eyes of the law anyway, they were innocent. West Side, however, was not the law. People had seen Charles just after the incident and Ed knew enough to be sure of their guilt.

After days of conferences and phone calls and meetings with everyone's parents but Rasheem's, it was agreed that Roland and Rasheem would be transferred to another alternative school in the city. The school specialized in finding full-time internships for their students and allowing them to earn credits toward graduation through work. Roland needed six credits, which he could earn in as many months if he set his mind to it. Rasheem had at least eighteen months to go, even at the most accelerated pace, and both Ed and Charl thought that he stood the best chance of succeeding if he could find something related to his art to get him through.

The problem was what to do with Maurice. He had only one-third of a credit left to go. If Ed threw him out, it would be September until he had the chance to earn that paltry figure even in another alternative school; with his mother's fury to contend with and the myriad other difficulties Maurice would clearly face in the interim, he might not ever make it. As much as he hated the idea of any preferential treatment, Ed felt he had no choice but to allow Maurice to stay on for the remainder of the year. It irked him, though, and he made certain that Maurice would not feel that he had gotten off lightly. For the last few weeks of school he would not be allowed to attend any classes or to roam around the school, attend Family Group, or talk to anyone other than the computer teacher, in whose room he would be confined from eight in the morning until three in the afternoon. He would have to bring his lunch with him and to ask permission even to go to the bathroom.

However arduous the terms of his stay were, his extension seemed like the ultimate betrayal to Rasheem and Roland. "I don't have no words for Ed," Rasheem told me. "I don't know. He's like nothing satisfies him. I mean, I already went through the whole system and then—you remember he's always been on my case, you remember the whole art thing? I don't know. Nobody knows how to mind they business in this school. Even though he's the principal he should still have boundaries—you can only go but so far when it comes to a student. I mean helping them out is one thing, but getting all into their business is another. And then when he said he was going to transfer me, I was like, wait a minute—we transferring you? Tha's a nice way of saying we kicking you to kingdom come. I no longer speak to Charyl, that's another person I don't want to speak to. She lied, right dead in my face. She said that they don't have no accusations against me, she said that I could go home, I was in the clear, that all they was going to do was to ask me some questions. I was like ah-right. Jean's another person I don't like. She's another nosy person. Remember that incident with Q. . . ?"

"I don't want to talk about that. Just leave it," Roland interrupted, and after a worried glance over to him, Rasheem did just that.

We were having lunch around the corner from the school when this conversation took place, trying to regain our composure after they had finally been told they were being transferred elsewhere. There was a strange formality about the meal, as though our friendships had died with their expulsion from the school and we were there just to polish things off, like a divorced couple after signing the final papers. Trying to settle on a neutral subject, I asked Roland what he was planning to do. Would he start up his menagerie again? "Nah nah nah. I'm into partying now. Been partying since Wednesday," he said, sounding as if he had already grown bored with his new pastime. "Party party party, tha's it." A few minutes later he added that he thought he might try life back out in California. He had spent the previous year there, he said, staying with an aunt who lived near the ocean. "There's no trouble out there," he said. "Seems like everybody out there I know and I don't get in trouble 'cause all I do is play dominoes inside the house, play cards inside the house, listen to music inside the house. The only reason we go outside is to drive around or go to the store or go to the beach, and there's no trouble in any of those things."

"What do you do here that gets you into so much trouble?" I asked.

"You can cross the street and get in trouble over here," he said. I thought of the shooting the month before and flailed around for another new subject.

"How's Maurice?" I asked after a pause.

"Fine." Rasheem shrugged. "He still at West Side."

"Does that bother you?" I asked.

"No, I'm glad to be leaving West Side. The only teacher who really gave me a run for my money was Rochelle. I finished that book. I finished it late, I admit, but I did finish that book." Roland didn't agree. He'd been hanging his head, slowly shaking it as he arranged french fries into a grid on the table in front of him. "Nah. Not me. Nah. I gotta say I like West Side," he said, softly. "I met a lot of people, you might as well say I know the whole school. And, Ed? Ed is the best person I met since I came to Manhattan—my best person. My best best best person I met in Manhattan and he brought me into the school and it was pretty good. I'm going to miss Ed. I'll come see him from time to time. I'm feeling bad that I let him down."

31

ONCE AGAIN IT seemed that all of us at West Side had been thrown face-to-face with our powerlessness. So many of the teachers and staff had gone out of their way to provide for the three boys: Ed had tried over and over to enroll Rasheem in weekend and afternoon art classes and had even arranged for him to meet with a designer at Marvel Comics; almost everyone looked out for Roland; and even Maurice had received special help and extra attention from various staff members. But whatever people at West Side had done—however encouraging Esther and Rochelle and Charyl and Ed had been—something else had gotten in the way, and we were all being forced to accept how tiny and bounded even our most forceful energies were in comparison with the great, distorted, sharp-edged world out there.

At least the end of the year was approaching; that's what I kept telling myself. I had been counting the days ever since I'd returned from Israel. But now I started to feel the way I used to while swimming a lap underwater when I was a sophomore in high school. We used to sneak into the school's pool in the mornings, when the cover was still pulled across and secured, and in some kind of adolescent daredevilry we would peel back one corner, and then swim all the way to the far end and back again. Halfway through I was always gripped with the panicked but sure conviction that I wouldn't make it. My lungs started to itch, then scratch, then burn, but with the cover pulled tight all you could do was keep swimming, push off the far wall as hard as you could, and then blow out whatever dribs of air were left in your lungs just before you reached the near one, so that as soon as you hit the air you could inhale—*ahhh*.

For Ed, though, and for the rest of his staff, what was left of the year held no such promise of relief. There were still the second round of RCTs to be completed, and minicycles and graduation preparations, not to mention the frantic worries and disappointments of the kids who weren't going to graduate. This was the time when a lot of them confronted the fact that all their absences and failed homework assignments and broken promises meant another year would go by without them moving on. Ed was the ultimate court of appeal for kids with issues like these, so he was even busier than usual.

In the thirty-eight minutes that followed Family Group one Tuesday morning, this is what Ed did: he left Family Group with James, intending to rework his schedule, and with a boy who called himself Sparks who hadn't been into school for over a month and who now wanted admittance to the adult-education classes on another floor in the building. On their way to the elevator, the three of them ran into Kalid, a basketball star, wandering aimlessly around the corridors. Ed sent him back to his classroom but twenty seconds later met him again, in another corridor. Before Ed could say anything, Lid raised his hand like a traffic policeman signaling for oncoming cars to stop: "You better stop dissing me, Ed. Every day you bin dissing me like this. I'm telling you now, nicely, to stop." Ed couldn't stand to be spoken to like this. He had already received a fair amount of flak for not having kicked Lid out earlier in the year after he'd been caught in a fight outside school, and by the time Ed had escorted him to Kathie's English class they were both so steamed up that Kathie herself had to interrupt. "I don't see how I can do any teaching at all under circumstances like this," she said, which brought Ed back to his senses.

Again he, James, and Sparks set off for the elevator. Halfway there they ran into another student who wasn't where he should be. This one was leaning against a windowsill, staring out at a brick wall, which was all that could be seen from there. After a couple of minutes of quiet interrogation Ed discovered that he was a new transfer to West Side—a superintendent's suspense, in fact—and that he didn't yet have a schedule and needed to go see someone in the special-education office. Now with three kids trailing him, Ed finally reached the seventh floor. He dropped off the transfer student in the special-ed office and then made a phone call to adult ed from the teachers' room and sent Sparks on his way. Just as he was going to turn his attention back to James, a teacher with some administrative questions needed his help. Then in walked Sean, the boy who'd smoked the tainted marijuana back before

Christmas and who'd more or less disappeared ever since. Ed finished with the teacher, greeted Sean, turned back to James, registered him for some American history classes that would prepare him for his upcoming RCT, and then wrote up an agreement for Sean to sign, which promised he would be present 88 percent of the time or else transfer out of West Side. It was the compromise he had reached with Charyl, the last, final chance for chronic truants who still showed at least some signs of wanting to be in school. Cheerfully warning Sean that he'd better show up tomorrow or else, Ed picked up the phone and called a girl who had just had a baby, then another whose mother and father had been arrested and hauled away in a highly publicized case involving child abuse; then he sat down to write a quick letter for Julio, the Latin King, who needed some personal references to help sway the judge in his case. As he was about to turn his attention to me for one of our regular scheduled interviews, he was called away by a frantic security guard to talk to a kid whose backpack had been found stuffed with bottles of Bacardi he was trying to sell.

I couldn't get over it. Even at this time of year Ed did more in thirty-eight minutes than most people did in a day. He never lost his cool either, and if he was a little short sometimes, maybe close to snapping when something displeased him, he managed to maintain such a calm, well-balanced approach to the chaos surrounding him that each person felt sure they were all he was thinking about for the few minutes they actually claimed his attention. He'd been through it all before, of course. The school year was like a marathon course that he'd run many times. He knew all the hills and valleys in advance, he'd say, and was able to get past them because he paced himself, and because he knew, too, that just on the other side there was the nice, gentle, downward slope into summer.

Besides, it was undeniably gratifying to see some of his kids prepare to graduate at last. The prom and commencement ceremonies were coming up soon, and the thought of his students participating in such gloriously mainstream rites of passage was his payoff for the whole grueling year. He had started to circulate catalogs filled with pictures of graduation rings and yearbooks and caps and gowns, and he and Esther had spent several weekends preparing for the prom: debating what the menu would be and what kind of nonalcoholic cocktails to serve, whether the waiters should wear short white jackets, how long the party should last, and how many dance floors they should have. They were like a pair of parents planning for their only daughter's wedding, and while Esther might have lost some sleep over the one-thousand-dollar deposit she had put down, and had spent almost a month walking round the school with "my heart in my hand, on my sleeve, in my mouth, wherever you want to put it," it looked now like all of their hard work would pay off. Posters of the glamorous fairy-lit cruise ship were stapled to every bulletin board in the school, and within a week Esther sold eighty tickets. When she opened the event to students from another alternative school and quickly sold the thirty more required to cover costs, she finally told Ed that they both could relax.

This was also the time of year that the Youthworks kids returned from Israel. Ed looked forward to their arrival because of the energy they provided his citybound students, and though they arrived at 5:30 on a Sunday morning every year, he was always there to greet them at the airport.

Remembering my own return, I was surprised by how many of them came to school the following day: Melissa, Raul, Naomi, Kamilah, Ylaria, Monica, Fred, Kenny, and Kevin had all showed up by eleven. Only Monica seemed depressed, but that was more because neither Kevin nor Reggie had spoken to her for the last two weeks than because she was back in New York. The rest seemed to be moving in a fog, not really sure what to make of the things they were suddenly seeing anew. Raul said he hadn't realized how he'd changed until he gotten on the subway that morning. He'd never had very good balance and had always held tightly to a pole or rail, but that morning he had done neither and was surprised to discover that he didn't lurch around or stumble or fall. Fred was shocked that he couldn't think of anything to say to his friends out on the corner. "You know how Stewart was always saying that when we got back it would seem like no one got off their asses since we even gone?" he said to no one in particular. "Well, he was right. It seemed like everyone just stayed in exactly the same place—my aunt's still in a homeless shelter, my other aunt still on welfare. . . ."

A lot of the kids were feeling equally disorientated. After ten minutes of listening to them reminisce in the Youthworks office that morning, I realized that the kids were in school for the very same reasons that I had stayed away. Just as I had, they were seeing the world differently now, and like poor-sighted people wearing corrective lenses for the first time, they wanted to reject what they saw. For me, that meant hiding out in cafés with friends. For them, it meant leaving their neighborhoods as soon as they could, to seek refuge at West Side, where at least they could be a group together again and reaffirm the reality of their trip and the fact that they had been away, seen people, walked places, and felt things that no one in the city seemed interested in.

As though afraid that they might slide back into the muck of lethargy that was suddenly so visible now, they were all approaching the day with the same, frantic "can do and will do it now" attitude. To this end, Raul spent most of his time on the phone to his sponsor, Jerry Blitzer, asking for help in finding a job; Ylaria chattered about her plans as fast as she could think of them, saying that she would go back to work at her old job while she looked around for something better; Fred insisted that whatever Ayala kept saying about the advantages of interesting over menial jobs, he didn't care what he did as long as he did something quick; and Kamilah just couldn't stand still.

Both Ayala and Stewart knew that the kids' energy would slacken as they began to confront the shadows of their former lives. Over the next few days they worked hard to preempt the inevitable plunge into disappointment with well-thought-out, straightforward pragmatism. If the kids really did want to change their lives, then they could, as long as they were prepared to work for it, Ayala insisted. And while Ed kept stopping into the office to chat with the kids and to look through the photos they were already compiling into albums, she used her contacts with companies in the city to line up a series of job interviews for those who wanted them.

Within a fortnight, Simon had been hired by a clothing store and had won the best-salesman award his first week there. Kamilah had applied for an animal-care program that Stewart had discovered, and Reggie had embarked on a series of interviews for a yearlong apprenticeship with a mechanic friend of a Youthworks board member. Surprisingly, Naomi was the most frantic of all. She kept saying that it was as if an epidemic had broken out in her neighborhood: everywhere she looked she saw strollers and babies and oversized pregnant girls. She compared it to Ebola, the virus she'd read about in a book while she'd been away, and she hoped and prayed that she wouldn't be struck next. In order to get out of there single and alive, she borrowed some of her mother's clothes and, after putting them together into acceptably professional outfits ("My mother likes to dress wild and Dominican, you know, so it's hard not to look bright"), she went out on one job interview after another—mostly to different branches of Lechters and the Gap.

Even after a couple of weeks, when their initial enthusiasm had worn down a little, most of the group remained impressively focused. When they gave a presentation to a group of students from the eleventh floor, it was almost like looking into a time warp. Just a few months before, the seven eager kids up at the front had been like the twenty or so gathered at the back, suspicious and irritated and mistrustful. But now they were sitting in front of their audience talking about controlling their lives and understanding others as well as themselves.

"What we need to know about her and her life for?" one girl asked loudly as Naomi tried to describe the pleasure of her late-night swing rides. Kamilah turned to the heckler and glared until she quieted down, and the girl didn't dare make a peep as Kamilah spoke about the zoo. Even Kenny talked movingly about how he had learned to laugh and to speak out—"No one will be able to respect or disrespect what you are thinking if you never say any of it," he said. "And I don't care anymore if people laugh at the way I speak—if a say a word wrong."

Some kids were having more trouble readjusting than others. Every year, Stewart had told me, one or two participants became dispirited upon their return. This time only Michelle seemed to have sunk into the directionless and vague negativity that had shrouded so many of them before they'd left. It was as if as soon as the barriers of her life in Israel had been removed she'd spilled out over too large a surface and lost herself. Heartbreak was part of it, I knew. Kirk had disappeared back into the mowed yards of his world almost as soon as they had returned, and while he had put in an appearance at Michelle's family's place, it had been clear that the bulky white linebacker with the shorn platinum hair didn't feel altogether at home with the conservatism of

Michelle's traditional Caribbean family. She hadn't heard from him for days, and the invitation had never been extended for her to visit his family across the river. Kirk had been the first real boyfriend she had ever had, and it seemed like his rejection had eclipsed the whole trip.

She didn't show up at West Side for a whole week after getting back from Israel. The first day she appeared in Family Group she slipped shyly into her chair, with her breakfast and her crooked smile and Dayna by her side. When Cristy insisted on being told at least how it was, all she said was "All right—it was OK—yea-ahh," and then twisted away just as she always did when she got nervous, looked down at her sausage-and-egg McMuffin and sighed halfheartedly, so that even Cristy knew not to push it.

With almost anyone else in his Family Group Ed would have been concerned by such a determined refusal to discuss what after all must have been a singularly profound and important experience. But he knew Michelle well. She already had more than enough credits to graduate, and even if she didn't go to college immediately, and took a job for a while to save up some money instead, he knew she would end up doing fine. Despite all the difficulties she had encountered, she'd managed to maintain an equilibrium over the past few years that would see her through, he knew. Because of the continued and sturdy support of her parents, she simply didn't need the comforting boundaries of West Side that most of the others in his group were clinging to right then.

Perhaps that was why Ed left her alone even when she turned down his invitation to the prom. He'd become increasingly bullish on the topic lately, and had taken to starting his Family Group with long descriptions of the open-air dance floors and the fine French cuisine that would be served on the ship. But however much the students continued to front that everything was fine and cool, their anxiety about leaving the school had only increased since Emilio had first brought it up almost a month before. So not a day had gone by when Ed hadn't reminded them that West Side didn't disappear when they graduated, and that they all had his phone number, and he'd be happy to see them anytime. Then he would return to the possibilities that were just now opening up for them, and reiterate that graduating was not something to be feared but a milestone to be celebrated with a prom and a fine graduation ceremony. His Family Group had grown bored with his cajoling weeks ago, but that didn't stop him as the day approached from redoubling his efforts to woo every graduate down to the prom, and from reminding them over and over about his offer to help with the cost of the tickets.

He'd already had some success. Emilio had instantly recognized the event as the kind of class act that he appreciated; he'd bought two tickets at their full price and was already looking through fashion magazines, studying outfits and trying to decide what to wear. Back before Maurice had been confined to the computer room, he had accepted a reduced-price ticket after pretending for a day or so to have been insulted by Ed's offer of charity. Though he couldn't go now either, Roland had gratefully pocketed two tickets as well, and Dayna, Tamiqua, and Alana had all finally accepted Ed's subsidies. Even James had finally asked for one.

Whatever Ed said, though, however much he begged and pleaded and argued, he simply hadn't been able to persuade Cristy to accept his help. Not that she didn't want to go. However happy she insisted she was staying home with Ray night after night, a prom on a fairy-lit luxury cruiser, her prom, her high school graduation prom, was a once-in-a-lifetime event. But even aside from the cost of the tickets, there were all the peripheral expenses to take into account: the cost of renting a tuxedo and buying a dress and transportation down to the boat and back. They could never afford to go together, and even if she wanted to, Ray would never let her go on her own. Nonetheless, over the next few days I saw her looking longingly through promotional photos of the boat and copies of the menus and lists of departure times in Esther's room. One afternoon I'd even heard her slam the book closed with the words "You think we all millionaires, Esther?"

The night of the prom Ed looked spectacular. Dressed in a fancy dark suit with a broad, bright tie, he stood between Esther and Marie and tried to contain his excitement as student after student made their way through the impromptu receiving line. The boat was everything the brochure had promised. There were two indoor dance floors and one outside roof terrace, a reception room, two decks, and three bars serving virgin margaritas, piña coladas, and daiquiris in classic James

Bond–style cocktail glasses with decorative umbrellas and maraschino cherries.

As the students arrived, their eyes drifted past their proud principal and up the sides of the boat, illuminated by spotlights somewhere out of sight. This was the first formal event many had ever attended, and they were filled with the knowledge that it was not only an important but an historic evening. The boys wore tuxedos mostly; the girls, evening gowns in deep, emerald greens, or golds or dazzling reds. Resting on their dates' arms, struggling to balance on the ridged gangplank in high heels, they walked onto the boat with their heads bowed in a mixture of concentration and embarrassed self-consciousness. Some of them didn't particularly like the sensation of rolling slightly on a boat, and many were nervous about being on the river at all. A few weeks before, the tabloids had given full play to a story about a barge colliding with a ship just like this one. But standing in small clusters not much beyond the entranceway, they were determined to enjoy themselves, and chatted politely, if formally, to one another until the boat finally pulled away from the pier and began to circle the lower tip of Manhattan.

Most of the Israel kids had arrived together, except for Enrique, who had come alone, nonchalant and bored, as if he'd been on a cruise ship a hundred times before, and Naomi and Raul, who had charged up the gangplank just seconds before the boat left the dock. They had missed a train and had spent twenty-five minutes waiting for the next one because of track work. Naomi had been in tears when they'd finally arrived. But she'd regained her composure now and was talking quietly to Carina, who looked striking in a long, red evening gown, and Ylaria, who had her hair braided so beautifully that Simon couldn't stop admiring it. Reggie had positioned himself near one of the cocktail tables on the upper deck and was kissing the hand of every girl who passed by. Bowing slightly in a response to each introduction, he'd say: "You look very beautiful tonight. I'm very pleased to meet you, Ma'am," with complete and straight-faced sincerity. Half an hour later, most of the party had followed him upstairs to mill around the rooftop bar and to get their photographs taken against the skyline.

Music had been playing since we'd boarded, but the volume was turned up once we got under way, and as the kids got accustomed to the novelty of their drinks and the finery of their friends, they began to converge on the dance floors. The Israel kids were the first to step out. And as I wandered between the decks in my own pair of too-high heels, taking photos of students dressed like extras in a movie and offering congratulations, I wished more of the kids in Ed's Family Group could have been a part of the fun. Dayna was there and Alana was down on the third floor, slow-dancing with her date. James, though, had pleaded sickness at the last minute, and while I'd hoped Cristy would change her mind after Ed had thrust two free tickets into her hand the afternoon before, she hadn't shown up either. She would have enjoyed the party more than almost anyone, and I couldn't help picturing her stuck in her pink bedroom, at home, watching television, or preparing dinner (steak, cooked long and slow the way her grandmother taught her, or rice and beans), thinking of us out here on the river having what she must have imagined was the night of our lives.

Emilio was there. Dressed in a crisp and expensive-looking white linen suit, he was holding court on the uppermost dance floor. I had never seen him dance before, and even as he smiled and winked at the women who surrounded him, it was clear that he wasn't very good at it. Stilted and awkward, he stepped heavily from side to side, clicking his fingers in only the vaguest time to the music, as if he had spent his life doing so much else that he'd never really learned how to dance and was only just trying to catch up now. He was still dealing, of course. His entire approach might have been more intelligent and calculating than Manny's, but his blind spot about the dangers inherent in the trade was more pronounced than Manny's fear would ever let his own become. After dancing for almost half an hour, he fetched me a cocktail and announced: "I love myself right now, I really do. I'm out there making my money and I'm still going to graduate like any other normal kid. What's my next step? Go to college, right? And what's the next step for normal kid? To go to college! I tell you, Tina, this is why I love myself so much! Plus, 'cause I'm not on the street," he added when I looked skeptical, "I only got like a five percent chance of being caught. Trust me. I belong in the real world," he said.

Watching him lean back against the ship's railing, with the dark, reflection-streaked water behind him, a beautiful girl gazing sweetly up at him on one side and Esther linking arms with him for a photo on the other, I almost believed that it might be true. There was certainly nothing threatening about the city we could see from the boat. Gliding up the East River now, we passed the Twin Towers, the Empire State, and the Chrysler building. We could see the Citicorp building, which looked grand and imposing that evening, and the smaller Con Edison tower on Fourteenth Street. Further downtown, Emilio picked out the lovely old Woolworth building, which no one recognized but he and Ed, who had joined us. After a few minutes of quiet contemplation, the two men heaved themselves up off the railing and headed downstairs for dinner.

Ed had finally chosen the Italian menu for the evening: shrimp to start, followed by pasta with chicken and broccoli, and cannolis and coffee for dessert. The large round tables had been covered with white tablecloths and candles and floral arrangements; heavy silverware and good china plates edged with gold had been set, too. Once again the kids were reduced to polite conversation as they took their places and tried to overcome the sensation that they really shouldn't be there.

The music didn't stop all night. Esther made sure there would be Latin songs mixed in among the hip-hop tunes, and as the boat turned around and began our last approach to the pier, there were even some oldies. I was surprised to see that all the kids knew how to sign the four letters above their heads in time to the Village People's "YMCA." They looked much more impressive doing the electric slide, though, a synchronized dance with oddly old-fashioned, western-style steps. All the girls lined up in rows for it, and at one point they had the whole thing going so beautifully that I couldn't resist stepping into a line. I was awful at it, and was relieved to be rescued by a samba line that had spontaneously formed and grew and then snaked its way down from the top deck to the bottom, around the two stairwells and past the bars and the dining tables, some of which were still laid with pastries, coffees, and teas.

In front of me, Ed danced for as long as his legs could hold out. Taking a break, he drifted to the top floor, where Emilio was again holding court. He danced with every girl up there. Then, starry-eyed, he headed back downstairs to the lower deck, which looked more like a club in Manhattan now as bow ties were loosened and shoes removed.

Sweating with his usual ease, Ed never once complained when he was pulled away and asked to stand in front of a fake, pink-leafed Japanese maple tree on the central floor, where Esther was taking Polaroids of proud couples. Whenever I saw him he was beaming. Weaving from one side of the boat to the other as if the seas were high, he kept saying, "Don't they all look so beautiful and handsome tonight? Don't they just all look beautiful?"

32

THE NEXT DAY Ed came into his classroom tired and saturated and happy. Greeting each member of his Family Group much as he had done standing at the bottom of the boat's gangplank, courteously, almost formally, and still awed by the splendor of the evening, he opened the class with a sigh.

"Last night we were in a world where accidents don't happen. There was a speech about it in a wonderful play I saw once—*Master Harold . . . and the Boys.* Danny Glover was in it, and he played a man who loved ballroom dancing. He said it was only in the ballroom where there are no collisions, where nobody trips or stumbles or bumps into anyone else; only there where everyone glides along in perfect time with each other instead of always bumping into each other the way we do in everyday life—and folks, it's worth all of you working hard and graduating, because I tell you, that was just how the prom was," he said. "An evening where no one bumped into anyone or anything else."

It was true that the prom had been a beautiful, almost perfect night. I had watched as the kids had grown with the realization that life might hold opportunities they had never before considered; even the Youthworks participants kids had finally relaxed into the knowledge that they could exist in the city as fully as they had on the kibbutz. Ed was right too, that if none of us ever had another night like it, it had at least offered an example of the way things should be, the way things could be, if we only kept striving for it. Those who had been on the ship strolled through the school for days afterward convinced they would never be the same again, and their poised optimism even started to spread to those who would have to return to West Side next fall for another year of school.

Most of the years' classes were over by then anyway. Finals had been graded and returned, and aside from the last minicycle leading up to the RCTs, and the niggling demands of planning a graduation ceremony, there was little left to do. The eighty-five students that were graduating that summer kept Rita, the college placement advisor, working overtime chasing down last-minute transcripts. But the rest of the teachers seemed to be focusing on wrapping up loose ends, concentrating on their advisees' upcoming summers, and making sure they had everything they would need. Summer school still looked as though it would be closed for everyone but graduating seniors because of cutbacks. Summer youth employment programs had been cut by more than fifty percent as well, so the outlook wasn't great, and many teachers were trying to hook up their students with special internships through friends as they planned their own, much-needed vacations. Rochelle would be going to the Caribbean for a few weeks with her husband, and David, the rapping math teacher, was negotiating the purchase of a house with a garden in Brooklyn. He had already bought a gas-powered barbecue in celebration.

Even most of the graduating seniors who hadn't gone to the prom had finally given in to the idea of their upcoming freedom and were beginning to lean actively toward it. But though Cristy had already passed her RCTs and was all set to graduate, she had been acting strange and oddly depressed recently. She still came to Family Group every day, but she hardly spoke and her mood was so isolating that it took a full week for her to tell me that her father had died. A long-time drinker with diabetes, her father had never left Salvador and she hadn't seen him for three years. They had quarreled then, but the day he died she collapsed, and her sense of isolation and loneliness was only increased when halfway through the night Ray got out of bed and called his father. "Just to say I love you pops," she heard him say into the phone.

For the past couple of days she had stayed at home keeping vigil and trying to figure out a way of getting "down to my country for the funeral." Ray promised $100 toward the ticket, but that wasn't nearly enough and, desperate to get out of the house, she had come back to school instead. In a new, bright green sweatshirt and with her hair neatly oiled and curled, tears welled up but didn't fall as she said "—I won't wear black for my father—I won't. I'll wear beautiful colors and get myself made up because he always like me to be happy and pretty and I won't wear black for him no matter what everybody says.

"He used to give me car rides for me to go to sleep. Every night a car ride—just him and me," she told me then. "We would go, imagine, like four blocks that way and like seven blocks that way and then round like it was a great big circle and every time I would be asleep by the time we got back and he would carry me to bed."

Ed tried to cheer her with praise and reports from other teachers about her incredible success at West Side, but graduation, suddenly, was besides the point. "I can't celebrate now—not with this. I don't deserve it Tina," she told me. Without the emotional energy to be either excited or frightened by the thought of leaving the school anymore, Cristy settled instead into the kind of quiet, regretful sadness that so often follows the death of a close but rarely seen family member. Subconsciously perhaps, she even started calling Ed "Pa," ("I adore him, he just like my father, you know, a big man with energy and kind like that," she'd told me once, months before) but she didn't cheer up even when he insisted on making her his family group assistant. "Oh, come on, Ed, what I got to teach them? They all my age or older," she said. And when Ed dragged her down to the art room one afternoon with Emilio and James and Michelle, she refused at first to even try on a graduation cap and gown because her mother had already told her that she wouldn't be going to the ceremony, and there was no way Ray was going to be able to take the time off from work.

The gowns were made of lightweight royal-blue polyester, and they hung strangely after having been folded for so long in their plastic bags. But as the students put them on even Michelle responded by rushing to the mirror and staring at herself in amazement. She hadn't gone to the prom either, and she still seemed to be keeping her distance from the rest of the Israel kids. But unlike Cristy, her mood was lifting as we approached the end of the year, and she had even found herself a summer job working in a lawyer's office. You couldn't tell it now, because the long blue gown hung all the way to the floor, but she had taken to coming to school wearing her new office clothes, skirt suits and flesh-colored panty hose and sensible leather shoes, as if testing out the persona that went best with them.

Emilio was right behind her, craning for a view of himself in the mirror and debating with Ed which side the silvery tassel on his pasteboard cap should hang. Cristy finally put on a gown and for a good ten minutes they all stood there, jostling for room in front of the skinny rectangle of mirror propped against the wall. They compared head sizes and smoothed out the seams and finally took money out of their pockets—two dollars, three, perhaps a five, to start paying off Esther for the cost of the gown and the yearbook and the graduation tickets. By the time the RCTs came around, most kids were walking around school as if they had already graduated.

Even the RCTs ran more smoothly this time around, and the lobby was totally calm on the first day of exams. There was no line of students waiting to be allowed in, and Margo was sitting quietly by herself at the desk, bathed in the sunlight that poured in through the open door, so relaxed that she could actually sit back and smile at me when I arrived. Jim occasionally came down to check on her progress and so did Charyl. Sometimes the phone even rang with requests for changes from upstairs. But there was none of the confusion of the previous January. With the list of kids permitted to take the exams neatly arranged in front of her, Margo explained that they had adjusted the system a little bit. If a student had a yellow card this time around, she let them in—no questions asked; if they didn't, and their name wasn't on the list, she sent them away. It was as simple as that. Ed had been called away, she told me straight-faced when I asked: "He's picking up some furniture that has been donated to the school from several warehouses up in the Bronx." There was a hovering millisecond before she burst out into a full-fledged, chest-pounding burst of laughter.

Who knows how the staff had finally prevailed on Ed to vacate the premises that day, but as a result of his trip, the seventh-floor lobby had been transformed by the following day. The furniture Ed had picked up was from an old Chemical Bank, and it had all been arranged: a tasteful blue sofa from the personal banking department, two little side tables, and a collection of wooden framed arm chairs. Ed hadn't been able to resist taking a notice board from the branch too, which announced their current mortgage and interest rates. Like a teacher in a one-room schoolhouse, he had displayed it in the center of the lobby, gathered a group of stray students around it, and was using the figures to practice percentages. Emilio was with him, desperately trying not to lose patience with a boy who couldn't make the leap from decimals to fractions. During the buildup to the exam, he had been giving extra math tutoring to a few kids who needed it. But his own RCT in global history was scheduled for that day as well, and as soon as the math exam began and the corridors emptied out, Emilio started to concentrate on his own history test. Sitting between two girls on the biggest, most overstuffed Chemical Bank love seat, he brimmed with confidence as he practiced answering questions from old papers one last time. A skinny, straight-haired girl with buck teeth read the questions out loud before turning adoringly to Emilio for the answer. Occasionally he became flustered, but more often he was sure of the answers and carefully articulated the correct response. Half an hour later, when Charyl started to circle the corridor, guiding kids to their appropriate exam rooms, Emilio was as ready as he was ever going to be. How could he not be, he said, as he walked into the room he'd been assigned: he had two well-sharpened No. 2 pencils, an eraser, and his brain.

James, however, was nowhere near as self-confident. I'd been keeping an eye on him since Ed had asked me to back in April, but he was an intensely private person, quiet, even demure at times, and he'd shown no sign that he'd wanted to talk until one afternoon when he'd tapped me on the shoulder and said, "Yo, Tina—wanna get some lunch?"

His life had been a roller coaster before he'd come to the school, he told me. A stint at a juvenile-detention center had been followed by a Catholic school on a basketball scholarship and then by a series of unsuccessful attempts at zoned schools. James had done well since arriving at West Side but he still wasn't convinced that things wouldn't fall apart on him once he left. Despite Ed's efforts, weeks of gloomy self-examination and surly disenchantment with the world and his place in it had led him to the irrefutable conclusion that he wasn't ready to leave West Side at all. He already had a slot at City College, but the only person he knew who'd made it to college was full of horror stories about how hard and constant the work was and how you needed to write long papers all the time, as well as hold down a job to make enough not only for living—for food and transportation and generally surviving—but for tuition too and schoolbooks. "College make me nervous," he said. "Well, not nervous, but yeah, nervous like in a panic? A lot of panic. They's just so much expectation on me. My mother, she says that as long as I get a job she'll be happy. But I know that she really wants me to go to college 'cause she never got to finish hers what with her having me so young—and then leaving home too. . . ." He stopped, looked down at his lap, and picked at the scab that had formed on the outside edge of his left hand. The weekend before his girlfriend had told him she was moving down South with another boy, and he had felt so hurt and betrayed and angry that he had wanted to hit her. He had never hit a girl, though, and after years of watching his stepfather mistreat his mother, he had always sworn that he never would. So he had turned and punched at a window instead. The window broke, and his hand had simply split, as if along a seam. "I'm scared, I guess. I'm just not ready for the rest of my life," he said.

Ed had anticipated this. He'd been hearing stories like these from many different students for months, and while most had been more vocal, James's fears had always been deeper. He had some learning difficulties too, and because Ed knew he would benefit from extra coaching, he made an exception and told James that he could stay on at West Side for another semester if that was what he really felt he needed. They agreed he would take college-prep classes in English and math, and maybe even tutor some younger kids too. And though Ed had made it clear that James should still graduate, that all he had to do was pass his RCT in global history to walk across the stage in front of his family, James clearly wanted to play it safe. Watching him as he waited to be shown into the examination room just before his last RCT, he looked nervous and guilty—like a junior high school kid trying to work up the courage to steal something from a store. When I wished him good luck he avoided eye contact and nodded at the floor in such a way that I knew he was going to do something stupid.

The test was the easiest one in years. No trick questions, no double meanings or purposeful traps. It was so straightforward that someone in the history department was prompted to suggest that when Republicans were a majority in the legislature they always made the test easier so they could claim credit for improvements in scores. The teachers did the same as they had the last time, gathering in a small room close to where their students were taking the exams, and at around four in the afternoon, when all but a handful of special-education students had finished, they once again gathered in a large, empty classroom to grade the tests. Unlike the English teachers, members of the history department marched their way in silence through the multiple-choice section before moving onto the essays, which they scanned line by line, checking valid points with a mark at the edge of the page and then counting them up for a score.

The results were gratifying. Almost 65 percent of the students who had taken the exam had passed, an extraordinary figure, given that global was traditionally the most difficult of the RCTs. The math scores were up as well, so although James had failed his test with a 27, a score so low he could only have done it on purpose, I couldn't understand why Ed looked so deflated the following day. He didn't even say hello when I walked into the room, and he was hunched over some paperwork with such apparent concentration that if I hadn't known him better I might have thought he was fascinated by what he was reading there.

"I see Emilio passed his global," I said, hoping to cheer him up.

"Yeah," he replied, perfectly matter-of-fact, by which I mean not terse or depressed or even surprised but almost amused in an existentially brave, laughing-at-the-gates-of-hell type of way. "Yeah, he passed his global yesterday, but he didn't even make it in for his American," he said. "And you know why he didn't? Because he was arrested yesterday afternoon for selling to an undercover cop."

I didn't say anything. Ed had come to associate Emilio with Javier over the past few months, I knew, and now it must have been as if the same awful tape were being played over again.

"Yeah," Ed continued, nodding the way he had when he'd first told me the story of Javier's suicide. "Yup. But they don't seem to know anything about his managerial role in the whole organization." With only the tiniest hint of desperation he added that he didn't think Emilio would serve time. "First of all, he has a clean record because all that other stuff was youthful offender and it all gets wiped clean, and second, he says he is thinking of joining a rehab program," he told me. "Getting arrested now could end up being the best thing that ever happened to him."

After all his maneuvering and careful plotting of his future, it was difficult to believe that Emilio had been stupid enough to stand out on the street and sell dope to an undercover policeman. When I asked him about it the following afternoon he only shrugged and said sheepishly that it was the first time he'd sold retail to anyone for years, and that he must have been out of touch. He had only done it because he'd been in such a good mood about his global that he thought he'd stay outside and make a little lunch money on the street for himself and some friends, he said. As if his recent academic success was enough to protect him, he hadn't even paid much attention to what he was doing, and he'd been busted and handcuffed before he knew what was happening. In the precinct building he'd been searched and fingerprinted and photographed and had then been left in the holding pen, or "catch room," where, he told me, averting his eyes in real shame now, he'd let another kid steal his sneakers. "This guy was acting hard, he was like, Yo yo yo, and making faces and I was just trying to chill, you know, and all of a sudden he pulled a knife out of his bootie and was saying like, 'Yo, I tell my peoples I representing, I need some kicks.' I was like, So? You ain't having mine. But he had this knife and he kept insisting, so in the end I was like ah-ight, here, take them. I had to ask for his so I wouldn't stay barefooted, and he laughed when he give me them. Old busted boots. Nasty boots. I felt so bad."

He'd been out on bail in less than twenty-four hours because they only had him for possession, he said. But that could mean jail time—"if I'm unlucky," and I had already heard that he'd collapsed into tears after speaking to a teacher named Carol for just a few minutes earlier on that morning. He'd seemed so unusually fragile that she'd ended up crying too, holding him in her arms and trying to comfort him.

"Just one week to go and I would have been *a high school graduate,*" he said. "I even invited my parents—my mom and my pops—to graduation, to try to make it up to them, you know? But all that's over now," he said. "All my work's been for nothing."

In a way he was right. Emilio no longer had any hope of graduating legitimately that summer. If he'd made it to his exam, the few credits he was missing would have been easy to waive, but now such a waiver was impossible. Even if he attended both sessions of summer school he would have to return to school in the fall. And yet, because Ed believed that graduation should serve not only as a congratulations but as a bridge across which his students could travel into a world of increased opportunity and real self-esteem, there was still a chance that Emilio would be given the opportunity to take part in the commencement ceremonies.

Ed did this every year for the handful of students who had been expected to graduate but who at the last minute ended up being a few credits, or a couple of RCTs shy. Most of Ed's teachers loathed this practice. It was just one of a number of what some staff members called his "egregious" abuses of the system. Forty credits were needed for graduation from a New York City high school, they insisted. Forty credits and passing scores on all of the RCTs. It was one thing when a student with thirty-nine credits and all their RCTs was allowed to walk across the stage with his or her peers, but they insisted that over the years Ed's proclivity to waive far larger gaps in requirements had became ridiculous. "I'm in a great minority here," he said in typical understatement as he prepared for the meeting in which each student's case would be considered.

There were nine of them this year, including Emilio. Each student was instructed to write a letter explaining why an exception should be made in their case, and then the letter was to be presented by the student's adviser. Staff members were so determined not to allow undeserving kids to "walk" that they had elected Rochelle, renowned for her tough, no-nonsense sense of fair play, to be their representative. She was determined to "represent the staff" to the best of her abilities, but Ed wasn't worried. However determined they sounded when discussing his impossible laxness in the teachers' room, he knew that what seemed egregious to his staff when they didn't know the kids seemed reasonable when they did. "The staff are a bunch of hypocrites," he said with a smile. "They hate the idea of any kid getting a break, but if it's one of their own they will fight to the death for them. And each one of these kids is somebody's."

Sure enough, one by one the advisers walked into the meetings declaring that in the case of their advisee an exception should clearly be made. One student had found out she was pregnant right in the middle of her RCTs; another had been ill on and off all year with chronic asthma and sickle-cell anemia; a third hadn't taken her exam at all because the paperwork had been faulty and she'd been wrongly advised. And as Ed quietly sat back and watched, Rochelle voted for a waiver each time, until almost every kid had been included in the graduation ceremony. Only one girl didn't make the final cut. She had only twenty-five credits and had lied about it, and even her own adviser argued against her being allowed to attend the ceremonies. Judged solely on his own merits Emilio might not have made it either, but in his case, Ed admitted, "I had two votes. I think it's very, very important for him to walk. And he will walk. I told Rochelle that no matter what she says, he will walk. Definitely."

33

IT WAS POURING with rain on graduation day. The festivities were officially supposed to start at 10:00. With much of the preparation work still to be done, however, Ed had asked me to get there as early as possible. Ed himself arrived at a little after 5:00 A.M., and hurrying along West 120th Street, trying to keep dry by hugging the overhanging walls of Columbia University, I ran right past him, camped out in his car in a T-shirt and sweat pants. He had a large cardboard box on his lap and another on the seat next to him, both filled with flat sheets of thick paper. Once folded, these would serve as programs for the ceremony. "You want to help? Here—" Ed said, and then handed me a couple of boxes from the back seat, which I carried into the building and passed to the first volunteer students I saw.

Esther was in the auditorium itself, up on the stage directing her kids in some last-minute decorating. They had already stuck flowers of blue tissue paper edged with glitter to the ends of the seat rows, like emergency-exit lights. But the front of the stage still needed to be decorated with strips of silver mesh, and a computer printout that read "West Side High School, Class of '95," had to be hung on the wall.

"Damn West Side, they don't plan for nothing. This shoulda all been done last night," Kevin said as he walked into the auditorium. Reggie was with him, but didn't answer; he had other things on his mind. His biological father had come all the way from Nevada to see him graduate and Reggie wasn't sure whether to be grateful or angry about the visit. His father hadn't been around for years, and wearing a white ten-gallon hat, a funky pair of gray-striped pants, and a short bolero jacket, he was attracting more than his fair share of attention from the handful of other people that had already arrived. It irked Reggie to think that after all those years of absence, the man had shown up now to share in his glory.

Out in the corridor, Michelle was also disgruntled and nervous. Her family had been there since half past eight, and she'd been posing for photographs ever since. Her sister Shawneequa had been given a pink skirt-suit to wear for the occasion and a little pillbox hat with a beaded veil that hung just past the eyes like her mother's. They had enjoyed posing together at first, their heads leaned together so that they met at the temples, but they had long since grown bored, and their smiles were now more forced than natural. Just behind them, in a similarly pink and shiny dress, Emilio's deaf and mute sister was also taking pictures. But despite the broad smile Emilio was giving, he seemed bemused by his nongraduating graduation. He hadn't lived at home since his father had thrown him out two years before, and I knew his mother would have had to fight to even be there that day. Looking at her now, all dressed up and beaming as her son wrapped his arm around her shoulders, I wondered if she knew he wasn't really graduating, or if Emilio had even told her he'd been arrested again. I guessed that he hadn't. He wouldn't have wanted to hurt her. Suddenly seeming to sense the transparency of his pose, and struggling to present a stronger, braver, more celebratory face to the world, he kissed both her cheeks and then winked at his sister, chucking her under the chin, before walking down the hall where the graduates were trying to arrange themselves in two long, alphabetized rows.

The balconies were about half full by then and the chairs on the floor had begun to fill up. In the aisles a few mothers and grandmothers in broad-brimmed hats and tight-fitting suits were still fussing over their charges, pinning flowers to buttonholes, straightening gowns, and adjusting collars, so they would be neat at least for the few seconds that the pictures were taken. Bringing up children had been hard for most here. Many had watched helplessly as their kids had floundered under the continual challenge of growing up poor and isolated in urban America, had seen them get pregnant, or expelled, or arrested. Some of their children had even gone to jail. But at West Side something had happened to each one of them that had stopped their free fall. And now, here they were, graduating. It was little short of miraculous, and perhaps because most of the people there weren't used to being at the center of a celebration, the atmosphere in the room was like that at a football game. They had been waiting for years for a moment like this to gather around and cheer.

With relatives, teachers, staff members, and dignitaries all gathered together, West Side looked like a community as solid as any that day. Sallejane Seif from the superintendent's office was there, as was the superintendent himself, a couple of representatives from the business community, and a handful of other people who had gone out of their way to help the school survive over the years. Doris Rosenblum was in the front row. She had founded the school twenty-seven years before, had never missed a graduation, and never tired of her work for Ed and his staff. The school had changed beyond recognition since she'd first walked into their original building on West End Avenue, but she was clear-sighted enough to see how important its well-being remained. After all, eighty-five once-troubled students were due to graduate that day because of the school she had created.

In a world where achievements were usually more ephemeral, it was incredible to see so many young people eagerly embarking on futures so much brighter than those they had grown up among. Of those graduating, nearly one-third were going on to college in the fall. Another third insisted they would enroll the following year. Some, like Simon, already had jobs, and for those who were the first in their families to complete high school, the simple fact of graduating was reward enough. Looking around, I could tell which families those were from the way the parents looked simultaneously abashed and proud, as though feeling unworthy themselves and gloriously fulfilled for their kids.

In the face of all this success, all this visible, countable, real achievement, it felt petty to think about the handful of kids who weren't there. But I couldn't help it. In this last-chance high school, I had spent most of my time with a particularly difficult group of kids. And though I still maintained that they were some of the most talented, bright, and energetic kids in the school, they hadn't provided me with much to celebrate that day. Not that all of them had failed. Emilio was there, and despite his arrest, he was close enough to graduating to be able to start college in September if he attended all of his classes that summer. West Side had done wonders for Cristy, too. Exceeding almost everyone's expectations, she had passed all of her RCTs and graduated. But at a time when her world should have been dramatically expanding it was shrinking, and though there was a diploma waiting for her on the stage, I knew she wouldn't be there to collect it.

Maurice wouldn't be there, either. He had walked out of the computer room just six days before graduation, and no one had seen him since. I'd half hoped he'd turn up now, in a freshly ironed blue graduation robe, with one of his demonic little-boy's smiles playing across his face. But I'd looked for him everywhere and had finally given up. With only a few days to go, he seemed to have thrown everything away as consciously as James had done when he'd deliberately failed his American history exam. But if they'd both turned themselves from successes into failures in the black-and-white world of sociological statistics, it was harder to pinpoint just where that line fell in the real world. The fact that James could have graduated if he'd chosen to spoke wonders both for him and for the school. Maurice had always been more complicated. He'd started at West Side with more problems than most and had a history so troubled that Ed had been warned not to take him on. If Maurice hadn't entirely succeeded, then at least being at West Side had provided him with an anchor outside the strictly regimented sphere of Williamson's. Maurice hadn't made all the choices Ed would have wanted him to make. But success, I had learned, was a relative term, and if it wasn't complete or even always visible, the achievement of a nonevent was as valid as, if less measurable than, the achievement of an actual event.

I had known this halfway through the fall, when I'd seen how isolated and horrifyingly coherent the lives of so many students were. Just hauling them to a neutral plane of calm, where they could relax and look around themselves for a time, required a massive effort. To encourage them to leap beyond that, into a world of positive results, was often impossible. During my past six months at the school I had learned to accept that. I'd had no choice. The pull of their chaotic pasts was just too strong. Roland, Rasheem, and Maurice had all succumbed. The absence of legitimate options had even forced Sandra, once so determined to change the world, to back away from her idealism. In the Netas, she had been dealing with teenagers from backgrounds as troubled as her own, kids with rap sheets longer than their years; nonetheless, she was courageous enough to try to reshape the organization and had continued to battle against the odds until she'd finally been overwhelmed, and had retreated into a pleasant but unchallenging domesticity. West Side had done its best to convince her of the plausibility of other options. But the school had not been enough. Until more mainstream institutions tried to bridge the boundaries others had created and she herself so readily believed in, she would continue to be outmaneuvered by the forces surrounding her. I remain convinced that that was what these kids needed more than anything: plausible, verifiable access to a place where wanting to change the world—or even just yourself—is rewarded with praise rather than arrest.

This wasn't easy, of course. Simply providing the opportunity was useless without solid preparation and the stamina to constantly reassure the kids that they would survive. But the eighty-five graduates waiting in the corridor that day proved it could be done. I could see Jeneena, the girl who had insisted on reading out her life story just before Christmas. She was on her way to City College in the fall, and there was no doubt that for her and Naomi and Reggie and Kevin this day really was a commencement. Standing next to Jeneena, Naomi was as wide-eyed and expectant as a high school graduate should be. She even had a new job at a midtown Gap that would start the following day. Reggie and Kevin were seriously thinking of joining the army; Michelle had a job lined up for the next year, and would then be headed south to a private college. Watching them straighten their gowns one last time before they marched into the room, I marveled at the escape route West Side had provided them.

Every teacher had helped. They had all done it differently, but each had convinced at least some of their kids to acknowledge and then activate their own potential. They were heroic; I had always known that. Taking on the most difficult students day after day was a wearing experience, especially as they were denigrated more often than praised for their efforts. As Ed had said, teaching was the only field in which taking on the most difficult cases was a cause for professional belittlement rather than reward. But despite this, and despite the hard-won knowledge that they might lose more students than they would help to succeed, they faithfully persisted in the belief that the difference they made in a handful of kids' lives was worth it.

West Side, in some sense, was a reflection of Ed's personality, of his inability to deal in any way except compassionately with the students' larger reality. As an institution, the school was more chaotic, less orderly, and less rigorously academic than many, and some of the teachers had taken issue with this over the course of my year there. But most often the disputes were a question of degree rather than substance. By being flexible enough to embrace the external lives of its students, West Side encouraged an individual give-and-take that most schools had neither the time nor the patience to deal with. If a child was sullen or withdrawn or angry, Ed and his staff would want to know why. If they were late, or perpetually absent, West Side would ask questions before responding. Taking a student's actions as symptoms rather than causes, they responded to each according to their needs. As Ed had said, the role his school most often performed was not intellectual, or even educational, but therapeutic. And it was because of this commitment to addressing the broader reality of the students that every kid had at least a chance of succeeding at the school.

Even Rasheem had nearly made it. Perhaps, with the help of another alternative school, he still would. But it had been awful to have to sit back and watch his drive to transform himself be derailed by what amounted to a series of unrelated and random incidents. There was nothing West Side could have done to prevent Roland from being shot, or from having his animals removed. Unforeseeable and profoundly impacting, those incidents were just bad luck, and in a world where random shootings are sad but not outrageous, what could a school like West Side do?

Then there were kids like Manny, who had grown up with the dual heritage of familial violence and drugs. What made him so tragic was that he had a vague, groping understanding that what he was doing scared him. But to have changed his life, he would have needed phenomenal powers of imagination and huge reserves of self-esteem. And he had neither. He had just an average amount of imagination, an average amount of self-esteem, and these weren't enough for him to do much more than straggle down to West Side when he remembered to. Until recently, he had still held out hope. One day he had talked for almost an hour about a friend of a friend whose uncle worked in construction. Such proximity to legitimacy excited him, and he'd twice told me that he'd asked his friend to talk to his uncle about it. But that had been before Lazarus was arrested. The last time I'd seen him, Manny had showed me a poem he had just written in Rochelle's class. She had assigned an autobiography, and Manny had composed the following:

Myself
Money sex and drugs
and the thugs
that I hang with.

He had given up. It broke my heart to admit it, but I'd seen it happen, slowly, over the past few months, and there was nothing I could do about it. Pitted against the chaos of generational poverty, underemployment, and a counterculture that had long since stopped looking to the mainstream for anything but the most crass commercialism, Manny faced problems just too numerous and large to overcome. Until these problems were collectively and concertedly addressed, West Side's reach would never be broad enough to catch all of its kids.

It wasn't just the influence of one world Ed was fighting against. No matter how hard Ed and his staff tried to convince their students that the mainstream was accessible and welcoming, there was no clearer lesson in how little the educational community and society at large cared for them than in the way West Side was treated. After three years in a temporary, leased space they no longer had even a decrepit old building to call their own. Worse, the lease on their office space now seemed in danger. And as they struggled on with insufficient funding and continued to pick up the slack for other schools, the public disrespect shown by the chancellor and others on the board never ceased. Ed continued to receive mail addressed to "Underachieving Schools," inviting him to special conferences. In the past month, he had been audited by a team from Albany, and he was also having to deal with representatives from the board roving through his corridors or sitting in on his Family Group, offering advice on how he could improve things. The last man who had shown up was a special assistant to the chancellor. He looked alternatively confused and bored as Ed's group had debated whether or not Alana should testify against her abusive husband in court. Ed was always polite. He attended the conferences and answered the phone calls and put in the hours at the remedial workshops in the hope that it might all lead to extra funding. But it never did, and no matter how much praise several programs in the school received, no matter how many kids they sent to Israel, or provided with jobs, or academically redeemed to the point where they would graduate, West Side still seemed to be viewed as a school as disposable as the students it served—a dumping ground for kids everyone wanted to forget.

But I hadn't met one kid at West Side who was disposable. Even the most antisocial of the students I'd come to know during my year were not, finally, so different from me. Some of them were confused and angry, but given the same circumstances, I was convinced that I would have turned out just like them. It was the difference in where we were born, and to whom, that separated us—not the difference of who we were. I had never had to watch my father chase my stepfather down the street, high on heroin and crying, the way Manny had, or to turn down collect phone calls from my father in prison. I had never been shot. Never been beaten or thrown out of my house; never spent even one night on the subway. I had never been encouraged in my own deviant behavior, either, the way so many kids at West Side had. And the only time I was ever shied away from, I remember as clearly as if it had happened yesterday. "I ain't getting on no bus with a stinking Paki," a boy standing behind me on line at the bus stop had said. But these things happened almost daily to the kids at West Side, and the never-ending barrage transformed young people just like me into young people who seemed very different—so different that a chasm of avoidance, misunderstanding, and fear now divided them from the rest of America.

But for all the attitude these kids had erected to protect themselves, they were still fantastically engaged in the struggle to survive, and to even excel at the roles they'd been handed. Since he was thirteen, Manny had been dogged in his attempts to become the best dealer on Knickerbocker Avenue; listening to his uncle the way most kids listen to their fathers, he had done everything in his power to step into the older man's shoes. Danny Figuera was struggling to be the best homeless kid ever by denying the grim loneliness of his situation and "representing," or "keeping it real." Sandra had done everything in her power to be the best Neta coordinator; Cristy, the best girlfriend; Roland, the best self-taught veterinarian; Alana, the best mother and wife to her husband. Even Maurice had put his all into being the best Casanova the girls at West Side had ever seen. In fact, it was because they spent so much energy trying to be the best that many of the kids I'd come to know well had no time to imagine how things might be if they acknowledged the grueling anxiety in their lives and set about trying to change it. As Emilio said, it wasn't that they didn't want to advance, it was just that they didn't know how.

As I looked out at the crowds still packed into the too small room with the homemade decorations and the unfolded programs, I no longer felt fear of, but fear for the eighty-five proud but anxious students about to enter the auditorium. They were starting down a path that could lead them out and away from the isolation that had hampered so many others. But even the most fortunate and well-adjusted of them still had so much to confront. They would need all the help they could get, and until more people recognize their shared, striving humanity, the larger social issues of poverty, racism, drugs, and violence will continue to represent obstacles that only the most heroic, and lucky, will surmount.

Many of the graduates that day were there only because Ed had followed them from group home to group home, shelter to shelter, from detention center to detention center, keeping the strand of possibility alive with a stream of letters and phone calls. It had been a lot of work, and it required a rare kind of commitment. But the fact remained that eighty-five once confused and angry kids, kids who at one time or another had been other schools' failures, were graduating now. More could have been if he and his staff had only had more help.

Epilogue

Since completing this book I have stayed in touch with a number of West Side students. The following list is not intended to be comprehensive, nor is it entirely up to date.

Sandra is living with Jose, with whom she has a baby girl. She is no longer involved with the Netas, and has recently re-enrolled both Jose and herself in high school.

Cristy enrolled in a professional training program, from which she graduated with honors. She is still living with Ray in her mother's apartment and is looking for a job close to home.

Manny ended up stealing from one of his drug "connecs" on Knickerbocker Avenue and was forced to change business locations. In the summer of 1996, he was arrested for assaulting one of his customers.

Danny was accepted by the job corps in Washington, D.C. He frequently visits New York City, where he gives motivational talks to teenagers incarcerated in Rikers Island.

Maurice didn't show up to the hearing for his role in the assault of Charles. I last spoke to his mother the fall of 1995; when I asked her if she had any idea where he might be, she replied: "Only Jesus has the answer to the question."

Roland became an inspirational rap singer who visits school and warns students of the dangers of hanging out with the wrong crowd.

Emilio is in prison upstate.

Michelle is working for an international not-for-profit company.

Naomi and Kamilah are roommates in college. They are both maintaining excellent grade-point averages.

Acknowledgments

This book could not have been written without the help, generosity, and trust of the staff and students at West Side High School. They took a huge risk in welcoming me into their lives. I hope I have not let them down. Among the teachers I would like to particularly thank are Rochelle, Esther, Rosa, Linda, Charyl, Marie, and Ann. Through their patience, their humor, and their obstinate persistence they helped me to understand what it means to work with kids, year after year. I would also like to thank Stewart and Ayala for welcoming me into the family of Youthworks, Margo for providing valuable overviews of the school, David for being around when I needed to let off steam, and the entire school security team for looking out for me. As for Ed, the inspiration and guidance he provided was an education in itself. I hope to always know him. He is a rock of wisdom and an endless source of generosity.

From the students themselves I learned more in one year than I ever thought was possible. I wish I could publicly acknowledge their courage and grace by thanking them here with their real names. Instead, all I can hope is that at least a portion of their intelligence, generosity, and warmth has managed to find a way into these pages. To have captured them entirely would have been impossible.